BUILDING FINANCIAL MODELS

SECOND EDITION

BUILDING FINANCIAL MODELS

SECOND EDITION

THE COMPLETE GUIDE TO DESIGNING, BUILDING, AND APPLYING PROJECTION MODELS

JOHN S. TJIA

New York Chicago San Francisco Lisbon London
Madrid Mexico City Milan New Delhi San Juan
Seoul Singapore Sydney Toronto

The **McGraw-Hill** *Companies*

To my wife, Charlotte, with love and kisses

3 4 5 6 7 8 9 0 DOC/DOC 1 5 4 3 2 1

ISBN: 978-0-07-160889-3
MHID: 0-07-160889-3

This book is printed on acid-free paper.

CONTENTS

INTRODUCTION

This book will teach you how to bring together what you know of finance, accounting, and the spreadsheet to give you a new skill—building financial models. The ability to create and understand models is one of the most valued skills in business and finance today. It is an expertise that will stand you in good stead in any arena—Wall Street or Main Street—where numbers are important. Whether you are a veteran, just starting out on your career, or still in school, having this expertise can give you a competitive advantage in what you want to do.

By the time you have completed the steps laid out in this book, you will have created a working, dynamic spreadsheet financial model that you can use to make projections for industrial/manufacturing companies. (Banks and insurance companies have different flows in their businesses and are not covered in this book.)

This second edition is an extensive rewrite of the first edition and includes an additional chapter on discounted cash flow valuation modeling. This edition uses screen illustrations from Excel 2007, the latest version from Microsoft Office available as of this writing. Although the instructions still apply to earlier versions, the illustrations are oriented more toward this latest incarnation of the world's most popular spreadsheet application.

FIRST, SOME DEFINITIONS

A spreadsheet can be used to tabulate and organize numbers, but it does not become a *model* until it contains data, equations, and specific relationships among the numbers that organize them into informational output.

The model becomes a *financial model* when it incorporates the relationships of operating, investing, and/or financing variables based on general accounting principles.

It can be called a *financial projection model* when it uses assumptions about future performance to give a view of what a company's future financial condition might be like. By changing the input variables, such a projection model becomes useful for showing the impact of different assumptions and/or strategies for the future.

TWO REQUIREMENTS FOR MAGIC

The task of developing a good spreadsheet model is a combination of many things, but primarily it is about good thinking and a sound knowledge of the tools at hand. These two attributes will put you on the right track for producing a model structure and layout that are robust yet easy and, yes, delightful to use. Arthur C. Clarke, the late renowned science writer, once said, "Any sufficiently advanced technology is indistinguishable from magic." I hope that after using the approaches and techniques for building models in this book, you too can look at your work and feel the magic you have created. And I certainly hope that your colleagues, managers, and clients will have the same reaction.

THIS IS A HANDS-ON BOOK

This book will lead you through the development process for a projection model. It is laid out in a step-by-step format in which each chapter describes a step. Each chapter covers a specific phase of building a model. This is a hands-on book. You will get the most out of this book if you perform the steps outlined in each chapter on your computer screen. By the end of the book, you will have the satisfaction of having built your own model. To this model you can then add you own changes and modifications.

BUILD MODELS WITH YOUR OWN STYLE

Building models is a fluid, creative activity, and there are as many ways to build a model as, say, to write a book. Most of them will result in working models, but not necessarily very good ones; there are, after all, bad books. But there are also excellent books with very different styles. The intent of this book is to show you the tools—the vocabulary and the syntax of model building, if you will—for developing a model that works properly, and so provide you with the foundation for developing other models. Just as you develop your own style of writing once you have learned the basics of language, you can then develop your own style of model building.

THE MODEL WE WILL BE BUILDING

The projection model we will be developing is one that you might find as the starting point in many forms of analysis. The model will have these key features:

- It will have historical and forecast numbers for modeling an industrial type of company or business. Forecast numbers can be entered as "hard-coded" numbers (e.g., sales will be 1,053 this year and 1,106 next year, etc.) or as assumptions (e.g., sales growth next year will be 5%, etc.).
- The income statement, balance sheet, and a cash flow statement are interlinked following general accounting principles.
- The balance sheet balances: the total assets must equal the total liabilities and net worth.
- Two mechanisms are introduced for balancing the balance sheet: the balance sheet method and the cash flow method.

- With the accounting interrelationships correctly in place, the cash flow numbers will also "foot," i.e., the change in cash from the total cash flow in any one year equals the change in the cash on the balance sheet from the prior year to the current year.
- There will be a "cash sweep" mechanism to automatically prepay outstanding debt with any excess cash on the balance sheet in the forecast years.
- The model drives a discounted cash flow valuation module. This module includes the standard methodology approaches for valuing a company.
- Additional outputs include common-size statements that show the income statement and balance sheet values as percentages of revenue and assets, respectively.

Once you have this model functioning, you can use it as the engine to drive other calculations such as your own ratios.

I have posted some of the models used in this book in the companion website www.buildingfinancialmodels.com.

MICROSOFT EXCEL

This book describes model building in Microsoft Excel 2007, but its core model-building concepts can be realized in earlier versions of Excel as well as any other model development language. Excel 2007 commands are organized in a "menu ribbon" at the top of the screen that reorganizes the placement of the commands seen in earlier Excel versions. For this reason, I give directions for operating the menus in both versions of Excel. Where I cover the menu commands from earlier versions of Excel, I refer to these earlier versions as "Excel 2003" for convenience. This reference should also be taken to mean versions of Excel from earlier years.

COMMANDS

Commands in Excel are described in this book using the ">" notation to indicate the menu selection process. Thus, the sequence for saving a file in Excel 2007 would be shown as *Office button> Save*, for example. (The Office button is the round icon at the far left in the Excel 2007 menu ribbon.) In Excel 2003, the same sequence would be *File>Save.*

ACKNOWLEDGMENTS FOR THE SECOND EDITION

My thanks to those who helped me as readers of the draft of this edition:

> Students in the finance class of Dr. Ben Sopranzetti at Rutgers University, including Ben Schmid, Saad Siddiqui, David Skibinski, Arthur King, Jorge Barreiro, and James McGrath.
>
> Readers of my first book who contacted me with valuable feedback include Peter McAniff and William H. Jarnagin.

ACKNOWLEDGMENTS FOR THE FIRST EDITION

This book is just a part of what I have learned in my career as a financial modeler in investment banking; so in thanking those who have helped me in the writing of this book, I must give thanks to all with whom I have worked, including the many hundreds of colleagues in J.P. Morgan (past) and JPMorgan Chase (present), who gave me encouragement and constructive feedback through all of the many generations of financial models I developed for that firm.

In looking back at my career and how I started to build financial models, I must return to the first time I saw a newfangled white box sitting on somebody's desk some time in the early 1980s. I remember asking, "What do you do with this?" And my then-colleague Lillian Waterbury said, "Type 'Lotus' at the C prompt sign." I did, and at this first PC I caught my earliest glimpse of the spreadsheet (it was Lotus 1-2-3 Release 1A). This would be a new direction for me. Thanks, Lillian.

Thanks to my friends and colleagues from the Financial Advisory Group. Sue McCain and Carol Brunner gave me my first chance to work as a modeler, and it made all the difference.

Juan Mesa taught me what clear thinking was about when we built a Latin American model with inflation financial accounting. Christopher Wasden was my guide in the arcane accounting for banks when we built a model for banks.

I worked together with Jim Morris and Humphrey Wu in New York and Mike Koster in London, and consider them as cohorts and comrades-in-arms in the arcane alchemy of finance, accounting, Excel, and Visual Basic for Applications that is the art of financial modeling. We all gave our best to produce modeling packages that were often more than the sum of their parts. Thanks, Jim, Humphrey, and Mike.

In the new JPMorgan Chase, Pat Sparacio, Marguerita Courtney, and Leng Lao were enthusiastic supporters of my work, and I thank them. Jay Chapin, an independent credit training consultant, read the manuscripts and cheered me on from his home base in Houston. Thanks, Jay. Fern Jones, a colleague and friend from my earliest days in finance so many years ago, also read the manuscript and encouraged me through the dark hours that probably every author experiences. Thanks also to Sumner Gerard, who took the time late into the night to look over the manuscript.

Finally, thanks to Susan Cabral, now of Cabral Associates, who in 1967 built in the mainframe computer the first financial projection model for J.P. Morgan, and quite possibly for Wall Street. Susan's model design was still in use 15 years later, and it was the starting point for me when I began modeling for the PC. Her design is present in almost all the models I have developed in my career. Thank you, Susan, for being the pioneer and for showing me the way.

BUILDING FINANCIAL MODELS

SECOND EDITION

CHAPTER 1

A Financial Projection Model

This book is about creating financial models, or more specifically, *integrated financial statement projection models*. Although a spreadsheet developed for any financial calculation or analysis can be called a model, an integrated financial statement model has the three financial statements for financial disclosure—the income statement, the balance sheet, and the cash flow statement—interlinked by accounting logic through Excel formulas. In essence, such a model is designed so that the future performance of a company, as defined by assumptions entered into the model, will be represented in the same manner and format as its historical financial statements.

The "financial model" discussed hereafter in this book will always mean an integrated financial statement model. Also, for simplicity, and unless otherwise indicated, I will assume that the financial model is an annual (and not a quarterly or some other periodicity) model set for fiscal years ending on December 31.

1.1 STRUCTURE

The integrated financial statement model follows the framework of accounting. The three statements are:

- The income statement
- The balance sheet
- The cash flow statement

1.1.1 The Income Statement

The income statement is a listing of revenues and expenses over the reporting period. The reporting period, or the periodicity, is typically 1 year. However, this can vary and can be quarterly, monthly, or whatever other periodicity is required. The financial model described in this book is for annual periods, but Chapter 19, Section 19.6 has some notes on the changes in the model's formulas that a nonannual periodicity would require.

The top line of the statement is the revenue line; the bottom line is the net income line, showing what the company has earned for the year after all expenses have been accounted for. Most companies' fiscal year coincides with the calendar year, that is to say, the reporting period ends on December 31. Others set their fiscal year to end on June 30 (e.g., Microsoft), or in fact any other month end. The main reason is to show the best possible seasonal condition. Many department stores, for example, use January 31 as their fiscal year end, a point after the year-end holiday sales when inventories are low and cash holdings are high.

An important point to note is that the income statement is a record over time. For any modeling in which you need to look at the income statement at some point in the year, you can usually take a prorated value to represent the income statement values up to that point. Thus, to look at a transaction done at September 30 in the year, you can assume that the year-to-date (YTD) sales would be 75% of the total for the year. This percentage can vary if the company's operations are highly seasonal. For example, a company that sells year-end holiday gifts would have its revenues heavily weighted to the last quarter in the year, and the YTD value at September 30 could be as low as 10% of the year's total.

This has implications if your model has to be converted into a foreign currency. Because the revenue and expense numbers are accrued over the reporting period, the foreign exchange conversion rate needs to use the average for that period, and not the period-end rate.

1.1.2 The Balance Sheet

The balance sheet is a snapshot of the company's periods at one point in time, specifically the end of the reporting period. Compare this with the income statement, which contains numbers that have been accumulated over the entire 12 months. The two statements have different time frames, but are presented as of the same day, at the end of the reporting period.

1.1.3 The Cash Flow Statement

The cash flow statement ties the two other statements together. This statement starts with the net income from the income statement, makes adjustments for noncash charges, and then keeps track of the changes in every account, except the cash account itself, on the balance sheet. (Chapter 12 covers building the cash flow statement.) The change is between the current year's balance sheet (Year t) and the prior year (Year t–1). Each change in each balance sheet account represents a source of cash (e.g., a sale of an asset or an increase in borrowing means there is more cash on hand) or a use of cash (e.g., an inventory increase or a repayment of debt means less cash on hand). At the end of the cash flow statement, we have a combined net source or net use of cash, equivalent to the *change* in cash between the current year and the prior year. This change should tie in with, or "foot" to, the difference in cash between Year t and Year t–1.

Because the cash flow statement needs to look at the current period's balance sheet *and* the prior period's to determine the changes, the first year column in the cash flow statement is typically left blank, since there is no "prior period" at the beginning of the modeling periods.

1.1.4 How They Are Interlinked

The following (Fig. 1-1) is a flowchart that shows the relationships. This may look cryptic at the moment, but don't worry; we will go

FIGURE 1-1

Flowchart of Interlinks Among the Three Financial Statements

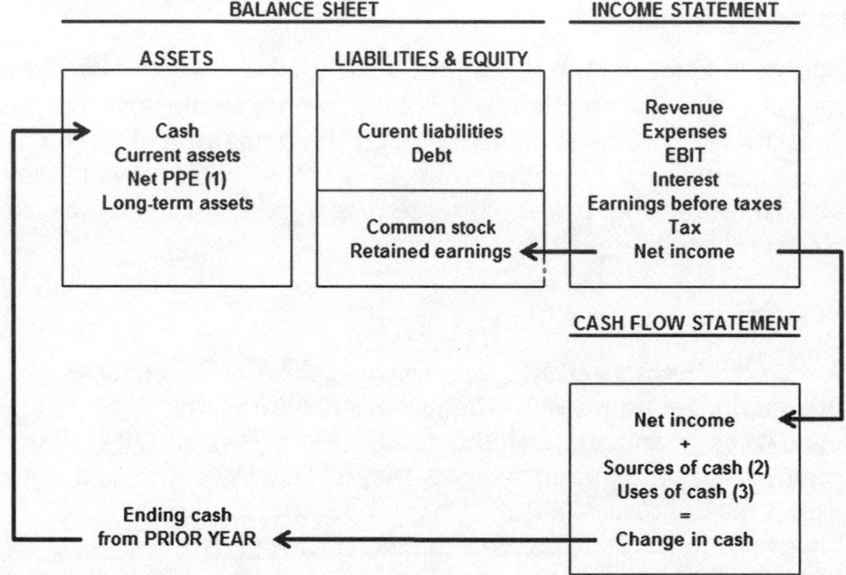

(1) PPE is Plant, Property, and Equipment.

(2) Sources of cash from decreases in assets or increases in liabilities between this year and the prior year (e.g., sale of assets, new debt).

(3) Uses of cash from increases in assets or decreases in liabilities or equity between this year and the prior year (e.g., buildup of working capital, repayment of debt).

through this again later as we go through the steps of building a financial model.

The main links are shown within the rectangle for the current year. For each year's cash flow statement, information from the prior year is needed, since we would need to look at the changes between the current year's balance sheet and the prior year's.

1.1.5 Other Parts of the Financial Model

Once the three statements are in place and working together, we have a modeling engine that can be put to good use to drive other forms of analysis, such as credit analysis, discounted cash flow valuation, and leveraged buyout (LBO) analysis. (Having two financial models to represent two companies, we can also combine them for a merger model.) We can add ratio pages to show the critical performance metrics, and also common-size statements. A common-size income statement shows the statement as percentages of revenue; a common-size balance sheet shows the line items as percentages of total assets.

1.2 AN ESTIMATOR, NOT A PREDICTOR

A financial model is not a crystal ball and its output does not dictate what the future will be. It is merely a tool to estimate what a company's future financial profile might be, given certain assumptions about its future performance. Its main utility is this: it is a way to test what needs to happen for one or more performance goals to be reached.

For example, a chief financial officer may say, "We will accumulate enough cash reserves in the next 3 years to retire $100 million of our debt." How can we test the validity of this statement? One way is to use a financial model and use the assumptions that the company has used. If the forecasts use conservative assumptions based on recent historical performance (although historical performance, as the investment fund advertisements always remind us, is no guarantee of future performance), the company's current reputation and position in the industry, then it might be a valid statement. However, if the $100 million accumulation is possible only through unrealistic and unprecedented increases in revenues, then it is more likely that we should discount the CFO's statement.

This role as a testing tool means that a financial model is best when we can change the inputs quickly for a series of sensitivity tests. What would the cash flow from operations be like if revenue went up by 8%, or 3%, instead of 5%, while margins: (a) held steady, (b) improved, or (c) worsened? Given the accounts in a model, the permutations of the sensitivities can be limitless. Chapter 19 gives a review of the main points to keep in mind in developing scenarios.

1.3 CRITICAL OUTPUTS

A financial model should allow you to reviews these measures of a company's performance:

- Earnings before interest and taxes (EBIT): EBIT is revenue less expenses directly related to its revenue-generating operations. Thus, EBIT is a measure of the earning power of its core operations. Nonoperating elements such as interest income or expense are not included.
- Earnings before interest and taxes, depreciation and amortization EBITDA: This is EBIT but without depreciation and amortization expenses, both of which are noncash expenses, so there is no actual cash that the company has to pay out. So EBITDA is a good way to arrive at cash earnings, the amount of cash generated by a company's core operations.
- Revenue and net income: This shows revenue-generating ability and profitability. Net income is basically EBIT less interest and taxes.
- Cash flow from operations: This shows net income plus addbacks of the noncash expenses less the cash that needs to be invested in the increase in operating working capital.
- Operating working capital: Working capital by definition is current assets minus current liabilities, but often the term "working capital" denotes current assets excluding cash, less current liabilities excluding short-term debt (both short-term notes payables and current portion of long-term debt). It might be useful to call this definition operating working capital (OWC). Thus OWC is a measure of the cash investments required to keep the company in operation. Cash and debt are separate financing decisions.

- Net plant, property, and equipment (PPE) and capital expenditures: Capital expenditures, or capex, is a major use of cash in the balance sheet. Capex is an ongoing expense because a company must continue to invest in its production equipment, which needs to be maintained, upgraded, or replaced over time.
- Levels of debt and equity: A company's level of debt may appear high or low relative to its equity, but the important measure is the company's ability to service the debt—to pay the ongoing interest expense and to repay the debt on a timely basis.

1.4 A ONE-OFF MODEL

Models can be built on a "one-off" basis or as a template model. One-off means that the model is built for a specific project, to be used only for that one purpose. It can be used again, of course, but it will probably require substantial modifications to accommodate the specifics of the next project. A one-off model is easier to build in one sense: because it is built for a specific project, there is no need to make room for multiple roles that a template model can have.

1.5 A TEMPLATE MODEL

A template model, on the other hand, is meant to be used again and again, as the analysis workhorse for a group or even a whole organization. Although there is no one model that will work in all cases, a good standardized template model should be sufficient for 80% to 90% of all the analytical work. One good way to extend the reach of a template model is to enable additional sheets to the modeling engine (Fig. 1-2). The sheets can be added to the front of the model (in the sense of the inputs, so that they can be made more granular) and the back of the model (to organize and supplement the output that the model is capable of producing on its own).

For example, a standard financial model will have only one revenue input. What happens if you need to work with a

FIGURE 1-2

Expanding the Capabilities of a Standardized Template Model

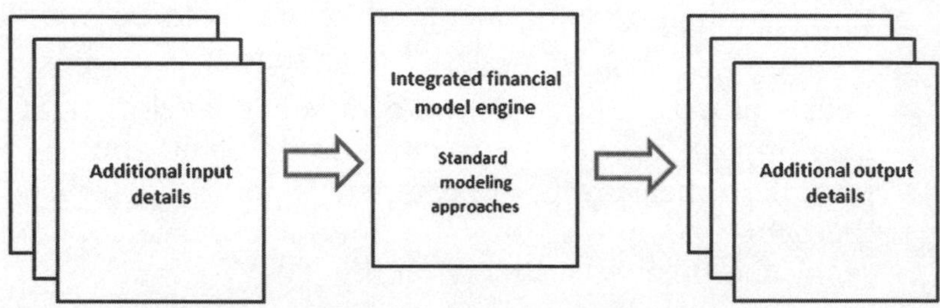

company that has multiple business segments? This approach of adding scratchpad sheets becomes useful in this case. On the new sheet, you can lay out the detailed assumptions and drivers for each of the business lines. Once you have a total for the revenue line, simply reference that back to the revenue input in the standard model. This approach can be repeated for other input lines in the financial model.

A standardized template model can be a powerful tool for a business team or the whole organization. Because it is designed to be used again and again, the developer and the users can continue to invest time in it to add features and enhancements, and also to comb out errors in the model. To the extent that the model is standard across a large group of users, it becomes much more than an analytical platform; it becomes a way to communicate thinking across diverse groups. A standardized model achieves this in several ways:

- A standardized analytical tool enables staff members to be placed in different projects quickly, with little or no time needed to have them be "desk ready." Such a tool also means that project startups can proceed quickly, with no lead time required to build a new model from scratch. Result: more projects done in less time and with greater clarity.
- It conveys to its users the analytical methodologies that others in the group are using, because those are

embedded in the model. This ensures a consistency in the analytical approach.

- It becomes in its own right a teaching tool, letting new users understand how the standard analysis should be conducted.
- As colleagues agree to use the same model, it becomes a common yardstick of analysis, a way to foster cooperation and partnership across groups.
- Credit and investment review committees who are familiar with the model can proceed to the qualitative analysis much more quickly and reach their decisions with greater facility. The economic returns can be significant: good (or better) decisions are made; bad decisions avoided altogether.

1.6 YOU AS THE MODEL DEVELOPER

1.6.1 Three Hats

As you start to build models, you will be wearing three hats:

1. You are the finance expert, working with the elements of the financial statements and your knowledge of accounting to produce the correct representation of the results.
2. You are the spreadsheet wizard, pushing Excel to squeeze the last ounce of performance out of your model.
3. You are the virtual architect, manipulating the screen and the structure of your model to produce a final product that is transparent (easy to follow), flexible (easy to change), and robust (hard to break down).

1.6.2 Three Versions

A good model takes time. Obviously, in the context of executing a project, you will need to work in a time-efficient manner. As you complete one model, you will sometimes find yourself saying: Next time, I'll do this part differently as I now understand it better. So a good model takes time and needs to pass through many versions. How many exactly? My experience is that you would need three to get to the solidly grounded model (and additional versions after that to continue to tweak it). The three are:

- Version 1: This is the first attempt, and involves gathering the required data and compiling the calculations. This model is not likely to be pretty and has lots of shortcuts and errors, but at least it gives a first picture of what the analysis should be like.
- Version 2: This corrects the errors as well as the shortcomings of Version 1. This version is easier to use and has more refinements in its calculations. After you develop this version and it has been in use for a little bit, suddenly you have a sense of what the model should have been doing all along, which leads to . . .
- Version 3: This version is the first "real" version. It is more elegant in structure and easier to use. Often, this is also a radical departure from Versions 1 and 2 and comes after a smack-your-forehead moment of insight ("Oh, I should have done it this way!"). This version is the one that satisfies the original concept of the model much more fully and elegantly.

1.7 SOME NOTES FOR WORKING BETTER

1.7.1 Two Monitors

Since the first edition of my book, I have begun to use two monitors for my work. I work with a laptop with Windows XP, and it is easy to set up an additional monitor that can serve not as a duplicate screen of the laptop, but as a second screen in addition to the laptop screen. The mouse cursor moves freely from one screen to the other. Moreover, the monitor screen can be set up as the primary screen.

With this setup, on one screen and on the other, it is possible to have combinations of:

- One model; and another model
- The worksheets of one model; the VBA code of the same model

- Excel on one; Word on the other
- E-mail on one; Microsoft Office on the other
- Or any other variation

The gains in productivity are real.

1.7.2 Mouse or Keyboard

You can operate the commands in Excel using either the mouse or the keyboard. For the latter, press the Alt key to begin, but there are some differences between Excel 2003 and 2007:

- In Excel 2003, look at the underscored letter in the command that you want to invoke.
- In Excel 2007, rather than an underscored letter, a small icon appears over the commands. The icon contains a letter, or a number, or a combination. Figure 1-3 shows the Excel ribbon at the Home tab after the Alt key is pressed. At this point, if I wanted to change the font, I would type "FF" as indicated in the icon over the font dropdown box.

Depending on how you learned Excel, a mouse is either an efficient interface design that allows an intuitive way to select from the commands visible on the screen (and the keyboard commands are a morass of seemingly random letters that you have to memorize), or the keyboard sequences are a quick and efficient way of operating Excel, with no time wasted on moving the hand away from the keyboard (and the mouse is a

FIGURE 1-3

The Excel Ribbon, Showing Letter or Number for Keyboard Commands When the Alt Key Is Pressed

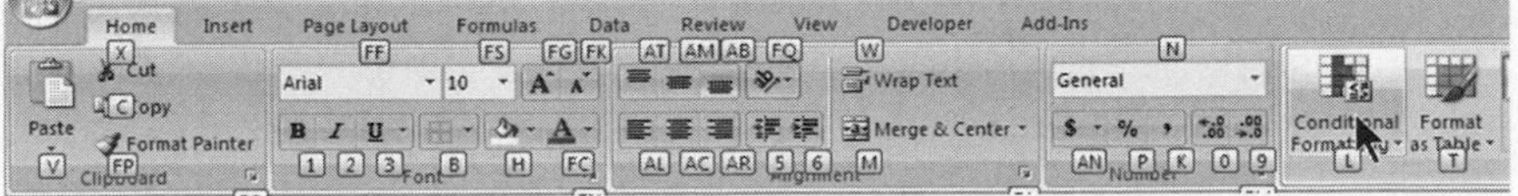

clumsy external device whose use can wrench wrists, elbows, and shoulders out of alignment). There is no one better way: the Excel developers know this, which is why the interface has both methods of input. Personally, I learned my Excel with the mouse, but I also make use of the shortcut keyboard commands for often-used commands such as Copy, Paste, and PasteValue (as formula, format, value, etc.). There is a benefit to knowing some of the keyboard commands, but if you still prefer to use the mouse, certainly no one can begrudge you that.

If you are a mouse user, I have two suggestions for you to consider. They are my own solutions for dealing with wrist, elbow, and shoulder pain that I had for many years due to using the mouse at the computer.

1.7.2.1 Mouse placement

The usual mouse position to the side of the keyboard puts the load of the arm and elbow on the shoulder, and this can lead to some soreness in the shoulder. One position that I found had worked to eliminate this is to place the mouse *in front of* the keyboard. Since the mouse is in front of the keyboard, with the cable going out to the left (I am right-handed), the action of my right hand from the keyboard to the mouse is not away from my body centerline (going out to the side of the keyboard, away from my torso), but rather toward it (coming nearer to my torso). In this way, it seems the whole arm is better supported at the shoulder.

Thus, between me and the computer screen, there is me the user, the edge of the desk, the mouse, the keyboard, and the screen. Of course, the keyboard will have to be placed a little bit farther out from the edge of the desk, but this also has the beneficial effect of creating more room to rest my forearms on the desk.

1.7.2.2 Vertical mouse

If you have soreness in your hand from using the mouse, it would be advisable to look into different mouse designs. The shape of the mouse determines the position that your hand is in whenever you are on the computer. Because a typical work day involves hundreds of clicks on the screen, you may start to get some soreness in the index finger, and also up your arm. I had this ache in the muscles of my forearm leading up to the elbow for many years, usually on the outside part of the elbow of my mouse hand. This was diagnosed as epicondylitis, usually known as "tennis elbow." It is an inflammation of the point of ligament attachment to the bone of the upper forearm. At its worst, which usually happened after a prolonged session of modeling, it was a burning sensation in the muscles.

The solution I found was something called the vertical mouse: it is essentially a mouse that has been turned sideways so that the buttons go down the side of the mouse. In using this mouse, the palm of the hand remains upright, rather than facing down. Because of this, the forearm remains in a more relaxed position with less tension in the muscles. The mouse that I use is made by Evoluent (www.evoluent.com). I have had no symptoms of the epicondylitis since I started using it. If you have been experiencing symptoms similar to mine, I recommend getting this mouse. (Note: I have no financial interest or connection to Evoluent.) If you are ordering one, make sure you specify whether you want the right- or left-handed model. Unlike a regular mouse, you cannot switch hands with the vertical mouse.

CHAPTER 2

Best Practices

This chapter contains my notes for best practices based on my experience of building models over the years.

One of the easiest traps to fall into is to start typing formulas into a blank screen as you start a model. This is understandable given the inviting screen that Excel presents, but resist this temptation! This is fine for worksheets for quick calculations, but for financial models that will be an analytical workhorse, following the principles outlined in this chapter will help make your models easier and faster to build and with fewer errors, and ultimately also more of a pleasure to use.

In building a model, the aim is to create a final product that from the user's point of view is accurate, fast, robust, easy to debug, and easy to use. In short, we want to have a model that is elegant, one that does its job in the cleanest and most direct way possible. A good model is one that "disappears." The model should be so well-attuned to its purpose that the user does not have to think about how to operate it, but simply uses it to get the desired results.

From a developer's point of view, there are many benefits for developing a well-designed and well-organized model:

- Both the developer (that's you) and other users can quickly find the information they need from the model. The confusion you avoid may be your own.

- Modifications or changes can be made easily.
- The final size of the model can be smaller, making it easier to transfer across platforms.
- The running time is faster than a poorly done model. The larger the model, the more apparent this discrepancy. In fact, a large but well-organized model often runs faster than a smaller and poorly organized one.

The pointers that follow may look like a lot to keep in mind. Put them into practice one by one, and by all means develop your own approaches to help you model effectively and efficiently. You will find that the more you follow best practices, the easier and more fun the work will be.

2.1 STARTING OUT

2.1.1 Have a Clear Idea of What the Model Needs to Do and Start Slowly

This is an absolute requirement. This may seem like an obvious point, but it is easy to start a model with a general idea that it should be, say, a "projection and valuation model." However, many questions still remain:

- What is the question that the model needs to answer?
- What is the level of detail that is required, or available? Does this need to be a full-blown model or is it a quick and dirty one? Or is it somewhere in between?
- Is this an annual model or some other periodicity?

The more questions you can raise, the better you can define the specific requirements for the model. This leads to a clearer picture of what the final products should be like, and will make the model-building process smoother and faster.

Once you have a clear idea, don't start just yet. Continue to think out the possible architecture. Sketch data flows on a piece of paper and share your thoughts with others. Create out a mock layout with labels and dummy numbers, so you can get a sense of what needs to be on the screens. Once you have a basic blueprint, build a small pilot model if you can to give yourself a proof of concept and to show to other team members as a reality check. Excel makes it easy to start working on your model, so it is all the more important that you spend some time up front developing the optimal path for building your model.

2.1.2 Understand the Users' Level of Expertise

Going hand in hand with defining a clear purpose for the model is understanding your users' level of expertise, in both the financial aspects of the analysis that your model is performing and Excel's functionalities.

Generally speaking, if your users already have a model or modeling format that they have used for some time, it is a good idea to make any (new and improved) model for the same analysis follow some of the layout and most of the analytical steps used in that model. Users generally like to stick with the familiar.

If you are creating a totally new model, much of a user's comfort level with your model depends on the user's own mental map of the analytical steps that the model is undertaking. For example, a discounted cash flow valuation model requires at least the following steps:

1. Specifying the date of the valuation for the discounting
2. Defining income statement forecasts down to the EBIT level, working capital levels and capital expenditure requirements
3. Estimating the weighted average cost of capital (WACC)
4. Selecting the terminal value approach
5. Setting the discounting method, i.e., whether using mid-period or period-end discounting

An analyst familiar with these steps and using your model will look for the sections representing these steps, and if you have done your modeling well, the analyst will find them easily. If you have done your job really well, the analyst will come across them precisely in the order expected. Of course, someone not familiar with this type of valuation will be lost, no matter how well you have designed your model.

Users who are not familiar with Excel can be intimidated by complex and seemingly incomprehensible formulas. In this case, it helps to keep the formulas as simple as possible, even if it means using additional rows. Of course, some formulas need to be complex to produce the result you want and cannot be reduced any further.

Also, check the version of Excel that your users have to ensure that your model will not have any compatibility problems. We are now in the era of Excel 2007, with a ribbon command interface that is quite different from the one users of earlier versions of Excel are accustomed to using. Although all the commands essentially still exist (with some additional bells and whistles here and there), veteran users will need to go through an adjustment period, with some implications of how you will need to write your user's guide. At the other end of the Excel lineage, we are now many years away from 1997, so one hopes that there are no users still using a pre-Excel 97 version. Versions earlier than Excel 97 are likely to have compatibility problems with current versions of Excel.

2.1.3 Set Your Global Settings First

Set the Excel stage properly, so that settings for fonts, numbers, the way the screen looks, etc., are out of the way, and you can concentrate on building your model without having to make continual small adjustments. See Chapter 3 on how to set the stage in Excel.

2.1.4 KISS

This stands for the well-known, if somewhat rude, saying: Keep It Simple, Stupid. When in doubt, make things less complex, rather than more complex. However, it does not mean that a model should be simplistic. It just means that for whatever your model needs to do, the best approach is always the simplest one.

2.2 LAYING OUT THE MODEL

2.2.1 A Logical Arrangement for an Audit Trail

A model needs to tell a "story": it must have a beginning, a middle, and an end of the analytical steps that it is designed to perform.

The easiest way to lay the story out is to put each step on different sheets, and arrange the sheets so that their tabs appear at the bottom of the screen in a left-to-right order, with the first sheets (on the leftmost tabs) carrying the inputs, and the last sheets (on the rightmost tabs) carrying the final outputs. Granted, there are times when calculations need to go "backward" in the flow of the sheets, but the more the user can feel that there is a direction of the flow in the model, the easier and more user-friendly the model will seem.

Sheet tabs can be renamed, so you can label them to tell a progression of steps (e.g., 1_ISInput, 2_BSInput, etc.) within your model. Because the sheet tab names are part of formulas that refer to the sheets, formulas are easier to read if the sheet tabs names short. Using shorter names also means that you can see more tabs across the bottom of the screen.

Excel also allows tabs to carry colors, so sheets with similar calculations can be marked with the same tab color. These become intuitively useful guides for anyone using your model.

2.2.2 Separate Input and Output Areas

There are many ways to organize a model in terms of inputs and outputs. At one end is the free-for-all that mixes the inputs and outputs willy-nilly throughout the model. At the other end is the highly organized approach where inputs reside in sheets clearly marked as inputs (perhaps with the use of color to designate input cells), and outputs are on sheets that are organized in a clean and presentation-ready formats.

The more you can work with separate input and output areas, the clearer and better organized your model will be.

2.2.3 Be Consistent

As much as possible, make the parts and the look of the model consistent across columns, and from sheet to sheet. In this way, you can not only achieve a clean and uncluttered look, but also minimize the frustration and potential for error that come from having to track the elements that are inconsistent with each other.

- Use the same formula across the columns. Write the formula in the first column containing formulas, and copy across. Where formulas are written to use the prior column's results (e.g., for a growth formula), you may not want to put this in the first column, since there is no "prior" year. However, a trick is to insert an additional blank column to the left of the first formula column, which can then serve as a "prior" (and blank) year. Keep the width of this blank column very small, so the additional column does not change the look of the layout very much. In this way, you can use the same formula across the columns. If you cannot write the same formula across, make it obvious where the formulas are different, by marking the column by some obvious formatting, such as lines or colors or adding a cell comment at the point of change.

- Use the same font, font size, and formatting (bold, italics, and underlines) to designate the same type of item. If you are using initial capitalization in your labels (each word begins with an upper case letter), do so consistently across your labels for added visual polish. If you are using colors in your fonts and cells, follow this consistency rule, too.
- Use the same arrangement of data across sheets, especially in the order of which column carries which year's data. If column F carries the data for 2008 (and column G for 2009, etc.), keep to this format so that cross-sheet references can be made easily, and a mismatch of column letters clearly indicates a referencing error. If one sheet needs an additional column so that its column reference becomes offset, it is worth putting in an additional column in all the other sheets, too. Again, reduce the width of these spacer columns so that they do not affect the visual layout of the model too much.

  (Consistent row references across sheets are more difficult to adopt, because sheets usually have different amounts of calculations requiring different number of rows.)
- Use the same label for the same account. Calling it "Cash Flow from Operations" on one sheet and "Cash Flow from Operating Activities" on another opens up room for confusion.

2.2.4 Keep Formatting Simple

Variations in formatting, in terms of font, font size, and colors of the font and the background, are ways to guide your users through the model's screens and informational content. However, be careful about being overly enthusiastic in adding these formatting embellishments, as this can result in a visual overload.

- Use the same typeface throughout, and just use variations in size and the combinations of bold, italic, and underline. Arial is the default typeface in Excel as part of the default style called "Normal," and has a clear, no-nonsense look. (A style is a named global format; changing an attribute of a style changes all instances of the style in a workbook.)
- Use pale colors for the cell background that convey a sense of differentiation without being florid. Combine these with differently colored fonts to convey other information. With black as the default font color, here are two color schemes that I have used and found to be well accepted:
    - Use a pale yellow background to mark cells that hold input data. The color background means that you can see which cells are the input cells even when there are no entries in them.
    - Use a blue font against the pale yellow background to further differentiate these cells as the input cells.
    - Use a dark green font against a white background for cells that show important data links from other areas of the workbook, or from other workbooks. This third format is not as important to use as the first two, however.
- Use strong colors to mark cells that you need to review again, such as cells that you are making temporary changes on to test the spreadsheet. Color the background of these cells, rather than just the fonts, so that you can spot them even when you are quickly going through the model's screens. Remove the colors once the cells have been corrected.

2.2.5 One Input for One Data Point

There should only be one input point for a data point. Entering the same data point—for example, the latest available stock price for use in a valuation calculation—in different locations means a duplication of work and, worse, the likelihood that you may have different and conflicting information with which the model is working.

Any formula that needs that data point should point to that one input location, whether directly or indirectly through one or more other formulas that ultimately read the input location.

2.2.6 Think Modular

If a model has a story, think of having the story told in "chapters": in separate distinct modules. In this modular approach, the blocks of your workbook perform discrete operations within them; each block's results are read by the next block, and so on. This makes it easy to put a model together and audit and check it later. It also makes changes easier to implement, since you can work within the modules and not have to roam over the whole model to change formulas.

2.2.7 Keep Formulas Simple

Keep your formulas simple, even if it means using additional rows to complete the calculations. If you write a formula and then have a hard time understanding it 10 minutes later, that is a sign that you might want to break up to formula into two or more separate components.

Of course, there are some cases in which the formula is going to be incomprehensible because of what you are asking it to do. In this case, once you have double-checked that it is performing its task correctly, let sleeping dogs lie.

2.2.8 No Hard-Coded Inputs in Formulas

Inputs that are used in formulas should be entered in separate cells, and not within the formulas themselves. If you are writing a formula that, say, calculates a tax of 36% on the EBT number in cell C40, don't write:

=C40*0.36

This hides the information that the tax rate is 36%, but more critically, it means extra work if you need to change the tax rate later, since you will have to go to the individual cells (assuming that you remember where all the hard-coded 36% entries are). A better approach in this case would be to write something like:

=C40*C41

where C41 contains the input for the tax rate.

2.2.9 Make All Calculations Visible

Avoid hiding columns and rows in the model to hide calculations; this only makes it difficult to understand what the model is doing. For a final printing, you might want to hide some rows for a better printout display, but once the printing is done, you should unhide them again. We will cover ways to quickly hide columns and rows in Chapter 19, Section 19.5.

Also, avoid setting an "invisible" font in which a cell's contents appear to be blank. This makes it vexing when checking formulas that read these invisible contents because the formulas seem to be working off empty cells (and you would need to go through an additional step of converting the invisible formatting into normal, visible formatting). It is also easy to create errors when these invisible rows are inadvertently deleted or overwritten as the model evolves.

Formulas are often set to be invisible when some required calculations need to be done, but the model designer does not want to mar the layout that has been worked out. Thus, a good solution for avoiding the need to have these invisible formulas is to have a good sense of where inputs should be placed, where calculations can be performed, and what the outputs should look like.

2.3 GUARDING AGAINST ERRORS

It is a fact of modeling life that however carefully you build a model, errors will creep in.

Dr. Raymond R. Panko, Professor of IT Management, Shidler College of Business, University of Hawai'i (http://panko.shidler.hawaii.edu/), shows that errors always occur in spreadsheets. The issue is not where there are any errors, but how many there are. Dr. Panko's research suggests that for tasks such as creating formulas in a spreadsheet, the error rate (defined as the number of errors made and undetected during the operation) is about 5%. The more complex the formulas and the larger the spreadsheet, the higher the rate and number of errors. Do not forget that the error rate goes up, too, whenever you become tired or bored.

Be aware of where errors creep in! It's a good way to keep the number of errors down and to as close to zero as possible.

2.3.1 Errors in References

These are very common. Typical errors are:

- Pointing the reference to the wrong cell. Using the arrow keys to place the cursor on the correct cell is one way to remedy this, but it is not always convenient when the cell you want to identify is not on the same screen or the same sheet.
- Wrong references can result if you have different formulas along a row. The principle of being consistent helps here: you should always try to have the same formulas working across a row. A change (e.g., the first three columns may be one formula, and the rest of the columns follow another, and there are no format variations or markers to indicate the change) invites errors when the cell in the starting column is inadvertently copied across all the columns in the row.
- Copying formulas across that causes the reference to be wrong. This may be a case in which the formula should include an absolute reference that fixes its source location as you copy across.
- Not noticing the use of absolute reference in the original formula, causing any copied cells to point to a fixed cell when it should point to be a relative cell. (This is the reverse of the third bullet point.) This is often the case

when you link into your worksheet a reference to another file: the reference comes with an absolute reference.

2.3.2 Errors in Functions

Avoiding these is a matter of being familiar with what each Excel function does. For example, if you want to count the number of cells that has content, regardless of whether it is a number or a text string, use COUNTA, rather than COUNT. If you use the latter, the final count will include only contents with numbers and not text, possibly giving you an undercount.

Errors in functions also include errors in entering the logical arguments. In the case of IF statements, probably the most commonly used function, take the time to think out clearly what needs to happen when the logical test is TRUE and when it is FALSE.

2.3.3 Errors in Range Definitions

Most functions use ranges, and although it is easy to type in the range, it is equally easy to mistype. To avoid typing errors, use the arrow keys to define ranges when writing functions.

Check that the final formula is correct. Use the F2 Edit key on a completed formula. Excel highlights the ranges read by the formula in differently colored boxes. This gives a quick visual check of the ranges.

Be careful when inserting rows and columns. Double check that these do not cause correct formulas already in the spreadsheet to suddenly become incorrect. For example, when you insert an extra row between a column of numbers and the summing cell at the bottom, the summing cell will not include this new row. Check that the summing formula includes the new inserted cell.

2.4 WORKING IN EXCEL

2.4.1 Become Familiar with Excel's Functions

Excel 2007's 343 functions (51 more than Excel 2003) give you an incomparable toolbox for analytical computations. Take heart—you will not need to know all of them. Chapter 6, Section 6.1 gives you a list of the 50-odd functions that I have found to be useful in my modeling work. When you find that you do need to use a function you are not already familiar with, Excel provides help through the Insert function. (It's the *fx* notation at the left end of the edit bar.)

Often, it is the combination of functions or the use of specific functions in unconventional ways that yields new modeling power. Here, the numerous Excel user forums on the Internet can give you information and tips. With the friendly give-and-take in these forums, you can also ask for help. Doing a Google search under "Excel forums" will quickly give you a list of these Web sites. One site I have found useful is www.groups.google.com/group/microsoft.public.excel. The site has subforums for general Excel questions, for functions and programming.

2.4.2 Document as You Develop

Documenting is one of the more onerous tasks of developing a model, but it is an unavoidable task once a model is complete and you have to explain to others, and just as importantly to remind yourself, what the model does and how it does it.

As a way to document various aspects of your model, use Excel's cell comment feature to add comments to cells as you work on your model. Cell comments can be used as a way to explain a particular feature of the model, remind yourself of changes to be made, or identify a source for a data point, among other things. The quickest way to insert a comment in a cell is to:

1. Right-click on the mouse
2. From the short menu shown, select Insert Comment…

Once placed in the cell, a comment makes itself known by a red triangle appearing discreetly in the top right corner of the cell.

2.4.3 Provide Ways to Catch Errors

Build in checks so that errors can be more easily detected. When working with a balance sheet, a parity check that checks that the two sides are balanced is an example of an easy and effective check.

2.4.4 Save and Save Often

Excel can crash; if it does, there goes the screen and your work! However, Excel now has the feature to automatically recover your work in progress. Make sure you turn on the AutoRecover feature:

To turn on AutoRecover:

1. *Tools>Options*, click on the Save tab.
2. Set the time interval for Excel to save your work. A setting of 10 or 15 minutes is reasonable. If there is a crash, Excel will use the file it last saved to restore your screen; you lose only the work between your crash and the last save.

At the same time, it is a good practice to save under a different name at regular intervals. Imagine the frustration if you have been working on a model for several days under the same name, and then it gets corrupted and is not recoverable. Since there is no other file under a different name, you will have lost a tremendous amount of work.

Change the name when you complete what you think is a significant change in the model. You should also change the name when starting a new work session (e.g., starting again in the morning, or even just after lunch and you want to separate the morning's work from the afternoon's). You can use a simple naming system that uses today's date and a letter to indicate the version on which you are working. Thus, for a model named "PILOT," for example, you can have PILOT1017a.xls, PILOT1017b.xls, etc., for the different versions of the work done in October 17. The next day, rename it PILOT1018a.xls, etc. (Here, the example uses the U.S. system of putting the month first before the day.) You can use spaces or underscores to make the name and time more visually separated as a matter of personal style.

CHAPTER 3

Setting the Stage

When Excel is up and running, it is inviting to rush in and start typing our formulas into Excel. However, a pause here to review and change some of Excel's settings will be helpful to our workflow and the look of the final product.

This chapter reviews the following topics:

- The appearance of the screen:
  - Gridlines
  - Colors
  - Column widths
- Workflow aids:
  - Toolbars
  - Styles
- Excel settings for:
  - Calculation
  - Editing
  - Autosaving

With the release of Excel 2007 with its ribbon command interface, this chapter will show the commands in both the new 2007 format and the classic pre-2007 versions. I will refer to the latter as Excel 2003, but instructions for this version are applicable for earlier versions of Excel, too.

There are quite a few Web sites that market add-ons that will allow the classic menus to appear in the Microsoft Office applications (Word, Excel, PowerPoint, and Access). If you are using any of these, then simply follow the instructions for the 2003 version.

3.1 THE APPEARANCE OF THE SCREEN

Many factors come into play for how well a model is received. Of course, it should be robust. It should contain all the analytical calculations to do the job at hand, and do them correctly. It should have a clear and easy-to-audit flow of calculations. It should have no excess baggage. These will make users want to use the model. But there are other—and more subtle—factors that can determine whether your users will like the product or not: how well the elements of the screen are laid out and how the screen itself looks. This first part goes over the settings for three elements of the appearance of the screen.

3.1.1 Gridlines

A plain screen can be more visually pleasing by reducing clutter, so let's have the screen *not* show the gridlines.

3.1.1.1 In Excel 2003 and Excel 2007

In Excel 2003: *Tools>Options*, then uncheck the Gridlines option in the lower left of the View tab (Fig. 3-1).

The Options settings form has 13 tabs, but there is no need to go through every single one of them. At most, we need concern ourselves with about half of them. On each of these, there are only a few settings to pay attention to. Everything else we can leave as they are.

In Excel 2007: Go to the View tab, then uncheck the Gridlines checkbox (Fig. 3-2).

If the gridlines do not appear on the screen, does it make it more difficult to locate a specific cell? Not really. Excel always shows the location of the cursor on the screen, whether the cells are marked by gridlines or not. Additionally, you have two indicators of what cell the cursor is in:

FIGURE 3-1

The Gridlines Checkbox in the Options Form

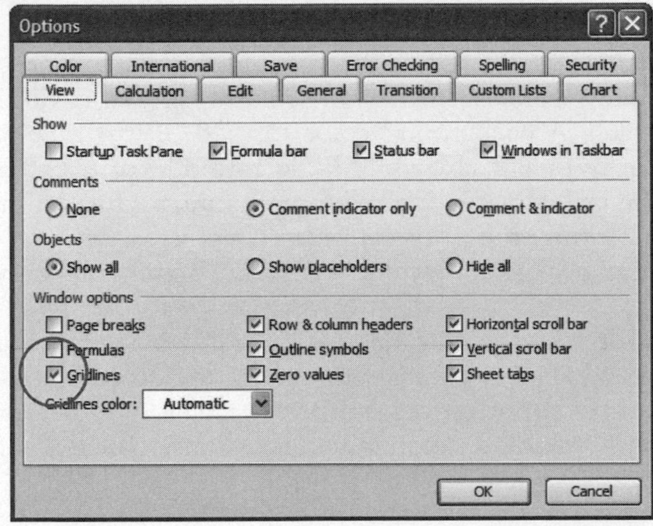

1. The row and column headings (on the frame at the left and top of the screen, respectively) indicate in bold the location of the active cell.
2. The active cell address is also shown in the name box just above the letter "A" on the column heading.

FIGURE 3-2

The Gridlines Checkbox Under the View Tab

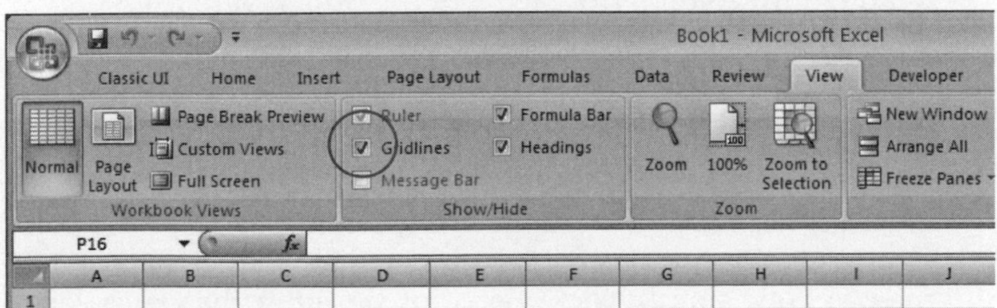

3.1.2 Colors

Excel allows you to apply colors in the cells (the background colors are called *Patterns*) and to the fonts being used. One of the easiest and visually pleasing ways to indicate an input cell in a model is to use a color as the cell background. For example, a light yellow color seems to work quite well as an indicator of an input cell. A background color instead of just a colored font (e.g., blue font against a white background) works better in that even if the cell is blank, the cell remains marked as an input cell. (During printing, the print setting can be set to black and white so that the background color does not appear as gray in the printouts.)

Excel 2003 and 2007 have different ways of dealing with color. Excel 2003 has global settings for the color palette, which you can then apply on a local basis. Excel 2007 has one color palette with standard colors and onto which you can add your own colors.

3.1.2.1 In Excel 2003

The background colors and the font colors can be set globally through *Tools>Options*. Once the colors are set, you apply them locally through *Format>Cells*.

In this section, we will first globally adjust a color. As an example, let's adjust the standard light yellow color so that it is a shade lighter. After this is done, we will apply it.

1. *Tools>Options*.
2. In the Options form, click on the Color tab (Fig. 3-3).
3. Click on the color in the palette to change. In this case, it's the third column from the left, the fifth square from the top.
4. Click on Modify. . .

You will see this (Fig. 3-4). Note there are two tabs: Standard and Custom.

The Standard way (Fig. 3-4): The current shade of the color is highlighted by the hexagonal marker. To adjust the color to a lighter yellow, simply click the color hexagon that is closer to

FIGURE 3-3

The Excel 2003 Color Settings in the Options Form

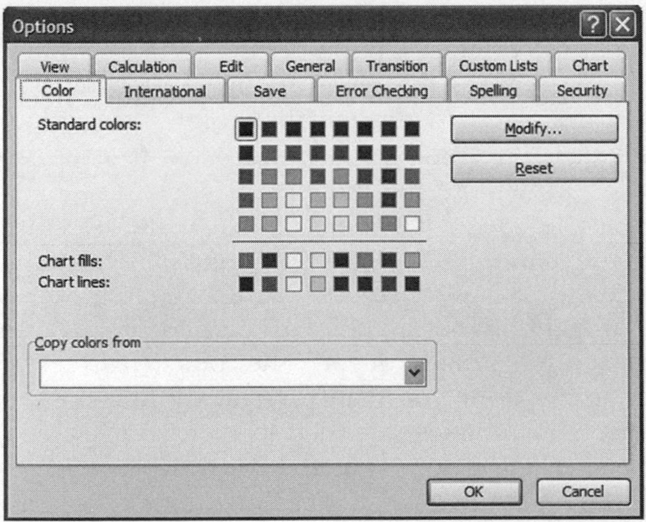

FIGURE 3-4

The Color Wheel Under the Standard Tab

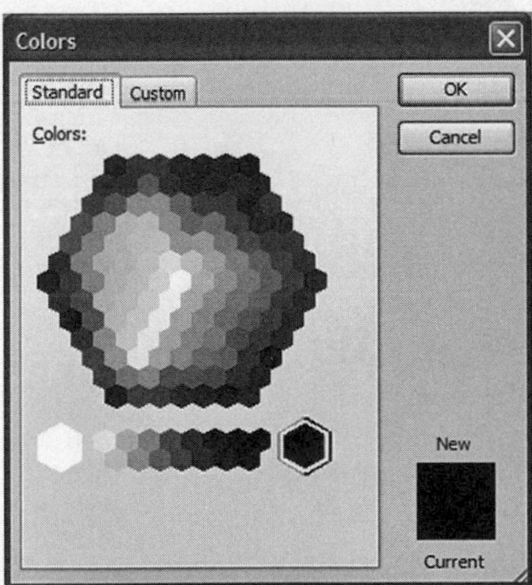

the center. You will see the change in the color in the square at the bottom right corner, where the "New" and the "Current" halves indicate the change in the color. In fact, if you want, you can choose a color that is not even yellow! In this case, the square in the original Options palette will be whatever color you select. This means that even though you have put the yellow pattern in place, to change that color, you simply change it at this global level and you do not have to change the cells individually throughout the model.

The Custom way (Fig. 3-5): You can make literally millions of colors by manipulating the red/green/blue settings or by moving the cross hairs on the spectrum and the arrowhead on the scale at right. To set a color, it helps to first set the arrowhead lower on the scale to deepen the color. This makes it easier to determine the color you want by just shifting the cross hairs. (The deeper color makes it easier to distinguish among hues.) Once you have the color, drag the arrowhead up again to get the shading you want.

Click on OK twice to get back to Excel.

FIGURE 3-5

The Custom Setting

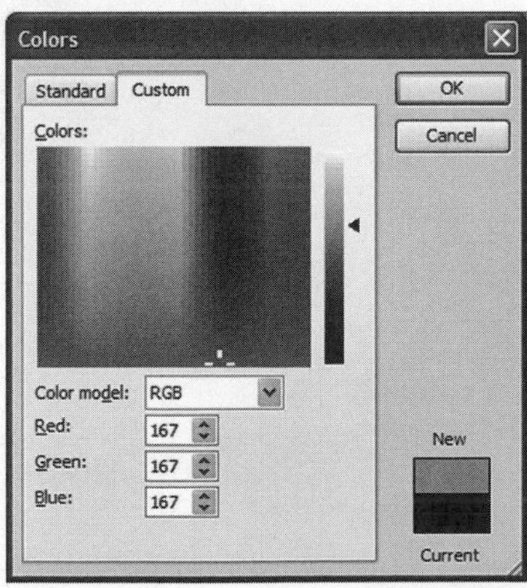

3.1.2.2 Applying colors locally in Excel 2003

Once the colors are set globally, you can apply it by highlighting the cell or cells you want to re-color. Then *Format>Cells,* go to the Pattern tab and select the color there.

3.1.2.3 In Excel 2007

The palette is available under the Home tab in the ribbon. Click on the Fill Color icon. (It looks like a tipping bucket of paint.) The current color setting is shown under the bucket, so if you click on the bucket (and not the dropdown arrow to its right), whatever cell or cells are highlighted will take on that color.

To change the current color, click on the dropdown arrow to see the palette (Fig. 3-6). Excel 2007 has a wider range of colors, listed as theme colors and standard colors.

If you do not see the color you want, click on the More Colors . . . option at the bottom, and you see the same Colors form with the standard and custom tabs as seen in Excel 2003 (see Figs. 3-4 and 3-5). Unlike Excel 2003, your choice of new colors does not replace the existing color squares, so you have a wider choice of colors.

FIGURE 3-6

The 2007 Palette

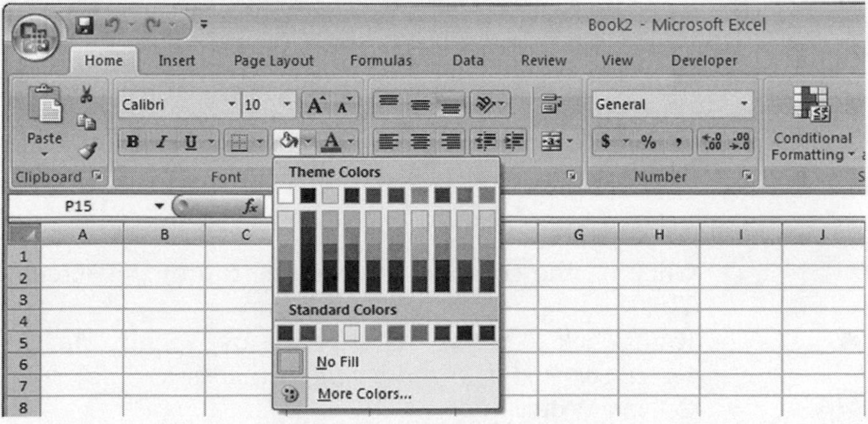

3.1.3 Column Widths

The default column width in Excel is 8.43 points. This is generally adequate for most purposes, but you may want to experiment with 10 or 12 point widths for the columns, and a wider (30–40 points) width for the labels.

To preserve the clean visual look of the screen, you should avoid changing the width of just one column across the screen. In a time series of columns, often this gives a jarring effect in which one column is clearly wider (or narrower) than the others.

It's a good idea to set the column width on the sheets to a uniform width that is set to the scale of numbers you are using.

3.1.3.1 In Excel 2003 and Excel 2007

In Excel 2003: To change column widths globally:

1. *Format>Column.*
2. Click on Standard Width and specify the width setting.

In Excel 2007: To change column widths globally:

1. Under the Home tab, go to Format.
2. Click on the down arrow, select Default width.

These commands will change the column widths globally. If you have manually changed a column width, a global change will not affect it. Excel considers such a column to be locally formatted, and thus are no longer affected by global changes.

For the column that carries the labels, a width of 30 to 35 is usually enough. You will have to change this column width manually, by either one of the two methods:

3.1.3.2 Manual adjustments to column width

For both Excel 2003 and Excel 2007:

- Method 1:
  - Click on the column letter at the top of the screen. This highlights the whole column.
  - Right-click to show the short mouse menu *while the cursor is still in the highlighted area,* and select Column Width.

- Specify the column width in the input box.
- Method 2:
    - Click on the column letter at the top of the screen. This highlights the whole column.
    - Click on the border to the right of the column letter block, and drag to the width desired.

3.2 TOOLBARS

Modeling is a continuous series of small steps. To the extent that you can take shortcuts in going through those steps, you will be able to work faster and with less fatigue.

Excel 2003 has toolbars that appear at the top of the screen, usually below the menu bar (Fig. 3-7). It is possible to customize these toolbars.

Excel 2007 introduces something called the ribbon, which expands on each of the default commands. Figures 3-8 and 3-9 show the ribbons under the first two of the default commands: Home and Insert. Other commands have other ribbons:

The default menu commands have also changed (Fig. 3-10).

What this means is that if you are switching from Excel 2003 to Excel 2007, you have some rewiring to do of your mental map of Excel. The menu trees between the two versions have some similarities, but mostly on the lower levels; the top-level interfaces are reorganized to a degree that guarantees drastically lower productivity at the keyboard when you first try it out. Admittedly, after some practice, it is likely that you will begin to sense the logic behind the new madness. It may also be that after the first two weeks, you will actually begin to like the new command tree. Excel 2007 does not provide a "classic" option

FIGURE 3-7

The Excel 2003 Default Toolbar

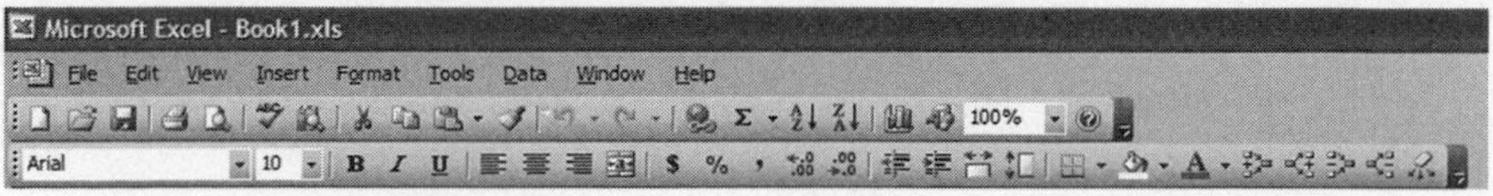

Microsoft Excel - Book1.xls
File Edit View Insert Format Tools Data Window Help
100%
Arial 10 B I U $ %

FIGURE 3-8

The Ribbon Under the Home Tab

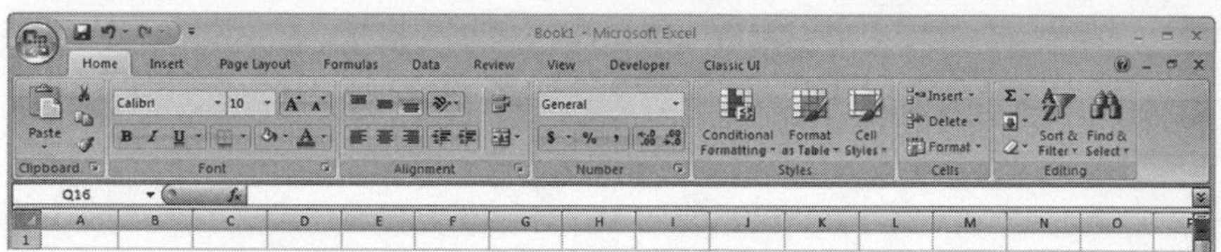

for the old menu, so when you make the upgrade, it will be a "cold turkey" change.

There are a number of Web sites that market add-ons to allow the Excel 2003 classic user interface (UI) to appear in Excel 2007. These give the same top-level commands as seen in Excel 2003, but the underlying tree follows what is available in Excel 2007. For example, even though you can use *Tools>Excel Options* (slightly different from the 2003 *Tools>Options*), the next screen shows Excel 2007's settings, and not Excel 2003's. Additionally, the Excel 2003 UI cannot be customized as in the real Excel 2003.

The 2003 UI add-ons may help in the transition to Excel 2007, but if the ribbon is the paradigm for Excel from now on, one might as well bite the bullet and start working with ribbons. That said, this chapter still covers the Excel 2003 menus as there is likely a majority of Excel users who have not upgraded to Excel 2007.

3.2.1 Excel 2003 Toolbars

Toolbars appear by default at the top of your screen and contain icons for quick short cuts to selected actions.

FIGURE 3-9

The Ribbon Under the Insert Tab

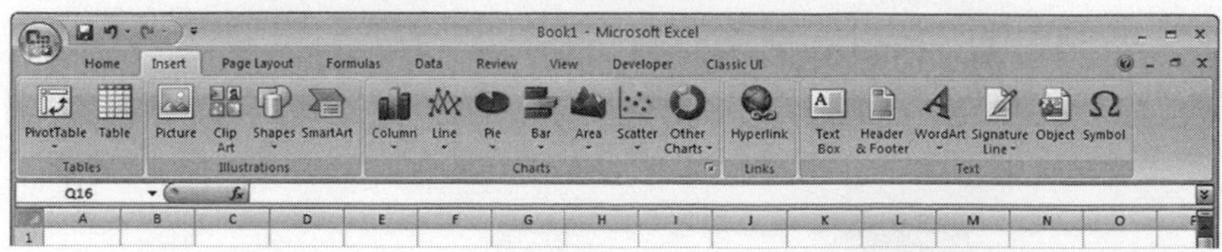

FIGURE 3-10

Comparison of Default Menu Commands

2003	File	Edit	View	Insert	Format	Tools	Data	Window	Help
2007	[Button]	Home	Insert	Page layout	Formulas	Data	Review	View	Developer

Excel has default toolbars as shown in Figure 3-11.

Here, the toolbars appear under the menu bar that shows the commands in Excel, and they appear on two rows. Each toolbar has a handle at the left edge, seen as a vertical stack of gray dots, that you can click on and drag. In this way, you can quickly rearrange the position of the toolbars relative to each other or elsewhere on the screen: the left edge, the right edge, the bottom, and even in the middle of the screen. You can park different toolbars at different locations.

You use the mouse to click on the icons, so toolbars are helpful only if you like to use the mouse.

If you have had some experience working with software icons, most of the Excel icons are self-explanatory. If an icon still looks cryptic, you can get a clue to what it does by putting the cursor of the mouse over an icon. A small text window should pop up with a word or two to explain the function. If you do not immediately see the pop-up text, move the cursor slowly around the bottom half of the icon. If you still do not see it, check that Excel is set to show these hints, called ScreenTips. Look at the section Other Settings for Toolbars (Section 3.2.1.3) in this chapter.

You can add additional toolbars and you customize a toolbar by adding or removing icons from the toolbar.

FIGURE 3-11

The Excel 2003 Toolbar

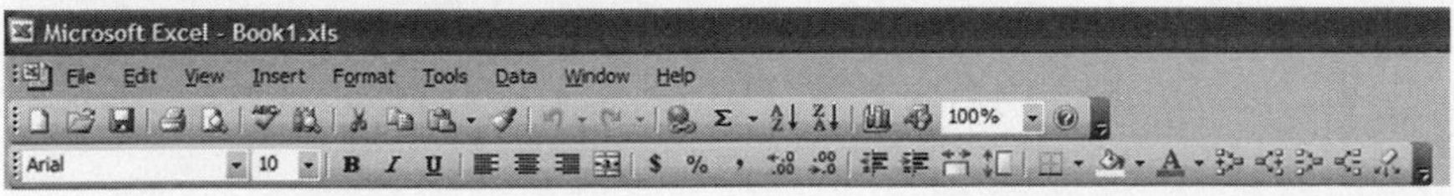

3.2.1.1 Adding toolbars

Use the sequence *View>Toolbars* to see the list of available toolbars.

Click on the toolbar(s) you would like to add to your screen. The illustration (Fig. 3-12) shows that the Standard and Formatting toolbars are currently on view. A second way to do this is to go to the Customize . . . command at the bottom of the menu, and make your selection from the Toolbars tab (Fig. 3-13). Note: This tab contains a wider selection of toolbars than is available from the first approach.

FIGURE 3-12

Customizing the Toolbar

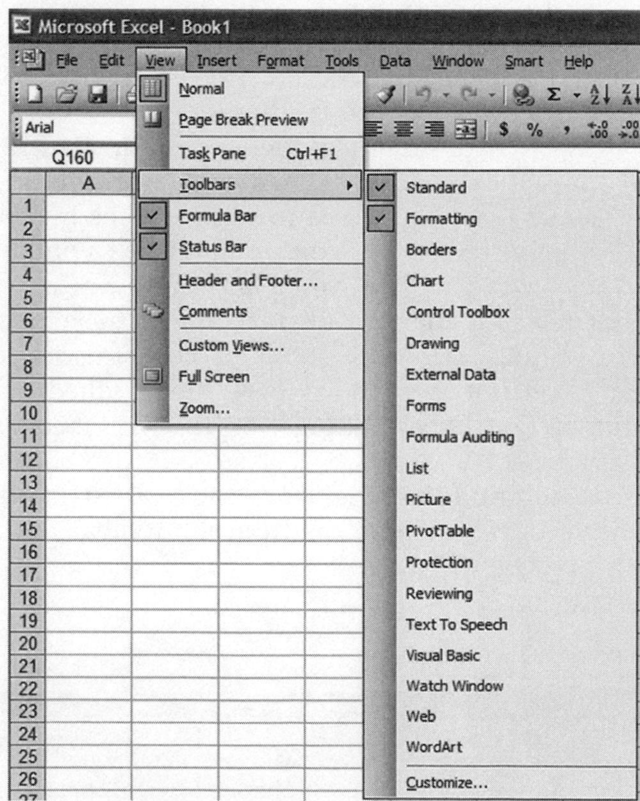

FIGURE 3-13

The Customize Form

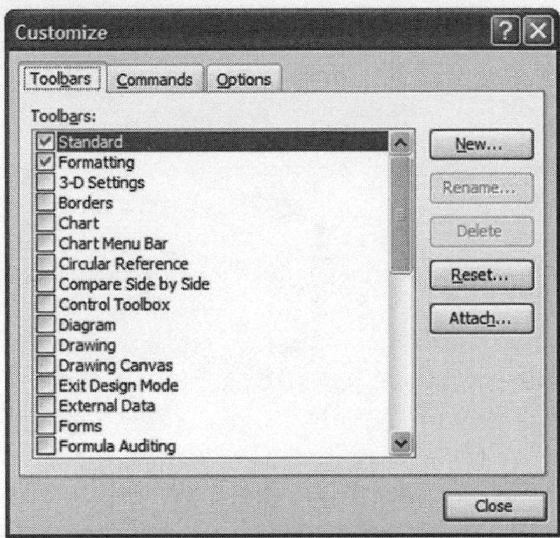

As you select new toolbars, they will appear in the middle of the screen. Use your personal preference to leave them there or to drag them to other locations.

Some toolbars you may want to add on a permanent basis: Formula Auditing is a good candidate for this. Others you may want to add only for the current stage of work.

The New button shown in Figure 3-13 allows you to create a new custom toolbar of your own.

3.2.1.2 Customizing a toolbar

Using the same sequence, click on the Customize . . .

The Commands tab shows the menu of available commands and icons (Fig. 3-14).

To add an icon to the toolbar:

1. Click on the type of command from Categories: box on the left.
2. Find the command you want from the Commands: box on the right.

FIGURE 3-14

Selecting Items to Customize the Toolbar

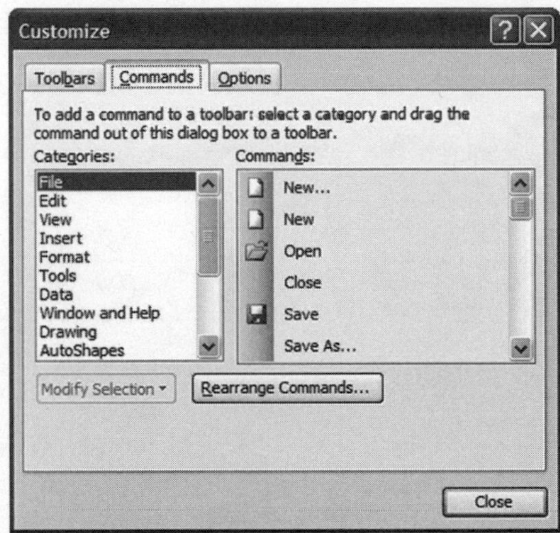

3. Click and drag the command and drag it into the toolbar section on the screen. Note: drag the icon into an existing toolbar (or the one you just created through the New button in the form seen in Fig. 3-13). Otherwise, it will not "stick."

To remove an icon from a toolbar:

1. Click on an icon in a toolbar and drag it out of the toolbar area.

Note: this works only if you are in the Customize mode.

3.2.1.3 Other settings for toolbars

Look at the Options tab (Fig. 3-15).

- Show Standard and Formatting toolbars on two rows: Check this checkbox to show the two toolbars on separate rows. Otherwise, they are strung out together as one row, and you have to search to the right for the icon you want.

FIGURE 3-15

Options for the Toolbar

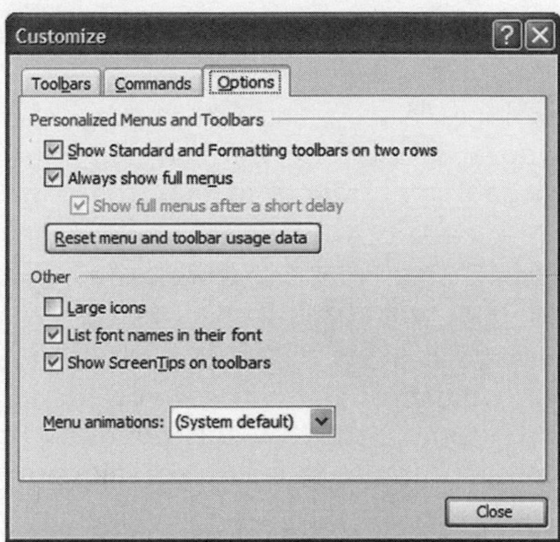

You should check this as you add more custom toolbars to have those toolbars appear on their own rows.

- Always show full menus: If you do not check this, a menu will be shown in the abbreviated format. For example, the Edit menu will appear like this (Fig. 3-16):

FIGURE 3-16

The Abbreviated Menu

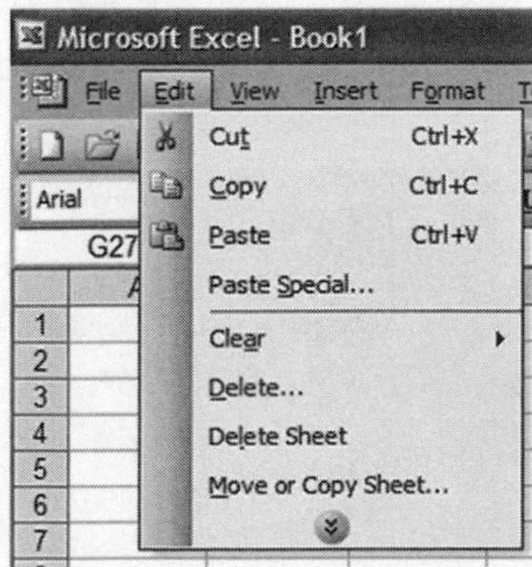

The full menu will not appear until you click on the double arrowheads at the bottom of the short menu (Fig. 3-16). After a slight pause, the full menu appears (Fig. 3-17):

- Large icons: This sets the icons to be large-sized on the screen.
- List font names in their font: Check this to have the font name appear in the font itself, so that you can see the different font appearances in the drop-down list of fonts.
- Show ScreenTips on toolbars: Check this to have Excel show hints of what each icon does.
- Menu animations: Select the method of menu animations. Select an animation that amuses you the most, but if you have a slow computer, this might add a delay to the menu appearance that is just long enough to be

FIGURE 3-17

The Expanded Menu

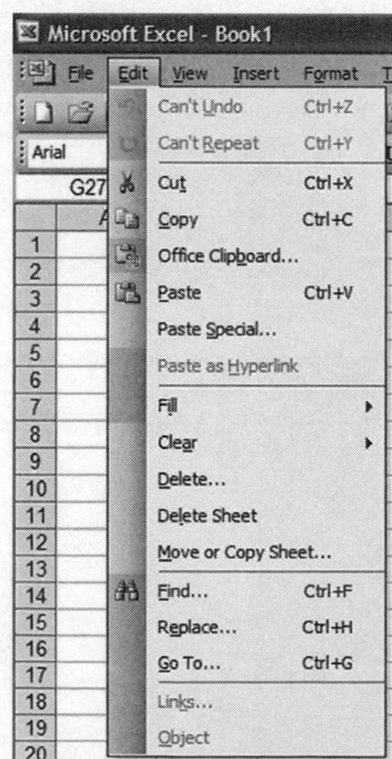

annoying. In this case, just stick to the system default setting.

3.2.2 Excel 2007 Quick Access Toolbar

In Excel 2007, the ribbons are essentially expanded toolbars. Even so, there is the Quick Access Toolbar (QAT) at the very top of your screen where you can insert icons that are shortcuts to the ribbon commands. In effect, you can recreate all your favorite Excel 2003 icons in this QAT (Fig. 3-18). There is only one line available, so if you have selected more icons than can be accommodated across the screen, the ones at the end will not be seen unless you click on the dropdown arrow at the right end of that toolbar.

The QAT can be set to be above the ribbon, or below it. As the ribbon itself can be minimized, you can get to an Excel 2007 screen that is space efficient and has most of your own icons visible at the top. So in terms of maximizing the spreadsheet real estate, this can be a workable arrangement.

3.2.2.1 Customizing the Quick Access Toolbar

To customize the QAT: *Office button* (the round Microsoft Office button at the top left corner of the screen)>*Excel Options*>*Customize* (Fig. 3-19).

Click on the dropdown box Choose Commands from, and you will be able to see a list of all possible commands by groupings. To get all commands, select All Commands. From this point, simply select the command from the left-hand listbox,

FIGURE 3-18

The Quick Access Toolbar Set Below the Minimized Ribbon

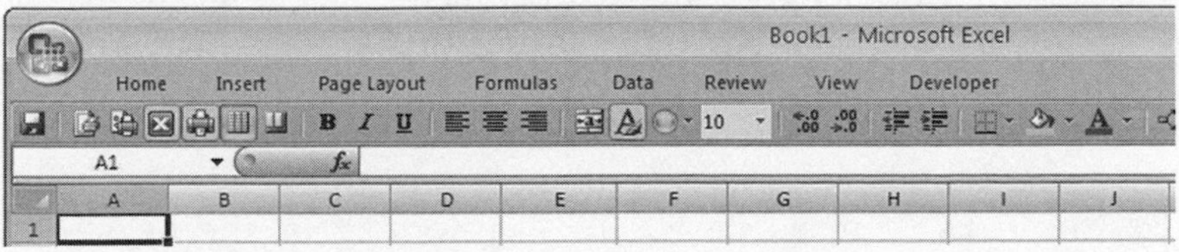

FIGURE 3–19

Customizing the Quick Access Toolbar

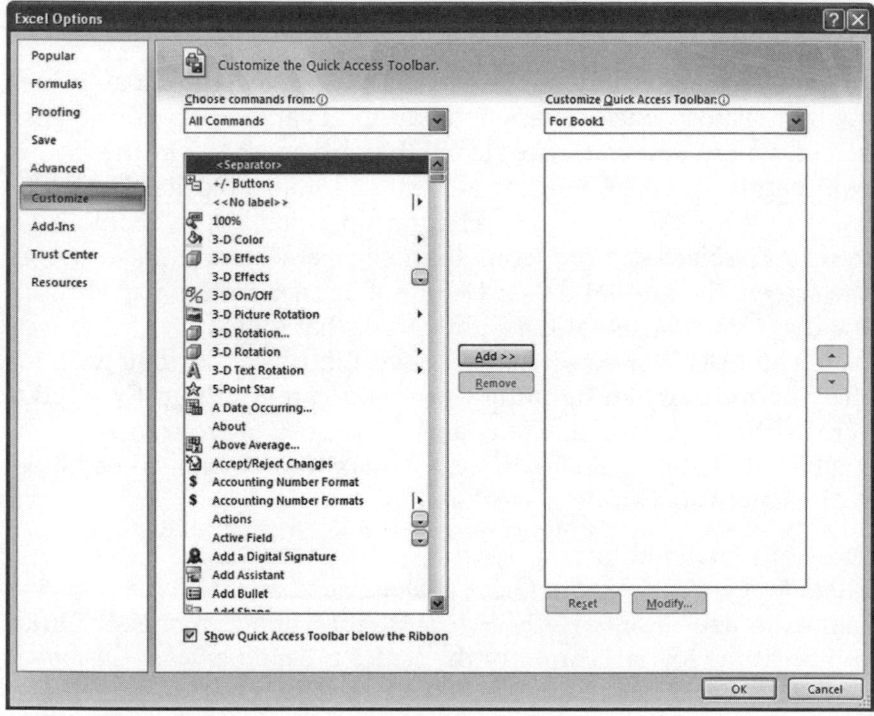

click on the Add button, and see it appear in the right-hand listbox. Use the <Separator> item on the top of the list to insert breaks in the icons you are adding to the QAT.

Check or uncheck the checkbox at the bottom left hand corner to specify whether you want to show the QAT above or below the ribbon.

You also have the choice for customizing the QAT only for the current workbook or for all documents. This setting is the dropdown box at the top right corner of the form. The default is for all documents.

Click on OK, and you are done.

Interestingly, you can use the keyboard to operate the icons. By the looks of it, as the QAT is customizable, the keystroke

FIGURE 3-20

Keystroke Indicators for Operating the Quick Access Toolbar After Alt Is Pressed

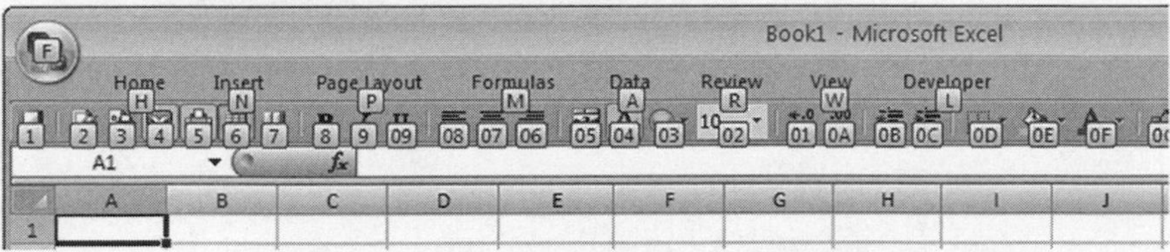

sequences for any particular action after the Alt key is pressed will vary depending on how the QAT has been set up. Figure 3-20 is an example of the keystroke sequences for operating the icons that are in the QAT customized as shown.

3.3 STYLES

A style is a named format that you can apply to cells in the workbook. A change in a style's format will change all the cells carrying that style. This is an example of a global setting. A local setting, by comparison, is one that only affects the current location.

In a new worksheet, the standard style is called Normal. It is possible that having set a global Normal style, you override it with a local change. In this case, if you make a change in the global Normal style, the Normal that has been changed locally will not follow the global change.

3.3.1 In Excel 2003 and Excel 2007

In Excel 2003:

- Use the *Format>Style* to define the global settings.
- Use *Format>Cells* to define the local settings.
- Once a global setting is changed locally, it no longer follows changes to the global setting.

The screen dialog boxes for both global and local settings are almost identical (the global sequence has a Style dialog box

FIGURE 3-21

The Style Form

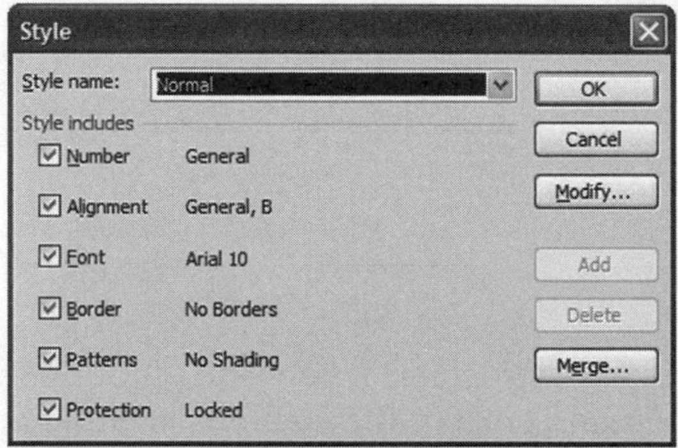

before everything else), so describing the setting for styles (global formatting) is the same as describing the formatting for cells (local formatting).

Press the sequence *Format>Style* to see this (Fig. 3-21):

Click on the Modify button to see the next step (Fig. 3-22):

FIGURE 3-22

Formatting within the Style

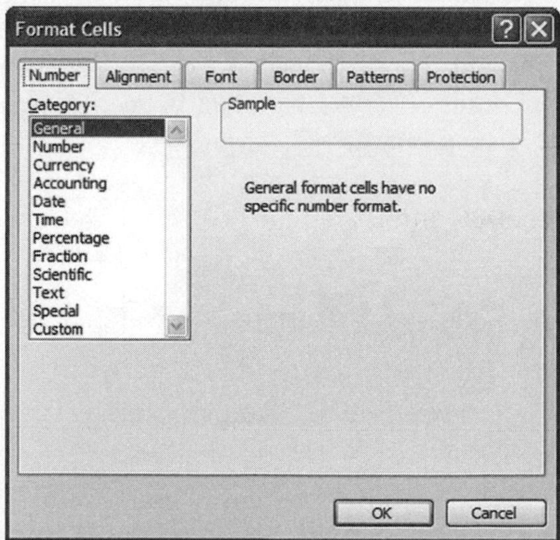

FIGURE 3-23

Setting Styles in Excel 2007

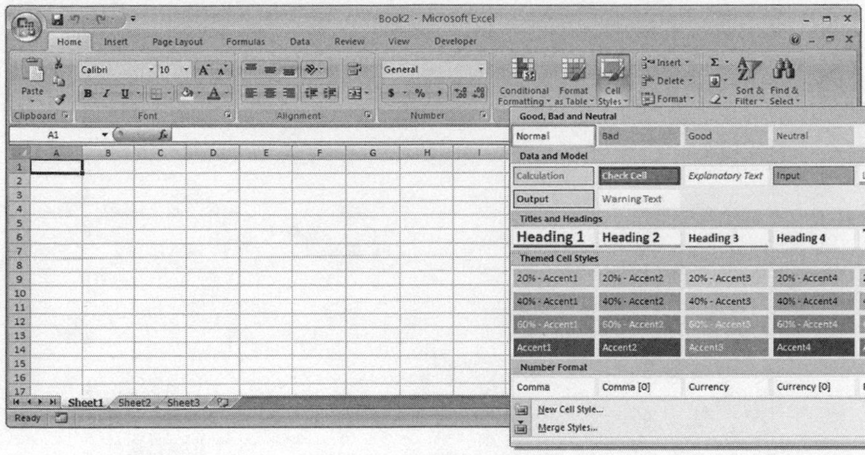

This step in Excel 2003 is similar to Excel 2007. Please skip down to section 3.3.2 to continue.

In Excel 2007:

Under the Home tab, in the Styles group, click on Cell Styles (Fig. 3-23). The Normal style is circled.

Right-click on the Normal button to see the menu to modify (Fig. 3-24):

Once the Modify is selected, you will see the form to format the various attributes of the style (Fig. 3-25):

FIGURE 3-24

Right Click on the Normal Style and Modify It

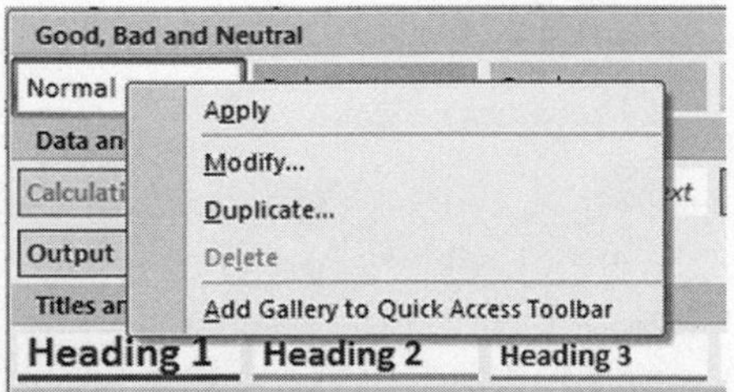

FIGURE 3-25

Modifying the Normal Style

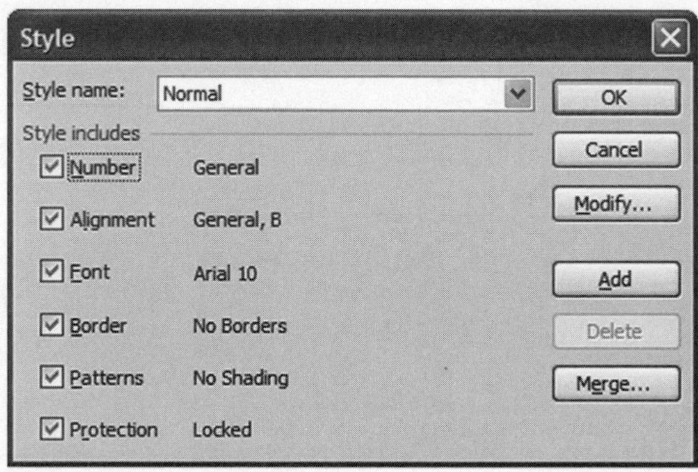

Click on the Format button and set the various attributes (Fig. 3-26).

3.3.2 Setting the Style

From this point on, the steps are the same in both versions. The dialog boxes are virtually the same, with only minor changes in layout and wording. Figures 3-26 and onward show the Excel 2007 dialog boxes.

Each style in Excel can be set in the six attributes of:

1. Number
2. Alignment
3. Font
4. Border
5. Pattern
6. Protection

You can set a style so that it carries any number from one to six attributes. Simply check the attributes that you want.

Let's go through all the settings for styles, just so we can fully cover the lay of the land. Remember, once past the Styles

FIGURE 3-26

Setting for Attributes

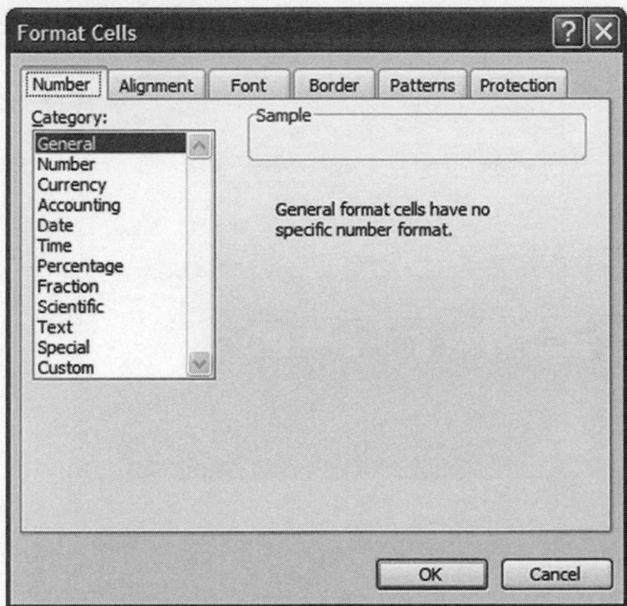

dialog box, the dialog boxes for the global settings and the local settings are identical—their titles all say Format Cells.

From the Styles dialog box, click on Modify . . .

3.3.2.1 Number

In the Number tab (Fig. 3-27), there are categories for number formats.

The General format is the default for numbers. It automatically sets the format according to how you make your entry. For example, if you entered 11.25%, then the format for that cell automatically becomes a percent format with two decimal places. A reference to this cell will cause that referring cell to also have this same format.

A cell set to General with a formula will show the result to as many decimal places as possible. If the formula is =1/4, then

FIGURE 3–27

The Format Cells Form

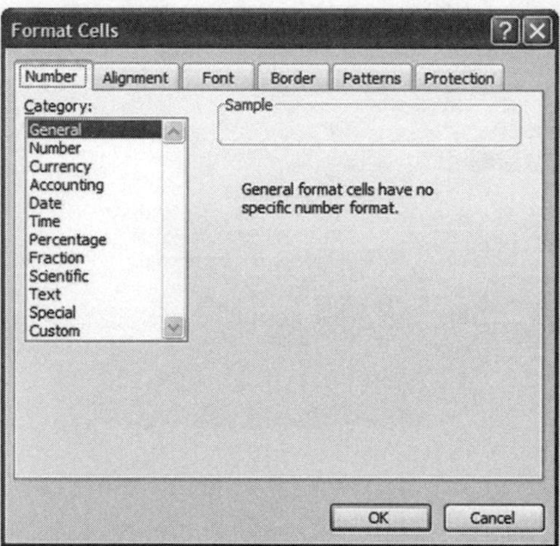

FIGURE 3–28

Setting the Parameters in the Number Tab

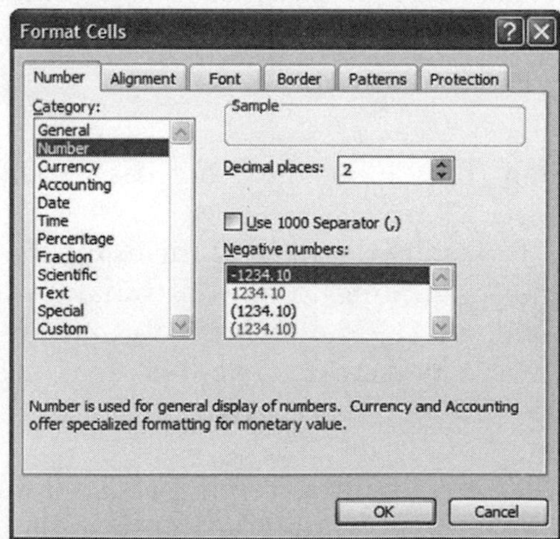

it will display 0.25. If the formula is =1/3, then it will display 0.33333. The actual number of digits visible depends on the column width.

The General format is a convenient feature for working up a small model or table of figures in Excel. However, for larger models where it would be beneficial to have a greater control of how the numbers are displayed, the Number attribute (Fig. 3-28) is useful:

The settings shown are for:

- One decimal place
- Use the comma separator for thousands (e.g., 1234.5 appears as 1,234.5)
- Parentheses for negative numbers. Shown is the selection for parentheses and in black font.

Feel free to explore the other settings. Other Number formats that would typically be used in financial modeling follow.

3.3.2.1.1 Currency This adds the currency symbols to the numbers, and you can set the number of decimal places that you want. Click on the Symbols list box to see the full list of symbols.

3.3.2.1.2 Accounting Accounting is a combination of Currency and additional formatting that puts the symbol at the start of the cell to the left and then numbers to the right.

3.3.2.1.3 Date This gives a selection of various date and time formats.

3.3.2.1.4 Percentage Percentage format, with decimal place settings.

3.3.2.1.5 Custom This setting is a good one for starting a format from scratch, or more importantly, for modifying an existing format. For example, you can select at first the Accounting format and enter your number in the cell. After this step, go through the format sequence again, but now click on the Custom format, and you will see the formatting codes that Excel uses for the Accounting format. With a little knowledge of what the codes mean (see Chapter 19, Section 19.3), you can then make changes in this format to get the final format that you want.

This kind of tweaking of formats can be done for any format already in place. The Custom setting is a good way to explore Excel's formatting functionalities.

3.3.2.2 Alignment

For global settings, there is nothing to change here (Fig. 3-29). For formatting specific cells (get to this form by *Format>Cells*), the text alignment and text controls settings are useful.

3.3.2.3 Font

This is the place for selecting the font and font size to use under the Normal style (Fig. 3-30).

FIGURE 3-29

The Alignment

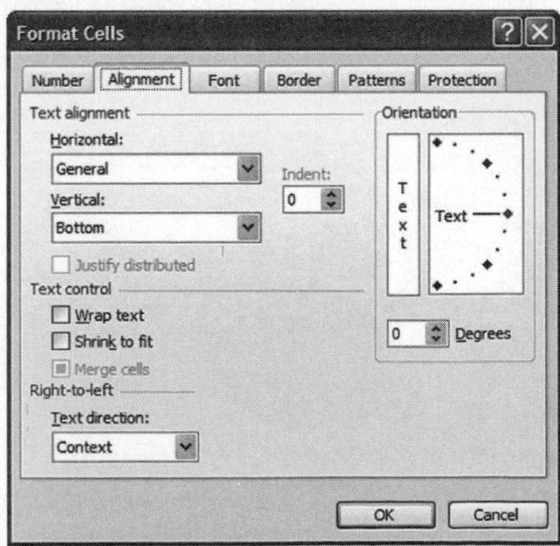

FIGURE 3-30

The Font

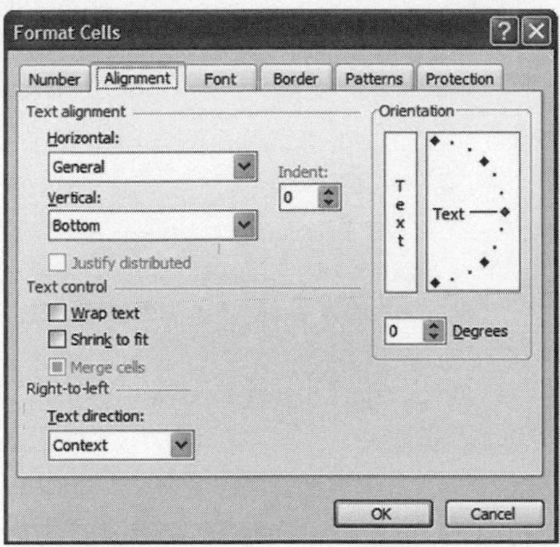

3.3.2.4 Border

For global settings, there is nothing to change here (Fig. 3-31). For formatting specific cells (get to this form by *Format>Cells*), the border settings are useful.

3.3.2.5 Fill

This tab (Fig. 3-32) is called Patterns in Excel 2003, and is more fully covered in the section on Colors (Section 3.1.2.1).

3.3.2.6 Protection

The Locked option (Fig. 3-33), if checked, protects cells in this format from changes, but only if the Protection option in the Tools menu has been turned on. In Excel 2003: *Tools>Protection>Protect Sheet*, or *Protect Workbook*. In Excel 2007: *Review tab > Changes group > Protect Sheet* button.

The Hidden option, if enabled by the same steps, will conceal the contents of the cell. Thus, formulas in a cell with the Hidden format enabled will not appear in the formula bar.

FIGURE 3-31

The Border Tab

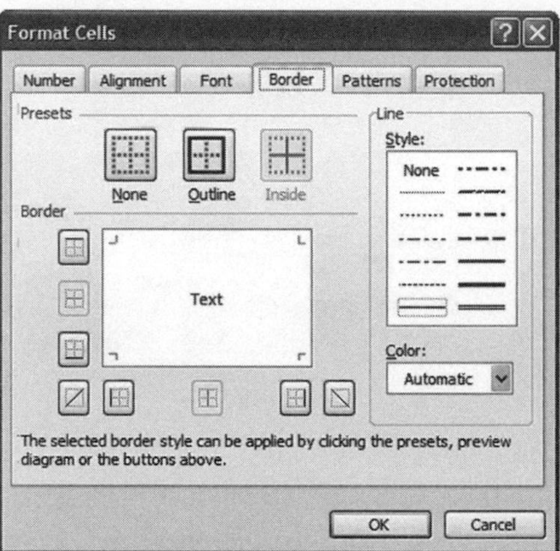

FIGURE 3-32

The Fill Tab

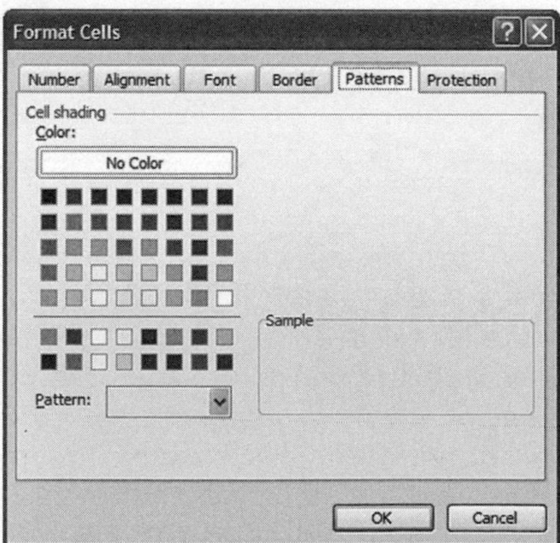

FIGURE 3-33

The Protection Tab

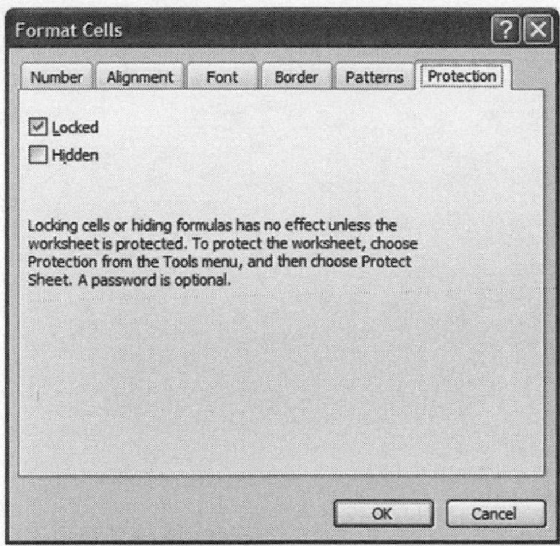

3.4 CALCULATION SETTINGS

3.4.1 Settings in Excel 2003 and 2007

In Excel 2003: *Tools>Options* form, *Calculation* tab (Fig. 3-34).

In Excel 2007: The *Office button>Excel Options>Formulas* (Fig. 3-35).

3.4.2 Automatic/Manual

With the Automatic option button selected, from the *Tools>Options* form, *Calculation* tab, Excel automatically recalculates all the numbers in the workbook every time there is a change in the workbook. Generally speaking, given the typical workbook size of about 5 megabytes or less and today's computer processor speeds, Excel can recalculate the workbook in an instant.

However, if the workbook is large and heavy with formulas and/or the computer you are using happens to have a slow processor speed, recalculation can take just long enough to disturb your workflow: every change you make is followed by a perceptible delay as Excel recalculates.

FIGURE 3-34

The Calculation Setting in Excel 2003

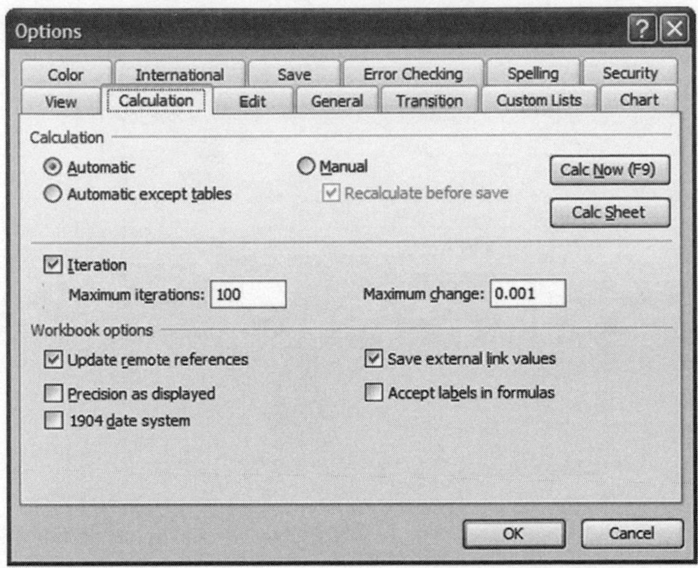

In this case, you might consider putting Excel on a manual calculation setting. If you do, you must make it a habit to press F9, the manual recalculation key, to update all numbers before you review the results. It is especially important to press F9 before any printing is done, so that the printout contains updated numbers.

Automatic except tables is a setting for automatic recalculation, except for the calculation of data tables. Data tables are a special way for Excel to create sensitivity tables, and are themselves calculation intensive. With this setting, the numbers in the worksheet are automatically recalculated, but in order to have the data tables calculate properly, you will have to press F9 for a manual recalculation.

3.4.3 Iteration

This subject is a special feature and is covered in a chapter on its own. Please turn to Chapter 7.

FIGURE 3-35

The Calculation Settings in Excel 2007

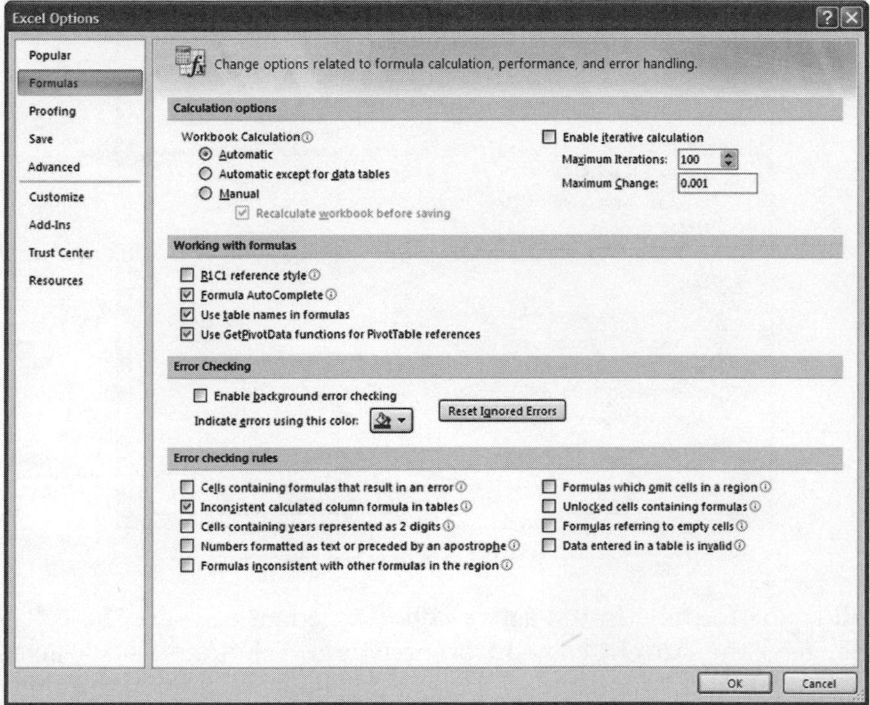

3.5 EDITING SETTINGS

3.5.1 Settings in Excel 2003 and 2007

In Excel 2003: *Tools>Options* form, *Edit* tab (Fig. 3-36).

In Excel 2007: *Office button>Excel Options>Advanced* (Fig. 3-37).

3.5.2 Edit Directly in Cell

With this checked, you can edit a formula by double-clicking on the cell. The formula appears as if overlaid on the cell. (It also appears in the formula bar.) You can then edit directly in the cell.

If this is unchecked, the formula appears only in the formula bar. However, if unchecked, there is another potential benefit: the double-click shows not the formula but the first precedent

FIGURE 3-36

The Edit Tab in Excel 2003

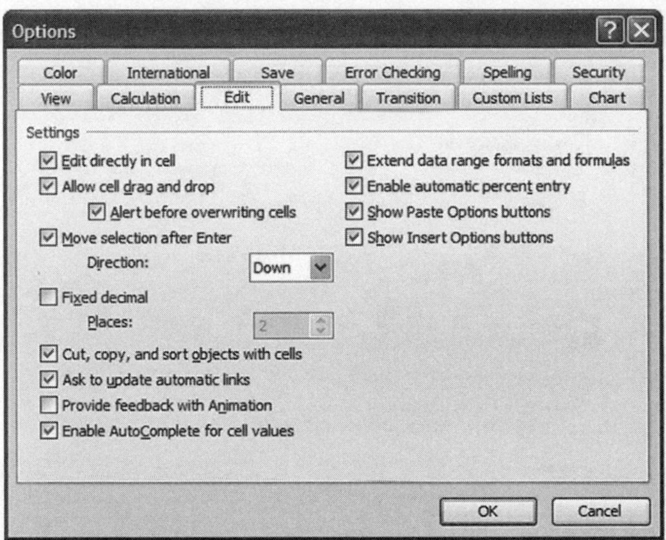

cell of the formula in the active cell. (Precedent cells are the cells that feed the current cell.) In other words, the double-click acts as a quick audit function of the first element in the current cell, so this is a useful setting. If you use this setting, press F5 to return from the precedent cell to the starting cell.

3.5.3 Move Selection after Enter

If this is checked, the cursor will move in the direction selected in the option. For certain tasks such as inputting a list of entries in a column, this can be helpful.

If unchecked, the cursor stays at the entry point. The setting here is usually a personal preference.

3.5.4 Enable Automatic Percent Entry

This is checked by default and is a good setting to have turned on. With this enabled, a cell that carries a percent format automatically divides your input by 100. Thus, to enter the value of 5%, you can

FIGURE 3-37

The Edit Settings in Excel 2007

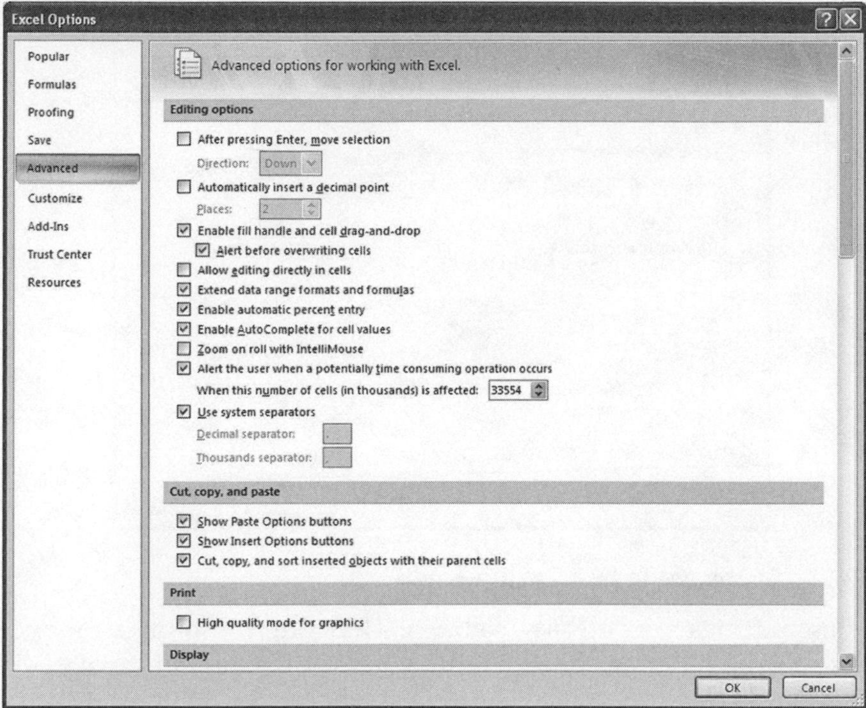

enter the number 5 into such a percent-formatted cell, and it will appear as 5%. (In reality, the value is 0.05, which is to say your entry has been conveniently divided by 100.) The only caveat is that if you want to enter the value below 1%, you have to make sure that you make the right entry: For 0.5%, you have to enter "0.5%"; entering "0.5" will result in 50%.

3.6 AUTOSAVE

3.6.1 In Excel 2003 and Excel 2007

In Excel 2003: *Tools>Options* form, *Save* tab (Fig. 3-38).

In Excel 2007: *Office button>Excel Options>Save* (Figs. 3-37 and 3-39).

FIGURE 3-38

The Save Tab in Excel 2003

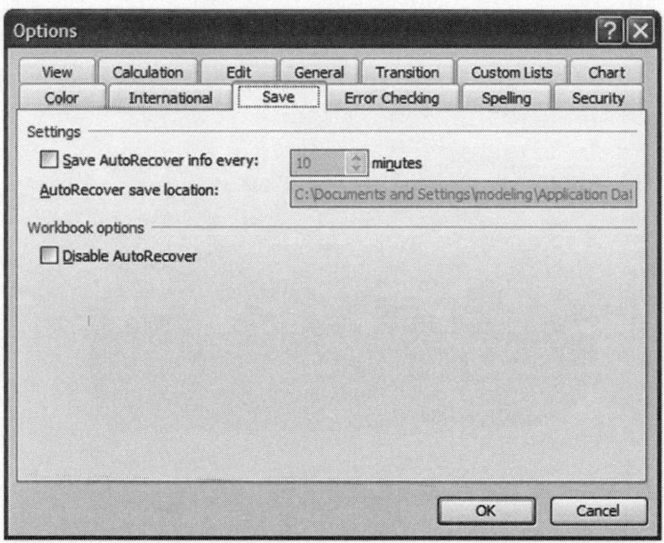

3.6.2 Autosave Is Not Saving

These settings are autosave settings. They are not settings to save your file on a regular basis, but they are settings to autosave your work in case Excel crashes. In that event, Excel will reopen and try to recover the last version that it has autosaved (which would be within the last 10 minutes by the settings shown in the illustration). This autosaved version will be available, even though the last full version that you saved manually may have been an hour ago.

Autosave is not an alternative to regular saving. If you have worked for an hour without saving and then turn off Excel (and ignore the prompt about saving the current workbook), all is lost, even if autosave has been running in the background every 10 minutes.

Remember to save your work manually, and save at regular intervals and under different names, especially if you have just completed a stage in your modeling work. In this way, you can also revert back to a clean working version of a model in case your next series of changes don't work out.

F I G U R E 3–39

The Save Settings in Excel 2007

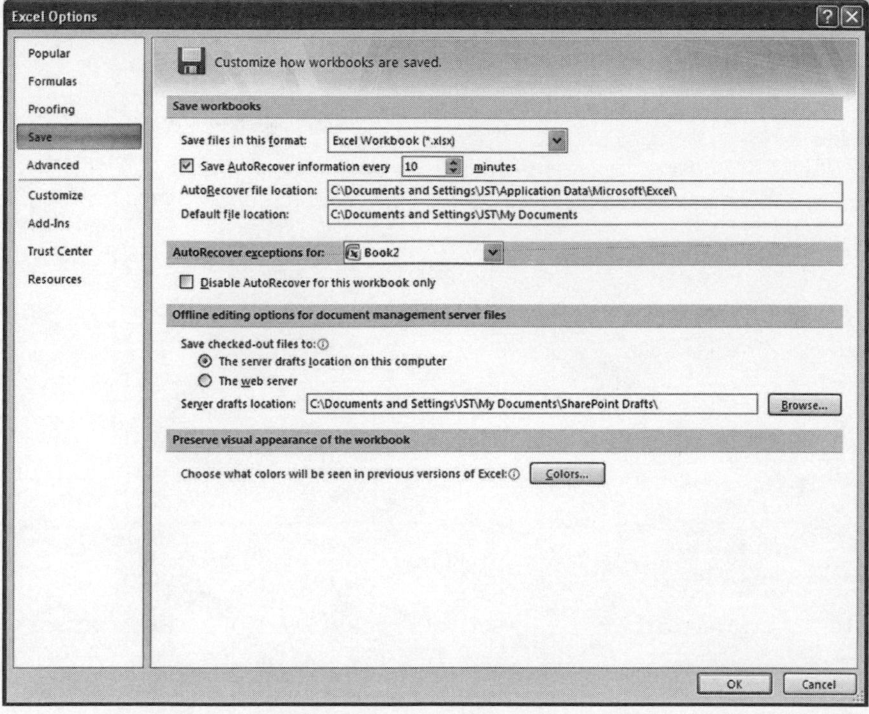

CHAPTER 4

Accounting for Modeling

To build a fully functioning model, we have to understand the accounting, because how the various parts of the model interact with each other follow general accounting logic. The accounting required for building good models is not difficult. In fact, if you think accounting is not your strong point, working with models is a good way to strengthen your grasp of the subject.

4.1 THE THREE FINANCIAL STATEMENTS

I describe them here in general terms.

The **income statement** keeps track of the revenues and expenses over the accounting period, typically a year, although the income statement can be prepared for shorter periods, such as a quarter or a month. The top line is revenue, and the bottom line is net income after dividends. If the company does not pay dividends, then it is just net income.

The **balance sheet** is a record of a company's holdings: its assets, liabilities, and equity at the end of the reporting period. The reporting period is typically at the end of the fiscal year, but balance sheets can also be prepared for shorter periods, such as at the end of quarters or even months. It is a snapshot of the company at this point in time. The total assets on the left side must equal total liabilities and the equity on the right side: the balance sheet must balance.

The **cash flow statement** shows how cash is being used during the year. The top line in the cash flow statement is the net income (before dividends) from the income statement. Subsequent lines show sources of cash (from revenues, selling assets or increasing liabilities or equity), and the uses of cash (in expenses or in buying assets or reducing liabilities in the balance sheet). The bottom line shows the total cash sources (or if the bottom line is negative, cash uses) in the company. If everything has been accounted for correctly, the total sources in the cash flow statement is the same as the increase in cash on the balance sheet between this year and the prior year. In this case, the cash flow statement is said to "foot" to the cash in the balance sheet. It may be that the total sources is negative—the company has been using up more cash that it generates—in which case cash on the balance sheet may drop to zero, and even to "negative cash." This means the need for more debt.

The cash flow statement puts the sources and uses of cash into three categories:

- Cash from operating activities
- Cash from investing activities
- Cash from financing activities

The full layout looks something like this:

Net income
+ Cash sources (uses) from operating activities
+ Cash sources (uses) from investing activities
+ Cash sources (uses) from financing activities
= Total cash sources (uses)
+ Beginning cash on the balance sheet
= Ending cash on the balance sheet

4.2 THE MAIN COMPONENTS

Figure 4-1 shows the main components of the three financial statements. Actual statements will have different names of the various accounts, but it is useful to view the statements as having these general types of accounts. These statements are for companies that can be described as industrial or manufacturing. Statements in other industries, such as finance and insurance, have a different set of accounts than those seen here.

4.3 THE ACCOUNTING EQUATION

This is the starting point for understanding the accounting in our modeling. In the balance sheet:

Total Assets = Total Liabilities + Shareholders' Equity

Visually, both sides must be the same height.

FIGURE 4-1

The Three Financial Statements

BALANCE SHEET

Assets	**Liabilities**
Cash	Accounts payable
Accounts receivable	Other current liabilities
Inventory	Debt
Other current assets	
	Equity
Net PPE	Common stock
Other long-term assets	Retained earnings

INCOME STATEMENT

Revenue
COGS
SGA

Interest
Taxes
Net income

CASH FLOW STATEMENT

Net income
+/- change in working capital

+/- change in investments

+/- change in financing

=+/- change in cash

Beginning cash
Ending cash

4.4 DOUBLE-ENTRY BOOKKEEPING

What the accounting equation also underscores is the principle of double-entry bookkeeping. This is to say that in the balance sheet, changes must happen in a one-two sequence. If something changes, something else must change also. In this way, the balance sheet is kept balanced. Figure 4-2 represents this graphically.

- Assets represent what we have
- Liabilities represent what we owe
- Equity (also called shareholders' equity or owners' equity) represents what we own

It is possible to "have" something without fully "owning" it. A house with a mortgage is a good example. The homeowner *has* it, but *owes* the part of the value that is represented by the mortgage. The bank holding the mortgage owns this portion of the value of the house. The homeowner *owns* only that part called the equity that represents his or her own money paid at the time of the transaction.

Generally speaking, the assets side represents the tangible physical asset in the world. The liabilities and equity side represents the intangible nature of the financing behind the asset, whether it is owned (equity) or financed by debt (liability). This is why even though there is only one thing in the physical world (the house), it affects both sides on the balance sheet.

FIGURE 4-2

The Balance Sheet, Balanced

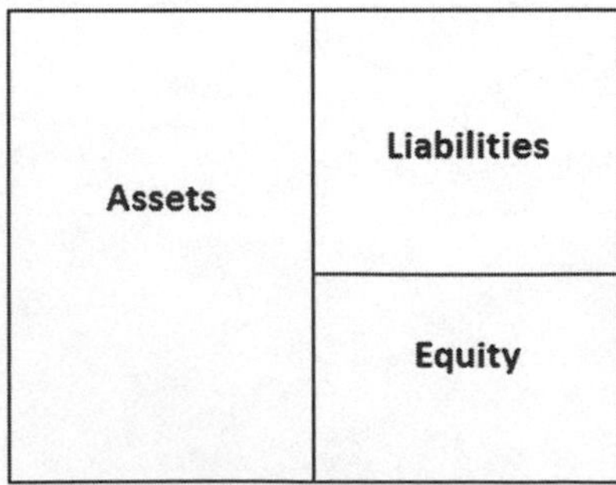

4.5 THE BALANCE SHEET OF A START-UP

Let's look at a start-up company to illustrate what the balance sheet shows.

4.5.1 At the Beginning

On Day 0 (Fig. 4-3), before it is established, the balance sheet shows $0 balances.

4.5.2 The Start of a Business

On Day 1, after the entrepreneur has decided to put in $5,000 of her own money into the venture and has taken out a $5,000 loan, the balance sheet looks like this (Fig. 4-4), with $10,000 of cash in hand. Cash is a physical asset, and this illustration shows how the entrepreneur comes to have the physical dollar bills in hand.

From this, we see that the right-hand side of the balance sheet is the funding side: increases in this side provide the cash to the left hand side of the balance sheet. In accounting terms, increases in the liabilities and equity side are *sources* of cash.

Likewise, decreases in the liabilities and equity side will require cash. So such decreases are *uses* of cash.

There is a direct relationship between the right hand side of the balance sheet and cash: when the former goes up, cash goes up; when the former goes down, cash goes down.

FIGURE 4-3

Before the Start Up

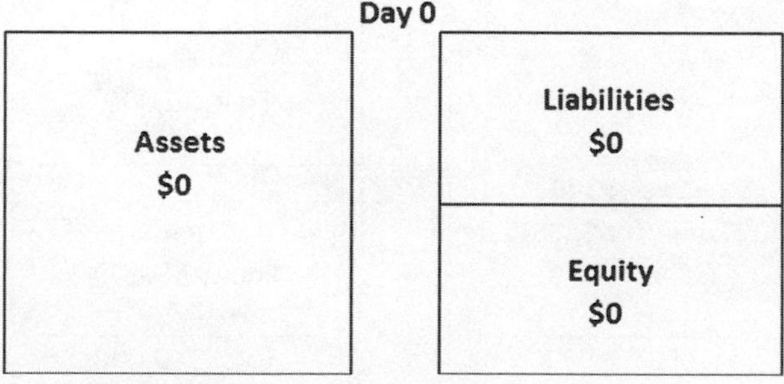

FIGURE 4-4

Increases in the Right-Hand Side Build Up Cash

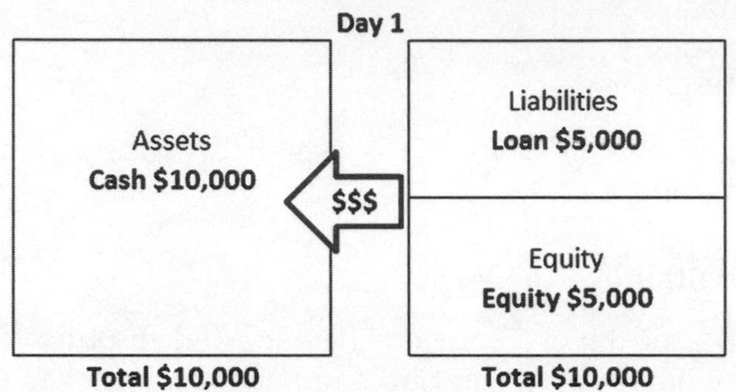

4.5.3 Using Cash for Purchases

Let's see what happens on Day 2 (Fig. 4-5), after our entrepreneur buys some office essentials.

Total assets remain the same at $10,000, but with each new asset, the cash goes down. After buying the desk, computer, and chair for $2,700, the cash account drops to $7,300. Here, we see that increases in the asset accounts (that are not cash) deplete cash.

FIGURE 4-5

Using Up Cash to Buy Assets

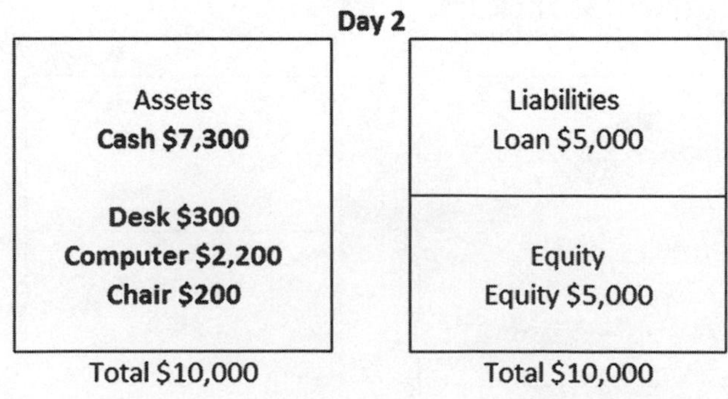

This makes sense: when we buy something, we use cash, so the cash account decreases, while the new asset account increases.

There is an inverse relationship between the left hand side of the balance sheet (the asset accounts excluding cash) and cash: when the former goes up, cash goes down; when the former goes down, cash goes up. These actions affect only the left hand side of the balance sheet; nothing changes on the right-hand side.

4.5.4 Retained Earnings

Aside from the starting loan and the equity, what other ways can the new business owner get cash? The third one is earnings from the business, and this is the lifeblood that will sustain the business over the long run. If the company is successful and makes profits, the earnings from the business are a continual source of cash over time.

Retained earnings are the accumulated earnings of the company. The earnings of the business from the income statement are recorded in the balance sheet as retained earnings. For a company that is just starting, the first year's retained earnings will be the same as its net income after dividends, if any. In subsequent years, the retained earnings is the accumulated net income after dividends of all preceding years plus the current year's net income.

Let's say that on Day 3 our entrepreneur receives a payment of $500 for a completed project. This shows up on the balance sheet as an item called retained earnings, which tracks the earnings of the business. This new entry increases cash and, therefore, the total assets by $500 (Fig. 4-6).

4.5.5 If Cash Runs Out . . .

What happens if the business owner now wants to buy a fancy car for $50,000 on Day 4? Schematically, we can present the balance sheet as follows (Fig. 4-7). This shows the balance sheet in the middle of the double-entry bookkeeping: (a) the car is bought, but (b) we have not done the second step of making the balancing entry.

FIGURE 4-6

A First Paycheck Adds Cash to the System

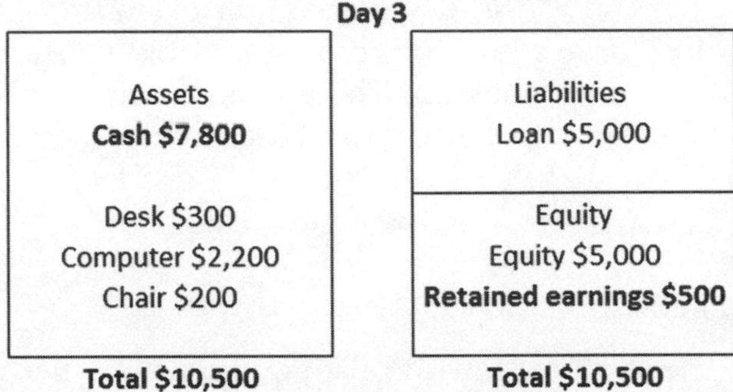

Day 3
Assets
Cash $7,800
Desk $300
Computer $2,200
Chair $200
Total $10,500
Liabilities
Loan $5,000
Equity
Equity $5,000
Retained earnings $500
Total $10,500

When there is insufficient cash, the name of the game is a rush to line up the funding required. In this case, the business owner can either apply for a loan or put more personal money or other investors' money into the balance sheet. This situation, in which there is a gap in funding, can be considered as a negative cash position. The negative cash means the need for more funding.

FIGURE 4-7

When Cash Runs Out

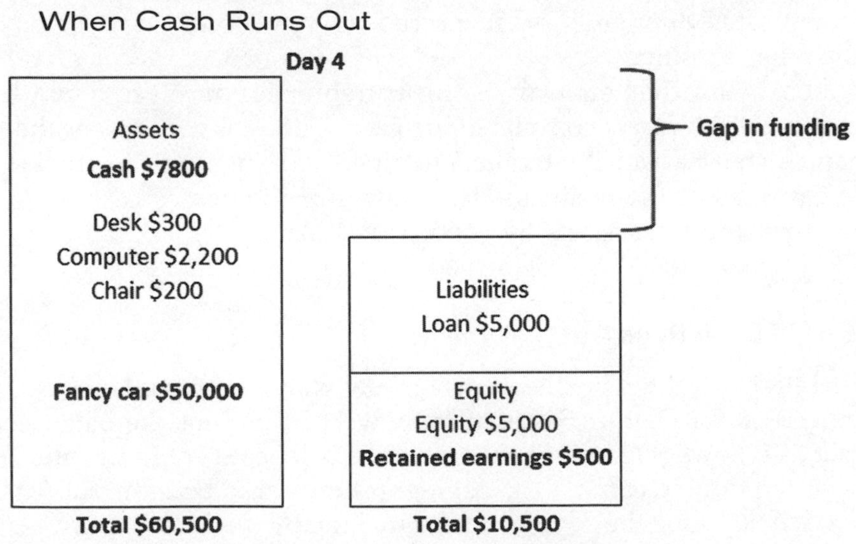

TABLE 4-1

Sources and Uses of Cash

	Asset	Liability or equity
Increase	Use	Source
Decrease	Source	Use

4.6 SOURCES AND USES OF CASH: DEBITS AND CREDITS

Table 4-1 summarizes the sources and uses of cash.

To link these to the accounting terms of "debits" and "credits" (used in T-accounts, which I will not go into here), it is enough as a guideline to know that when an account transaction is a "debit," it always means a use of cash. Likewise a "credit" always means a source of cash.

4.7 DOUBLE-ENTRY BOOKKEEPING AND CHANGE IN CASH

The preceding examples show how the balance sheet remains balanced with double-entry bookkeeping. Additionally, the second action in double-entry bookkeeping can be said to be in essence a change in cash, because any change in an asset, liability, or equity is either a source or a use of cash.

In certain transactions where an asset is acquired directly through debt (think of buying something using your credit card), one can think of this as two transactions, each with its own double-entry sequence that still follows the idea that the "second action is a change in cash":

Transaction 1: First entry: Put down your credit card for an instantaneous loan. Second entry: get cash. So your personal credit card debt account goes up; and your cash account likewise goes up.

Transaction 2: First entry: Give the cash electronically to the merchant. Second entry: Get the item you are buying in return. The asset account for that new item goes up; your cash account goes down.

4.8 CHANGE IN CASH AND MODELING

In spreadsheet financial modeling, the next step to take is simply to make the model *do the second action in the double-entry bookkeeping—keeping track of the change in cash.* This frees us to work with the assumptions we want to include in the model without having to worry whether the numbers are getting out of balance. A working integrated financial statement model will ensure that the balance sheet will always be balanced, and by extension, the changes in cash in the cash flow statement always foot to the changes of cash in the balance sheet.

4.9 BALANCING THE BALANCE SHEET

In modeling, balancing the balance sheet uses "plugs" (Fig. 4-8). Just to be clear, this term does not mean a manually hard-coded number that is entered in the spreadsheet to balance the balance sheet. The term "plug" as used in this book means a dynamic number automatically calculated by the formulas we write in Excel. This number is Excel in action as the second step in double-entry bookkeeping.

The plug on the asset side is called "excess cash" and is assumed to be cash. Historical numbers have only one cash line, but in forecasts we can also continue to assume a level of cash required for operational purposes; this line would then be called "cash" or "minimum cash." Any cash produced by the interactions of the forecast assumptions above this minimum cash would be "excess," which is why this is called "excess cash."

Excess cash comes into play when the modeling assumptions produce a liabilities and equity side that outpaces the assets side. In other words, there is more cash than can be used in buying assets. We saw this in our entrepreneur's balance sheet for Day 1 (Fig. 4-4). The cash would be the "excess cash" plug.

The plug on the liabilities side is called a "revolver" and is generally assumed to be debt. A revolver is a credit line that a

FIGURE 4-8

Excess Cash and Revolver as Balancing Numbers

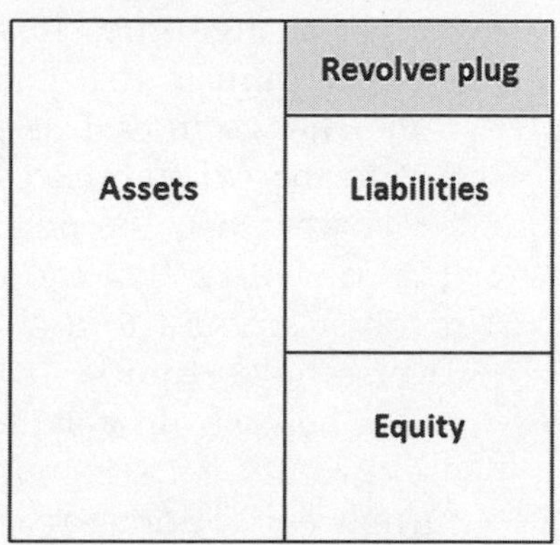

company has with a financial institution: the company can borrow on it when required and then repay it if it has cash on hand. The credit line is renewed regularly, so it "revolves" from year to year, and that is why it is called a revolver. For modeling purposes, this plug could be made an equity plug, but most of the time it is in the form of debt because in real life, short-term liquidity needs are met by bank financing, not by share issuances.

The revolver comes into play when the modeling assumptions result in an assets side that outpaces the funding side: more assets to be bought, but not enough funding. In the preceding example for Day 4 (Fig. 4-7), the gap in the funding would be filled by a revolver plug of $50,000.

4.10 TWO WAYS OF BALANCING

From the modeling point of view, there are two ways of balancing the balance sheet:

- Use only the balance sheet and the income statement. This is a mechanistic way that involves checking one side of the balance sheet against the other and putting in either an excess cash or a revolver number to make both sides balance. This approach requires only the current year's income statement and balance sheet.

- Use the balance sheet, the income statement and the cash flow statement. This is a more accounting-oriented approach. The cash flow statement is used to determine the net change in cash with the change in each balance sheet account in the assets, liability and equity sections. If the change in cash is positive, then the model adds that to the existing excess cash number. If the model has a revolver, then the positive cash reduces that revolver. It may well be that the positive cash changes a prior revolver amount to a current excess cash amount. The reverse holds true if the change in cash is negative. To build the cash flow statement in this approach requires the current year's income statement and both the current and prior year's balance sheets.

The income statement plays a role in both cases because the net income flows into the retained earnings on the balance sheet, and net income is the first item in the cash flow statement. However, its importance in the balancing depends on how we wish to calculate the interest from the excess cash and the revolver. If we wish to calculate the interest on the average levels of the plugs, then the income statement will be a part of the balancing system, since the net income will change depending on the effects of the plug interest. (However, this approach brings us into the issue of circular references. See Chapter 8 for more on this.) If the interest is based on the prior levels of the plugs, then the income statement is not part of the balancing system.

Both approaches produce the same numbers in the balance sheet (Figs. 4-9 and 4-10). The role of the income statement in the following illustrations is in the increase in the retained earnings.

The balancing formula excludes excess cash and revolver (both of which are the plugs that the formula is seeking to determine) to avoid circular references.

This second approach involves a few more steps than the first one. Nevertheless, both arrive at the same result. When we start building our pilot models (Chapter 7) we will include both approaches.

Note that the first approach of looking at the balance sheet only arrives at the balancing number in one step. The second

FIGURE 4-9

Balancing with the Balancing Sheet Only

ASSETS	Year 1	Year 2	Year 2
Excess cash	100		60
Accounts receivable	130	140	140
Inventory	140	150	150
Net PPE	500	600	600
Other assets	80	60	60
Total	**950**	**950**	**1,010**
LIABILITIES AND EQUITY			
Revolver	0		0
Accounts payable	80	70	70
Other current liabs	120	140	140
Debt	220	200	200
Common stock	400	440	440
Retained earnings	130	160	160
Total	**950**	**1,010**	**1,010**
Total assets (excl excess cash)			950
Total liabs (excl revolver)			1,010
Excess cash (revolver)			60

approach first looks at the *change* in cash, which must then be added to the prior year's balancing cash or revolver number to arrive at the current balancing number.

The illustration here looks at the excess cash plug. The approach would be similar for the revolver plug. The following is another illustration (Fig. 4-11) showing the case in which the prior year's excess cash changes to the current year's revolver, because the buildup of assets (uses of cash) outpaces the funding arrangements (sources of cash).

4.11 PRODUCING CASH: PROFIT FOR MORE PROFIT

How does a business last? The answer is in the first principle of running a business: "Don't run out of cash." One way not to run out of cash is to make lots of it. Figure 4-12 is an illustration of the cash generation cycle in a business. These flows are part of any

FIGURE 4–10

Balancing Through the Cash Flow Statement

ASSETS	Year 1	Year 2	Source (use) between Year 1 and Year 2	Year 2
Excess cash	100			60
Accounts receivable	130	140	(10)	140
Inventory	140	150	(10)	150
Net PPE	500	600	(100)	600
Other assets	80	60	20	60
Total	**950**	**950**		**1,010**
LIABILITIES AND EQUITY				
Revolver	0			0
Accounts payable	80	70	(10)	70
Other current liabs	120	140	20	140
Debt	220	200	(20)	200
Common stock	400	440	40	440
Retained earnings	130	160	30	160
Total	**950**	**1,010**		**1,010**
Total sources			110	
Total uses			(150)	
Change in cash			(40)	
Beginning excess cash (revolver)				100
Change in cash				(40)
Ending excess cash (revolver)				60

good financial model, and this is why such a model can serve a very useful purpose for any business owner who wishes to better understand the dynamics of his or her business.

A successful business will have a circular flow shown in the arrowed lines between its balance sheet and income statement:

1. A company's productive assets, whether a factory producing physical widgets or office space with smart employees providing intellectual services, produce revenue.
2. Operating expenses, interest, taxes, and dividends are subtracted from revenue.

FIGURE 4-11

Excess Cash Plug Changes to Revolver Because of High Use of Cash

ASSETS	Year 1	Year 2	Source (use) between Year 1 and Year 2	Year 2
Excess cash	100			0
Accounts receivable	130	160	(30)	160
Inventory	140	170	(30)	170
Net PPE	500	700	(200)	700
Other assets	80	60	20	60
Total	**950**	**1,090**		**1,090**
LIABILITIES AND EQUITY				
Revolver	0			80
Accounts payable	80	70	(10)	70
Other current liabs	120	140	20	140
Debt	220	200	(20)	200
Common stock	400	440	40	440
Retained earnings	130	160	30	160
Total	**950**	**1,010**		**1,090**
Total sources			110	
Total uses			(290)	
Change in cash			(180)	
Beginning excess cash (revolver)				100
Change in cash				(180)
Ending excess cash (revolver)				(80)

3. Net income, after dividends, flows into the balance sheet's retained earnings account.
4. The increase in equity adds more cash to a company's balance sheet. Any additional increases in debt financing or any equity issuances also add cash.
5. The cash can be used to purchase more productive assets to add to its capacity to produce revenue and support working capital needs. The remaining unused cash is useful as a cash account for general day-to-day operations.
6. With more productive assets, more revenue is produced.

FIGURE 4-12

The Cash Generation Cycle

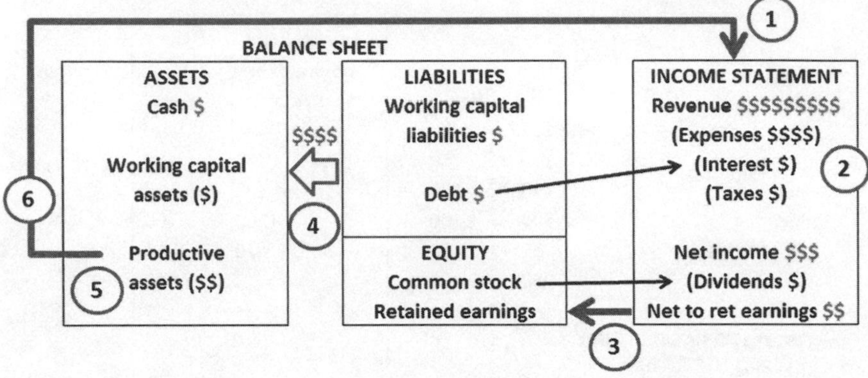

At the same time, debt has interest expense and equity (usually) has dividends. Both reduce the available flow to net to retained earnings.

If this cycle is running properly, there is a virtuous cycle of profit begetting more profit. As more cash is available, better and more productive assets create more revenues, which result in more net income to add to the balance sheet of the business, which allows the owner to invest in more productive assets . . . and so on.

If it is not, then the cycle is a vicious one. As less cash is produced, there is less investment in the business, productive capacities shrink, and the top-line revenue shrinks, leading to smaller net profit. Attempts to shore up the cash position by borrowing more increase interest expense, which has negative effects on the net income. If the business continues on this vicious downward cycle, the business runs out of cash and goes bankrupt.

4.12 MANAGEMENT LEVERS IN THE CASH GENERATING CYCLE

These are the key levers that management can work to keep profits high:

- Increase sales and keep profit margins high
    - Market to and price for the clientele you want
    - Control expenses
    - Explore tax efficiencies
- Control working capital
    - Limit receivables; get cash from customers as quickly as possible
    - Manage inventories
    - Take advantage of trade discounts
    - Stretch out payables, within limits
- Invest in efficient production facilities
- Balance debt/equity
    - Keep within coverage limits, seek lower-cost financing
    - Limit dividends

If you look at Figure 4-12, the key is to increase any point that has a positive $$$ sign, and to decrease any point that has a negative parentheses ($$$) sign.

4.13 MODELING FOR BUSINESS MANAGEMENT

From this, we can see that modeling is not only an accounting exercise, but is also a useful tool for understanding the nature of businesses. The management levers mentioned in the preceding section can be measured by ratios and other metrics on the model. In historical performance, we can see management's track record. In looking at projected performance, we can then deduce what the company's health may be like in the future if we used the same assumptions going forward. At the same time, if we wanted particular financial targets to be reached, we can then explore how those levers would need to be changed to hit those goals. By this modeling approach, we can then arrive at a conclusion on whether the company is on a feasible path toward a positive cash generation cycle.

CHAPTER 5

The Model Building Toolbox: F Keys and Ranges

This chapter goes over specific keyboard controls and looks at how Excel considers blocks of cells in the spreadsheet area. Specifically:

- The F keys on your keyboard
- Range names in Excel

5.1 F KEYS

Along the top row of your keyboard is a series of keys marked F1 to F12. Each of these "F keys" launches specific commands in Excel, but you will find that the ones you will be using often are really only about half of the F keys. The ones used more often are shown in bold:

- F1 Help
- **F2 Edit the active cell**
- F3 Paste a name into a formula
- **F4 Repeat the last keyboard action**
- **F5 Go to**
- F6 Move to the next pane

- F7 Check spelling
- F8 Anchors the start of a range
- **F9 Calculate all sheets in all open workbooks**
- F10 Make the menu bar active
- F11 Create a chart
- F12 Save As . . . command

Additionally, there are four other frequently used sequences that use the F keys in combination. In these combinations, press F2, release, and then press the second F key. (The step is shown with the comma; a + means that the two keys need to be pressed simultaneously.) These are:

- F2, F4 Cycle through absolute references
- F2, F5 Trace back to formula sources
- F2, F9 Recalculate portions of formulas
- Shift + F9 Recalculate the current sheet only
- Ctrl + Alt + F9 Forced calculation

In addition to these, Excel gives you even more commands if these F keys are used with Shift, Ctrl, Alt, Ctrl + Shift, or Alt + Shift. Most of these are not often used if you rely on the mouse, but you should explore the full list of functions by going to F1 Help. Type any of the F keys (e.g., F1) in the input box at the top of the Find tab. Then select the "Function keys in Microsoft Excel" in the list of items shown in the list box at the bottom of the form for a full list of the function keys in Excel.

5.1.1 F1: Help

This is the key you use to get help from Excel.

5.1.2 F2: Edit

Pressing this key will bring you to the "edit mode." It will allow you to edit the cell that your cursor is on. Pressing this key and other F keys will have other results (see the following).

In the F2 Edit mode, you can choose to edit the formula directly in the cell that the cursor is on, or in the formula bar near the top of the screen. In both cases, the cells of the precedent cells (the cells that feed the current cell, i.e., the ones carrying data that "precede" the current cell) will be highlighted by different-colored borders. The setting to determine this is in the *Tools>Options>Edit* tab, with the check box marked "Edit directly in cell." In Excel 2007, this is set through *Office Button>Excel Options>Advanced>Allow editing directly in cells.*

This choice is a matter of personal preference, but there is also one important difference. If the "Edit directly in cell" is checked, double-clicking a cell has the same effect as pressing F2; it just gets you into the Edit mode. However, if this is not checked, double-clicking on a cell will "jump" you to the precedent cell (or the first precedent address if there is a long formula in that cell). A precedent cell is the cell that contains data that are being used in the cell that you are on. The opposite of this, referring to the cell that makes use of the data in the current cell, is the dependent cell.

5.1.2.1 F2, F4: Cycle through absolute references

Cell addresses in Excel change automatically when you copy them from cell to cell. The cell in B3 (Fig. 5-1), which has the formula =A3, will change as it is copied into different cells. Across the same row, the column letter reference will change; down the same column, the row number reference will change.

The references do not change when B3 is moved by cut-and-paste, as opposed to copied by copy-and-paste.

In some instances, it would be preferable not to have this relative referencing work. When we copy the cell to other places,

FIGURE 5-1

Copying Cell B3 with No Absolute References

	A	B	C	D	E	F
1						
2						
3		=A3		=C3	=D3	=E3
4		=A4				
5						

we can make an absolute reference. We do this by putting the dollar sign ($) in front of the column letter or the row number. The $ sign makes the letter or number static as you copy the cell. There are four possibilities for specifying the address, and pressing F4 successively after you are in the F2 Edit mode will cycle you through these settings.

As you copy Cell B3, the formula:

- A3: Both the column letter and the row number will move (Fig. 5-1).
- $A$3: Both stay unchanged (Fig. 5-2).
- A$3: The column letter will change, but the row number will stay unchanged (Fig. 5-3).
- $A3: The column letter stays unchanged, but the row number will change (Fig. 5-4).

You can also insert the $ symbol manually by typing it into the appropriate place(s) in the cell address.

5.1.2.2 F2, F5: Tracing back to formula sources

Once in the edit mode with the F2 key, you can highlight a cell address and then press F5. This is a quick "go to." This is most helpful for tracing back to the source(s) when the cell you are editing contains a long formula.

5.1.2.3 F2, F9: Recalculating portions of a formula

Press F2 while you are in a cell with a long formula, then highlight a portion of the formula with your mouse and press F9. The high-

FIGURE 5-2

Copying Cell B3 with Row and Column Absolute References

	A	B	C	D	E	F
1						
2						
3		=$A$3		=$A$3	=$A$3	=$A$3
4		=$A$3		=$A$3	=$A$3	=$A$3
5						

FIGURE 5-3

Copying Cell B3 with Row Absolute Reference

	A	B	C	D	E	F
1						
2						
3		=$A3		=$A3	=$A3	=$A3
4		=$A4		=$A4	=$A4	=$A
5						

lighted portion of the formula will be shown as the result. This is a great way to check if your formulas are calculating correctly, because you can highlight increasingly larger portions to follow the sequence of calculations.

Here's an example (Fig. 5-5):

1. Press F2 to edit the formula in E6. Highlight D2 in the formula. You can highlight this by placing the cursor within D2 and double-clicking; Excel will highlight this unit (Fig. 5-5).
2. Press F9. D2 now changes to 0.6, the contents of the cell D2 (Fig. 5-6).
3. Now highlight E2 in the formula and press F9. E2 changes to 140, the number it contains (Fig. 5-7).
4. Now highlight the expression 0.60*140 . . . (Fig. 5-8).
5. . . . and when you press F9, this expression changes to its result of 84 (Fig. 5-9).

You can continue doing the successive highlighting and pressing F9 through any formula, no matter how long. F2 and F9 will always show you the result.

FIGURE 5-4

Copying Cell B3 with Column Absolute References

	A	B	C	D	E	F
1						
2						
3		=A$3		=C$3	=D$3	=E$3
4		=A$3		=C$3	=D$3	=E$3
5						

F I G U R E 5-5

Recalculating Formula Portions, Step 1

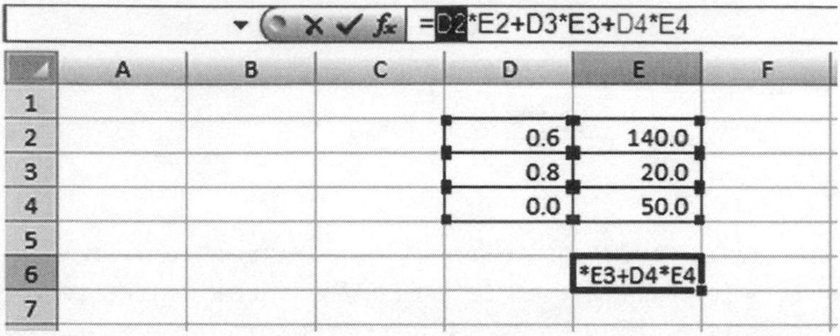

=D2*E2+D3*E3+D4*E4

	A	B	C	D	E	F
1						
2				0.6	140.0	
3				0.8	20.0	
4				0.0	50.0	
5						
6					*E3+D4*E4	
7						

Be careful. After you have finished your checking, make sure you press the Esc key and not the Enter key. Pressing Esc will undo all the results and revert the formula to its original form. Pressing Enter will convert the portions of the formula you have been editing in this way into the result. If you pressed the Enter key after step 5, the formula will now be permanently changed to = 84 + D3*E3 + D4*E4. Fortunately, you can still reverse this action by pressing Ctrl+Z, for Undo.

Excel also has an additional feature to show calculations in a formula. This is the Evaluate command. In Excel 2003, this is seen as part of the Formula Auditing toolbar. In Excel 2007, this is under the Formulas tab, Evaluate Formula (Fig. 5-10). The icon is *fx* under a magnifying glass.

F I G U R E 5-6

Recalculating Formula Portions, Step 2

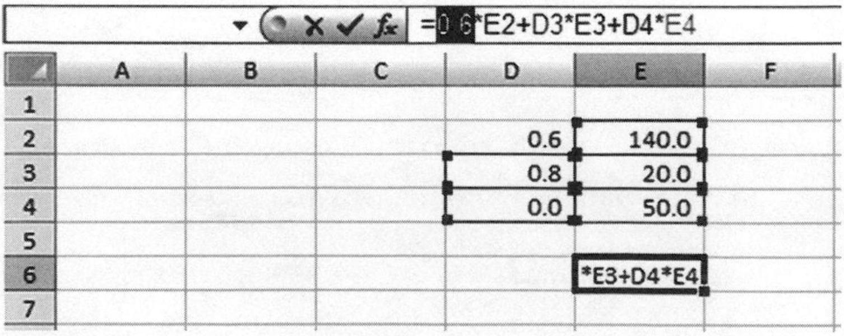

=0.6*E2+D3*E3+D4*E4

	A	B	C	D	E	F
1						
2				0.6	140.0	
3				0.8	20.0	
4				0.0	50.0	
5						
6					*E3+D4*E4	
7						

FIGURE 5-7

Recalculating Formula Portions, Step 3

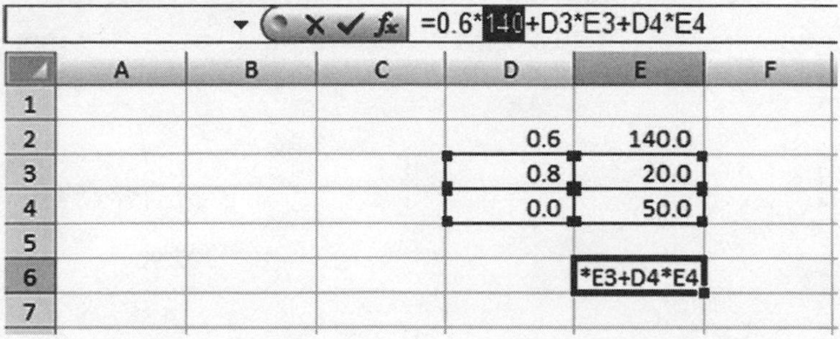

=0.6*140+D3*E3+D4*E4

	A	B	C	D	E	F
1						
2				0.6	140.0	
3				0.8	20.0	
4				0.0	50.0	
5						
6					*E3+D4*E4	
7						

To use this, place the cursor in the cell containing the formula you want to evaluate. You will see the Evaluate Formula form pop up (Fig. 5-11). Then click on the Evaluate button, or press E, to step through the formula. Instead of the button, you can also just press E on the keyboard.

The Evaluate Formula goes through the formula from left to right, converting each calculation unit into its final value, very much like the successive steps we did with the F2, F9 sequence. The F2, F9 sequence may still be useful if you have a long formula and you want to see the results of a specific portion within the long formula, and you don't want to run through the evaluation of the whole formula.

FIGURE 5-8

Recalculating Formula Portions, Step 4

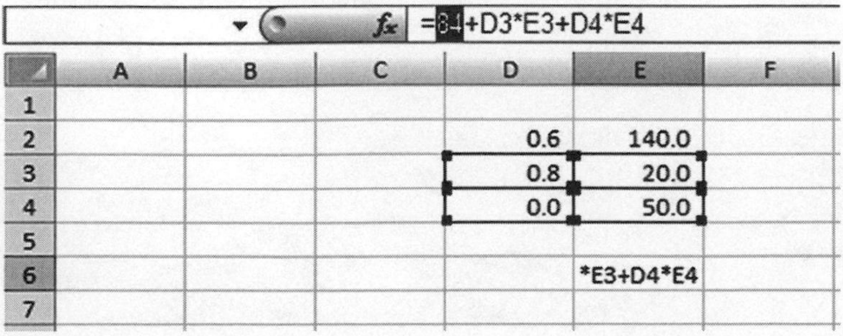

=84+D3*E3+D4*E4

	A	B	C	D	E	F
1						
2				0.6	140.0	
3				0.8	20.0	
4				0.0	50.0	
5						
6					*E3+D4*E4	
7						

FIGURE 5-9

Recalculating Formula Portions, Step 5

IF | =84+D3*E3+D4*E4

	A	B	C	D	E	F
1						
2				0.6	140.0	
3				0.8	20.0	
4				0.0	50.0	
5						
6					*E3+D4*E4	
7						

5.1.3 F3: Paste a Name into a Formula

This function pastes a name from the list of range names into a formula (see the section on Ranges later in this chapter). As you write or edit the formula, press F3 and a "Paste Name" dialog box will pop up on your screen. From this, you can select the range name you want to paste into the formula. Once you click on OK, then Excel returns you to the formula and you can continue working with the formula.

5.1.4 F4: Repeat the Last Action

F4, by itself, will repeat the last command. This can be a shortcut sequence, like Ctrl+B for bold, or even the keyboard sequence equivalent, *Format>Cells>Font>Bold*. This is a time-saving key when you need to do something that involves hitting multiple keys across many cells in your sheet, and this is worth remembering.

FIGURE 5-10

Evaluate Formula Icon

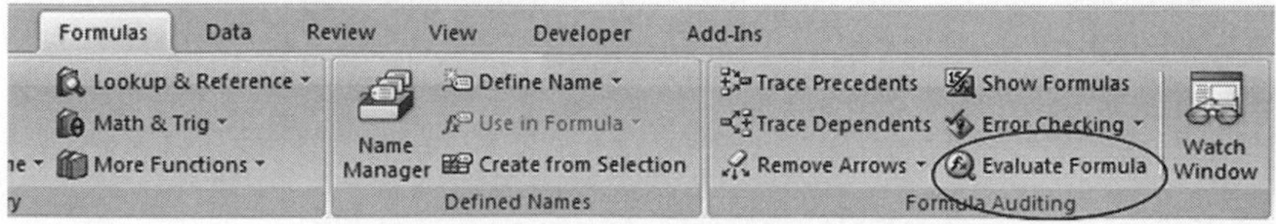

FIGURE 5-11

The Evaluate Formula Form

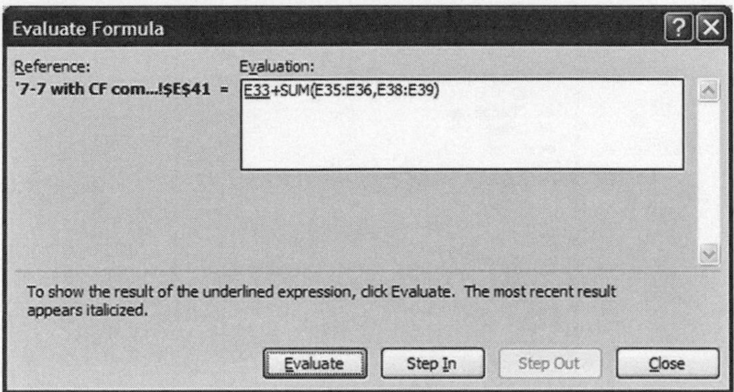

If you are doing a sequence that requires two operations (e.g., selecting a row across the worksheet, and then performing an Insert command to add a whole row across), F4 will only repeat the last command. This means that you will be inserting a row on only one column (the last command), since F4 does not also select the whole row (the second-to-last command). In such a case, exploring the keyboard alternative may prove useful. The keystroke sequence for inserting a whole row is *Alt>Insert>Rows*. Your cursor can be on any column in the row to do this. Now when you press F4, this sequence is repeated and you can then quickly insert rows anywhere else on the worksheet.

5.1.5 F5: Go To

Pressing F5 will show you this form. If you have a file that has no range names, the "Go To:" box will be blank. If you have range names, they will be shown, as shown in Figure 5-12.

If there are range names (see Section 5.2 in this chapter), and you want to go to a particular one, just highlight it and then click on OK. If you want to go to another address, type it in the "Reference" box. Here is a feature to remember: once you get to your destination, you can press F5 again and just press OK to return to your starting point.

FIGURE 5-12

The Go To Form, in a Model with Many Range Names

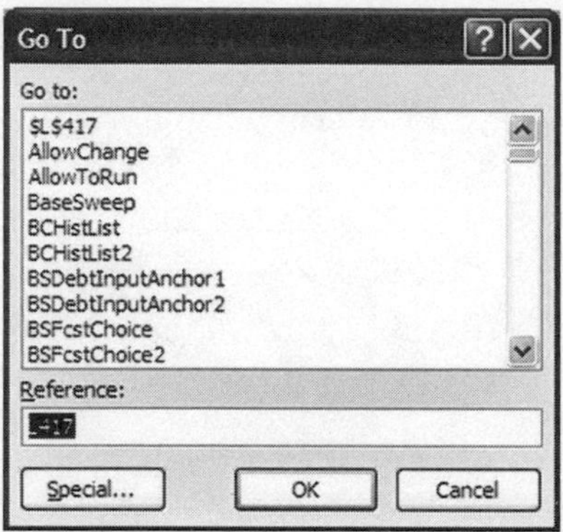

Click on the "Special" key to see another form that lists other destinations to go to with the F5 key (Fig. 5-13).

The Go To Special form is more of a specialized "find" function. It is a "go to" function to go to cells that meet the condition that you have selected from the option buttons. Most of the options are self-explanatory.

Note the following options:

- Row differences. If you have two or more columns of numbers and you want to check if any of the cells are different across the rows, highlight the columns and then choose this option. It will show you all the rows where the numbers are not identical.
- Column differences. This is the same idea as with Row differences, but only for differences across columns.
- Last cell. This shows you the cell at the bottom right-hand corner of the area of the screen that you have used. You use a cell by changing its contents or format. The more cells you use, the more memory that your file needs (and the bigger the size of the file). For this reason, if you have been working on a sheet and making many changes, it is a good idea to check where the last cell is, so that the sheet is not any bigger than it needs to be. The keyboard alternative to check this is Ctrl+End.

FIGURE 5-13

Go To Special

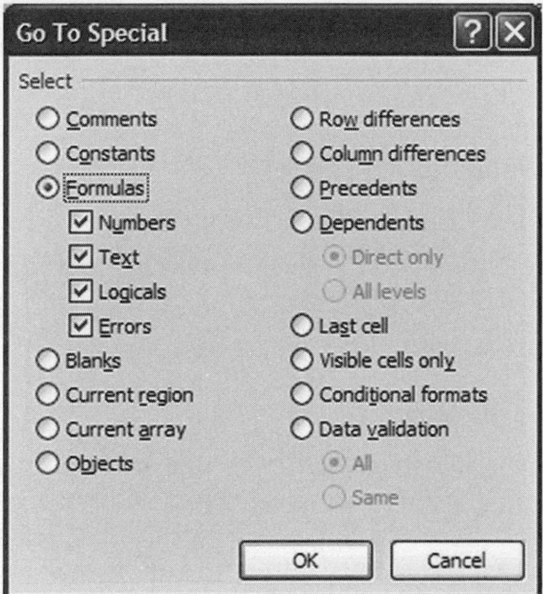

To reduce the used area on your sheet, do the following:

1. Select the row just below the last row with data and highlight all the rows below it to the last row being used. Do this by clicking and dragging on the row numbers on the left of the screen.
2. Delete the highlighted rows. You can do this by a right-click on your mouse and selecting Delete.
3. Do the same with columns by selecting the column just to the right of the last column of data and highlighting all the used columns to the right of that. Do this by clicking and dragging on the column letters on the top of the screen.
4. Delete the highlighted columns. Again, you can right-click on your mouse and selecting Delete.
5. Save the file and close it. When you reopen it, the used area will have reduced itself.

Another way to see the used range and one that does not use the F5 key at all is to go to cell A1. You can do this by pressing Ctrl+Home. Then press the Shift+End+Home keys together. This will highlight the used range. Pressing End+Home alone will make the cursor go to the last used cell, without highlighting the used range.

5.1.6 F6: Move to the Next Pane

If you have split the screen (Excel 2003: *Windows>Split;* Excel 2007: *View>Split*) so that it has up to four areas or panes, then pressing F6 will move you from one pane to another in a clockwise direction.

5.1.7 F7: Spelling Command

This launches a spell check for the active sheet only. If you want to check the spelling on other sheets, you will have to go to those sheets and press F7 again. F7 is the shortcut for *Tools>Spelling* in Excel 2003. In Excel 2007, the command is *Review>Spelling*.

5.1.8 F8: Anchor the Start of a Range to Extend a Selection

This is not a well-known key but it is useful when you want to highlight a large range. Whereas highlighting a small range can be easily done with the mouse, anything beyond one screen wide and one screen high is a little tricky. To highlight, say, 80 columns across and 2000 rows down, use the F8 key in this way:

1. Go to the top left corner of the range you want to highlight, and then press F8. This anchors the start of the range.
2. If you use the keyboard arrow keys, the highlighted range automatically expands as you move the cursor any way from the starting point. If you are using the mouse, go to the bottom right corner of the range and then click to define it.
3. When you are ready to define the range, press Enter, and the active cell becomes the top left corner, even as the whole range remains painted on your screen.

If you change your mind about highlighting a range after you pressed F8, just press Esc.

5.1.9 F9: Recalculate

This key recalculates the whole file, and any other file that is also open in Excel. If you have set your worksheet to have automatic calculation, this key is not critical, as that setting means that Excel will always be refreshing the worksheet to take into account any changes that have been made.

If you have set the calculation setting to "Automatic except for tables," then you must press this F9 key if you want to update your data tables. Other calculations outside the data tables will be refreshed automatically.

If your setting is for manual calculation, then you must remember to press this key to ensure that the screen shows the latest set of calculated numbers, including for the data tables. This is especially important prior to any printing.

5.1.9.1 Ctrl + Alt + F9 or Shift + Ctrl + Alt + F9 for forced calculation

As your model becomes more complex and sizable, Excel must keep track of the myriad of calculations in it. Occasionally, although not very often, you may find that the numbers do not seem to be updating properly. One reason is that Excel has an "intelligent recalculation" feature that is supposed to minimize the recalculations it has to do (i.e., it "knows" when cells do not need to be recalculated because the results will not change with further recalculations). This feature can lead to a situation in which the recalculation does not happen when it should. In this case, use this sequence to override the intelligent recalculation feature and force Excel to go through a refresh.

Hint: As we go deeper into modeling, we will be using circular references. To use these, you will need to set Excel to the calculation setting to allow iterations. If you find that the numbers are not recalculating, no matter how many times you press F9 or Ctrl+Alt+F9, check that the iteration setting has been enabled. If you have circular references and the iteration setting is off, the recalculation cannot proceed.

Shift+Ctrl+Alt+F9 is a more extensive forced recalculation in Excel. This sequence forces Excel to recreate its "calculation dependency tree," the record of interlinked formulas in the model that provides the priorities for recalculation. Forcing a recreation of the calculation tree can useful in resetting Excel's calculations, especially in very large models in which the calculation tree has been filled to this maximum capacity.

5.1.10 F10: Make the Menu Bar Active

F10 allows you to select items on the menu bar by the keyboard. In Excel 2003, when you press F10, you will see that the File menu item on the menu bar seems to be on a raised level. This indicates that the menu item can now be selected by pressing the keys on the keyboard that correspond with the underlined letter in the menu item.

In Excel 2007, small letters will appear in the menu ribbon. Enter a letter that corresponds to the menu command you want to invoke.

F10 is equivalent to just pressing the Alt key.

5.1.11 F11: Create a Chart

This is the key that will quickly show a set of numbers that your cursor is on as a chart.

5.1.12 F12: Save As Command

This is the alternative of *File>Save As* command in Excel 2003, or the *Office Button>Save As* command in Excel 2007. F12 allows you to save a file quickly, but potentially under a different name than it has. This is different from Ctrl+S, or *File>Save*, which saves the file under the name it already has.

5.2 RANGES

In Excel, we often work with a block of cells for various operations. Such a block is called a range. The top left corner of a range is defined by one cell, and the bottom right corner is defined by another. In this way, a range is always rectangular and in fact can only have this four-sided shape. One cell can also be thought of as a range, whose top left address is the same as the bottom right. Likewise, the whole sheet from A1 to IV65536 (in Excel 2003) or A1 to XFD1048576 (in Excel 2007) is a range.

A range can also be a whole row or a whole column. In the former, the range would be defined as, say, "10:10" for Row 10, without the use of column letters. The latter would be defined as "A:A" (to name Column A), without the use of row numbers.

Once you have a range, you can name it, and this is where it becomes a powerful tool for your model building.

In Figure 5-14, we see an example of the use of a range name. Cell C4 contains the value 35%, and this is the tax rate that will be applied to the numbers in Row 2 to calculate the provision for taxes.

In Column C, there are two formulas. The first one, in Cell C5, shows the cell addresses being used to calculate the provision for taxes. The second one use the range name TaxRate for Cell C4. In fact, you can see the range name of a cell in the upper left hand corner of the screen, right next to the formula bar. In this example, you can see that the cursor is resting on the cell that has been named TaxRate.

5.2.1 Defining a Range Name Quickly

When defining a range name, use the Name Box at the upper left-hand corner just above the corner where the column letter A and the row number 1 meet. Use the following steps:

FIGURE 5-14

Using a Range Called TaxRate

TaxRate | fx 35%

	A	B	C	D	E	F	G	H
1			2010	2011	2012	2013	2014	
2	Taxable income		200.0	220.0	242.0	266.2	292.8	
3								
4	Tax rate		35%					
5	Provision for taxes		70.0	=C4*C2				
6	Provision for taxes		70.0	=TaxRate*C2				
7								

1. First, highlight the cell or cells that you want to name.
2. Click on the dropdown box in the Name Box, type the range name, and press Enter
3. This quick shortcut is good for naming any size range.

Do not use any spaces in a range name, and do not begin a range name with a number. These kinds of range names are not accepted. Use the underscore if you wish to separate the name (e.g., "Tax_Rate"). Range names also have absolute addresses by default, so that if you copy this across, the range name TaxRate will continue to point to cell B3. This named range becomes convenient to use when you are further down in the spreadsheet and need the input number. You can just type TaxRate instead of having to find the exact cell address.

Even if the Cell C4 is named TaxRate, you can still use the cell address itself to write a formula that uses this cell. The cell address approach can be useful if you want relative references in subsequent formulas that use the initial cell.

5.2.2 The Long Way of Naming Ranges

If we do not use the Name Box for naming ranges, we have to use the sequence *Insert>Name>Define* (Excel 2003) or *Formulas>Define Name* (Excel 2007) to get to the user form that will allow us to define, or name, the range. As you can see, this requires more steps.

5.2.3 Naming Many Ranges at the Same Time

A variation of this longer sequence is actually useful and is a time saver when you want to name many ranges at the same time. This can occur when you need to set some toggle ranges, for example. Here's how to do it (Fig. 5-15):

1. Type the range names that you want to create in the spreadsheet. For our example, write them down vertically. In this example, we are going to name the cells in Column C with the names that we have entered in Column B. Note that you can create ranges that are more than one cell wide in this way by highlighting a wider range, e.g., B2: D6.

FIGURE 5-15

Naming Range Names

	A	B	C	D
1				
2		StartDate		
3		EndDate		
4		NoOfYears		
5		TaxRate		
6		TaxUSOForeign1		
7				

2. Highlight the range B2 to C6 and press *Insert>Name>Create* in Excel 2003. In Excel 2007, the command is *Formulas>Create From Selection*.
3. A user form like that shown in Figure 5-16 will appear.
4. Click on OK.

Done! The user form explains that Excel is creating the named ranges based on the names in the left column of the block you have highlighted. By this approach, you could also have created named ranges based on labels you have into the top, bottom, or right of the highlighted block.

5.2.4 Making Range Names More Informative

Use range names that are clear and spell out the name as much as possible, while keeping it easy to type. In the example, "TaxRate"

FIGURE 5-16

Create Names from Selection

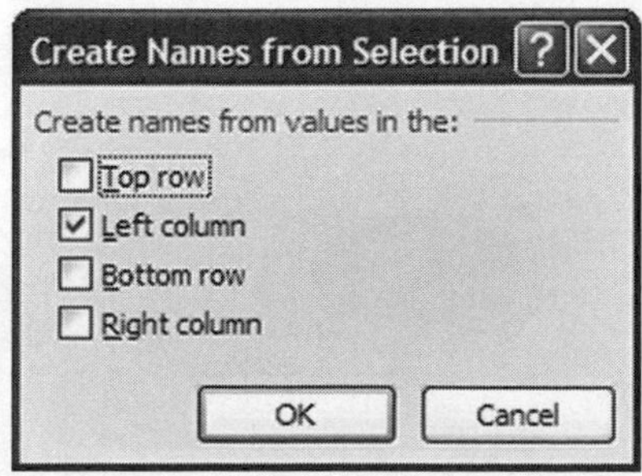

is more immediately clearer than "TxRt." If you are going to be typing this range name many times as you develop your model, strike a good balance between clarity and ease of typing.

You can also use range names to describe switches. For instance, you may have a cell that holds the switch for the use of a U.S. tax rate or a foreign tax rate for a tax calculation, which will be either a 0 or a 1, respectively. In this case, you might try using the name "TaxUS0Foreign1". When you write the IF statement, you can remember without fail that the first argument of the statement =IF(TaxUS0Foreign1=0, . . . is for using a U.S. tax rate.

5.2.5 Deleting a Range Name

To delete a range name, do the *Insert>Name>Define* sequence. At the dialog box that you see, select the range name in the list box and then click on the Delete button.

FIGURE 5-17

The Name Manager

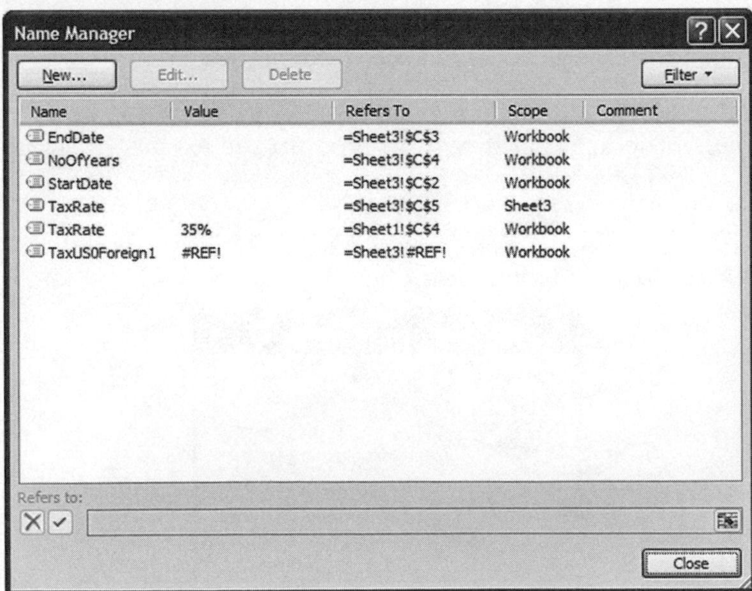

Excel 2007 has an improved range name manager in *Formulas> Name Manager*. The form that appears (Fig. 5-17) lists the name, value, cell(s) that the range refers to, the scope and comment.

The scope refers to the fact that you can create multiple range names with the same name in one workbook. The first range name has the Workbook scope. This means that it applies to the whole workbook. The second (and subsequent) duplicate range names carry the scope of the sheet name where the second duplicate name was created. As shown, you can see the two scopes for the name TaxRate.

The Name Manager also shows the range names that are in error. The TaxUS0Foreign1 range name is in error here. One nice addition to the Name Manager seen in Excel 2007 and not in earlier versions is the ability to filter on the range names (Fig. 5-18). In a model in which there may be hundreds of range names, you can filter on Names with Errors to see the list of range names that have ERR indications (Fig. 5-19). You can then highlight any or all of them by clicking on them and deleting them in one go by clicking on the Delete button.

FIGURE 5-18

Filtering Range Names

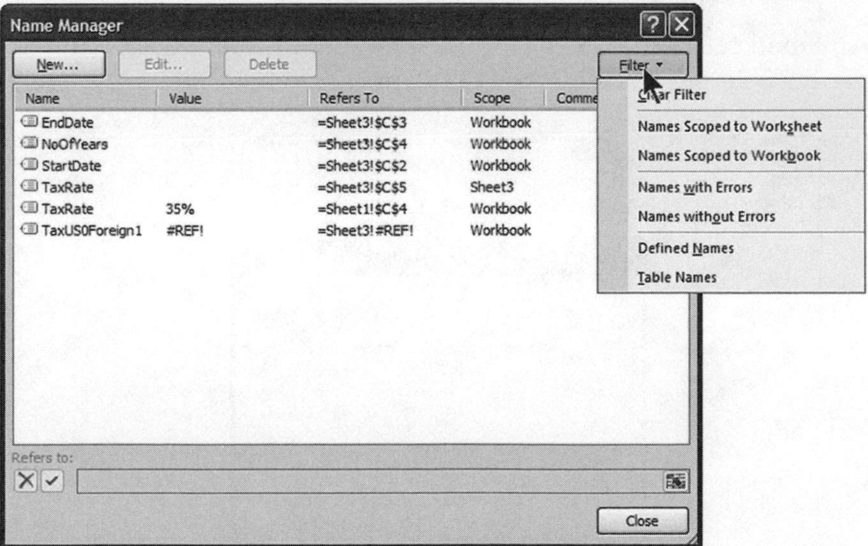

FIGURE 5-19

Filtering on Names with Errors, Ready to Delete

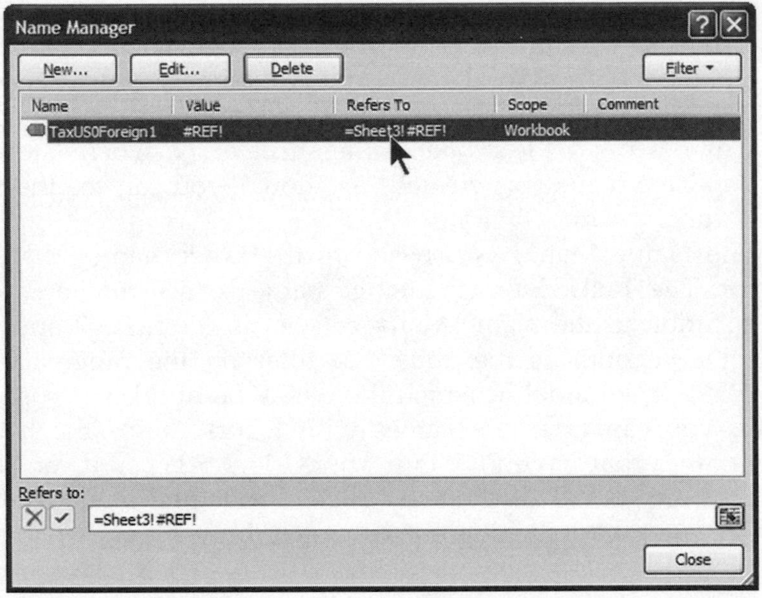

5.2.6 A Named Range Does Not Have to Refer to a Range of Cells

A named range can exist without a reference to a cell or a range. Figure 5-20 shows the form that appears when you press New

FIGURE 5-20

A Named Range Without a Cell Reference

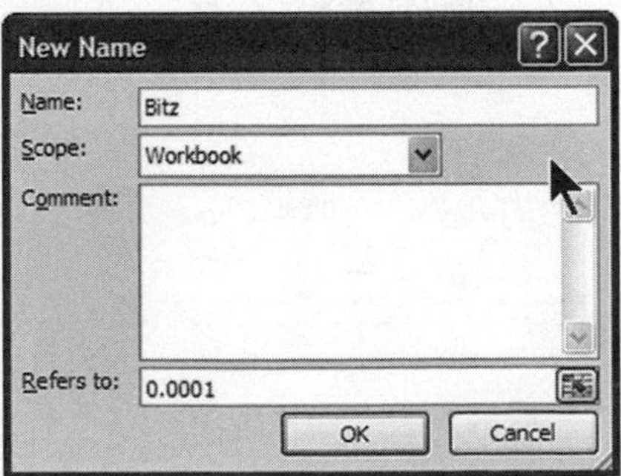

in the Range Manager form. Here, rather than specifying a cell or range address in the Refers to box, the entry is simply a factor 0.0001 for the range name "Bitz." Now in the workbook, I can write a formula such as =A1*Bitz and the result is whatever value is in Cell A1 multiplied by 0.0001.

5.2.7 A Range Name Can Be a Formula

You can use a named range as a formula. To do this, define the formula in the Refers to input in the Range Manager form.

In Figure 5-21, we start by placing the cursor in Cell C6. From the Name Manager form, click on the New button at the top left

FIGURE 5-21

Starting from the Name Manager

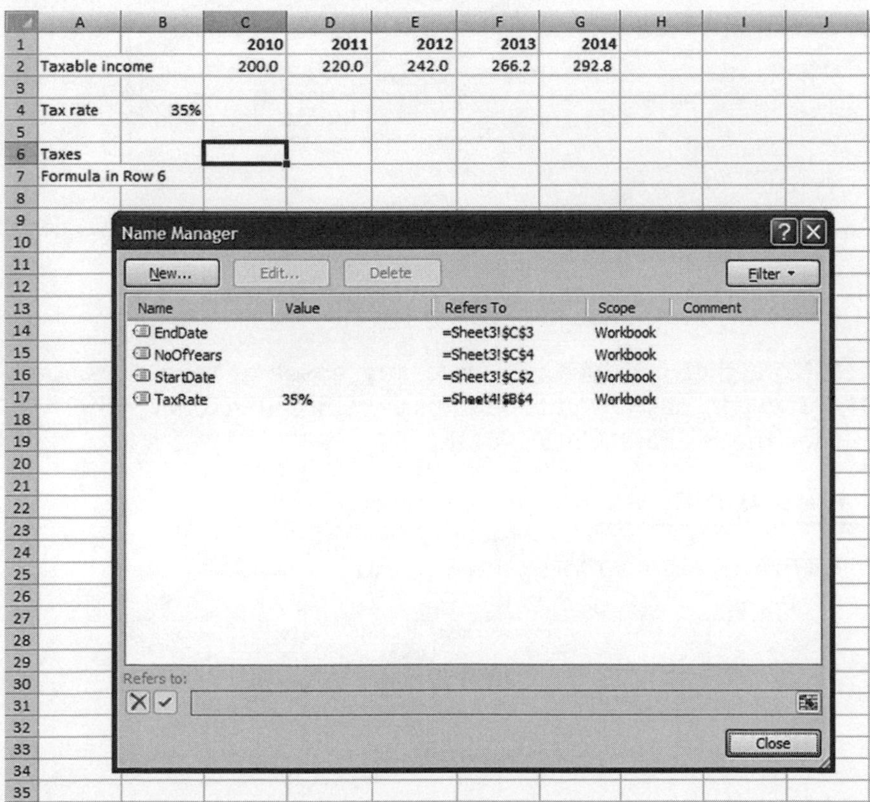

FIGURE 5-22

The New Name Form, with the Formula We Want in the Refers to Input Box

	A	B	C	D	E	F	G	H
1			2010	2011	2012	2013	2014	
2	Taxable income		200.0	220.0	242.0	266.2	292.8	
3								
4	Tax rate	35%						
5								
6	Taxes							
7	Formula in Row 6							

New Name

Name: TaxCalc

Scope: Workbook

Comment:

Refers to: =c2*$B$4

OK Cancel

corner. In the New Name form (Fig. 5-22), name the new range TaxCalc and in the Refers to input box, enter the formula:

=C2*$B$4

Note that C2 does not have any absolute references. Cell B4, however, has absolute references, since it refers to the one cell for the tax rate. Click on OK.

FIGURE 5-23

A Range Name Can be a Formula

	A	B	C	D	E	F	G	H
1			2010	2011	2012	2013	2014	
2	Taxable income		200.0	220.0	242.0	266.2	292.8	
3								
4	Tax rate	35%						
5								
6	Taxes		70.0					
7	Formula in Row 6		=TaxCalc					
8								

FIGURE 5-24

TaxCalc Across the Columns

	A	B	C	D	E	F	G	H
1			2010	2011	2012	2013	2014	
2	Taxable income		200.0	220.0	242.0	266.2	292.8	
3								
4	Tax rate	35%						
5								
6	Taxes		70.0	77.0	84.7	93.2	102.5	
7	Formula in Row 6		=TaxCalc	=TaxCalc	=TaxCalc	=TaxCalc	=TaxCalc	
8								

Now back in the worksheet, you enter the formula =TaxCal in Cell C6 (Fig. 5-23) and the calculation works.

If you copy =TaxCalc across the columns to Columns D:G, it also works correctly for each of the columns (Fig. 5-24).

5.2.8 Excel Can Multiply Two Multi-Column or Multi-Row Ranges

Excel can perform operations with multi-cell ranges if their dimensions are the same. In Figure 5-25, Row 2 has a range called TaxableIncome that spans columns C to G. Likewise, if Row 4, it has a range called TaxRate_Yrs that spans the same columns. In Cell C6, we can write the formula:

=TaxableIncome*TaxRate_Yrs

And the result for Cell C5 is shown. Copy this same formula across to columns D:G. Excel keeps track of which value

FIGURE 5-25

Operations with Multi-Cell Ranges

	A	B	C	D	E	F	G	H	I	J	K
1			2010	2011	2012	2013	2014				
2	Taxable income		200.0	220.0	242.0	266.2	292.8	<== This is the TaxableIncome range			
3											
4	Tax rate		35%	35%	35%	35%	35%	<== This is the TaxRate_Yrs range			
5											
6	Taxes		70.0	77.0	84.7	93.2	102.5				
7	Formula in Row 6		=TaxableIncome*TaxRate_Yrs								
8											

in each range array and performs the requested operation with the matched equivalents in the two ranges.

Using the same principle, the ranges can span the whole row or the whole column. It is possible to have a range that is defined, say, as "10:10". This means that the whole row from Column A10 to Column FXD10 (or A10 to IV10 in Excel 2003) has the range name. Likewise, it is possible to name a whole column a range by specifying, say, "A:A" for column A, from Row 1 to the bottom of the worksheet.

CHAPTER 6

The Model Building Toolbox: Functions

Functions are pre-formatted formulas in Excel. You can view the list of functions in Excel by clicking on the icon that looks like *fx* on the formula bar. This brings up the Insert Function form. The form is also accessible through the *Insert Function* button in the *Formulas* tab in Excel 2007.

Functions allow you to do arithmetic and other operations quickly and conveniently For example, in order to add together numbers in the range A10 to A20, you can add each individual cell by using the + sign:

```
A10+A11+A12+A13+A14+A15+A16+A17+A18+A19+A20
```

or you can use the SUM function:

```
=SUM(A10:A20)
```

Excel's functions can work in many ways. The SUM formula for the task can also work when written like this:

```
=SUM(A10,A11+A12,A13:A14,A15+A16,
    SUM(A17,A18,SUM(A19:A20)))
```

A function always starts with the name of the function, followed by a set of parentheses. If the function is the first entry in the cell, you will need a beginning equal sign (=) to indicate to Excel that the function and any other functions that you are writing in that cell is a formula. Within the parentheses, you need to specify the type of information, called *arguments,* that the function needs. Some functions, such as =NOW(), which returns the current time setting, do not need any arguments, but you will still need to type the parentheses. Others need one or more arguments, with some of them being optional; i.e., you can enter them or omit them.

Within a function, arguments can be:

- A number or a text string
- A cell or range reference, or multiple references, such as the SUM function shown above
- A whole column: COUNT(A:A)
- A whole row: MAX(20:20)
- A range name: AVERAGE(Revenues)
- Another formula or expression: SUM(250/3,12*43.5)
- Other functions: SUM(AVERAGE(C1:C10),AVERAGE (C21:C30))
- Optional with a marker: OFFSET(B1,0,2) or OFFSET(B1,,2). The space between the double commas is where the 0 has been left out. Excel considers such an omission to be the same as 0.
- Optional without a marker: HLOOKUP(D5,B2:B3,2) or HLOOKUP(D5,B2:B3,2,TRUE). Excel considers the omission of the last argument as being the equivalent of the TRUE argument.
- Any combination of the preceding.

6.1 LIST OF USEFUL FUNCTIONS

In Excel 2007, there are 343 functions, 51 more than was found in Excel 2003. New categories of Engineering and Cube have been added. The good news is that of this number, you need to be familiar with only about 45 or so (and you do not have to venture into the new Engineering and Cube functions).

Here is a list of 46 functions that are useful to know:

Logical	Lookup	Date	Information	Math	Special	Financial	Text
IF	CHOOSE	DATE	ISERROR	INT	SUMIF	NPV	TEXT
SUM	OFFSET	YEAR	ISBLANK	MOD	SUMPRODUCT	IRR	LEFT
AVERAGE	MATCH	MONTH	ISNUMBER	ROUND	COUNTIF	XNPV	RIGHT
COUNT	INDEX	DAY	ISTEXT	MROUND		XIRR	MID
COUNTA	VLOOKUP	EOMONTH					UPPER
MIN	HLOOKUP	DAYS360					LOWER
MAX	INDIRECT	NOW					PROPER
AND		DATEVALUE					LEN
OR							

6.1.1 Exponential Power

Much of the power in using functions comes knowing how to combine them in multiple ways. It is better to know 15 functions and how to combine them in various combinations, than to know 30 functions but only be able to work with them singly.

6.2 WORK NOTES

The following are notes to help speed up your work, whether by saving a keystroke here and there or otherwise streamlining your work flow.

6.2.1 Rows Before Columns

In functions that require row and column arguments, the order is always *row* and then *columns*. Thus, when you see =OFFSET(K10,2,1) (see Section 1.5.2 for more of this function), the 2 is the row specifier and the 1 is the column specifier.

The row and column specifiers start together at either 0,0 or 1,1. There are no functions that use 0,1 or 1,0 as the row and column specifiers.

6.2.2 Period Instead of Colon

When you have to type in an argument that is a range reference, e.g., A1:A10, you can type the range by using the period (.) rather than the colon (:) that Excel displays, as the separator. Excel will automatically convert that period to a colon. In this way, you save one keystroke as you need to press only one key, rather than two (the Shift key and the semicolon key to get the colon).

6.2.3 Leave Out <>0 When the Condition "is not a zero"

When you write a condition that something is not a zero (<>0), you can leave this out. Thus when you need to write:

```
=IF(A1<>0,B1,C1)
```

. . . you can write it more simply as follows. This will save you four keystrokes:

```
=IF(A10,B1,C1)
```

6.2.4 No Need for Capitals

When you write the function, you do not have to use capital letters. Excel will display them as capitals. Of course, if you are writing string arguments, such as the "Sell" and "Hold," they will appear exactly as you type them. You will save one keystroke as you will not need to press the Shift key.

6.2.5 No Need for Spaces Between Arguments, but They Can Be Helpful

There is no need to put spaces between arguments, but on long formulas with many arguments, and especially if they contain embedded functions, it can be visually helpful to put in spaces. Thus, instead of this:

```
=IF(A10,B1,IF(C1<0,C5,D5))
```

it can look like this:

```
=IF(A10,B1,  IF(C1<0,C5,D5))
```

6.3 LET'S START

Because the purpose of this chapter is to have you become familiar with the functions in the context of their use, the following is organized a little differently from the list of categories that Excel has. We will talk about them in the following way:

1. The starting point: IF
2. Alternatives to IF
3. Functions for adding
4. Functions for counting
5. Functions for dates
6. Functions for looking up data
7. Dealing with errors
8. Other functions to know

6.4 THE STARTING POINT: IF

6.4.1 IF

If you can only know one function in Excel, if should be IF. This is the function that turns Excel from purely a calculator to a spreadsheet capable of making different types of "what-if" calculations based on different conditions. It has three arguments, and the syntax is as follows:

=IF(ThisConditionIsTrue, DoThis, ElseDoThis)

As an example, you can have the condition: If Cell A1 contains a value other than 0, show the contents of Cell B1; otherwise, show the contents of Cell C1:

=IF(A1<>0,B1,C1)

Let's look at the formula carefully:

- Functions are formulas, so you should begin with the equal (=) sign. This in effect tells Excel: "Get ready to calculate whatever is after the = sign." If you write the above formula without the equal sign, it will appear as text, a string of characters that will not calculate.

The formula shows the contents of Cell B1 or C1, depending on the condition in Cell A1. We can, however, have the choices occur in the IF function itself. Thus, we could write:

```
=IF(A1<>0,10,22)
```

- We can put other operators (=, >, <, <=, >=) in place of the <> sign in the condition. We can also show the choices as text, rather than numbers. In this case, we have to put double quotes around the text:

```
=IF(A1>0,"Sell","Hold")
```

6.4.1.1 It's TRUE or FALSE

When Excel tests whether something is true or not (e.g., in A1>0, is it true that A1 is greater than 0?), it actually returns the condition TRUE or FALSE. You can see this by writing in the number 10 in Cell A1. Next to it, in Cell A2, write the following:

```
=A1=10
```

Remember to put the = sign at the beginning. We want Excel to calculate this. Cell A2 will now show:

```
TRUE
```

If you change Cell A1 so that it contains a number other than 10, a text string or a blank, then Cell A2 will show:

```
FALSE
```

These words appear even though you did not type them in. The words TRUE and FALSE are *keywords* in Excel, and are part of Excel's own vocabulary of words with distinct meanings in Excel. All the names of functions (IF, SUM, etc.) are also keywords. To avoid confusion, do not use keywords when naming range names.

What this means is that in any IF statement, such as:

```
=IF(A1<>0,B1,C1)
```

Excel was really testing:

=IF(TRUE,B1,C1)

What the formula returns is based on whether the test is TRUE or FALSE.

6.4.1.1.1 Booleans: The value of TRUE or FALSE

TRUE or FALSE have values in Excel: TRUE is 1 and FALSE is 0. The English mathematician George Boole (1815–1864) introduced a system of algebraic logic that returns a 1 when two values being compared are equal, and a 0 when they are not. This is now known as Boolean logic.

We can use this Boolean logic as another way to write an IF test—without writing IF. Here is an example when we want to have a statement that says: Return the value 300 when Cell A10 is 22. Write in Cell A11:

=(A10=22)*300

You will need the parentheses around the A10=22 to make it clear to Excel that this is a Boolean test. Otherwise, if will try to test that A10=22*300.

In this Boolean statement, when A10=22 and is TRUE (and thus carries the value of 1), the formula returns 300, since the logic is equivalent to 1*300. If A10 is not 22 and the statement A10=22 is FALSE (with a value of 0), then the formula returns 0 because it is now 0*300.

The equivalent formula with an IF statement would be:

=IF(A10=22,300,0)

Of course, when the IF statement contains two arguments that are not a number or a 0, such as the formula:

=IF(A10=22,300,888)

Then you would need two Booleans:

=(A10=22)*300+(A10<>22)*888

In this case, you might as well use the IF statement.

Booleans (as they are called for short) are nice to use when you want to put a simple switch to turn a cell's numeric contents on and off. The only caveat is that they are not often used, and will confuse people unfamiliar with them.

6.4.1.2 Nested IF statements

You can write an IF statement with other IF statements within them. This is called a *nested* IF statement, and it is useful when you have more than one condition that leads to two choices. In other words, if *one condition* is true, *do this*; otherwise, if a *second condition* is true, *do that*, otherwise do a *third thing*.

Here is an example of a nested IF statement:

```
=IF(A10=1,100,IF(A10=2,200,999))
```

Excel can have up to seven levels of IF statements. However, if you write such a formula, you will find that it would be very difficult to keep track of the nested logic.

6.4.1.3 A zero may not be a zero

One main use of an IF statement is to test whether a cell 0 or not, and this will drive the result of the formula. In the example:

```
=IF(D17=0,D25,D28)
```

where D17 is the result of a calculation, keep in mind that a 0 may appear as a 0 on the worksheet, but it can actually be a small number, such as 0.0000000015. This is the result of how Excel computes its calculations, which are done in a base-16 or hexadecimal number, and then converted back to the base-10 basis for the display. A slight discrepancy may result in this translation process, generally of such a small scale as to be not material to your calculations. However, it does mean that if this miniscule number is present, the test D17=0 will return a FALSE, when in fact it should be a TRUE.

In this case, use the ROUND function (see Section 6.11.1), which rounds the result to a specified number of decimal places. A modified formula is shown in the following.

```
=IF(ROUND(D17,2)=0,D25,D28)
```

6.4.1.4 The last argument is the default

In an IF statement, the last argument is the default, the result of the formula when none of the conditions has been met. For example, when you write an IF statement for designating currency scale (Thousands, Millions, and Billions), it would be useful to have the last argument be the most condition that you will see the most of. Let's assume that this is Millions. The IF statement would then be:

```
=IF(C5="B","Billions",IF(C5="T","Thousands","Millions"))
```

In this way, if the Cell C5 does not have B or T, or contains any other letter or number, or is blank, the setting will default to Millions.

6.4.1.5 Be consistent in the condition

If you are writing many IF statements in a workbook to test a condition, be consistent in writing out the test condition. For example, if you have two settings in the model for an accounting approach ("Purchase" or "Recap"), always keep the test in one form IF(D4= "Recap", . . .) and do not switch to IF(D4= "Purchase", . . .). Being consistent means that if the input cell has an incorrect entry or is blank, the model will continue to be internally consistent.

6.5 ALTERNATIVES TO IF

- Consider CHOOSE if the IF statement is being used to specify an item from a list of selections. The selections do not have to be in contiguous cells. This function is useful when the list is more that 7 items (the limit for nested IF statements) and fewer than 29 (the limit for CHOOSE).
- Use OFFSET or INDEX if the IF is being used to select an item from a list of contiguous cells. These two are useful of lists of more than 29 items.
- Use MIN or MAX if the IF statement is being used limit the appearance of numbers to above or below certain thresholds, such as a 0 value.

- Use AND or OR, or combinations, to reduce nested IF statements. The shorter IF statement may not necessarily be easier to read, however.

6.5.1 CHOOSE

CHOOSE is a good alternative to IF for selecting an item from among a list.

Instead of writing an IF statement like this for making a selection based on a number in Cell C10:

```
IF(C10=1,"Apples",IF(C10=2,"Bananas",IF(C10=3,"Cherries","Dates")))
```

We can write this:

```
= CHOOSE(C10,"Apples","Bananas","Cherries","Dates")
```

So if C10 contains the value 2, then the formula returns "Bananas."

The choice is based on an index number that is the first argument in the function:

```
= CHOOSE(Index_Number,Choice1,Choice2, . . . ,Choice29)
```

Based on the index number (the first argument), CHOOSE selects from the values listed.

CHOOSE is that much more straightforward compared to IF. Note that CHOOSE does not work with ranges. You cannot write CHOOSE(C10,D10:G10), for example. This is not all that bad: what this means is that you can move the positions of the choices in the worksheet. You have to specify the items to select individually, up to the limit of 29. Thus, the index number must be between 1 and 29. The index number cannot be a 0.

6.5.1.1 Specifying 0 for "No choice"

To have the option of entering a 0 in order not to select any value, and since the index number cannot be a 0, use the following variation. You can enter 0 in the specifying cell C10, but it is read by the CHOOSE function as 1. In turn, the first argument is "", or blank. Since this argument is used, you can only list 28 other options.

```
= CHOOSE(C10+1,"","Apples","Bananas","Cherries","Dates")
```

6.5.2 OFFSET

Instead of IF, you can also use OFFSET as a way to select items from a range. In fact, it works only when the items to choose from are in a range; you cannot pick choices from different parts of a worksheet or from different worksheets the way you can with CHOOSE. However, you can actually select from a lot more choices than CHOOSE.

The syntax is:

= OFFSET(Reference,RowsOffset,ColumnOffset)

At its core, OFFSET is a function of finding a cell that is so many rows and so many columns away from a starting reference cell. We can use this ability to pick a remote cell as a way to choose, but it is important to remember this is a far more powerful function. Here's how it works.

The formula (in Cell B10 in Figure 6-1)

= OFFSET(B4,3,2)

returns 402, or the contents of Cell D7. This is the cell 3 rows down and 2 columns to the right of the reference cell B4.

The first number after the reference cell is the number of rows away from the reference cell. A positive number means the row is below the reference cell; a negative number means it is above. The second number is the number of columns away: a

FIGURE 6-1

The OFFSET Function

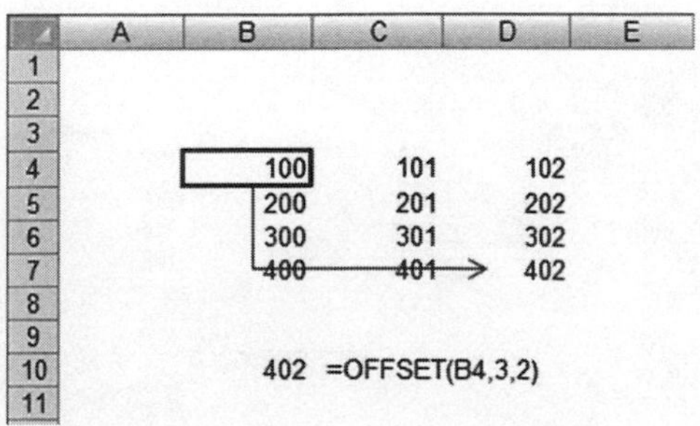

	A	B	C	D	E
1					
2					
3					
4		100	101	102	
5		200	201	202	
6		300	301	302	
7		400	401	402	
8					
9					
10		402	=OFFSET(B4,3,2)		
11					

positive number means to the right of the reference cell; a negative number means to the left.

You can have both row and column counts to be positive, both to be negative, or have a negative row count and a positive column count, and vice versa.

OFFSET(B7,–3,1) as seen in Figure 6-2 has a negative row and a positive column specified. This formula from the base of B7 (the boxed cell) returns the value in Cell C4, because that cell is three rows above and one cell to the right of the base cell.

If we write:

OFFSET(B7,0,0)

we get the contents of B7 itself, because the formula is asking for 0 rows and 0 contents away from Cell B7.

6.5.3 Comparing IF, CHOOSE, and OFFSET

Here is a comparison of IF, CHOOSE, and OFFSET (Fig. 6-3). These are set to work an input toggle in Cell A3. All these will return "Apples" if A3 is 1, "Bananas" if it is 2, and so on.

With OFFSET, the list of items has to be in a contiguous range, because the function is simply counting how many cells away from the data cell is from the reference cell. In the illustration, the OFFSET row specifier is B3 minus 1, since "Apples" occupies the 0 offset position from Cell B1, "Bananas" occupies the 1 offset position, and so on.

FIGURE 6-2

The OFFSET Function with a Negative Offset

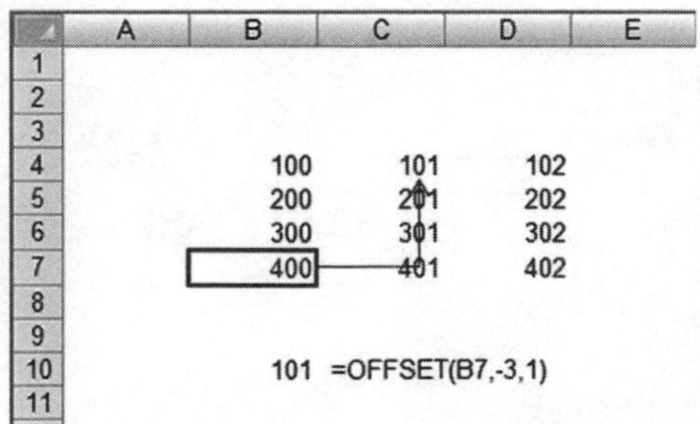

FIGURE 6-3

Comparing IF, CHOOSE, and OFFSET

	A	B	C	D	E	F	G
1	**Apples**	**Bananas**	**Cherries**	**Dates**			
2							
3		2	Bananas	=IF(B3=1,A1,IF(B3=2,B1,IF(B3=3,C1,D1)))			
4							
5			Bananas	=CHOOSE(B3,A1,B1,C1,D1)			
6							
7			Bananas	=OFFSET(A1,0,B3-1)			
8							

In the next example (Fig. 6-4), there is another important point to note. If we move (not copy) the list of items to a vertical range, the IF and CHOOSE references will automatically change, but we would need to manually adjust the OFFSET formula to flip the row and column specifiers.

6.5.4 AND

As part of writing the IF statement, you can use the AND function, which combines the conditions. It is not an alternative to IF as such, but you could say that it is an alternative to a second IF. Rather than writing a nested second IF, you could combine the conditions with one AND, and write just one IF. The AND syntax is:

AND(Condition1,Condition2, . . .)

FIGURE 6-4

OFFSET Must Be Edited when the Layout Is Moved

	A	B	C	D	E	F	G
1	**Apples**						
2	**Bananas**						
3	**Cherries**	2	Bananas	=IF(B3=1,A1,IF(B3=2,A2,IF(B3=3,A3,A4)))			
4	**Dates**						
5			Bananas	=CHOOSE(B3,A1,A2,A3,A4)			
6							
7			Bananas	=OFFSET(A1,B3-1,0)			
8							

Notice that the AND precedes everything and the conditions are enclosed in parentheses. The function will return a TRUE if all the conditions in the function are true, and it will return a FALSE if even only one is not true. AND can contain up to 30 conditions.

AND is very helpful if you need to write a formula for the following, for example: If the employee's age is 50 or more, and his age plus length of employment is 70 or more, then he can retire. In the formula, "Age" and "Employment" are range names for individual cells containing the relevant data.

```
=IF(AND(Age>=50,Age+Employment>=70),
"See retirement counselor","Keep working")
```

6.5.5 OR

OR has the same syntax as AND:

```
OR(Condition1,Condition2, . . .)
```

Again, notice that OR precedes everything. Any one of the conditions must be true before the OR function returns a TRUE.

6.6 FUNCTIONS FOR ADDING

6.6.1 SUM

The SUM function allows you to add ranges and/or individual numbers quickly. A simple SUM would be:

```
=SUM(D10:D150)
```

Note that with SUM, you can sum big ranges, which would be tedious to do if you had to use the plus sign to string all the elements together. You can specify the elements to sum as individual elements, either as cell references or the numbers themselves, as ranges of numbers, and even nested SUM statements:

```
=SUM(D10,D11,D15:D20,12+D23+D24,
SUM(D30:D35,12*4)/365)
```

One difference between SUM and just using the + sign is that SUM is more forgiving when adding text string such as "na" (Fig. 6-5).

FIGURE 6-5

Comparing SUM with the + Sign

	A	B	C	D	E	F	G
1							
2		243			243		
3		469			469		
4		863			863		
5		na			na		
6		25			25		
7							
8		**1,600**	=SUM(B2:B6)		**#VALUE!**	=E2+E3+E4+E5+E6	
9							

The range in SUM will automatically expand as you insert intervening rows (or columns, if you are SUMming across a table). However, you must be careful to recheck the range if you have been inserting or deleting rows at the top or bottom (or left and right edges) of the table.

6.6.2 SUMIF

This is a combination conditional and summing function. It will add the items in a range of values only if they fulfill a condition. The syntax is:

= SUMIF(Range,Criteria,SumRange)

Range is a list of items. *Criteria* is a condition related to Range. *SumRange* consists of the items that will be summed depending on the results of Criteria and Range.

Here's an example (Fig. 6-6): We want to find out the total items related to the listing for Alex, and the formula in F2 is:

= SUMIF(B2:B7,E2,C2:C7)

The first range in B2:B7 is the Range. The Criteria is the cell E2, in which we have entered the word "Alex." (You could also just enter the test "Alex" directly into the formula.) The formula sums all the items in C2:C7, the SumRange, that is associated with "Alex." And the answer is 6.

FIGURE 6-6

SUMIF

	A	B	C	D	E	F	G	H	I
1									
2		Alex	3		Alex	6	=SUMIF(B2:B7,E2,C2:C7)		
3		John	2						
4		Alex	1						
5		Lena	4						
6		Hillary	5						
7		Alex	2						
8									

SUMIF does not work with multiple conditions. You cannot write SUMIF(B2:B7,AND("Alex","John"),C2:C7), for example. However, if you wanted this result, the easy solution is to write the formula again, first using "Alex" and then using "John":

SUMIF(B2:B7,"Alex",C2:C7)+SUMIF(B2:B7,"John",C2:C7)

6.6.2.1 Variation of SUMIF

In the following illustration (Fig. 6-7), SUMIF is being used to sum the cells that meet a quantitative condition, in this case the condition of "over 3." Note the Range is now defined as the range of numbers, rather than the list of names.

Range is the same as SumRange. Because Range is the same as SumRange, we can actually write the formula in an abbreviated form:

= SUMIF(C2:C7,E2)

FIGURE 6-7

Variation of SUMIF

	A	B	C	D	E	F	G	H	I	J
1							**Referencing Cell E2**			
2		Alex	3		>3	9	=SUMIF(C2:C7,E2,C2:C7)			
3		John	2			9	=SUMIF(C2:C7,E2)			
4		Alex	1							
5		Lena	4				**Writing ">3" directly into SUMIF**			
6		Hillary	5			9	=SUMIF(C2:C7,">3",C2:C7)			
7		Alex	2			9	=SUMIF(C2:C7,">3")			
8										

If you want to write the condition within the formula itself, you have to put it as a text string (i.e., put it in quotes):

= SUMIF(C2:C7,">3")

6.6.2.2 SUMIF for summing rows with a unique characteristic
You can use SUMIF in a particularly powerful way: as a way to total rows that share a unique identifier (e.g., account descriptions) in a model, especially when they are separated by intervening rows and where you expect the model to have rows added or deleted by the user.

Let's say you have a sheet for listing divisional revenues (Fig. 6-8). Rather than summing the revenues at the bottom using SUM, use SUMIF. The illustration shows a listing of three divisional revenues in rows 3, 8, and 13. In row 18, we put the SUMIF formula. The formula shown is the contents of Cell B18.

FIGURE 6-8

Summing Rows Sharing a Unique Characteristic with SUMIF

	A	B	C	D	E
1		**2009**	**2010**	**2011**	
2	**Division 1**				
3	Revenue	100	120	140	
4	COGS	81	87	98	
5	SGA	7	9	12	
6					
7	**Division 2**				
8	Revenue	60	70	80	
9	COGS	45	48	53	
10	SGA	5	6	7	
11					
12	**Division 3**				
13	Revenue	40	45	50	
14	COGS	31	33	36	
15	SGA	3	4	6	
16					
17	**Total Company**				
18	Revenue	200	235	270	
19		=SUMIF($A$2:$A$15,$A18,B$2:B$15)			
20					

We copy this formula across that line to Columns C and D. Note four important points:

1. The formula in Cell B18 has absolute references for the column in Range ($A$2:$A$15) since this stays fixed.
2. The formula in Cell B18 for the Criteria has an absolute reference only for the column ($A18), since we want the reference to the title column even if we copy this formula across the screen. However, if we want to copy it to another row, the reference should then point to that row.
3. The formula in Cell B18 for the SumRange has absolute references only for the row ($B2:$B15). When we copy this cell to other columns or rows, we want the reference to be to different columns but to the same set of rows.
4. The two ranges must be of the same size: A2:A15 and B2: B15, and aligned. If they are not of equal size and are not aligned, this formula gives wrong answers.

If you add more divisional sales lines between rows 1 and 15, they will automatically be part of the sum of Total Company's revenue. You must be careful to include the new rows as part of the range shown in the SUMIF function. By the same magic, if you delete any divisional sales segments, the total will continue to work and will not return any error messages.

6.6.2.3 SUMIF for aggregating into annual periods

When you are working with quarterly or other non-annual periods, it is useful to show an aggregated annual sum. SUMIF provides an easy way to do this (Fig. 6-9).

Under the range of dates for the quarterly periods, we add an additional row for the year of the quarter. We can use the YEAR function (see Section 6.8.2).

For the annual periods, we use the SUMIF formula (shown for Cell B9) that sums the SumRange of $B$4:$I$4 based on whether Row 3 in each column matches the Criteria in the annual column.

6.6.3 SUMPRODUCT

This is a quick way to multiply two ranges of numbers together. The syntax consists of two or more ranges, both of which must

FIGURE 6-9

Aggregating Non-Annual Periods Using SUMIF

	A	B	C	D	E	F	G	H	I
1									
2		Mar-09	Jun-09	Sep-09	Dec-09	Mar-10	Jun-10	Sep-10	Dec-10
3	=YEAR(B2) ===>	2009	2009	2009	2009	2010	2010	2010	2010
4	Quarterly Revenue	110	120	130	140	150	160	170	180
5									
6									
7		Dec-09	Dec-10						
8	Annual Revenue	500	660						
9		=SUMIF($B$3:$I$3,YEAR(B$7),$B$4:$I$4)							
10		This is the formula in Cell B7; Copy to Cell C7							
11									

be the same size, and the function multiplies each element in one range with the corresponding element in the other range.

The illustration (Fig. 6-10) shows how the SUMPRODUCT accomplishes the task of deriving the total interest expense from a list of debt items and their individual interest rates.

In this one cell, we can accomplish what otherwise would take separate multiplications of each debt by each interest rate and then the summing of the products.

6.7 FUNCTIONS FOR COUNTING

6.7.1 COUNT

This counts the items in a range. An important point to note is that the COUNT function counts only numbers. It will disregard entries of text.

In Figure 6-11, the formula in Cell C6 returns 3, the number of times numbers appear in the range B2: C4.

FIGURE 6-10

SUMPRODUCT

	A	B	C	D	E	F	G	H
1		Debt	Interest Rate		Interest Expense			
2		100	3.0%		42	=SUMPRODUCT(B2:B5,C2:C5)		
3		200	4.0%					
4		300	5.0%					
5		400	4.0%					

FIGURE 6-11

COUNT and COUNTA

	A	B	C	D	E
1					
2		Adam	12		
3		Billy	3		
4		Charlie	5		
5					
6		COUNT	3	=COUNT(B2:C4)	
7					
8		COUNTA	6	=COUNTA(B2:C4)	
9					

6.7.2 COUNTA

Unlike COUNT, COUNTA counts both numbers and text. The second function in Figure 6-11 shows COUNTA(B2:C4) returning the number 6.

6.7.3 COUNTIF

This is a combination conditional and counting function. It is similar to the SUMIF but returns a count of the items that meet the condition, rather than the sum. It only has two arguments. The syntax is:

= COUNTIF(Range,Criteria)

Range is a list of items. Criteria is a condition related to Range.

The following (Fig. 6-12) shows three examples.

In Example 1, COUNTIF returns the number of items related to the category "Alex." Note that the range is not limited to just the column of names. Here, the range covers both names and values but it still returns the correct number of instances of "Alex."

In Example 2, COUNTIF returns the number of items that are above 25. The criteria is entered as a string ">25". It does not matter that the range includes names and values.

In Example 3, COUNTIF is used as a master alert system (in Cell B14) that returns an "Error" message if a range that it

FIGURE 6-12

COUNTIF

	A	B	C	D	E	F	G	H	I
1		**Example 1**							
2		Alex	3	=COUNTIF(G2:H7,B2)			Alex	32	
3							John	27	
4		**Example 2**					Alex	19	
5		>25	4	=COUNTIF(G2:H7,B5)			Lena	43	
6							Hilly	51	
7							Alex	22	
8									
9									
10		**Example 3**							
11		OK	OK	OK	Check	OK			
12									
13		MasterAlert							
14		Error	=IF(COUNTIF(B11:F11,"Check"),"Error","OK")						
15									

looks to contains a message that triggers it, in this case the word "Check." (The range in Example 3 could be a series of functions that tests that values in those five columns have no discrepancies, for example.)

6.7.4 AVERAGE

This is really the SUM and COUNT functions together, or even more basic, the sum of the elements, divided by the number of elements. The syntax is:

= AVERAGE(number1,number2,... ,number30)

The number arguments are numbers, arrays, or references that contain numbers. If the argument is a text, AVERAGE will consider it the same as a blank. Some points to note when using AVERAGE:

- A blank cell is totally disregarded in the averaging calculations. A cell with a 0 is part of the calculations (Fig. 6-13).
- If the elements all point to blank cells, you will have a #DIV/0! error. This is the result of the denominator

FIGURE 6-13

AVERAGE

	A	B	C	D	E	F	G	H	I
1									
2		10			10		10	=AVERAGE(B2:E2)	
3									
4		10	0	0	10		5	=AVERAGE(B4:E4)	
5									
6									
7							#DIV/0!	=AVERAGE(B7:E7)	
8									

count being zero. However, if the function points to at least one cell that contains a value, even if that value is 0, then it will work.

6.8 FUNCTIONS FOR DATES

Dates can be simple four-digit numbers that go up by 1 with each column, representing years. Occasionally, you may have to enter quarterly dates or work with days, months, and years. If we want to have a good control of the dates in the column so that we can easily change them, then we will have to understand how dates work in Excel.

6.8.1 How Excel Keeps Track of Dates

Excel keeps track of dates by assigning a number, or a *serial value*, to a date, starting with the number 1 for January 1, 1900. The upper limit is the serial value 2,958,465 for December 31, 9999. Excel's formatting takes this another step. By using different data formats, you can make the serial value appear in the date format you want, including non-U.S. dates ("31/12/2003"), or even as times of the day or the day of the week.

Even with serial values for dates, we cannot just add 30 or 30.42 (that's 365/12) to a starting date if we want to make it go up by one month at a time. Adding 30.42 to December 31, 2009, will give us January 30, 2010, and not January 31. Adding 30.42 to January 31 will give us March 1, not the end of February.

The solution is to work with years, months, and days. If we want to go up one month, we simply add 1 to the month designator, no matter what the length of the month is. Likewise, to go up 1 year, we add 1 to the year designator, leap year or not. We can do this in Excel, because Excel will show you what year, month, or day it is for any serial value representing any time between January 1, 1900 and December 31, 9999.

6.8.2 To Get the Year, Month, and Day from a Date

The functions YEAR, MONTH, and DAY if used on a serial value will return the respective information. Thus, if we picked a serial value like 40543:

= YEAR(40543)

returns 2010;

= MONTH(40543)

returns 12; and

= DAY(40543)

returns 31.

This is to say that December 31, 2010 is the date represented by 40,543. This date is 40,543 days away from December 31, 1899 (January 1, 1900, being day 1 in the serial value, is 1 day away). We would get the same results if we actually used the date 12/31/2010. Note that we are using it as a text string, shown between two double quotes:

= YEAR("12/31/2010")

returns 2010;

= MONTH("12/31/2010")

returns 12; and

= DAY("12/31/2010")

returns 31.

For our overseas readers: we are using here the U.S. convention for dates, which uses the order of month/day/year. Excel can be set to show different dating formats so that the serial value will appear with the correct order of days, months, and years (Fig. 6-14).

In Excel 2007, on the *Home* tab, go to *Format>Format Cells> Number* and select Date in the "Category" list box. Look at the drop-down box for "Locale (location)."

In earlier versions, go to *Format>Cells>Number* and select Date in the "Category" list box. Look at the drop-down box for "Locale (location)."

You will have to use the double quotes on the date to mark it as a text string. However, if the date were placed in another cell and the function referenced that cell, you do not have to worry about double quotes.

FIGURE 6–14

Formatting Dates

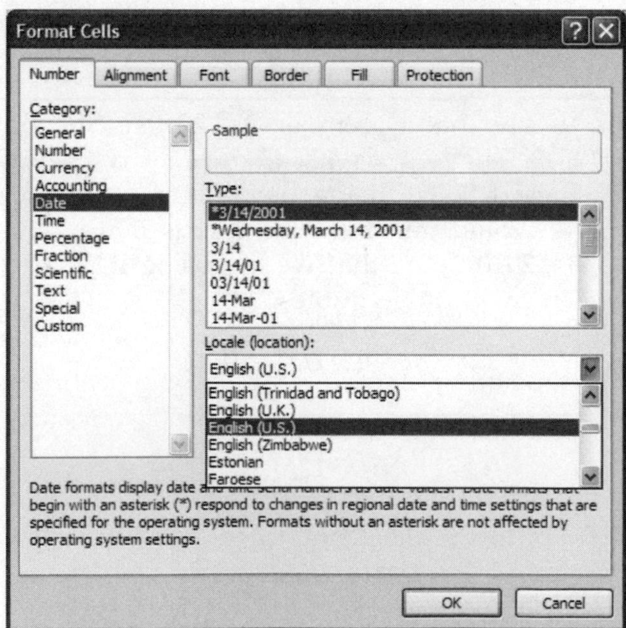

6.8.3 To Get a Date from the Year, Month, and Day

Going the other way, to arrive at a date based on given inputs for the year, month, and day, we use the DATE function.

= DATE(2010,12,31)

This returns the serial value 40543, which can be formatted to appear as 12/31/2010.

Because Excel functions can use the results of other functions, we can write the following in Cell C1. Let's put 12/31/2010 in a separate cell, say, Cell B1:

= DATE(YEAR(B1),MONTH(B1),DAY(B1))

This returns the same date: 12/31/2010.

6.8.4 Monthly Dating

Here is a simple dating problem: How do we make a date go up by one month? Or more specifically, how do we get from the end of one month to the end of the next month?

We start with 12/31/2010 in B1. To make it go up by one month, we add 1 to the MONTH. In C1, we write:

= DATE(YEAR(B1),MONTH(B1)+1,DAY(B1))

This will return 1/31/2011 (January 31, 2011). Success! Building on this, let's try the next column again. In D1 we add another digit to the MONTH(C1):

= DATE(YEAR(C1),MONTH(C1)+1,DAY(C1))

This returns 3/3/2011 (March 3, 2011)! This is not quite right. What's happening? The problem arises because January has 31 days and with this formula we are asking Excel to give the date for something like February 31, 2004 because the date we specified for days was DAY(C1), which was returning 31, for January. We had no trouble with the first formula for January, because that month has the same number of days as December. Since February in this year only has 28 days, Excel keeps counting until the "day 31" of February, and comes up with the equivalent March 3. Excel's datingsystem is intelligent enough that it does not go into error when you specify a day that is beyond the month's number of days.

How do we find the ending day of each month, given that months' lengths vary? Instead of trying to find the ending day of each month, we could look for the first day of the next month and then subtract one day. Since the first day is always day 1, this is quite easy. So January 31 is really February 1 minus 1 day; February 28 is March 1 minus 1 day, and so on. Since Excel can deal with something like "February 31" to return March 3 (or March 2 in a leap year), can Excel consider January 31 as being "February 0," and February 28 as "March 0"?

Yes, in fact, it can. So now we have a solution for our dating problem. We add an extra month to the month interval we want to go up, but specify 0 for the DAY.

Let's have 12/31/2010 in B1 again. In C1, to make the date go up by one month, we write:

```
= DATE(YEAR(B1),MONTH(B1)+2,0))
```

to get "February 0, 2011," which is 1/31/2011.

In D1, to continue to the next month, we write:

```
= DATE(YEAR(C1),MONTH(C1)+2,0)
```

to get "March 0, 2011," which is 2/28/2011.

After this tour of the ins and outs of dates, the EOMONTH function is a shortcut. The function stands for "end of month." The syntax is EOMONTH(Start_date, the number of months before or after the start_date). These two formulas:

```
= EOMONTH("12/15/2010",0)

= EOMONTH("12/31/2010",0)
```

both return 12/31/2010, since this is the end of the month that is 0 months from the start date. EOMONTH works to get to the last day of the month, but if you need to have a date a certain number of days, months, and years from a starting date, you will still need to work with the more complicated date functions.

6.8.5 Yearly Dating

Increasing dates by 1 year is fairly simple matter now. Just add 1 to the YEAR number. We will use the same table, with 12/31/03, in cell B1. In cell C1, we would use the formula:

= DATE(YEAR(B1)+1,MONTH(B1),DAY(B1))

We will not have to worry about the DAY being off, since we are dealing with the same month in the year, just a year apart. However, if we are working with a February year-end, this formula will not return the leap day of February 29 in the leap years, since the DAY will always be based on the count of 28 for 2011 (or 29 if the starting year had been a leap year). We could use the approach of using the 0 day of the next month, however:

= DATE(YEAR(B1)+1,MONTH(B1)+1,0)

This is the approach to use if you want the leap day to appear on the leap years. Alternatively, instead of adding 1 to the YEAR number, we can add 13 (12 + 1) to the MONTH and still use 0 for the DAY. That will bring us to exactly a year later.

= DATE(YEAR(B1),MONTH(B1)+13,0)

For a date of a year earlier, we would use subtract 11 months (from –12 + 1) to the MONTH function:

= DATE(YEAR(B1),MONTH(B1)-11,0)

6.8.6 Nonannual Intervals

Using the MONTH part makes it easy to change the periodicity of your model from annual to quarterlies, or to some other nonannual interval. When you do this, it is a good idea always to use the "+ 1" approach to the MONTH and use 0 for the DAY, because the intervals you have can bring you to months with dissimilar ending days.

6.8.6.1 Finding the number of days between dates

Because of the serial value system, it is easy to find the number of days that have elapsed from one date to the next. For example, to find the number of days between August 17, 1953 and October 1, 2010, we do the following:

= DATE(2010,10,1)-DATE(1953,8,17)

which returns 20,864 days.

Alternatively, we can represent the actual date as a serial value by using the DATEVALUE function, which converts the text of the date to the serial value:

= DATEVALUE("10/1/2010")-DATEVALUE("8/17/1953")

which returns 20,864 days.

6.8.6.2 Finding the number of months between dates using DAYS360

Finding the number of months between two dates is a little tricky, because of the different lengths of the months in the interval. In the last example we could divide 20,864 by the average number of days in a month (i.e., 365/12, or 30.42), but this is inelegant. A better way is to use the DAYS360 function. With DAYS360, Excel considers each year to be 360 days by assuming that there are 12 months, each composed of 30 days. So Excel has a way of considering the ending days of each month so that everything falls into line properly. The syntax is:

= DAYS360(BeginningDate,EndingDate)

The beginning date can be one defined by the DATE function, but DAYS360 is also smart enough to take the text of the dates:

= DAYS360(DATE(1953,8,17),DATE(2010,10,1))

which returns 20,564 days. Or

= DAYS360("8/17/1953","10/1/2010")

which returns the same number: 20,564. Compare this with the actual number of days of 20,864. The number of interval days is fewer than the previous calculation because each 360-day year is 5 days shorter than the actual year (6 in a leap year). This is not a problem if we are looking to get a sense of the portion of the month or the year using this method. To find the number of months, we simply take the interval in days in a 360-day year and divide it by 30. Now, to get the number of months or the number of years:

20,564/30=685.47 months

20,564/360=57.12 years

6.8.6.3 *When to use DAYS360 in a model*

DAYS360 is useful in calculating a portion of the year. Let's say that a transaction happens on June 14, and we just want to get a value for the stub portion, or the portion of the year remaining after the deal. Let's assume a December 31 year-end:

= DAYS360("6/14/2010","12/31/2010")/360

which returns 197/360, or 0.55.

6.8.6.4 *Solving a problem with DAYS360*

In some situations, DAYS360 does not give you a 30-day month. Take the case where cell A1 has the date of 12/31/2010 (the end of December) and cell A2 has the date 2/28/2011 (the end of February in a non-leap year):

= DAYS360(A1,A2)

The formula returns 58 days.

Under the logic that each month is 30 days, the function should return 60 days for the two full months' interval. It does not in this case because Excel looks at the end of the month and tries to fit the 28-, 29-, 30-, and 31-day endings into some order, and somehow the 28-day ending is confusing it. We can help Excel get unconfused by bringing the dates into the beginning of the month, where the interval algorithm is more straightforward. We do this by adding the number 1 to the cell references. In this way, we also do not need to change the dates themselves:

DAYS360(A1+1,A2+1)=60 days

Assuming that you are always using period-end dates, adding 1 to the components of DAYS360 is a good way to make sure that the function works properly.

6.9 FUNCTIONS FOR LOOKING UP DATA

Looking up data is really pinpointing the location of the data point that you want, whether it is from a collection of alternatives or from its location as defined by rows and columns.

Two of the functions for looking up data have been introduced as variations of the IF functions: CHOOSE and OFFSET.

6.9.1 CHOOSE

See section 6.5.1.

6.9.2 OFFSET

See section 6.5.2.

6.9.3 MAX and MIN

MAX (return the largest number given a list of arguments) and MIN (return the smallest number from a list of arguments) are alternatives to IF when you need to test against certain limits.

To show results that are always above zero, you can write it with an IF statement:

```
=IF(A10>0,A10,0)
```

This means that if A10 is over 0, then show it, otherwise (if it is a zero or negative number), just show a zero. You can write it with the formula that is more efficient, like this:

```
= MAX(A10,0)
```

This reads: Show the maximum in the given range of arguments, in this case, A10 and 0. Thus, if A10 is a negative number, 0 is the greater number, and that is the result you will see. If it is positive, then A10 will be the number displayed.

Likewise, the following are equivalents hold true:

```
= IF(A10<0,A10,0)
```

```
= MIN(A10,0)
```

Here is the variation if you want to say: Show A10 only if it is less than zero, but show it as a positive number:

=IF(A10<0,–A10,0)

Note the minus sign in front of A10.

=–MIN(A10,0)

Note the minus sign in front of the MIN.

Or an alternative using MAX:

=MAX(–A10,0)

Note the minus sign in front of A10.

MIN and MAX become a much better choice over IF when there are more elements:

= MAX(A10,B10,C10,0)

or

= MAX(A10:C10,0)

An equivalent IF statement would be:

=IF(AND(A10>= B10,A10>= C10,A10>=0),A10,IF(AND(B10>= A10,B10>= C10,B10>=0),B10,IF(AND(C10>= A10, C10>= B10,C10>=0),C10,0)))

As you can see, this tortuous formula is horrendously difficult to write correctly and check, and this is only to test just three cells against the value 0.

In the case where we want to find the maximum or minimum values of a range or a row, there is no other way but to use MAX or MIN:

= MAX(A1:G16)

= MIN(10:10)

6.9.4 MIN and MAX Together

If you want to show the value only as between 0 and 5, you can use the two together in the same formula:

= MIN(MAX(A10,0),5)

In this way, any number that is in A10 will be shown only as a number between 0 and 5. The MAX function will show only numbers in A10 that are equal to or greater than 0. Potentially, this could be, say, 27. The MIN will show that result only between 0 (the bottom limit of the MAX) and 5 (the limit set by the MIN). So this is a way to limit the number that is being read elsewhere in the model to only the values between 0 and 5.

Another way is to put a limit on the input cell so that only this range of values can be entered. You can do this through the Data Validation feature of Excel (see Chapter 19).

6.9.5 MIN and MAX with Negative Numbers

MIN will always return the lowest value, in positive or negative numbers; MAX likewise returns the highest value.

If the range named TestRange contains 1,2,3, then:

= MIN(TestRange) will return 1

= MAX(TestRange) will return 3

Note the results for negative values. If the range named TestRange contains –1, –2, –3, then:

= MIN(TestRange) will return –3

as –3 is the lowest value:

= MAX(TestRange) will return –1

as –1 is the highest value.

Because of this, be careful with using MIN and MAX with negative numbers. If your intent is to find a negative number that is closest to zero, use MAX; for a negative number farthest from zero on the numbers scale, use MIN.

6.9.6 MATCH

Use MATCH if you are looking for the location of a specific number or text in a range. Depending on how you write the formula, this function will return either the row or column number (but not both) within the range that you specified. The syntax is:

= MATCH(LookUpValue,LookupArray,MatchType)

LookUpValue is the item that you want to look up. This can be a number, a text, or a reference to another cell that holds the LookUpValue.

LookUpArray is a contiguous range of cells, or a range name.

MatchType can be either 1, 0, or –1. If it is 1, the MATCH will find the largest value that is less than or equal to the LookUpValue. In this case, the items in the LookUpRange must be arranged in ascending order.

If it is –1, it will find the smallest value that is greater than or equal to the LookUpValue. The data must be in descending order.

If it is 0, then it will find the exact match for LookUpValue. The data can be in any order. MATCH is very useful in this mode, and this is what we illustrate below (Fig. 6-15).

In this simple example, let's find the location of the word "Carol" from the list of names.

The argument "Carol" is written directly into the function formula, but it could well have been a reference to another cell that actually holds that word. The range in the middle specifies the one-column block. The "0" at the end indicates we are looking for the exact match for "Carol."

In this instance, the formula will return the value of 2, meaning that it has found Carol in the second row of the target range, which in this case is row 7 on the sheet. MATCH finds only the

FIGURE 6-15

MATCH

	A	B	C	D	E	F	G
1							
2				**Location of Carol within the range**			
3				2	=MATCH("Carol",B6:B10,0)		
4							
5							
6		Bob		**Location of Carol within the column**			
7		Carol		7	=MATCH("Carol",B:B,0)		
8		Ted					
9		Alice					
10		Bob					
11							

first instance of the lookup value. If we had set the MATCH function to look for "Bob", it would only return the value of 1 in this example, disregarding the second instance of "Bob."

If we make a slight change to the formula and made the target range be the whole column, then the function will return 7, since "Carol" is now in the fourth row of this "range."

= MATCH("Carol",B:B,0)

There is an interesting point: we have just identified the actual row number in the sheet of where "Carol" is located (or at least the first instance of "Carol"). Being able to identify a row number of a data point can be useful in other instances, especially if we already know which column it is in.

6.9.7 INDEX

INDEX returns the value of a cell within a range, by locating its row position and its column position. The syntax is:

= INDEX(Array,RowNumber,ColumnNumber)

The Array is any range storing the data.

The RowNumber is an integer starting from 1 that specifies which row within the Array the data point is in. RowNumber 1 means that the data point is on the first row of the Array. This can be omitted if the Array is a one-row range.

The ColumnNumber likewise is an integer starting from 1. It specifies which column the data point is in. ColumnNumber 1 means that the data point is on the first column of the Array. You can omit this if the Array is a one-column range.

In Figure 6-16, if we define the Array as B2: E5, then INDEX(B2:E5,1,1) will return the value in the top left corner of the range (i.e., "Bob"). Using this table, we will get the following results from these other variations:

= INDEX(B2:E5,3,1)

returns "Ted".

= INDEX(B2:E5,4,3)

returns "PhD".

FIGURE 6-16

Using INDEX to Get Different Data Points from an Array

	A	B	C	D	E	F	G	H	I
1			Age	City	Degree				
2		Bob	43	San Francisco	JD				
3		Carol	36	New York	MBA				
4		Ted	39	Los Angeles	MA				
5		Alice	38	Boston	PhD				
6									
7		Array column no				Array column no			
8		1				2			
9	Array row no					Age	=INDEX($B$1:$E$1,1,F$8)		
10	4	Alice	=INDEX($B$2:$E$5,$A10,B$8)			38	=INDEX($B$2:$E$5,$A10,F$8)		
11									

See also the kinds of information you can get out of the table by having inputs that specify the row and column numbers (bold boxes). Cell F9 shows "Age" from an index that looks at a different array, Cells $B$1:$E$1.

When you use INDEX, the row and column numbers must specify positions within the Array. If they point to a location outside the range, you will get a #REF error message.

6.9.8 Using MATCH and INDEX Together

The power of Excel functions can be magnified by using them together. Because MATCH can locate a row number based on matching it with a specific label or value, you can use the result of MATCH as a row parameter in INDEX. In the following illustration (Fig. 6-17), we specify the company "Charlie" in cell E7. The following formula in cell E8 returns the stock price for the company:

```
= INDEX(E2:E5,MATCH(E7,B2:B5,0))
```

The INDEX Array range is a one-column range, so we do not have to specify the Column number argument.

6.9.9 HLOOKUP/VLOOKUP

HLOOKUP and VLOOKUP are functions that work together in the same way as MATCH and INDEX in searching for a data point

FIGURE 6-17

Using INDEX and MATCH Together

	A	B	C	D	E	F	G	H	I
1		**Company**			**Stock Price**				
2		Alpha			$ 12.25				
3		Baker			$ 8.50				
4		Charlie			$ 22.00				
5		Delta			$ 17.35				
6									
7		Enter company name			Charlie				
8		Stock price			$ 22.00	=INDEX(E2:E5,MATCH(E7,B2:B5,0),1)			
9									

in data range. HLOOKUP is for searching the data range horizontally, by columns; VLOOKUP is for searching vertically, by rows.

HLOOKUP and VLOOKUP are powerful functions and are often used when simpler functions such as OFFSET or INDEX will do just fine. These functions are most useful when the answer does not depend on an exact match with your search parameters. The syntax for HLOOKUP is as follows:

= HLOOKUP(LookUpValue,TableArray,RowNumber, LookUpType)

The LookUpValue is the value to be looked up in the first row of the TableArray.

The TableArray contains the data for the lookup.

The RowNumber is the row that contains the data to be returned by the function.

The LookUpType is optional. If omitted or TRUE, this means than an approximate match can be returned if there is no exact match. The approximate match will be based on the value that is less than the LookUpValue.

In Figure 6-18, three examples show how HLOOKUP works.

In the first instance (Cell D6), the applicable tax rate returned is 28% because the income entered is over $2,500 but below $25,000. The LookUpType is not entered, so this is equivalent to TRUE. If the LookUpType were set to FALSE, the formula HLOOKUP (D5,$A$2:$E$3,2,FALSE) would result in an #N/A error because there is no exact match to the entry of $14,750.

FIGURE 6-18

HLOOKUP

	A	B	C	D	E	F	G
1							
2	Income	$0	$2,500	$25,000	$50,000		
3	Tax rate:	15%	28%	31%	36%		
4							
5		Enter income:		$14,750			
6		Applicable tax rate:		28%	=HLOOKUP(D5,$A$2:$E$3,2)		
7							
8		Enter income:		$24,999			
9		Applicable tax rate:		28%	=HLOOKUP(D8,$A$2:$E$3,2)		
10							
11		Enter income:		$25,000			
12		Applicable tax rate:		31%	=HLOOKUP(D11,$A$2:$E$3,2)		
13							

The second instance (Cell D9) returns the same 28%.

The third instance (Cell D12) returns a new rate of 31%, since the income has reached the threshold of $25,000.

VLOOKUP uses the same syntax, but the table has to be arranged vertically (Fig. 6-19):

FIGURE 6-19

VLOOKUP

	A	B	C	D	E	F	G
1							
2		Income	Tax rate:				
3		$0	15%				
4		$2,500	28%				
5		$25,000	31%				
6		$50,000	36%				
7							
8		Enter income:		$14,750			
9		Applicable tax rate:		28%	=VLOOKUP(D8,$B$2:$C$6,2)		
10							
11		Enter income:		$24,999			
12		Applicable tax rate:		28%	=VLOOKUP(D11,$B$2:$C$6,2)		
13							
14		Enter income:		$25,000			
15		Applicable tax rate:		31%	=VLOOKUP(D14,$B$2:$C$6,2)		
16							

6.10 HANDLING ERRORS

As we develop the formulas in our model, Excel has a way of telling us when we are going about it the wrong way. The four most common error messages that Excel will show are the following:

- #DIV/0!
- #VALUE!
- #NAME?
- #REF!

6.10.1 #DIV/0! Errors

Excel will display this error when you attempt to divide a number by 0. It is easy to write a formula that inadvertently divides by zero because as you develop the formula, you may be using some test numbers. However, once you clean up the model, these test numbers go away and you will have formulas that then show the #DIV/0 errors. It may be that as the model starts to be used, there will be values coming in that will make these formulas calculate properly again. However, it is sometimes quite disconcerting for a new user unfamiliar with your model to see these error messages. For this reason, for any formula you write that involves a division, you should take steps to do an error trap by using an IF statement.

Thus, instead of the formula:

```
= D10/D12
```

we should write it as:

```
=IF(D12,D10/D12,0)
```

Remember that D12 is the short way of writing D12<>0. Another variation is this formula:

```
=IF(D12,D10/D12,"na")
```

This formula will return the text "na" if D12 is zero. This is fine, unless there is the chance that this formula will be read by another cell as part of the calculation in that cell. If the first cell shows "na," then the calculation in the second cell will run into trouble because it will not be able to use this text in its calculations. That second cell will show the #VALUE! error (see 6.10.2).

One trick you can use if you do want the "na" to show but avoid having other cells running into calculation problems is to use the first formula that returns a 0. To do this, we use Excel's formatting capabilities to show "na" when it is the value for 0. Please turn to Chapter 19 to see how this is done.

6.10.2 The #VALUE! Error

The usual occurrence of this error message is when you have written a formula whose components include a text. Essentially, this is Excel saying: "I don't want text. I want values only, please."

6.10.3 The #NAME? Error

You will get this error if your formula uses a range name that does not exist. This can be because of a misspelled range name, or a range name that you have created and used before but that has now been deleted. A misspelled function name will also give you this error.

6.10.4 The #REF! Error

This happens when the formula uses an invalid cell reference. For example, start with a formula in cell A10 like this:

= A1+10

If you copy this up one row, the formula will return a #REF!. In copying, Excel will try to keep the relative referencing, so as you go up one row, it changes the reference to A0. Since A0 does not exist, the error message shows up.

You will also get this error if you are in a situation where a formula, looks like this:

= B10+C10

and you cut and paste something into B10 and/or C10. Copying and pasting will not cause a #REF! error, however.

6.10.5 The ISERROR Function for Trapping Errors

Errors in a spreadsheet are generally easy to find and correct. Understanding what the error messages mean allows us to get an idea of what kind of error to look for and make the necessary corrections.

When we build a model, however, errors can be a little more troublesome. As you will see when we start developing the formulas in the model, we will be using circular references.

A circular reference occurs when a formula refers to itself, whether directly or indirectly. For example, if you enter =SUM(A1:A10) in cell A10, you would get a circular reference because every time A10 is calculated, it must include itself in the SUM calculation, in a never-ending cycle.

When you create such a circular reference, Excel will give you a warning message (Fig. 6-20):

There are two ways of dealing with circular references and Excel's attempts to warn you about them:

1. One way is to correct the inadvertent circular references. Clicking on the OK on this message form will get Excel's circular reference toolbar to show, which will help you to start to zero in on where the troublesome reference is.
2. The second way, and this is only if you actually want to have circular references, is to set Excel's calculation to the iteration mode by the following sequence: *Tools>Options >Calculation>Iteration*. This will set Excel to allow circular references. An iteration is simply a cycle of calculation in which you can imagine a "wave" of calculation sweeping through the whole model, sheet by sheet.

FIGURE 6-20

Circular Reference Warning

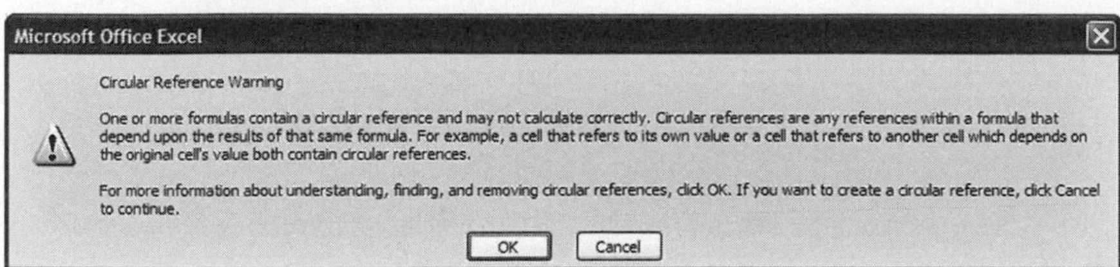

Why do we want iterative circular references? Simply put, it is a simple way to get the model to converge on its calculations of interest expense. As you will see in the next chapters, in the forecast years the model will be creating "plug" numbers to balance the balance sheet. A plug number that is assumed to be debt will create an additional interest expense, which will affect the plug number itself. The model then has to recalculate (or iterate) to adjust for this increase, which in turn will create another, but incrementally smaller, increase. The iteration will go through several more cycles before there is convergence within the limits set in the model.

So, circular references can be used to good advantage. The dangerous thing is that as there is now a calculation loop in the model, if there is an error that gets inadvertently introduced into the calculations, this error message will continue to cycle around in the loop. Even after the source of the error has been removed, the error message continues to be caught in the loop! In this case, there are two ways to correct the situation:

1. Manually change one of the formulas in order to "break" the calculation loop. Make sure that the source of the original error is corrected, and recalculate the model again to clear out the error message. Once this is done, restore the formula again.
2. A more elegant way is to use the ISERROR function to trap the error. Simply put, at a location in the calculation loop, we write a formula that returns a 0 when it encounters an error condition. Let's say we put this in cell C51:

```
=IF(ISERROR(C50),0,C50)
```

Cell C50 is a cell that is part of the loop, as is Cell C51. If there is an error in the loop, this formula in Cell C51 will revert to a 0, which is then read by the rest of the calculations. The 0 breaks the circular loop and gives the error message a chance to be cleared out, so that when C51 calculates again, it does not see the error sign and automatically reconnects to C50. The loop is restored.

6.11 OTHER FUNCTIONS TO KNOW

6.11.1 ROUND, MROUND, INT, and MOD

Working with parts of numbers:

- ROUND(number, number of digits) rounds the number to the specified number of digits. =ROUND(1.564,1) will return 1.6, for example. Likewise, =ROUND(1.564,0) will return 2.
  Neat trick 1: You can put a negative number for the number of digits: –1 will round the number to the nearest ten, –2 to the nearest hundred, –3 to the nearest thousand, etc. Thus, =ROUND(1,234.2, –2) will return 1,200.
- MROUND(number, multi-le) rounds to the nearest multiple. To round to the nearest 5 cents in a price, =MROUND($1.96,0.05) returns $1.95. MROUND is a function that is part of the Analysis ToolPak. You can check whether it is enabled or not by the sequence *Tools>Add-Ins* in Excel 2003. In Excel 2007, it's *Office Button>Excel Options>Add-Ins,* and then click on the Go button at the bottom of that form.
- INT(number) will get you the integer part of the number, the part to the left of the decimal point.
- MOD(number, divisor) will return the remainder of the number after it has been divided by the divisor. To get to the part of a number to the right of the decimal point you must use 1 as the divisor; thus, =MOD(1.564,1) will return 0.564. You can use other divisors for other results. For example, =MOD(1.564,0.5) returns 0.064. The divisor can be any number except 0.

6.11.2 ABS, CEILING, FLOOR, ROUNDUP, ROUNDDOWN

Working with numbers in a direction:

We can imagine that numbers lie on a line, with the 0 point separating the negative and the positive numbers. The following functions work in identifying or shifting numbers on the numbers line.

- ABS(number) returns the value of a number without the sign. Thus =ABS(–5) and ABS(5) will both yield 5, or the measure of the distance of 5 from the 0 point on the numbers line.
- CEILING(number, significance) returns the number rounded away from zero. For a positive number, this means it is rounded up. =CEILING(2.01,1) returns 3. For a negative number, it is rounded down, so it becomes more negative. CEILING(–2.01,–1) returns –3. Both the number and significance must have the same sign. If they do not, a #NUM! error results.
- FLOOR(number, significance) is similar to CEILING, but rounds the number toward zero. FLOOR(1.99,1) returns 1. FLOOR(–1.99,–1) returns –1. Similar to CEILING, both the number and significance must have the same sign. If they do not, a #NUM! error results.
- ROUNDUP(number, number of digits) behaves like ROUND, but rounds a number away from zero (in this sense it also works like CEILING). The number of digits can be a positive or negative number, and works exactly the same way as in ROUND.
- ROUNDDOWN(number, number of digits) is similar to ROUNDUP, but rounds the number toward zero.

6.11.3 ISNUMBER, ISTEXT, ISBLANK

These functions are useful for determining the kind of information with which you are dealing.

- ISNUMBER(Value) will return a TRUE if value is a number and a FALSE if it is a text or is blank. One example where this is useful is when you are writing an IF statement where you want the formula to read the entry in a cell, even if it is a zero. (The usual IF statement testing for the value "if it is not a 0" will return a FALSE when it encounters the number 0.)
- ISTEXT(Value) will return a TRUE if the value is a text string.

- ISBLANK(Value) will return a TRUE if the value refers to an empty cell.

6.11.4 LEFT, RIGHT, MID, LEN, LOWER, UPPER, PROPER, TEXT, VALUE

Working with Text:

These functions are useful when you work with text strings. In these functions, the space between words counts as one character.

- LEFT(Text, number of characters) returns the leftmost portion of the text consisting of the number of characters defined. =LEFT("Good Morning",7) returns "Good Mo".
- RIGHT(Text, number of characters) returns the rightmost portion of the text, consisting of the number of characters. =RIGHT("Good Morning",7) returns "Morning".
- MID(text, start number, number of characters) returns a portion of the text from the letter of the start number. The portion will have the length of the number of characters. =MID("Good Morning",2,5) returns "ood M".
- LEN(text) returns the number of characters in the text. LEN is short for "length." =LEN("Good Morning") returns 12.
- LOWER(text) returns the text all in lowercase. =LOWER("Good Morning") returns "good morning".
- UPPER(text) returns everything in uppercase. =UPPER("Good Morning") will result in "GOOD MORNING".
- PROPER(text) returns text with the first letter of each word in uppercase and the remaining letters in lowercase. =PROPER("goOd moRNing") returns "Good Morning".
- TRIM(text) removes leading and trailing spaces, and reduces multiple spaces between words to one space. =TRIM("Good morning") returns "Good Morning".

- TEXT(value, format) is a useful function for creating dynamic labels that include values. Excel is able to handle text strings and values together, but if you want the values to carry a particular format when you want to show the two together, you must use TEXT and define the format of how that value will appear.
- =TEXT(1.386, "$0.00") returns "$1.39." Note that the conversion also includes a rounding effect. The "$1.39" is now a text string, so that you can link it to other text strings by using the ampersand (&) symbol. Amazingly, you can still apply an operation to this text string so that it still performs as a value, but the format does not work on the result. TEXT(1.386, "$0.00") * 2 returns "2.78," not "$2.78." The rounding effect in TEXT also causes 1.386 to become 1.39.
- VALUE(text) converts the text of a number into the value of that number. However, you do not really need this function as Excel can convert text to values as necessary.

6.12 FINANCIAL FUNCTIONS: NPV, XNPV, IRR, XIRR

NPV (net present value) and IRR (internal rate of return) are the necessary functions to know when you start working with cash flows and estimating the returns of various projects. Both these functions deal with the time value of money. Time value of money is a way of saying that a dollar today is not worth the same value as a dollar will be in the future, or as it was in the past. No, we are not talking about inflation here. We are talking about the fact that money can earn interest.

Let's take a brief detour: Let's say that we can earn 5% interest every year on our dollar. Thus, our $1.00 today will be worth $1.05 next year (the arithmetic is simple: $1 ×1.05 = $1.05), and $1.1025 ($1 × 1.05 × 1.05) a year after that. By the same token, to have our $1.00 today, we actually needed to have only $0.9524 last year ($1.00 divided by 1.05. The proof that we have the right answer is $0.9524 × 1.05 =$1.00) and $0.9070 two years ago.

The important point to remember is that the values seen in Table 6-1 represent the same time value of $1.00 at a 5% rate. This rate is called the discount rate. So to rephrase what we said in the previous paragraph, a dollar today is the same as something more than a dollar in the future, and something less than a dollar in the past. The term for adjusting the $1.00 across time to become a higher future number is called future valuing; reducing it by going backward in time is present valuing. Present valuing is also called discounting, although you can use it to describe future valuing by saying "discounting forward."

Back to our functions. You should keep in mind the following points. If you are dealing with annual periods, the NPV and IRR functions will work perfectly for your calculations. These functions use the spacing of the columns, with data in each column regarded as 1 year's data, as the annual timing for the calculations. If you have a year in which there are no flows and you want these functions to include that year, you must have a 0 there. The NPV and IRR functions disregard blanks. However, if you are dealing with uneven flows—they do not happen every year, or they happen at irregular intervals across the years, or both—then you should use the XNPV and XIRR functions. These more powerful functions look not just to the flows in each column, but also to the date labels in each column, and calculate the results based on the time intervals.

NPV and IRR are in the standard set of functions in Excel. However, XNPV and XIRR are part of the extended set of functions that are available only when the Analysis ToolPak Add-In is enabled. You can check whether it is enabled or not by the sequence *Tools>Add-Ins* in Excel 2003. In Excel 2007, it's *Office*

TABLE 6-1

Time Value of Money

2 Years Ago	1 Year Ago	Now	Next Year	2 Years Later
$90.70	$95.24	$100.00	$105.00	$110.25

Button>Excel Options>Add-Ins, and then click on the Go button at the bottom of that form.

6.12.1 NPV

NPV(rate, value1,value2, . . .) returns the net present value of the annual flows represented by the values. These values can be positive or negative numbers, representing, by the usual convention, inflows and outflows of cash, respectively. Instead of individual values, you can use a range of values. Rate is the annual discount rate.

Be very clear about the timing of the discounting when you use the NPV function, because the values are assumed to occur at the end of each year. So you have to be careful about whether you want to discount the first value in the function. In the following illustration (Fig. 6-21), Cell C7's NPV of 151.34 shows the result of the first value of (100)—representing an investment outflow of 100 at the end of 2009—being part of the NPV function. This means that it is also being discounted at 10.0% (entered in Cell B1). Thus, this shows the NPV as of the beginning of 2009 for the cash flows that occur at the end of the year for the period 2009–2013.

FIGURE 6-21

NPV at the Beginning, Ending, and Midpoint of the Investment Year

	A	B	C	D	E	F
1	Discount rate	10.0%				
2						
3		Dec-31-09	Dec-31-10	Dec-31-11	Dec-31-12	Dec-31-13
4	Cash flows	(100)	50	60	110	130
5		All flows at the end of the year				
6						
7	NPV at beginning of 2009		151.34	=NPV(B1,B4:F4)		
8						
9	NPV at the end of 2009		166.48	=B4+NPV(B1,C4:F4)		
10	NPV at the end of 2009		166.48	=C7*(1+B1)		
11						
12	NPV at the midpoint of 2009		158.73	=C7*(1+B1)^0.5		
13	NPV at the midpoint of 2009		158.73	=C9/(1+B1)^0.5		
14						

In contrast, the formula for Cell C10 shows that the first value in cell B4 is simply added to the columns C to F that is part of the NPV function. Thus, the (100) is not being discounted at all, and Cell B10's value of 166.48 represents the NPV of the flows at the end of 2009, at the time the investment is being made.

6.12.1.1 NPV at mid-year

The NPV function assumes that the cash flows occur at the end of the year. However, a business or project produces flows throughout the year, so it would not be correct to say that the flow suddenly appears at the end of the year. A more accurate conceptual representation would be to recognize them at the middle of the year. This midpoint is the average of the timings of the flows throughout the year.

In Figure 6-21, Rows 12 and 13 show the NPV values if we recognized the flows at the midpoint of each year. We can get to the NPV by either future valuing (increasing) the NPV at the beginning of the year by half a year's discounting factor (see Cell C12), or present valuing (decreasing) the NPV at the end of the year by the same factor. Either way, we get to the same result.

6.12.2 XNPV

XNPV(rate,values,dates) returns the net present value occurring at the dates specified.

The illustration (Fig. 6-22) shows how the XNPV can work with different discounting approaches by changing the data timelines.

In the first example, the XNPV is set to discount the flows to the beginning of 2009 (as shown by the date January 1, 2009 in Cell B3). The result of 151.34 is identical to the one seen in the NPV illustration (Fig. 6-21).

In the second example, the XNPV is set to discount the flows to the end of 2009. We change the date in Cell B3 to be December 31, 2009. Even though this is a duplicate of the next column, XNPV continued to work and returns the value 166.43. This is slightly different from the result in the NPV calculation

FIGURE 6–22

XNPV

	A	B	C	D	E	F	G	H
1	Discount rate	10.0%						
2								
3		**Jan-1-09**	**Dec-31-09**	**Dec-31-10**	**Dec-31-11**	**Dec-31-12**	**Dec-31-13**	
4		0	(100)	50	60	110	130	
5	XNPV	151.34	=XNPV(B1,B4:G4,B3:G3)					
6								
7		**Dec-31-09**	**Dec-31-09**	**Dec-31-10**	**Dec-31-11**	**Dec-31-12**	**Dec-31-13**	
8		0	(100)	50	60	110	130	
9	XNPV	166.43	=XNPV(B1,B8:G8,B7:G7)					
10								
11		**Jan-1-09**	**Jun-30-09**	**Jun-30-10**	**Jun-30-11**	**Jun-30-12**	**Jun-30-13**	
12		0	(100)	50	60	110	130	
13	XNPV	158.79	=XNPV(B1,B12:G12,B11:G11)					
14								

of 166.48, and is due to the days actually being calculated in the XNPV function.

In the third example, we are discounting the flows to January 1, 2009, but are recognizing the flows at the midpoint of the year. We change the date timelines to follow accordingly. The result is 158.79, again slightly different from the NPV calculation of 158.73 due to the calculation using the actual number of days.

The dates in XNPV can have irregular intervals of months or years.

6.12.3 IRR

IRR(values,guess) returns the internal rate of return on the range of values. An IRR is the rate that would bring the NPV on a set if it flows to 0. The values must contain at least one number that is positive and one that is negative. The guess rate is a rate you can enter, such as 0.10 (10%), to help the function to begin its calculations correctly. You can omit this guess, in which case Excel will begin its calculations with the guess rate of 10%.

In Figure 6-23, the flows represent an investment (say, a loan) of \$100 at December 31, 2009. Each year, the loan has \$8

FIGURE 6–23

IRR

	A	B	C	D	E	F	G
1							
2		Dec-31-09	Dec-31-10	Dec-31-11	Dec-31-12	Dec-31-13	Dec-31-14
3		(100)	8	8	8	8	108
4	IRR	8.0%	=IRR(B3:G3,10%)				
5							

in interest. At the end of the fifth year, the principal amount is repaid, along with the interest for that year. Not surprisingly, the IRR calculates a yield of 8.0%.

Each column in the IRR range is assumed to be one year. A blank column will not be counted as a year. If you want that column to be counted, then it must have 0 in it. The same is true for rows if you set the flows in a vertical fashion in a column.

6.12.4 XIRR

XIRR(values,dates,guess) returns the IRR on a range of values associated with the dates. These two ranges must span the same columns so that Excel will know which period's data are associated with which period. The dates in XIRR can have irregular intervals of months or years.

In Figure 6-24, four examples show how XIRR is versatile in its calculations in timelines. The first example is similar to the IRR example seen earlier.

In the second, it is possible to have two columns with the same date: in this case, it means that there was a net investment of only (92) on Dec 31, 2009. Therefore, the IRR is higher than 8.0%.

In the third, this is the IRR if the investment was made at the beginning of the year, and the returns are recognized at the middle of the year. The IRR is higher than 8% because the cash flows are being returned 6 months earlier than in the first example.

In the fourth example, we see that XIRR can be used to calculate returns even when the timing of the flows is highly uneven.

FIGURE 6–24

Irregular Periods Are Possible with XIRR

	A	B	C	D	E	F	G
1							
2		**Jan-1-09**	**Dec-31-09**	**Dec-31-10**	**Dec-31-11**	**Dec-31-12**	**Dec-31-13**
3		(100)	8	8	8	8	108
4	XIRR	8.0%	=XIRR(B3:G3,B2:G2)				
5							
6		**Dec-31-09**	**Dec-31-09**	**Dec-31-10**	**Dec-31-11**	**Dec-31-12**	**Dec-31-13**
7		(100)	8	8	8	8	108
8	XNPV	10.5%	=XIRR(B7:G7,B6:G6)				
9							
10		**Jan-1-09**	**Jun-30-09**	**Jun-30-10**	**Jun-30-11**	**Jun-30-12**	**Jun-30-13**
11		(100)	8	8	8	8	108
12	XNPV	9.1%	=XIRR(B11:G11,B10:G10)				
13							
14		**Jun-30-09**	**Mar-15-09**	**Jul-3-09**	**Nov-17-11**	**Aug-17-12**	**Dec-31-15**
15		(100)	8	8	8	8	108
16	XNPV	6.8%	=XIRR(B15:G15,B14:G14)				
17							

CHAPTER 7

Building a Pilot Model

As a first step to building a full integrated finance model, let's start by building a small pilot model to explore the various connections between the income statement, balance sheet and the cash flow statement.

We will build the pilot model in two versions for balancing the balance sheet:

- The balancing uses only the balance sheet and the income statement,
- The balancing uses the balance sheet, the income statement, and the cash flow statement

7.1 HOW TO READ THE ILLUSTRATIONS

The screen shots in this book are from Excel 2007. Except for the cosmetic look, the views they show are identical to Excel 2003 and earlier versions.

To the right of the last column in the illustration (Fig. 7-1) is text that describes the formula being used in the same row of the last column.

Cells that have hard-coded inputs are shaded, and the row also carries the label "Input" (e.g., see Cells E3–E5). When you

FIGURE 7-1

Historical Year. Cells in Gray Contain Hard-Coded Input Numbers and Do Not Have Formulas

	A	B	C	D	E	F
1				Hist		
2		INCOME STATEMENT		Year 1	Formulas in column E	
3		Revenue		160.0	Input	
4		COGS		80.0	Input	
5		SGA		29.0	Input	
6		EBIT		51.0	=D3-SUM(D4:D5)	
7						
8		Interest: Excess cash	3.0%	0.0	Input	
9		Interest: Revolver	6.0%	0.0	Input	
10		Interest: Debt	6.0%	19.2	Input	
11		EBT		31.8	=D6+D8-D9-D10	
12						
13		Tax	40.0%	12.7	Input	
14		Net income		19.1	=D11-D13	
15						

FIGURE 7-2

Historical Year (Year 1) and the First Projected Year (Year 2)

	A	B	C	D	E	F	G	H
1				Hist	Proj			
2		INCOME STATEMENT		Year 1	Year 2	Formulas in column E		
3		Revenue		160.0	200.0	Input		
4		COGS		80.0	90.0	Input		
5		SGA		29.0	45.0	Input		
6		EBIT		51.0	65.0	=E3-SUM(E4:E5)		
7								
8		Interest: Excess cash	3.0%	0.0	0.0	=$C$8*D18		
9		Interest: Revolver	6.0%	0.0	0.0	=$C$9*D23		
10		Interest: Debt	6.0%	19.2	20.1	=$C$10*AVERAGE(D24:E24)		
11		EBT		31.8	44.9	=E6+E8-E9-E10		
12								
13		Tax	40.0%	12.7	18.0	=$C$13*E11		
14		Net income		19.1	26.9	=E11-E13		
15								

are building your own model, you may want to use a light background color such as light yellow to highlight the input cells as shown. The color makes it easy later on to locate the input areas, especially if no data have been entered and they remain blank.

Cell E6 shows the formula that is contained in D6. Likewise in Figure 7-2, which shows the model with the first projected year now occupying column E, there are formulas in Rows 8 to 10 and on Row 13 where there were only inputs in the historical year.

7.2 TO START, ADD A NEW BLANK WORKBOOK IN EXCEL

Open Excel. A new workbook is ready for you.

7.2.1 Set the Normal Style

Set the Normal style to have the following format:

- One decimal place
- Use thousand separators
- Black parentheses for negative numbers

7.2.2 Gridlines

Select whether or not you want to see gridlines in the workbook. In the illustrations, the gridlines are turned off.

7.3 PILOT MODEL NO. 1

In this example, we will build a model whose balance sheet balances without the use of a cash flow statement. Lay out the following lines in your new workbook (Fig. 7-3):

- Column A has a width of 1.5.
- Column B has a width of 26.
- Column C has a width of 5.
- Columns D and onward have a width of 10.

FIGURE 7-3

The Historical Year Column

	A	B	C	D	E	F
1				Hist		
2		INCOME STATEMENT		Year 1	Formulas in column D	
3		Revenue		160.0	Input	
4		COGS		80.0	Input	
5		SGA		29.0	Input	
6		EBIT		51.0	=D3-SUM(D4:D5)	
7						
8		Interest: Excess cash	3.0%	0.0	Input	
9		Interest: Revolver	6.0%	0.0	Input	
10		Interest: Debt	6.0%	19.2	Input	
11		EBT		31.8	=D6+D8-D9-D10	
12						
13		Tax	40.0%	12.7	Input	
14		Net income		19.1	=D11-D13	
15						
16				Hist		
17		BALANCE SHEET		Year 1		
18		Excess cash		0.0	Input	
19		Current assets		200.0	Input	
20		Long-term assets		350.0	Input	
21		Total assets		550.0	=SUM(D18:D20)	
22						
23		Revolver		0.0	Input	
24		Debt		320.0	Input	
25		Common stock		50.0	Input	
26		Retained earnings		180.0	Input	
27		Total liabs and equity		550.0	=SUM(D23:D26)	
28						
29		Balance sheet check		0.0	=D27-D21	
30						
31		Assets without excess cash				
32		Liabs, equity without revolver				
33		Excess cash (revolver) as calculated				
34						

These widths are not critical; you can vary them. However, to match the column lettering in the illustration, please have the same columnar layout in your workbook as in the illustrations.

Use the same numbers for the moment. Later on, when the model is working, you can test it by entering your own set of numbers. The historical year's balance sheet should be balanced, as indicated by the balance sheet check on Row 29. The model does not do anything to balance any discrepancies. In fact, the model should not do this for the historical years since you would want such discrepancies to be apparent, and corrected.

The interest expense for excess cash and revolver are hard-coded 0 inputs for this column, since there should not be any balancing plugs to produce the interest.

Now let's add another column. The easiest would be to copy column D to the right to column E, and make the appropriate changes as shown in the boxed rows (Fig. 7-4):

Now we begin the magic of balancing.

The marked areas show how the balancing mechanism works. We start from the bottom, Rows 31 and 32:

1. We first calculate what the excess cash/revolver plug number should be in order to balance the balance sheet. The labels indicate the rows are assets *without* the excess cash and liabilities + equity *without* the revolver. We then write the latter minus the former to get a value that is the excess cash if it is positive, or a revolver if it is negative (Row 33). It is important to exclude the plug values in order to arrive at the excess cash/revolver number, in order to avoid a circular reference. See Chapter 8 for a fuller description of circular references. As a side note, rather than [liabilities + equity] – assets, we could have done the reverse: asset – [liabilities + equity]. The resulting value would then be excess cash if negative, and revolver if positive. The signs for the plugs in this case would be slightly counterintuitive, hence the approach described in the screen shot.
2. The excess cash/revolver result in Row 33 ("Excess cash (revolver) as calculated") is then referenced back to the balance sheet. We see in Row 18 ("Excess cash") the formula:

```
= MAX(E33,0)
```

FIGURE 7-4

The Second Column: The First Projected Year

	A	B	C	D	E	F	G	H
1				Hist	Proj			
2		INCOME STATEMENT		Year 1	Year 2	Formulas in column E		
3		Revenue		160.0	200.0	Input		
4		COGS		80.0	90.0	Input		
5		SGA		29.0	45.0	Input		
6		EBIT		51.0	65.0	=E3-SUM(E4:E5)		
7								
8		Interest: Excess cash	3.0%	0.0	0.0	=$C$8*D18		
9		Interest: Revolver	6.0%	0.0	0.0	=$C$9*D23		
10		Interest: Debt	6.0%	19.2	20.1	=$C$10*AVERAGE(D24:E24)		
11		EBT		31.8	44.9	=E6+E8-E9-E10		
12								
13		Tax	40.0%	12.7	18.0	=$C$13*E11		
14		Net income		19.1	26.9	=E11-E13		
15								
16				Hist	Proj			
17		BALANCE SHEET		Year 1	Year 2			
18		Excess cash		0.0	31.9	=MAX(E33,0)		
19		Current assets		200.0	250.0	Input		
20		Long-term assets		350.0	375.0	Input		
21		Total assets		550.0	656.9	=SUM(E18:E20)		
22								
23		Revolver		0.0	0.0	=-MIN(E33,0)		
24		Debt		320.0	350.0	Input		
25		Common stock		50.0	100.0	Input		
26		Retained earnings		180.0	206.9	=D26+E14		
27		Total liabs and equity		550.0	656.9	=SUM(E23:E26)		
28								
29		Balance sheet check		0.0	0.0	=E27-E21		
30								
31		Assets without excess cash			625.0	=SUM(E19:E20)		
32		Liabs, equity without revolver			656.9	=SUM(E24:E26)		
33		Excess cash (revolver) as calculated			31.9	=E32-E31		
34								
35								

This brings Row 33 into Row 18 only if it is positive. The MAX function simply returns the greater (the maximum) of the value in E33 or 0. If E33 is negative, then it returns a 0.

3. Likewise in Row 23 ("Revolver"), we see the formula:

   = –MIN(E33,0)

   This brings Row 33 into Row 23 only if it is negative, but the minus sign in front of the MIN means that this negative number as calculated in Row 33 appears in Row 23 as a positive.

4. Now we have to connect the interest income and interest expense from the excess cash and the revolver. This is done in Row 8 ("Interest: Excess cash") and Row 9 ("Interest: Revolver"). The interest at this point looks to the *prior* period, not the current period, in order to avoid circular references. We discuss this a little more in Chapter 8.
   The interest for debt is set as an average of the outstanding in the first projected year and the prior (historical) year. In the absence of any other information, it is assumed that the debt outstanding amount changed at the mid-point of the year, and this is captured by the average function for the interest expense calculation.

5. One last point: Make sure you connect the income statement to the balance sheet by adding the net income line (Row 14) to the retained earnings line (Row 26) for the formula for the projected year. The formula in Row 26 takes the prior year's retained earnings and adds that to the current year's net income number.

At this point, the balancing mechanism is complete. Copy the column to the right, and enter the test numbers as shown as a check. Once you are satisfied that this pilot is working, input other assumptions into the model and the balance sheet will always dynamically balance itself (Fig. 7-5).

7.4 PILOT MODEL NO. 2

Let's move on and build the model that balances the balance sheet through the cash flow statement.

FIGURE 7–5

The Complete Pilot Model No. 1

	A	B	C	D	E	F	G	H	I
1				Hist	Proj	Proj			
2		INCOME STATEMENT		Year 1	Year 2	Year 3	Formulas in column F		
3		Revenue		160.0	200.0	390.0	Input		
4		COGS		80.0	90.0	190.0	Input		
5		SGA		29.0	45.0	80.0	Input		
6		EBIT		51.0	65.0	120.0	=F3-SUM(F4:F5)		
7									
8		Interest: Excess cash	3.0%	0.0	0.0	1.0	=$C$8*E18		
9		Interest: Revolver	6.0%	0.0	0.0	0.0	=$C$9*E23		
10		Interest: Debt	6.0%	19.2	20.1	20.7	=$C$10*AVERAGE(E24:F24)		
11		EBT		31.8	44.9	100.3	=F6+F8-F9-F10		
12									
13		Tax	40.0%	12.7	18.0	40.1	=$C$13*F11		
14		Net income		19.1	26.9	60.2	=F11-F13		
15									
16				Hist	Proj	Proj			
17		BALANCE SHEET		Year 1	Year 2	Year 3			
18		Excess cash		0.0	31.9	0.0	=MAX(F33,0)		
19		Current assets		200.0	250.0	350.0	Input		
20		Long-term assets		350.0	375.0	400.0	Input		
21		Total assets		550.0	656.9	750.0	=SUM(F18:F20)		
22									
23		Revolver		0.0	0.0	42.9	=-MIN(F33,0)		
24		Debt		320.0	350.0	340.0	Input		
25		Common stock		50.0	100.0	100.0	Input		
26		Retained earnings		180.0	206.9	267.1	=E26+F14		
27		Total liabs and equity		550.0	656.9	750.0	=SUM(F23:F26)		
28									
29		Balance sheet check		0.0	0.0	0.0	=F27-F21		
30									
31		Assets without excess cash			625.0	750.0	=SUM(F19:F20)		
32		Liabs, equity without revolver			656.9	707.1	=SUM(F24:F26)		
33		Excess cash (revolver) as calculated			31.9	(42.9)	=F32-F31		
34									

The easiest thing to do, rather than replicate setting up a new model, is to copy Model No. 1 onto another sheet in your workbook. We will be changing the bottom part of the model to convert it to pilot Model No 2.

1. Delete the rows used for the balancing in Model No. 1 (Rows 31-33). Keep the balance sheet check row, though.
2. Write in the cash flow rows as shown (Fig. 7-6). Leave the first column blank, because the cash flow statement looks

FIGURE 7-6

Modifications for Pilot Model No. 2

	B	C	D	E	F	G	H
1			Hist	Proj			
2	INCOME STATEMENT		Year 1	Year 2	Formulas in column F		
3	Revenue		160.0	200.0	Input		
4	COGS		80.0	90.0	Input		
5	SGA		29.0	45.0	Input		
6	EBIT		51.0	65.0	=E3-SUM(E4:E5)		
7							
8	Interest: Excess cash	3.0%	0.0	0.0	=$C$8*D18		
9	Interest: Revolver	6.0%	0.0	0.0	=$C$9*D23		
10	Interest: Debt	6.0%	19.2	20.1	=$C$10*AVERAGE(D24:E24)		
11	EBT		31.8	44.9	=E6+E8-E9-E10		
12							
13	Tax	40.0%	12.7	18.0	=$C$13*E11		
14	Net income		19.1	26.9	=E11-E13		
15							
16			Hist	Proj			
17	BALANCE SHEET		Year 1	Year 2			
18	Excess cash		0.0	31.9	=MAX(E44,0)		
19	Current assets		200.0	250.0	Input		
20	Long-term assets		350.0	375.0	Input		
21	Total assets		550.0	656.9	=SUM(E18:E20)		
22							
23	Revolver		0.0	0.0	=-MIN(E44,0)		
24	Debt		320.0	350.0	Input		
25	Common stock		50.0	100.0	Input		
26	Retained earnings		180.0	206.9	=D26+E14		
27	Total liabs and equity		550.0	656.9	=SUM(E23:E26)		
28							
29	Balance sheet check		0.0	0.0	=E27-E21		
30							
31			Hist	Proj			
32	CASH FLOW		Year 1	Year 2			
33	Net income			26.9	=E14		
34							
35	(Increase) decrease in current assets			(50.0)	=D19-E19		
36	(Increase) decrease in long-term assets			(25.0)	=D20-E20		
37							
38	Increase (decrease) in debt			30.0	=E24-D24		
39	Increase (decrease) in common stock			50.0	=E25-D25		
40							
41	Total change in cash			31.9	=E33+SUM(E35:E36,E38:E39)		
42							
43	Beginning cash (revolver)			0.0	=D18-D23		
44	Ending cash (revolver)			31.9	=E41+E43		
45							

FIGURE 7–7

The Completed Pilot Model No. 2

	A	B	C	D	E	F	G	H	I
1				Hist	Proj	Proj			
2		INCOME STATEMENT		Year 1	Year 2	Year 3	Formulas in column F		
3		Revenue		160.0	200.0	390.0	Input		
4		COGS		80.0	90.0	190.0	Input		
5		SGA		29.0	45.0	80.0	Input		
6		EBIT		51.0	65.0	120.0	=F3-SUM(F4:F5)		
7									
8		Interest: Excess cash	3.0%	0.0	0.0	1.0	=$C$8*E18		
9		Interest: Revolver	6.0%	0.0	0.0	0.0	=$C$9*E23		
10		Interest: Debt	6.0%	19.2	20.1	20.7	=$C$10*AVERAGE(E24:F24)		
11		EBT		31.8	44.9	100.3	=F6+F8-F9-F10		
12									
13		Tax	40.0%	12.7	18.0	40.1	=$C$13*F11		
14		Net income		19.1	26.9	60.2	=F11-F13		
15									
16				Hist	Proj	Proj			
17		BALANCE SHEET		Year 1	Year 2	Year 3			
18		Excess cash		0.0	31.9	0.0	=MAX(F44,0)		
19		Current assets		200.0	250.0	350.0	Input		
20		Long-term assets		350.0	375.0	400.0	Input		
21		Total assets		550.0	656.9	750.0	=SUM(F18:F20)		
22									
23		Revolver		0.0	0.0	42.9	=-MIN(F44,0)		
24		Debt		320.0	350.0	340.0	Input		
25		Common stock		50.0	100.0	100.0	Input		
26		Retained earnings		180.0	206.9	267.1	=E26+F14		
27		Total liabs and equity		550.0	656.9	750.0	=SUM(F23:F26)		
28									
29		Balance sheet check		0.0	0.0	0.0	=F27-F21		
30									
31				Hist	Proj	Proj			
32		CASH FLOW		Year 1	Year 2	Year 3			
33		Net income			26.9	60.2	=F14		
34									
35		(Increase) decrease in current assets			(50.0)	(100.0)	=E19-F19		
36		(Increase) decrease in long-term assets			(25.0)	(25.0)	=E20-F20		
37									
38		Increase (decrease) in debt			30.0	(10.0)	=F24-E24		
39		Increase (decrease) in common stock			50.0	-	=F25-E25		
40									
41		Total change in cash			31.9	(74.8)	=F33+SUM(F35:F36,F38:F39)		
42									
43		Beginning cash (revolver)			0.0	31.9	=E18-E23		
44		Ending cash (revolver)			31.9	(42.9)	=F41+F43		
45									
46									

at the variance between the current and the prior balance sheet years. For the first year of the balance sheet, there is no "prior" year.

The "Beginning cash (revolver)" line (row 43) bears some explanation. Note the formula:

= D18–D23

Row 43 ("Beginning cash (revolver)") shows the beginning values—this is same as the prior year's ending values—for excess cash (Cell D18) and revolver (Cell D23). It is the catch-all for both excess cash and revolver, and where a revolver is represented by a negative number. However, the prior year's revolver in the balance sheet is shown as a positive. To have it represented in Row 43, we have to put a negative sign on Cell D23. Hence the final formula =D18 – D23.

3. Connect the balance sheet excess cash (Row 18) and revolver (Row 23) to the ending cash (revolver) line in the cash flow statement (Row 44) with the formulas shown.
4. Add another year for all three statements by copying the whole column E to column F to finish the pilot model (Fig. 7-7).

7.5 TESTING THE MODELS WITH YOUR OWN NUMBERS

Now that you have completed the models, feel free to test them by varying the inputs. The balancing mechanism should work when you vary your inputs.

You can also begin to see that outside of the balancing formulas, you can now expand these models. For example, in the balance sheet, instead of one line for current assets, you can now break it into receivables, inventory, and other current assets. You can apply the same type of changes for the income statement. When you expand the model in this way, make sure the new lines are included in the SUM formulas for the various sections, and that the cash flow statement also takes them into account.

7.6 SOME NOTES ON THE PILOT MODELS

- These are simplified models, but they serve well enough to illustrate how to build an integrated model. Despite the fact that they use different balancing approaches, they arrive at the same final answer. Chapter 4, Section 4.10 gives the background for this.
- The interest calculation for the excess cash and revolver is basic and does not look at the interest produced by the plugs in each current year. Doing so will produce a circular reference. This is a perennial problem in modeling. There are ways to avoid using circular references, but there is none that avoids circular references completely and at the same time is simple and returns a "correct" calculation (that is, it calculates the ongoing interest from the plug, which necessarily is a circular calculation). See Chapter 8 for a fuller discussion, and also a variation of pilot Model No. 1 (Section 8.8.1) that not only uses but *requires* circular references for its balancing.
- The balance sheet and cash flow statement accounts are simplified. In real life, they carry more detail. The real-life cash flow statement in particular has its own organization, showing the sources and uses of cash by categories of operations, investment, and financing. This is described more fully in Chapter 12. Nevertheless, this simplified cash flow does use the convention of a positive number to show a source of cash, and a negative number to show a use of cash. More importantly, the pilot models capture the essential links among the three financial statements, and the proof that they have been captured correctly is that in either case the balance sheet is balanced.

CHAPTER 8

Circular References and Iterative Calculations

At its simplest, a circular reference is a formula that references itself. The reference is circular because the cell's output is its input, which is used to produce its output, which is used as its input, and so on. In modeling, a circular reference could be a cell that references itself, or a starting cell that references a string of other formulas, the last one of which references the starting cell. The circularity is referred to as the formula loop.

8.1 TO USE OR NOT USE

The starting point in modeling is: don't use it. Circular references are to be avoided.

That said, the one generally accepted use of circular references is in the calculation of average interest for the excess cash or revolver plugs for balancing a balance sheet. We will cover this a little later in this chapter.

8.1.1 Don't

The main arguments against using circular references are:

- If Excel is not set to use iterations and the model has iterations, Excel will hang (it appears stuck on the screen).

- If there is an error, such as #DIV/0! Or #REF!, it spreads uncontrollably throughout the model. Even if the source of the error is corrected, the error message is forever caught in the loop and the model remains inoperable. Getting this message out requires a cumbersome manual process of deleting a cell in the circular reference loop and then recreating it again.
- If iteration is on for a specific and known calculation, there is no way of detecting other unintended circular references put in by mistake since the use of the iteration setting disables Excel's circular reference detection system.
- People think circular references are a sign of bad modeling.

8.1.2 Maybe

Each of the objections to circular references can be countered:

- Put a macro that launches on opening to turn on the iteration setting. A message box to inform the user that the iteration has been turned on is also helpful. A reasonably adept user of Excel can also turn this setting on manually.
- Put an ISERROR error trap in the loop. See Section 8.7.2. This stops the error message from propagating throughout the model. Correct the source of the error and the model automatically clears out the error messages.
- Put in an IF statement switch that turns off the intended loop and turns off the iteration setting. In this way, any rogue circular references will be detected. Turn the loop back on to continue working.
- If your work team is used to circular references, they will know that it is in fact a sign of advanced modeling.

Circular references, specifically to calculate the average interest on the balance sheet plugs, are often used in investment banking models, as this produces the correct results (see Section 8.4).

8.1.3 Yes

Use circular references if not using them results in material discrepancies in the results. But in this case, make sure that everyone who works this model is comfortable with its use.

8.1.4 On the Other Hand

There are some workarounds you can use that avoid circular references but produce results close to what you would get if you had used circular references. You can use a manual cut-and-paste value to get to the same result, but this is tedious. A macro solution to automate this reduces the time required for cutting and pasting, but you will need to remember to refresh the calculation every time there is a change in the numbers. See Chapter 18.

8.2 TURNING ITERATIONS ON IN EXCEL

To use iterative calculations in Excel, you have to set Excel so that it can work with circular references.

In Excel 2003: *Tools>Options, Calculations* tab, check the *Iterations* checkbox.

In Excel 2007: *Office>Excel Options>Formulas,* check *Enable iterative calculation* checkbox.

In both versions, leave the maximum iterations at 100 and the maximum change at 0.001. The maximum iterations setting is the number of repeated calculations that Excel will run before it stops, whether the answer has been reached or not. (The maximum for both Excel versions is 32,767.) For the kind of iterative calculations that we will be using, Excel should be running no more than 10 iterations or so to converge on the solution. If it needs more than that, chances are there is an error.

The maximum change is the amount of absolute change in each value in the workbook above which Excel will continue to iterate. If the change is less than this, then Excel considers the solution to have been reached (i.e., the numbers are no longer moving to any discernible degree) and it will stop calculating—even before the maximum number of iterations is reached.

8.3 WHAT HAPPENS IN ITERATIVE CALCULATIONS

With the iteration setting on, Excel is able to use the results of a prior calculation in its current calculation. A good way to visualize how it does this is to imagine that Excel calculates iterative formulas by the order of its elements. Let's step back and first see what happens when the iteration setting is *not* on.

8.3.1 In the Normal Setting (Iteration Off)

In this setting, Excel seeks to calculate all parts of the worksheets simultaneously. This works well if all formulas are working sequentially off each other, i.e., there are cells that will calculate first, the results of which are used by subsequent cells that then feed other cells that display the final result. But a circular referencing formula throws this process out of kilter. If the cell A1 contains a formula that reads itself, such as the formula = A1 + 1, this disrupts the sense of the "first" and "subsequent" order that Excel needs to do its work.

$$\text{Cell A1} = \text{Cell A1} + 1$$

Excel looks at both A1 values, but one side has a +1. This leads to an irresolvable contradiction, and Excel stops.

8.3.2 With Iteration On

In this setting, Excel looks at the formula in sequence from left to right. As it begins, Cell A1 is 0, so that is the value it uses. As it continues to the right in the formula, it encounters A1 + 1. In this case, because A1 is held in memory as 0, A1 + 1 is 1.

$$\text{Cell A1} = \text{Cell A1} + 1$$

$$0 = 0 + 1$$

Therefore, the end result is 1.

As it iterates, or begins the second sequence, Cell A1 is 1, and so A1 + 1 must be 2.

$$\text{Cell A1} = \text{Cell A1} + 1$$

$$1 = 1 + 1$$

Therefore, the end result is 2.

At the beginning of the third sequence, Cell A1 is now 2, so A1+1 must be 3. And so on. . . .

Cell A1 = Cell A1 + 1

2 = 2 + 1

Therefore, the end result is 3.

This will continue until the maximum number of iterations is reached. Note that the change after each iteration is 1, well above the 0.001 default maximum change, so Excel will keep iterating.

The idea that a cell can be adding to itself is rather odd and perhaps is the reason why there is a natural tendency to dislike this "wrong" construction. However, those who have worked with Excel's macros in VBA (Visual Basic for Applications) and have coded in other programming languages know that the statement x = x + 1 is a good programming structure that does not raise any issues of circularities.

8.4 AN EXAMPLE: AN INTEREST CALCULATION

Here's an illustration for the calculation for the interest on the revolver plug. In this example, the iteration setting is on.

With each iteration, the revolver, which represents a funding shortfall, increases as the revolver itself produces interest expense (which in turn increases the funding shortfall). In the example that follows, the change after each iteration becomes progressively smaller, until it is less than 0.001, at which time Excel stops (0.001 is the setting for maximum iterations).

The principle is the same when the plug is excess cash, which represents excess funding. In this case, the excess cash increases as it produces interest income that adds to the retained earnings, leading to more excess cash.

8.4.1 Iteration 0

Figure 8-1 shows a balance sheet with a revolver of $10 before any calculations begin. This, as you recall from Chapter 7 on building pilot models is a dynamic plug number calculated by Excel, based

FIGURE 8-1

At Iteration 0

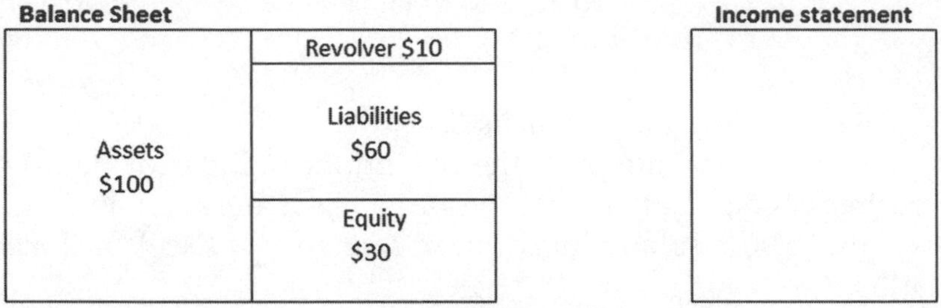

Balance Sheet	
Assets $100	Revolver $10
	Liabilities $60
	Equity $30

Income statement

on the difference between the left and right sides of the balance sheet. This is a modeling situation in which the company has more assets than its funding capacity; therefore, the model makes up for the funding shortfall by inserting the revolver number.

The revolver is debt. Let's assume the interest rate is 10%. For ease of illustration, let's also assume there are no taxes in the income statement, so any change in the interest expense is reflected in the net income by the same degree. Total assets, and also total liabilities and equity, start at $100 on the balance sheet.

8.4.2 Iteration 1

In the first iteration (the first cycle of calculation), we begin with the revolver at $10. With 10% interest, the revolver produces $1 of interest expense ($10 of beginning revolver × 10% interest). This will *reduce* the net income by $1. (We assume there are no taxes.) In turn, this *reduces* the equity by the same amount. Consequently, the revolver now has to *increase* by this additional shortfall, as shown by the ending revolver amount of $11 (Fig. 8-2). The circular loop of this iterative calculation is shown by the fact that we start and end with the revolver.

8.4.3 Iteration 2

The second iteration begins with the revolver at $11. The same calculations result in an ending revolver of $11.1 (Fig. 8-3).

FIGURE 8-2

Revolver Increases by $1 at the End of Iteration 1

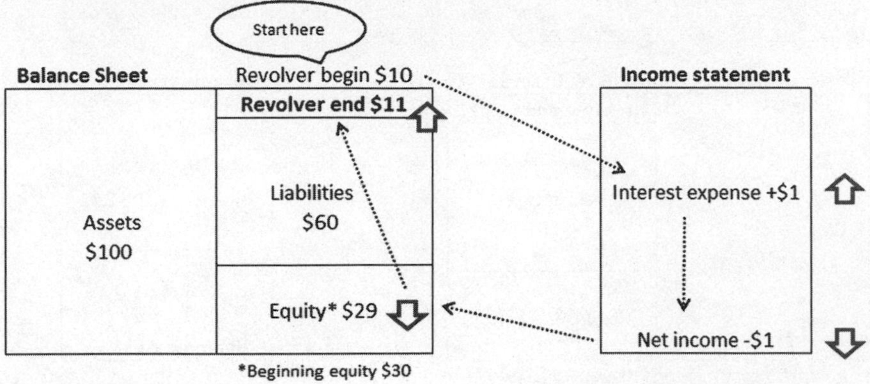

8.4.4 Iteration 3

The third iteration begins with the revolver at $11.1. The same calculations result in an ending revolver of $11.11 (Fig. 8-4).

8.4.5 And So On. . . .

At the end of Iteration 4, the revolver will be $11.111; at the end of Iteration 5, $11.1111, etc.

FIGURE 8-3

At the Completion of Iteration 2

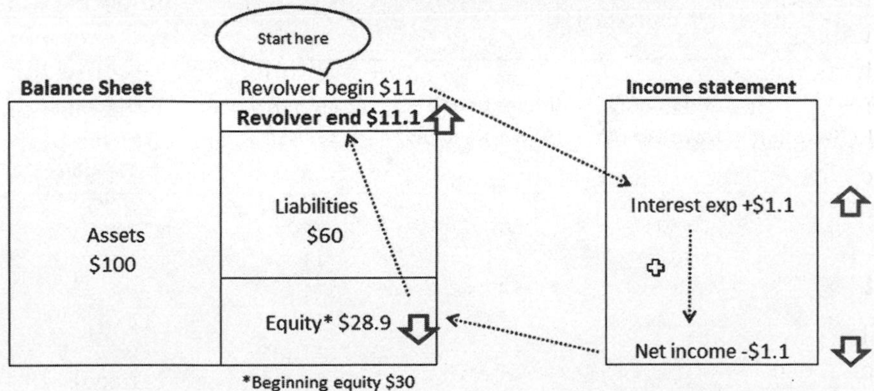

FIGURE 8-4

At the Completion of Iteration 3

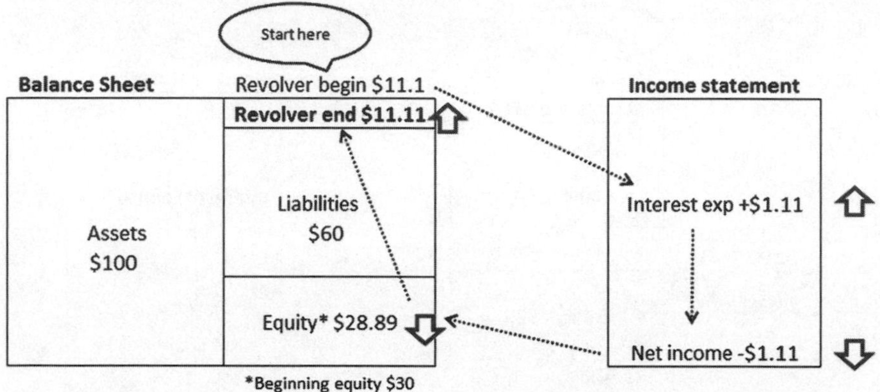

You can see that with each go-round (Table 8-1), the revolver increases by the interest (10% of the starting amount). If the maximum change in the iteration setting is at 0.001, the value is reached at iteration 4. At the fifth iteration, the change is 0.0001, less than the maximum setting, and Excel stops its iterating calculations.

TABLE 8-1

Results of Iterations

Iteration	Beginning Revolver (A)	Interest at 10% (B) = 10% × (A)	Ending Revolver (C) = $10 + (B)	Incremental Change in Revolver
0	$10	$0	$10	$0
1	10	1	11	1
2	11	1.1	11.1	0.1
3	11.1	1.11	11.11	0.01
4	11.11	1.111	11.111	0.001
5	11.111	1.1111	11.1111	0.0001

TABLE 8-2

Results of Iterations with an Effective After-Tax Interest Rate of 6%

Iteration	Beginning Revolver (A)	After-Tax Interest (B) = 6% × (A)	Ending Revolver (C) = $10 + (B)	Incremental Change in Revolver
0	$10	$0	$10	$0
1	10	0.6	10.6	0.6
2	10.6	0.636	10.636	0.036
3	10.636	0.63816	10.63816	0.00216
4	10.63816	0.6382896	10.6382896	0.0001296

8.4.6 If There Is a Tax Effect

If there had been a 40% tax rate, the increment with each cycle would be only 6% [10% interest rate * (1%–40% tax rate)] of the starting amount, and the maximum change increment would be reached sooner at iteration 4 (Table 8-2).

8.5 AVERAGE INTEREST CALCULATION

The preceding illustrations use an interest expense calculation based on the full revolver amount for the current period. In modeling, the more typical approach is to use the average values of the current period and the prior period, to take into account the change in the outstanding amount over the period. This applies to not just the plug calculations for excess cash or revolver, but to all the accounts that produce interest income or interest expense. Let's look at a debt account as an illustration. We might see, for example, the forecast numbers shown in Table 8-3:

For the interest expense for 2010, we can use $200 * 10% and have $20. This assumes, though, that the $200 debt has been at that level for the whole year between Jan 1 and December 31. However, looking at the outstanding debt in the prior year, we can see that it was $100 at December 31, 2009. In all likelihood,

TABLE 8-3

Debt and Interest Rates

	2009	2010
Debt	100	200
Interest rate	10%	10%

the additional $100 of debt did not get added to the balance sheet the very next day. In the absence of any other additional information then, we assume that it was done at the mid-point of the year. So the interest calculation is the average of $100 and $200 (or ($100 + $200)/2 = $150) multiplied by 10% interest, which gives $15.

If the debt is for a revolver, we can go through the same thinking, and assume that the funding shortfall arises out of the ongoing needs through the whole year. Again, in the absence of any additional information, we assume that the revolver increased steadily in a linear fashion through the year. The average calculation would be correct again for this assumption.

Average interest calculations for interest-yielding (cash and investments) and interest-bearing (debt) accounts *other than the excess cash and revolver plugs* do not present any problems with circular references. These non-plug numbers do not change with each iteration, because their interest does not change the ending current period's numbers used in the average interest calculations.

8.5.1 Using a Partial Year Factor

This average formula of ($100 + $200)/2*10% can also be written as ($100*0.5 + $200*0.5)*10%. The 0.5 represents the mid-point of the year. If we did have additional information that the debt increase was made on, say, September 30, 2009, which is the three-quarter point in the year, we can apply that factor for a more precise calculation of the interest expense: ($100 * 0.75 + $200 * (1 – 0.75)) * 10%, which gives $12.50. This is an interesting feature to put in a financial model, and is a more accurate way to forecast.

8.6 AVOIDING CIRCULAR REFERENCES

Having gone through an introduction of circular references, here are ways of avoiding them.

8.6.1 Use the Prior Year's Plug

Figure 8-5 shows the flows in using the prior year's plug. For Year 2 (the bottom half of the illustration), the interest expense is driven by the revolver in Year 1, and does not affect Year 2's revolver. The effect of this interest expense, although reflected in the ending revolver, does not go to the income statement again. In this way, so there is no circular loop. Continuing the calculations, the ending revolver in Year 2 is not used for the interest calculation in Year 2. Instead, it is used in the interest calculation in Year 3.

Although this works, notice that the interest expense calculation is not "correct": rather than \$0.5 (\$5 * 10%) it should be a little over \$0.75 ((\$5 + \$10)/2 * 10%, plus the effect of interest on interest). This

FIGURE 8-5

Using the Prior Year's Plug

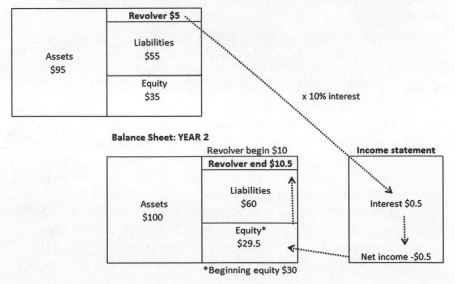

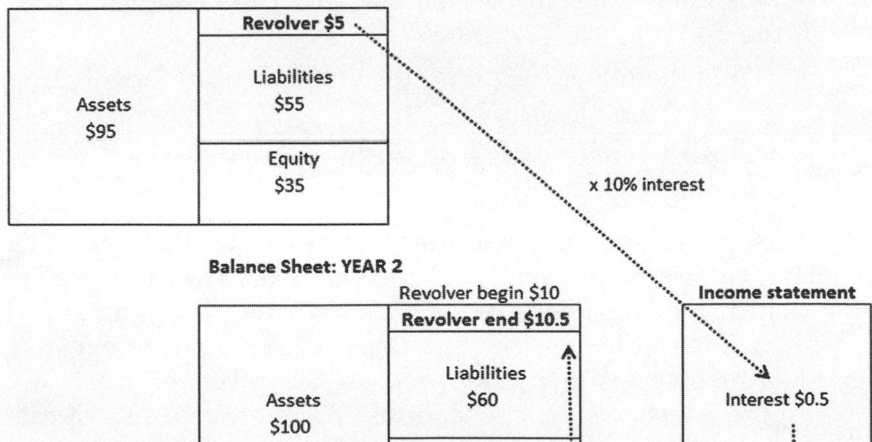

approach is acceptable if the plug numbers in the balance sheet are small relative to the reset of the numbers, or the plug does not vary much from year to year since each prior year more or less represents the current year's plug. More likely, however, the discrepancy can be significant, and all the more so if the unit being used changes from thousands to millions or even billions of dollars.

8.6.2 Create a Proxy for the Current Year's Plug

This technique should be considered if the change in the plugs is big enough from year to year. The secret is to develop a proxy plug where the liabilities and equity side, specifically the retained earnings account, does not include any flows based on the real (as opposed to the proxy) plug.

The proxy retained earnings = The prior year's actual retained earnings + a proxy net to retained earnings.

A proxy net to retained earnings is created by a proxy EBT * (1 – tax rate).

A proxy EBT is created by:

- The current year's EBIT
- Plus interest income on the *prior* year's excess cash (this is the plug account)
- Plus interest income on the current year's cash (this is the non-plug cash account)
- Minus the interest expense on the *prior* year's revolver (this is the plug account)
- Minus the interest expense on the current year's non-plug debt

This proxy retained earnings is added to the liabilities (which includes the revolver) and then compared with the assets side (which includes the excess cash), and the plug is thus derived. The interest income (if the plug is excess cash) or expense (if it is a revolver) is then calculated on this proxy plug.

Figure 8-6 shows the calculations. There are two sets of calculations for the excess cash/revolver: the proxy calculations are shown in a rounded box below the balance sheet. The formulas in the income statement for interest income/expense on the

FIGURE 8–6

Formulas for Calculating Proxy Plugs (Boxed)

	A	B	C	D	E	F	G	H
1				Hist	Proj	Proj		
2		INCOME STATEMENT		Year 1	Year 2	Year 3	Formulas in column F	
3		Revenue		160.0	200.0	390.0	Input	
4		COGS		80.0	90.0	190.0	Input	
5		SGA		29.0	45.0	80.0	Input	
6		EBIT		51.0	65.0	120.0	=F3-SUM(F4:F5)	
7								
8		Interest: Excess cash	3.0%	0.0	1.0	0.5	=$C$8*AVERAGE(E36:F36)	
9		Interest: Revolver	6.0%	0.0	0.0	1.3	=$C$9*AVERAGE(E37:F37)	
10		Interest: Debt	6.0%	19.2	20.1	20.7	=$C$10*AVERAGE(E24:F24)	
11		EBT		31.8	45.9	98.5	=F6+F8-F9-F10	
12								
13		Tax	40.0%	12.7	18.3	39.4	=$C$13*F11	
14		Net income		19.1	27.5	59.1	=F11-F13	
15								
16				Hist	Proj	Proj		
17		BALANCE SHEET		Year 1	Year 2	Year 3		
18		Excess cash		0.0	32.5	0.0	=MAX(F42,0)	
19		Current assets		200.0	250.0	350.0	Input	
20		Long-term assets		350.0	375.0	400.0	Input	
21		Total assets		550.0	657.5	750.0	=SUM(F18:F20)	
22								
23		Revolver		0.0	0.0	43.4	=-MIN(F42,0)	
24		Debt		320.0	350.0	340.0	Input	
25		Common stock		50.0	100.0	100.0	Input	
26		Retained earnings		180.0	207.5	266.6	=E26+F14	
27		Total liabs and equity		550.0	657.5	750.0	=SUM(F23:F26)	
28								
29		Balance sheet check			0.0	0.0	=F27-F21	
30								
31		**Basis for proxy plug interest calculations**						
32		Proxy retained earnings			206.9	267.1	=E26+(F6-F10)*(1-$C$13)	
33		Assets without excess cash			625.0	750.0	=SUM(F19:F20)	
34		Liabs, proxy equity excl revolver			656.9	707.1	=F24+F25+F32	
35		Proxy excess cash (revolver)			31.9	(42.9)	=F34-F33	
36		Proxy excess cash			31.9	0.0	=MAX(F35,0)	
37		Proxy revolver			0.0	42.9	=-MIN(F35,0)	
38								
39		Actual balancing						
40		Assets without excess cash			625.0	750.0	=SUM(F19:F20)	
41		Liabs, equity without revolver			657.5	706.6	=SUM(F24:F26)	
42		Excess cash (revolver)			32.5	(43.4)	=F41-F40	
43								

proxy plugs are also shown in a rounded box. The balance sheet balancing numbers are calculated separately and use the "real" (non-proxy) numbers.

As the table shows (Table 8-4), the proxy numbers are quite close to the actual numbers:

However, there are issues to look out for with this approach:

- Getting to the proxy net to retained earnings becomes more complex if you have tax rates that vary because of the effects of tax loss carryforwards.
- Other accounts between the EBT and the final net to retained earnings number can be problematic if they rely on the relative calculations. For example, a dividend payout may be calculated as a percentage payout of net income. Since the net income is typically the plug interest values, we would have to create a proxy net income on which to calculate dividends. Another way to avoid this would be calculate dividends as a dividend per share assumptions × the number of outstanding shares.

8.6.3 Cut and Paste Value Each Iteration's Results

In this approach (Fig. 8-7), the plug calculations are created as usual (Row 33, "Excess cash (revolver) as calculated"), but this is then copied onto the next row as values (Row 34, "Excess cash (revolver) as values"). Use the Cut/Paste-Value sequence in Excel: the keystrokes are Ctrl+C, and then Alt, E, S, V. These sequences

TABLE 8-4

Comparison of Proxy Versus Actual Results

	Proxy	Actual
Excess cash	31.9	32.5
Revolver	42.9	43.4

FIGURE 8-7

Cut and Paste Value the Excess Cash/Revolver Calculation

	A	B	C	D	E	F	G	H	I	J
1				Hist	Proj	Proj				
2		INCOME STATEMENT		Year 1	Year 2	Year 3	Formulas in column F			
3		Revenue		160.0	200.0	390.0	Input			
4		COGS		80.0	90.0	190.0	Input			
5		SGA		29.0	45.0	80.0	Input			
6		EBIT		51.0	65.0	120.0	=F3-SUM(F4:F5)			
7										
8		Interest: Excess cash	3.0%	0.0	0.5	0.5	=$C$8*AVERAGE(E18:F18)			
9		Interest: Revolver	6.0%	0.0	0.0	1.3	=$C$9*AVERAGE(E23:F23)			
10		Interest: Debt	6.0%	19.2	20.1	20.7	=$C$10*AVERAGE(E24:F24)			
11		EBT		31.8	45.4	98.5	=F6+F8-F9-F10			
12										
13		Tax	40.0%	12.7	18.2	39.4	=$C$13*F11			
14		Net income		19.1	27.2	59.1	=F11-F13			
15										
16				Hist	Proj	Proj				
17		BALANCE SHEET		Year 1	Year 2	Year 3				
18		Excess cash		0.0	32.2	0.0	=MAX(F34,0)			
19		Current assets		200.0	250.0	350.0	Input			
20		Long-term assets		350.0	375.0	400.0	Input			
21		Total assets		550.0	657.2	750.0	=SUM(F18:F20)			
22										
23		Revolver		0.0	0.0	43.7	=-MIN(F34,0)			
24		Debt		320.0	350.0	340.0	Input			
25		Common stock		50.0	100.0	100.0	Input			
26		Retained earnings		180.0	207.2	266.3	=E26+F14			
27		Total liabs and equity		550.0	657.2	750.0	=SUM(F23:F26)			
28										
29		Balance sheet check			0.0	0.0	=F27-F21			
30										
31		Assets without excess cash			625.0	750.0	=SUM(F19:F20)			
32		Liabs, equity without revolver			657.2	706.3	=SUM(F24:F26)			
33		Excess cash (revolver) as calculated			32.2	(43.7)	=IF(ISERROR(F32-F31),0,F32-F31)			
34		Excess cash (revolver) pasted as values			32.2	(43.7)	Hard-coded number			
35										
36										

Plugs refer to row 34, not 33

work in both Excel 2003 and 2007. Do this until the line for the balance sheet check (Row 29, "Balance sheet check") shows zeros.

8.6.3.1 Manual steps or macro

Doing the copy and paste-value sequence for the lines works but is a manually tedious way of arriving at the answer. The next step, of course, would be to put an on-screen button that would launch a macro to do the task automatically, and stop when the balance sheet check row reads zeros. Please refer to Chapter 18, Section 18.10 for a macro approach to do this.

8.7 USING CIRCULAR REFERENCES: PRECAUTIONARY MEASURES

Having seen all the steps trying to arrive at an "accurate" average interest income and expense for the balancing plugs without the use of circular references, one might arrive at the point at which it might be useful to just use the circular references! If you have in fact decided to try using circular references, and assuming that you have passed the test that your users agree to the use of iterations, then read on.

8.7.1 Turn the Iteration Setting on Upon File Opening

If your model uses iterations, it's a good idea to include an Workbook_Open macro in the ThisWorkbook sheet object that automatically turns the iteration setting to on when the model is opened. (The older approach, and one that still works just as well, is to use an Auto_Open macro that can be stored in any of the VBE modules.)

However, it is also true that Excel's circular reference detection is faster than the Workbook_Open macro. Consequently, the user will see the Excel warning of a circular reference upon opening (Fig. 8-8).

It's only until you press OK from this that the Workbook_Open macro launches to set the iteration on, making this warning moot.

8.7.2 Always Use Error Traps

Because circular references create unending calculation loops, an error message in the calculations will be caught in the loop. Even when the source of the error is removed, the error message (such as a #DIV/0! or #REF!) will continue to be present. One way to remove this is a manual interruption of the loop: erase one formula, make sure the workbook recalculates to clear out the error message, and then write the formula back in. This works, but is a rather tedious way to repair the error.

FIGURE 8-8

The Circular Reference Warning (As Seen in Excel 2007)

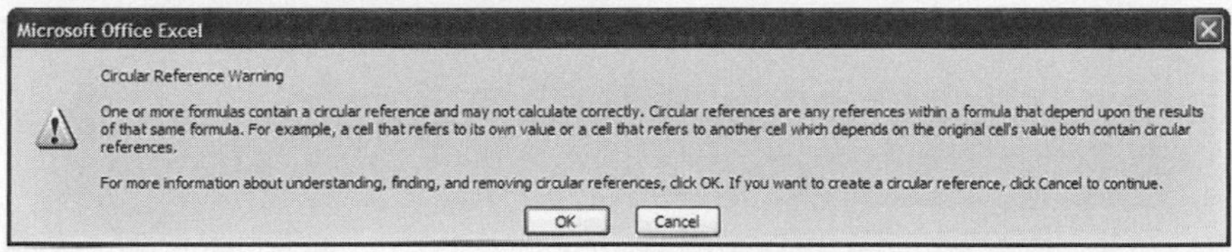

Another way is to put in an error trap by using an IF statement with an ISERROR function. Writing it is simple: simply put the IF statement around the original formulas as follows:

=IF(ISERROR(original_formula),0,original_formula)

When there is an error message, the ISERROR test becomes TRUE, and consequently the formula returns a 0.

As an example, look at cell F32 in Figure 8-9. The original formula is:

F29-F30

With the ISERROR test, the formula becomes:

=IF(ISERROR(F29-F30),0,F29-F30)

At this point, you can correct the source of the error. As Excel recalculates, the formula's test for ISERROR is FALSE (there is no error), and so it reverts back to the original formula to reestablish the circular reference for the iterative calculations (Fig. 8-10).

This self-recovery ability makes models with iterative calculations that much more manageable.

8.7.3 Use a Check to Isolate Any Unintended Circular References

If you are still skittish about using circular reference, here is something you can do. Put in the model an IF statement switch that can turn the plug interest calculation from average (circular reference) to prior period (no circular references) and back again (Fig. 8-11).

FIGURE 8–9

Use of an Error Trap (Row 32)

	A	B	C	D	E	F	G
1				Hist	Proj	Proj	
2		INCOME STATEMENT		Year 1	Year 2	Year 3	Formulas in column F
3		Revenue		160.0	200.0	390.0	Input
4		COGS		80.0	90.0	190.0	Input
5		SGA		29.0	45.0	80.0	Input
6		EBIT		51.0	65.0	120.0	=F3-SUM(F4:F5)
7							
8		Interest: Excess cash	3.0%	0.0	0.5	0.5	=$C$8*AVERAGE(E18:F18)
9		Interest: Revolver	6.0%	0.0	0.0	1.3	=$C$9*AVERAGE(E23:F23)
10		Interest: Debt	6.0%	19.2	20.1	20.7	=$C$10*AVERAGE(E24:F24)
11		EBT		31.8	45.4	98.5	=F6+F8-F9-F10
12							
13		Tax	40.0%	12.7	18.2	39.4	=$C$13*F11
14		Net income		19.1	27.2	59.1	=F11-F13
15							
16				Hist	Proj	Proj	
17		BALANCE SHEET		Year 1	Year 2	Year 3	
18		Excess cash		0.0	32.2	0.0	=MAX(F33,0)
19		Current assets		200.0	250.0	350.0	Input
20		Long-term assets		350.0	375.0	400.0	Input
21		Total assets		550.0	657.2	750.0	=SUM(F18:F20)
22							
23		Revolver		0.0	0.0	43.7	=-MIN(F33,0)
24		Debt		320.0	350.0	340.0	Input
25		Common stock		50.0	100.0	100.0	Input
26		Retained earnings		180.0	207.2	266.3	=E26+F14
27		Total liabs and equity		550.0	657.2	750.0	=SUM(F23:F26)
28							
29		Balance sheet check			0.0	0.0	=F27-F21
30							
31		Assets without excess cash			625.0	750.0	=SUM(F19:F20)
32		Liabs, equity without revolver			657.2	706.3	=SUM(F24:F26)
33		Excess cash (revolver) as calculated			32.2	(43.7)	=IF(ISERROR(F32-F31),0,F32-F31)
34							
35							

Note: You should link this switch, preferably through a macro and an on-screen button, so that the "Y" and "N" setting for the IF statement also sets the iteration on and off, respectively.

- Run the model with no circulars (interest is calculated on each prior period's plug). When you are ready to print and want the hard-copy printouts to show the "correct" interest calculations, change the setting to circular references. After printing, the switch is turned off again.

FIGURE 8–10

How the ISERROR Error Trap Works

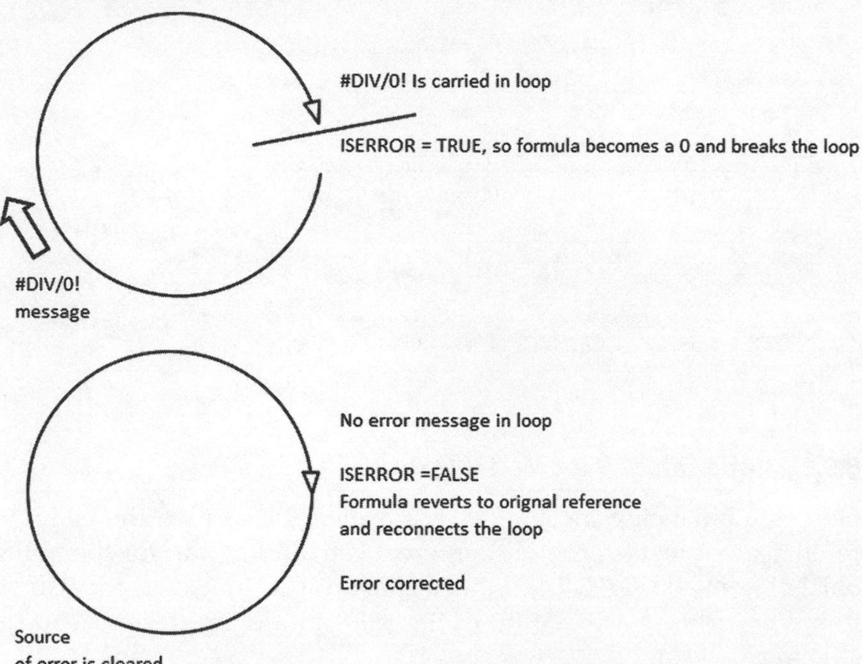
#DIV/0! Is carried in loop
ISERROR = TRUE, so formula becomes a 0 and breaks the loop
#DIV/0!
message
No error message in loop
ISERROR =FALSE
Formula reverts to orignal reference
and reconnects the loop
Error corrected
Source
of error is cleared

- Do the opposite: Run the model with circulars. But before printing, turn the iteration off. This step is *only* to see if there are unintended circular references elsewhere in the model. If there are (Excel will show its circular reference warning), then correct them. Then set the iteration back to on, make sure the model recalculates to have the "correct" numbers again, and print. This step has the advantage of the on-screen model is always working with the correct numbers from the iterative calculations.

8.8 FUN WITH CIRCULAR REFERENCES

The examples below use circular references and *require* that the iteration setting is on.

FIGURE 8-11

Switch for Average ("Y") or Prior Period ("N") Interest. Note Variances in Results

	A	B	C	D	E	F	G	H	I	J	K
1				Hist	Proj	Proj					
2		INCOME STATEMENT		Year 1	Year 2	Year 3	Formulas in column F				
3		Revenue		160.0	200.0	390.0	Input				
4		COGS		80.0	90.0	190.0	Input				
5		SGA		29.0	45.0	80.0	Input				
6		EBIT		51.0	65.0	120.0	=F3-SUM(F4:F5)				
7		Use circular?	Y								
8		Interest: Excess cash	3.0%	0.0	0.5	0.5	=IF($C$7="Y",$C$8*AVERAGE(E18:F18),$C$8*E18)				
9		Interest: Revolver	6.0%	0.0	0.0	1.3	=IF($C$7="Y",$C$9*AVERAGE(E23:F23),$C$9*E23)				
10		Interest: Debt	6.0%	19.2	20.1	20.7	=$C$10*AVERAGE(E24:F24)				
11		EBT		31.8	45.4	98.5	=F6+F8-F9-F10				
12											
13		Tax	40.0%	12.7	18.2	39.4	=$C$13*F11				
14		Net income		19.1	27.2	59.1	=F11-F13				
15											

8.8.1 Variation of Pilot Model No. 1

Here is a balancing mechanism for a model that uses the circular reference not just for the plug interest calculation, but for the main balancing itself (Fig. 8-12). In fact, this approach *requires* the use of iterations. This is a variation of the pilot model no. 1 described in Chapter 7 (Section 7.3).

The variation from the earlier pilot model no. 1 is shown in the boxed area. Here, the formulas use total liabilities and equity (*including* the revolver) and total assets (*including* excess cash). It then arrives at the difference between the two (Row 33, "Difference"). The excess cash (revolver) is calculated in Row 34 ("Excess cash (revolver)") by summing Row 33 with Row 34 itself!

The ISERROR function is added to trap errors. Since circular references are already in use by the balancing mechanism, the interest calculations on the plugs can use the average calculations. (As noted in Section 8.5, the interest calculation on average plugs by itself produces circular references.)

8.8.1.1 How does it work?

Let's examine the steps in this iterative calculation. One way to do this is to set Excel maximum iteration setting to 1, rather than the

FIGURE 8–12

Magic Balancing

	A	B	C	D	E	F	G	H	I	J
1				Hist	Proj	Proj				
2		INCOME STATEMENT		Year 1	Year 2	Year 3	Formulas in column F			
3		Revenue		160.0	200.0	390.0	Input			
4		COGS		80.0	90.0	190.0	Input			
5		SGA		29.0	45.0	80.0	Input			
6		EBIT		51.0	65.0	120.0	=F3-SUM(F4:F5)			
7										
8		Interest: Excess cash	3.0%	0.0	0.5	0.5	=$C$8*AVERAGE(E18:F18)			
9		Interest: Revolver	6.0%	0.0	0.0	1.3	=$C$9*AVERAGE(E23:F23)			
10		Interest: Debt	6.0%	19.2	20.1	20.7	=$C$10*AVERAGE(E24:F24)			
11		EBT		31.8	45.4	98.5	=F6+F8-F9-F10			
12										
13		Tax	40.0%	12.7	18.2	39.4	=$C$13*F11			
14		Net income		19.1	27.2	59.1	=F11-F13			
15										
16				Hist	Proj	Proj				
17		BALANCE SHEET		Year 1	Year 2	Year 3				
18		Excess cash		0.0	32.2	0.0	=MAX(F34,0)			
19		Current assets		200.0	250.0	350.0	Input			
20		Long-term assets		350.0	375.0	400.0	Input			
21		Total assets		550.0	657.2	750.0	=SUM(F18:F20)			
22										
23		Revolver		0.0	0.0	43.7	=-MIN(F34,0)			
24		Debt		320.0	350.0	340.0	Input			
25		Common stock		50.0	100.0	100.0	Input			
26		Retained earnings		180.0	207.2	266.3	=E26+F14			
27		Total liabs and equity		550.0	657.2	750.0	=SUM(F23:F26)			
28										
29		Balance sheet check			0.0	0.0	=F27-F21			
30										
31		Total assets			657.2	750.0	=SUM(F18:F20)			
32		Total liabilities and equity			657.2	750.0	=SUM(F23:F26)			
33		Difference			0.0	0.0	=F32-F31			
34		Excess cash (revolver)			32.2	(43.7)	=IF(ISERROR(F33+F34),0,F33+F34)			
35										
36										

Plugs refer to row 34, not 33

default 100. Then set the calculation to manual. This way, we can see each one step in the iteration by each tap of the Enter key.

The principle is that each cell in Row 34 ("Excess cash (revolver)") with the formula that adds Row 33 ("Difference") to itself, acts as a sort of a bucket. The bucket holds the initial difference, and then keeps adding any incremental difference to that main bucket. In this way, the plug number is built up, and the total after each incremental increase is read by the balance sheet. By doing so, the difference in the balance sheet sides becomes less and less. The iteration continues until the incremental difference passes the Excel maximum change test, and Excel stops calculating.

Here is a schematic of the iterative calculations. The concept would be the same if the plug is the excess cash plug.

Iteration count		**0**	**1**	**2**	**3**	**4**
A	Excess cash	0	0	0	0	0
B	Assets	200	200	200	200	200
C=A+B	Total assets	200	200	200	200	200
D	Revolver	0	0	20	20	22
E	Liabs & equity	180	180	180	178*	178
F=D+E	Total liabs & equity	180	180	200	198	200
G=F−C	Difference	0	−20	0	−2	0
H=G+H	Accumulated difference	0	−20	−20	−22	−22

*In iteration 3, this is due to reduction in retained earnings from the revolver interest expense.

To illustrate step by step in the model:

8.8.1.1.1 At Iteration 0 Let's look at the last column (Year 3) in Figure 8-13. At the start of the balancing sequence, there is an imbalance in the balance sheet, as shown by the balance sheet check on Row 29 of (42.9). By our convention, the negative difference indicates that this is a revolver plug.

The difference row (Row 33) is where the balancing begins. At this first iteration, this has not calculated and remains at 0.

8.8.1.1.2 At Iteration 1 As the calculation continues, Row 33 shows the difference between the two sides of the balance sheet (Fig. 8-14). Excel calculates in the iteration mode in a column-by-column manner, going from left to right, and in each column it goes from top to bottom. The calculation has not reached the next row yet.

As the iteration continues, the calculation now reaches Row 34 (Fig. 8-15). This line is where the excess cash or revolver is calculated.

FIGURE 8–13

At Iteration 0. See Imbalance on Row 29

	A	B	C	D	E	F	G	H
16				Hist	Proj	Proj		
17		BALANCE SHEET		Year 1	Year 2	Year 2		
18		Excess cash		0.0	32.2	0.0	=MAX(Q34,0)	
19		Current assets		200.0	250.0	350.0		
20		Long-term assets		350.0	375.0	400.0		
21		Total assets		550.0	657.2	750.0	=SUM(Q18:Q20)	
22								
23		Revolver		0.0	0.0	0.0	=-MIN(Q34,0)	
24		Debt		320.0	350.0	340.0		
25		Common stock		50.0	100.0	100.0		
26		Retained earnings		180.0	207.2	267.1	=P26+Q14	
27		Total liabs and equity		550.0	657.2	707.1	=SUM(Q23:Q26)	
28								
29		Balance sheet check			0.0	(42.9)	=Q27-Q21	
30								
31		Total assets			657.2	750.0	=SUM(Q18:Q20)	
32		Total liabilities and equity			657.2	707.1	=SUM(Q23:Q26)	
33		Difference			0.0	0.0		
34		Excess cash (revolver) as calculated			32.2	0.0		
35								

8.8.1.1.3 At Iteration 2 As the second iteration starts (Fig. 8-16), the revolver line in the balance sheet reads the plug as calculated in Row 34. It looks like everything is balanced.

8.8.1.1.4 At Iteration 3 However, at the next recalculation, the balance sheet goes a bit off balance again (Fig. 8-17). This is because the interest expense from the revolver has come into the flows. This is shown by the retained earnings numbers, which is lower than what was seen in Figure 8-16.

This lag in the calculations, where the balance sheet appears to be in balance but then goes off balance again, is due to the fact that the interest expense formula in the income statement is referencing the revolver line (Row 23) in the balance sheet. So the interest formula has to wait for the revolver line to reflect the plug as calculated in Row 34. We can eliminate

FIGURE 8-14

At Iteration 1. Row 33 Shows a Difference

	A	B	C	D	E	F	G	H
16				Hist	Proj	Proj		
17		BALANCE SHEET		Year 1	Year 2	Year 2		
18		Excess cash		0.0	32.2	0.0	=MAX(Q34,0)	
19		Current assets		200.0	250.0	350.0		
20		Long-term assets		350.0	375.0	400.0		
21		Total assets		550.0	657.2	750.0	=SUM(Q18:Q20)	
22								
23		Revolver		0.0	0.0	0.0	=-MIN(Q34,0)	
24		Debt		320.0	350.0	340.0		
25		Common stock		50.0	100.0	100.0		
26		Retained earnings		180.0	207.2	267.1	=P26+Q14	
27		Total liabs and equity		550.0	657.2	707.1	=SUM(Q23:Q26)	
28								
29		Balance sheet check			0.0	(42.9)	=Q27-Q21	
30								
31		Total assets			657.2	750.0	=SUM(Q18:Q20)	
32		Total liabilities and equity			657.2	707.1	=SUM(Q23:Q26)	
33		Difference			0.0	(42.9)	=Q32-Q31	
34		Excess cash (revolver) as calculated			32.2	0.0		
35								

this lag by pointing the interest expense formula directly to –MIN(Row 34,0), instead of Row 23. The –MIN means that the revolver will use that number only it is a negative, and then will show it as a positive.

Likewise, if the balancing number is for excess cash, then the interest income calculation could look directly to MAX(Row 34,0), instead of Row 18.

The formulas were set without this direct reference for ease of following the flows. The additional step in the calculation does not add materially to the time required for the calculations.

8.8.1.1.5 At Iteration 4 With the fourth iteration, the balance sheet comes back into balance (Fig. 8-18). Additional iterations at this point may refine the interest expense calculation, but the incremental changes from each iteration is small, and Excel stops recalculating.

FIGURE 8–15

Iteration 1 Continues, and Row 33 and Row 34 Show a Value

	A	B	C	D	E	F	G	H	I	J
16				Hist	Proj	Proj				
17		BALANCE SHEET		Year 1	Year 2	Year 2				
18		Excess cash		0.0	32.2	0.0	=MAX(Q34,0)			
19		Current assets		200.0	250.0	350.0				
20		Long-term assets		350.0	375.0	400.0				
21		Total assets		550.0	657.2	750.0	=SUM(Q18:Q20)			
22										
23		Revolver		0.0	0.0	0.0	=-MIN(Q34,0)			
24		Debt		320.0	350.0	340.0				
25		Common stock		50.0	100.0	100.0				
26		Retained earnings		180.0	207.2	267.1	=P26+Q14			
27		Total liabs and equity		550.0	657.2	707.1	=SUM(Q23:Q26)			
28										
29		Balance sheet check			0.0	(42.9)	=Q27-Q21			
30										
31		Total assets			657.2	750.0	=SUM(Q18:Q20)			
32		Total liabilities and equity			657.2	707.1	=SUM(Q23:Q26)			
33		Difference			0.0	(42.9)	=Q32-Q31			
34		Excess cash (revolver) as calculated			32.2	(42.9)	=IF(ISERROR(Q33+Q34),0,Q33+Q34)			
35										

FIGURE 8–16

The Revolver Line in the Balance Reads the Plug

	A	B	C	D	E	F	G	H	I	J
16				Hist	Proj	Proj				
17		BALANCE SHEET		Year 1	Year 2	Year 2				
18		Excess cash		0.0	32.2	0.0	=MAX(Q34,0)			
19		Current assets		200.0	250.0	350.0				
20		Long-term assets		350.0	375.0	400.0				
21		Total assets		550.0	657.2	750.0	=SUM(Q18:Q20)			
22										
23		Revolver		0.0	0.0	42.9	=-MIN(Q34,0)			
24		Debt		320.0	350.0	340.0				
25		Common stock		50.0	100.0	100.0				
26		Retained earnings		180.0	207.2	267.1	=P26+Q14			
27		Total liabs and equity		550.0	657.2	750.0	=SUM(Q23:Q26)			
28										
29		Balance sheet check			0.0	0.0	=Q27-Q21			
30										
31		Total assets			657.2	750.0	=SUM(Q18:Q20)			
32		Total liabilities and equity			657.2	750.0	=SUM(Q23:Q26)			
33		Difference			0.0	0.0	=Q32-Q31			
34		Excess cash (revolver) as calculated			32.2	(42.9)	=IF(ISERROR(Q33+Q34),0,Q33+Q34)			
35										
36										

FIGURE 8–17

At Iteration 2. Row 29's Imbalance Is from Interest Expense Flowing into the Balance Sheet

	A	B	C	D	E	F	G	H	I	J
16				Hist	Proj	Proj				
17		BALANCE SHEET		Year 1	Year 2	Year 2				
18		Excess cash		0.0	32.2	0.0	=MAX(Q34,0)			
19		Current assets		200.0	250.0	350.0				
20		Long-term assets		350.0	375.0	400.0				
21		Total assets		550.0	657.2	750.0	=SUM(Q18:Q20)			
22										
23		Revolver		0.0	0.0	42.9	=-MIN(Q34,0)			
24		Debt		320.0	350.0	340.0				
25		Common stock		50.0	100.0	100.0				
26		Retained earnings		180.0	207.2	266.3	=P26+Q14			
27		Total liabs and equity		550.0	657.2	749.2	=SUM(Q23:Q26)			
28										
29		Balance sheet check			0.0	(0.8)	=Q27-Q21			
30										
31		Total assets			657.2	750.0	=SUM(Q18:Q20)			
32		Total liabilities and equity			657.2	749.2	=SUM(Q23:Q26)			
33		Difference			0.0	(0.8)	=Q32-Q31			
34		Excess cash (revolver) as calculated			32.2	(43.7)	=IF(ISERROR(Q33+Q34),0,Q33+Q34)			
35										

FIGURE 8–18

At Iteration 4. Row 29 Comes Back into Balance

	A	B	C	D	E	F	G	H	I	J
16				Hist	Proj	Proj				
17		BALANCE SHEET		Year 1	Year 2	Year 2				
18		Excess cash		0.0	32.2	0.0	=MAX(Q34,0)			
19		Current assets		200.0	250.0	350.0				
20		Long-term assets		350.0	375.0	400.0				
21		Total assets		550.0	657.2	750.0	=SUM(Q18:Q20)			
22										
23		Revolver		0.0	0.0	43.7	=-MIN(Q34,0)			
24		Debt		320.0	350.0	340.0				
25		Common stock		50.0	100.0	100.0				
26		Retained earnings		180.0	207.2	266.3	=P26+Q14			
27		Total liabs and equity		550.0	657.2	750.0	=SUM(Q23:Q26)			
28										
29		Balance sheet check			0.0	0.0	=Q27-Q21			
30										
31		Total assets			657.2	750.0	=SUM(Q18:Q20)			
32		Total liabilities and equity			657.2	750.0	=SUM(Q23:Q26)			
33		Difference			0.0	0.0	=Q32-Q31			
34		Excess cash (revolver) as calculated			32.2	(43.7)	=IF(ISERROR(Q33+Q34),0,Q33+Q34)			
35										

8.8.2 Keeping Track of Scenarios

You can use circular references for displaying the results of multiple scenarios that you are running in the model.

Figure 8-19 shows a worksheet for an IRR calculation. The inputs for the flows are shown in Rows 2–4. A case toggle (the case input in Cell C6) sets the row that is being calculated through the use of the CHOOSE function. The CHOOSE formula is in all six columns. The formula for the last column (Cell H7) is shown. The IRR result is shown in Cell C10.

Usually, using the case toggle will only allow one set of results to appear. Here is where we can use a circular reference. Look at the formula in Cell C13 for Case 1:

=IF($C$6=1,$C$10,C13)

This formula says: if the case input is set to 1, read the IRR calculation in Cell C10, otherwise read itself.

The formula in Cell C14 for Case 2 is:

=IF($C$6=2,$C$10,C14)

FIGURE 8-19

Circular References in Rows 13–15 Retain the Results of Each Case

	A	B	C	D	E	F	G	H	I	J	K
1			Year 0	Year 1	Year 2	Year 3	Year 4	Year 5			
2		Case 1 flows	(300.0)	100.0	110.0	121.0	131.0	144.0			
3		Case 2 flows	(300.0)	100.0	105.0	127.0	115.0	137.0			
4		Case 3 flows	(300.0)	98.0	103.0	116.0	156.0	166.0			
5											
6		Case input	1								
7		Case used	(300.0)	100.0	110.0	121.0	131.0	144.0	=CHOOSE($C$6,H2,H3,H4)		
8											
9											
10		IRR	27.0%	=IRR(C7:H7)							
11											
12		IRR results									
13		Case 1	27.0%	=IF($C$6=1,$C$10,C13)							
14		Case 2	25.6%	=IF($C$6=2,$C$10,C14)							
15		Case 3	28.2%	=IF($C$6=3,$C$10,C15)							
16											

This says: If the case input is set to 2, read the IRR calculation in Cell C10, otherwise read itself. The formula in Cell C15 for Case 3 is along similar lines.

These formulas read the IRR results for their particular case. But when the case is changed, each formula retains the result for its particular case. In this way, all three formulas show the results of all cases, regardless of the current setting in use in the model.

One note of caution, though: If you use this, you must make sure that you cycle through all the cases, in order to "load" the results into each formula. If you make changes during the modeling, before the final printing of your results, you should cycle through all the cases again, to refresh all the results.

CHAPTER 9

Variations on Balancing Plugs

Now that we know how to create the balancing plugs in the balance sheet, it is an easy next step to derive the variations. Again, just to repeat, the "plug" here is a dynamic number created by the balancing formulas on the balance sheet or cash flow statement. The plug is *not* a hard-coded number that you have to enter manually for balancing purposes.

Let's look at the different ways we can make use of the balancing plugs in out model:

- How to modify the revolver calculation seen in the last chapter so that it acts as an equity plug, not a debt plug.
- How to have the excess cash plug as a dividend in the income statement and effectively does not appear on the balance sheet at all.

9.1 WORKING WITH BALANCE SHEET BALANCING NUMBERS

In the following illustrations, the changes for the various plug variations are shown using the balancing method of using the balance sheet only. This is because trying to determine an equity plug or an excess cash dividend does not quite fit in with the intent of the cash flow statement, which is designed to track cash. Determining these values from the mechanistic balance sheet only view is much simpler.

Once the balance sheet is balanced, the cash flow statement can be constructed. Recall that the cash flow statement can be viewed as reconciliation view of the flows from the income statement and the changes in the balance sheet accounts.

9.2 THE LIABILITIES PLUG DOES NOT HAVE TO BE A REVOLVER

We have been considering the plug on the liabilities side as debt, but a more useful way of thinking about this plug is that it is a shortfall in financing. From the modeling—and from the business point of view, too—it does not have to be debt, as long as it provides the necessary financing for the company. The plug can well be an equity plug (Fig. 9-1). This has its own quirks, as described in Section 9.2.1.

The plug is typically viewed as debt because in the real world, when a company needs funding, the easiest thing to do

FIGURE 9-1

The Equity Plug

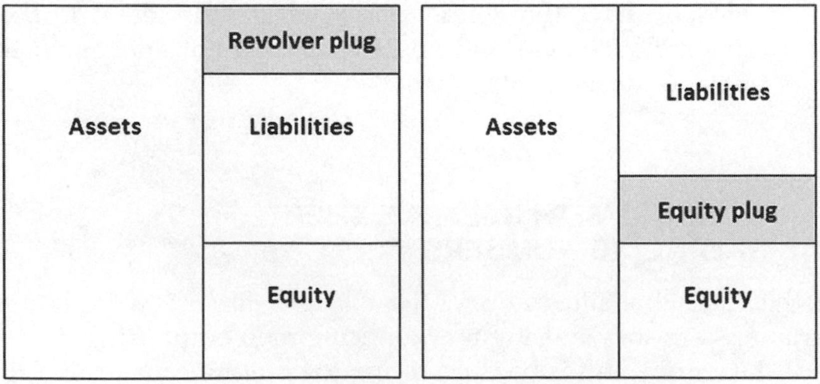

Revolver plug
Assets
Liabilities
Equity

Liabilities
Assets
Equity plug
Equity

is to borrow money, rather than issue stock. Likewise, the debt is readily repayable when the company has cash on hand.

9.2.1 The Equity Plug

When the financing plug is a revolver, we can let it vary from year to year, depending on the financing shortfalls as a result of our projections. Revolver lines of credit allow for this: the company can draw down if it needs financing, and then repay when it has excess cash. In this way, the revolver is best viewed as a short-term debt of the revolving kind. The revolver can be placed in the long-term debt category, but the potential for sudden increases and decreases does not make it act like a long-term debt.

If we want to use the plug as an equity plug, the main difference is that the equity plug can increase when there is a need for additional financing, but it should *not* decrease when there is excess cash. In real life, companies do issue equity to meet financing needs, although not for short-term needs. They certainly would not buy back its equity as a short-term response to having excess cash. Both issuing equity and buying back shares are complicated and fairly time-consuming processes.

FIGURE 9-2

A Mix of Revolver and Equity Plugs

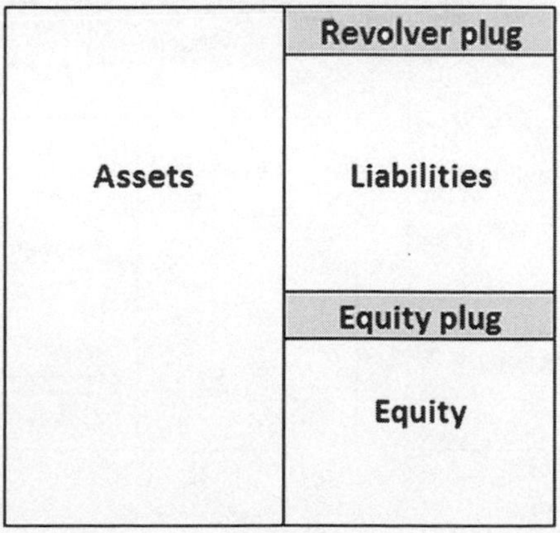

Assets
Revolver plug
Liabilities
Equity plug
Equity

Why have an equity plug? Do this when you are modeling a start-up company when the sources of debt financing are limited. Once past the formative years, we can make the plug shift to a revolver plug, either in a yes/no switch or a percentage mix (Fig. 9-2). We cover this in Section 9.4.

9.2.2 Effect on Dividends

When we do use an equity plug, we should consider that there may be extra dividends that the company will issue, as the equity plug implies additional shares. We would have to have assumptions of share prices to convert the equity plug to an increase in shares, and the dividend rate per share, to calculate the increase in dividends.

9.3 THE ASSET PLUG DOES NOT HAVE TO BE EXCESS CASH

The excess cash plug is a way of adding cash to the assets side of the balance sheet so that the two sides balance. Where there is excess financing (liabilities and equity too high) and/or not enough investments in assets (assets other than cash too low), the excess

FIGURE 9-3

Dividending Out the Excess Cash Amount to Balance the Balance Sheet

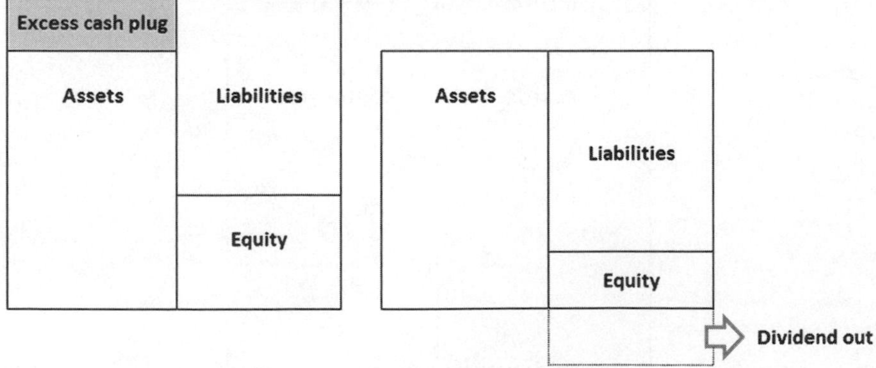

FIGURE 9-4

A Partial Dividending Out, with Some of the Excess Cash Remaining on the Balance Sheet

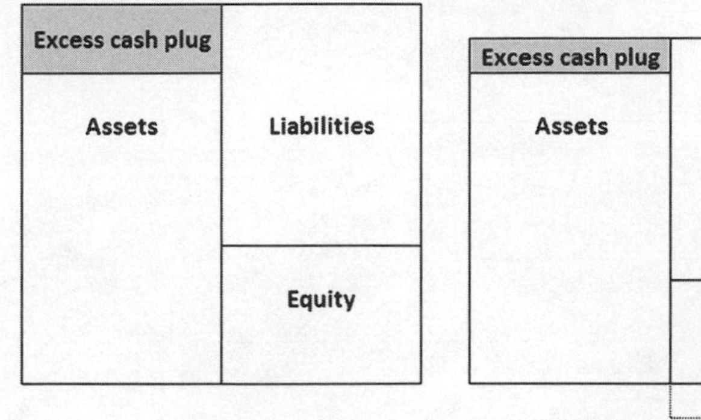

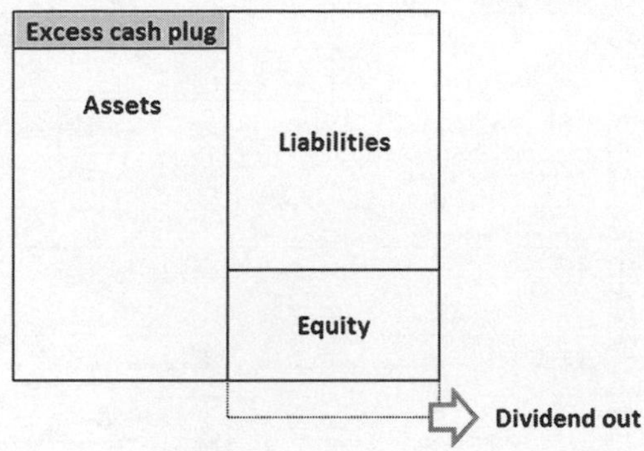

cash plug comes into play. Another way to balance such a balance sheet is to *reduce* the liabilities and equity side, by dividending out what would be the excess cash plug out of the retained earnings account (Fig. 9-3).

We can also do a partial dividending out, where a percentage of the excess cash plug remains on the balance sheet (Fig. 9-4). The percentage can be an input. Section 9.5 covers this.

9.3.1 Formula Changes for the Equity Plug

Figure 9-5 shows the model the changes for the equity plug. Numbered notes in the illustration correspond with the points that follow. This is based on the completed model at the end of building Pilot Model No 1 in Chapter 7, Section 7.3 (Fig. 7-5). The income statement formulas remain the same. The changes made were:

1. Row 23, for the revolver, has been hard-coded as 0s but remains in place. This is done since we will be using this row again later on in this chapter.
2. A new row has been inserted for the equity plug, and this appears as Row 25. Note that the formula looks to the

FIGURE 9-5

Changes for the Equity Plug

	A	B	C	D	E	F	G	H	I	J
1				Hist	Proj	Proj				
2		INCOME STATEMENT		Year 1	Year 2	Year 3	Formulas in column F			
3		Revenue		160.0	200.0	390.0	Input			
4		COGS		80.0	90.0	190.0	Input			
5		SGA		29.0	45.0	80.0	Input			
6		EBIT		51.0	65.0	120.0	=F3-SUM(F4:F5)			
7										
8		Interest: Excess cash	3.0%	0.0	0.0	0.0	=$C$8*E18			
9		Interest: Revolver	6.0%	0.0	0.0	0.0	=$C$9*E23			
10		Interest: Debt	6.0%	19.2	20.1	20.7	=$C$10*AVERAGE(E24:F24)			
11		EBT		31.8	44.9	99.3	=F6+F8-F9-F10			
12										
13		Tax	40.0%	12.7	18.0	39.7	=$C$13*F11			
14		Net income		19.1	26.9	59.6	=F11-F13			
15										
16				Hist	Proj	Proj				
17		BALANCE SHEET		Year 1	Year 2	Year 3				
18		Excess cash		0.0	0.0	0.0	=MAX(F34,0)			
19		Current assets		200.0	300.0	350.0	Input			
20		Long-term assets		350.0	375.0	400.0	Input			
21		Total assets		550.0	675.0	750.0	=SUM(F18:F20)			
22										
23		Revolver		0.0	0.0	0.0	This row is hard-coded as 0		1	
24		Debt		320.0	350.0	340.0	Input			
25		Equity plug		0.0	18.1	43.5	=E25-MIN(F34,0)	2		
26		Common stock		50.0	100.0	100.0	Input			
27		Retained earnings		180.0	206.9	266.5	=E27+F14			
28		Total liabs and equity		550.0	675.0	750.0	=SUM(F23:F27)			
29										
30		Balance sheet check		0.0	0.0	0.0	=F28-F21			
31										
32		Assets without excess cash			675.0	750.0	=SUM(F19:F20)			
33		Liabs, equity with prior year's equity plug			656.9	724.6	=SUM(E25,F24,F26:F27)		3	
34		Excess cash (revolver) as calculated			(18.1)	(25.4)	=F33-F32			
35										

balancing formula in Row 34, but also adds the *prior year's* equity plug. This is important, and is the reason why the equity plug must be at least as high as the prior year's number. Remember, the equity plug increases to meet a funding shortfall, but it does not decrease if there is excess funding.

3. The balancing formulas in Row 32 are the liabilities + equity + the *prior year's equity plug*. This line does not have the revolver number. Row 32 and Row 25 work together for the equity plug calculation.

9.4 USING BOTH THE EQUITY PLUG AND A REVOLVER

Now that we have the equity plug, we can also add a percentage factor input (see note 1 in Fig. 9-6) that will distribute the plug accordingly. In Figure 9-6, even though the distribution is set to 50%, the plug appears uneven: 12.7 for the revolver and 30.8 for the equity plug. However, the equity plug has the prior year's number of 18.1 embedded in it. If we subtract this out of the 30.8, we get the same number as the revolver (30.8 – 18.1 = 12.7).

FIGURE 9-6

The Plug as Both Debt and Equity Plugs

	B	C	D	E	F	G	H
1			Hist	Proj	Proj		
2	INCOME STATEMENT		Year 1	Year 2	Year 3	Formulas in column F	
3	Revenue		160.0	200.0	390.0	Input	
4	COGS		80.0	90.0	190.0	Input	
5	SGA		29.0	45.0	80.0	Input	
6	EBIT		51.0	65.0	120.0	=F3-SUM(F4:F5)	
7							
8	Interest: Excess cash	3.0%	0.0	0.0	0.0	=$C$8*E18	
9	Interest: Revolver	6.0%	0.0	0.0	0.0	=$C$9*E23	
10	Interest: Debt	6.0%	19.2	20.1	20.7	=$C$10*AVERAGE(E24:F24)	
11	EBT		31.8	44.9	99.3	=F6+F8-F9-F10	
12							
13	Tax	40.0%	12.7	18.0	39.7	=$C$13*F11	
14	Net income		19.1	26.9	59.6	=F11-F13	
15							
16			Hist	Proj	Proj		
17	BALANCE SHEET		Year 1	Year 2	Year 3		
18	Excess cash		0.0	0.0	0.0	=MAX(F34,0)	
19	Current assets		200.0	300.0	350.0	Input	
20	Long-term assets		350.0	375.0	400.0	Input	
21	Total assets		550.0	675.0	750.0	=SUM(F18:F20)	
22		Percent debt					
23	Revolver	50.0%	0.0	0.0	12.7	=-MIN(F34,0)*$C$23	(2)
24	Debt	(1)	320.0	350.0	340.0	Input	
25	Equity plug		0.0	18.1	30.8	=E25-MIN(F34,0)*(1-$C$23)	(3)
26	Common stock		50.0	100.0	100.0	Input	
27	Retained earnings		180.0	206.9	266.5	=E27+F14	
28	Total liabs and equity		550.0	675.0	750.0	=SUM(F23:F27)	
29							
30	Balance sheet check		0.0	0.0	0.0	=F28-F21	
31							
32	Assets without excess cash			675.0	750.0	=SUM(F19:F20)	(4)
33	Liabs, equity with prior year's equity plug			656.9	724.6	=SUM(E25,F24,F26:F27)	
34	Excess cash (revolver) as calculated			(18.1)	(25.4)	=F33-F32	
35							

9.4.1 Changes for the Equity Plug and Revolver

1. Create a percentage input cell in Cell C23.
2. Create the formula for the revolver and multiply Cell C23 into to the formula to multiply in the percentage factor.
3. On the equity plug (Row 25), multiply (1-C23) to the formula to multiply in the portion of the percentage factor that is not a revolver.
4. The balancing formula in Row 32 does not require any changes.

9.5 DIVIDENDING OUT THE EXCESS CASH

Now we turn our attention to the excess cash plug. In this case, instead of using the plug as a number that will add to the left side (the assets side) to make the balance sheet balance, we use the plug as an additional dividend in the income statement. This has the effect of reducing the net to retained earnings flow, essentially reducing the right-hand side of the balance sheet. In this way, the balance sheet becomes balanced.

9.5.1 Changes for Dividending Out Excess Cash

The steps are (Fig. 9-7):

1. Add the two rows in Row 16 and Row 17. Put the excess cash formula in the dividends line, or Row 16.
2. Hard-code the excess cash row as 0. We will be using this again in the next section.
3. The liabilities, equity, and revolver line needs to be changed so that it is equal to: debt, common stock, and *the prior retained earnings + net income before the dividends*. The reason for the last part is that the dividends line is now equivalent to the balancing number, so we want to exclude that when we want to find out the balancing amounts.

FIGURE 9-7

Dividending Out Excess Cash to Balance the Balance Sheet

	A	B	C	D	E	F	G	H	I	J
1				Hist	Proj	Proj				
2		INCOME STATEMENT		Year 1	Year 2	Year 3	Formulas in column F			
3		Revenue		160.0	200.0	390.0	Input			
4		COGS		80.0	90.0	190.0	Input			
5		SGA		29.0	45.0	80.0	Input			
6		EBIT		51.0	65.0	120.0	=F3-SUM(F4:F5)			
7										
8		Interest: Excess cash	3.0%	0.0	0.0	0.0	=$C$8*E21			
9		Interest: Revolver	6.0%	0.0	0.0	0.0	=$C$9*E26			
10		Interest: Debt	6.0%	19.2	20.1	20.7	=$C$10*AVERAGE(E27:F27)			
11		EBT		31.8	44.9	99.3	=F6+F8-F9-F10			
12										
13		Tax	40.0%	12.7	18.0	39.7	=$C$13*F11			
14		Net income		19.1	26.9	59.6	=F11-F13			
15										
16		Dividends		0.0	31.9	0.0	=MAX(F36,0)	1		
17		Net to retained earnings		19.1	(5.0)	59.6	=F14-F16			
18										
19				Hist	Proj	Proj				
20		BALANCE SHEET		Year 1	Year 2	Year 3				
21		Excess cash		0.0	0.0	0.0	This row is hard coded as 0		2	
22		Current assets		200.0	250.0	350.0	Input			
23		Long-term assets		350.0	375.0	400.0	Input			
24		Total assets		550.0	625.0	750.0	=SUM(F21:F23)			
25										
26		Revolver		0.0	0.0	75.4	=-MIN(F36,0)			
27		Debt		320.0	350.0	340.0	Input			
28		Common stock		50.0	100.0	100.0	Input			
29		Retained earnings		180.0	175.0	234.6	=E29+F17			
30		Total liabs and equity		550.0	625.0	750.0	=SUM(F26:F29)			
31										
32		Balance sheet check		0.0	0.0	0.0	=F30-F24			
33										
34		Assets without excess cash			625.0	750.0	=SUM(F22:F23)			
35		Liabs, equity without revolver			656.9	674.6	=SUM(F27:F28,E29+F14)		3	
36		Excess cash (revolver) as calculated			31.9	(75.4)	=F35-F34			
37										

9.5.2 Changes for Partially Dividending Out Excess Cash

We can set the model so that it dividends out less than 100% of excess cash. (Fig. 9-8): The steps are:

1. Add an input cell to specify the percentage factor, 75.0% in this case. In the illustration, this is in Cell C16.
2. Multiply Cell C16 into the dividends line in Row 16.

3. Multiply (1 minus Cell C16) into the excess cash line in the balance sheet, in Row 21.
4. The balancing formula in Row 34 remains the same as in Figure 9-7.

FIGURE 9-8

Partially Dividending Out Excess Cash

	A	B	C	D	E	F	G	H	I
1				Hist	Proj	Proj			
2		INCOME STATEMENT		Year 1	Year 2	Year 3	Formulas in column F		
3		Revenue		160.0	200.0	390.0	Input		
4		COGS		80.0	90.0	190.0	Input		
5		SGA		29.0	45.0	80.0	Input		
6		EBIT		51.0	65.0	120.0	=F3-SUM(F4:F5)		
7									
8		Interest: Excess cash	3.0%	0.0	0.0	0.2	=$C$8*E21		
9		Interest: Revolver	6.0%	0.0	0.0	0.0	=$C$9*E26		
10		Interest: Debt	6.0%	19.2	20.1	20.7	=$C$10*AVERAGE(E27:F27)		
11		EBT		31.8	44.9	99.5	=F6+F8-F9-F10		
12									
13		Tax	40.0%	12.7	18.0	39.8	=$C$13*F11		
14		Net income		19.1	26.9	59.7	=F11-F13		
15		(1)	Percent dividended						
16		Dividends	75.0%	0.0	24.0	0.0	=MAX(F36,0)*$C$16	(2)	
17		Net to retained earnings		19.1	3.0	59.7	=F14-F16		
18									
19				Hist	Proj	Proj			
20		BALANCE SHEET		Year 1	Year 2	Year 3			
21		Excess cash		0.0	8.0	0.0	=MAX(F36,0)*(1-$C$16)	(3)	
22		Current assets		200.0	250.0	350.0	Input		
23		Long-term assets		350.0	375.0	400.0	Input		
24		Total assets		550.0	633.0	750.0	=SUM(F21:F23)		
25									
26		Revolver		0.0	0.0	67.3	=-MIN(F36,0)		
27		Debt		320.0	350.0	340.0	Input		
28		Common stock		50.0	100.0	100.0	Input		
29		Retained earnings		180.0	183.0	242.7	=E29+F17		
30		Total liabs and equity		550.0	633.0	750.0	=SUM(F26:F29)		
31									
32		Balance sheet check		0.0	0.0	0.0	=F30-F24		
33									
34		Assets without excess cash			625.0	750.0	=SUM(F22:F23)	(4)	
35		Liabs, equity without revolver			656.9	682.7	=SUM(F27:F28,E29+F14)		
36		Excess cash (revolver) as calculated			31.9	(67.3)	=F35-F34		
37									

CHAPTER 10

Preparing to Build a Full Model

We have explored balancing mechanisms, circular references, and variations on the plugs. Now let's start to build a full model.

10.1 EXPANDING FROM THE PILOT MODEL

The pilot model has worked well as a simplified model to test the modeling design. From this core design, we can add more accounts to the model without affecting its balancing mechanisms. The following lists the typical accounts for a full model for companies in the industrial/manufacturing sector. Other sectors (financial institutions, insurance, etc.) have different business flows, and so their models have different categories of accounts in all statements. In those other types of models, the balancing principles remain the same, however.

As we saw in Chapter 7 in developing the cash flow statement for Pilot Model No. 2 (Section 7.4), selected income statement and changes from almost all balance sheet accounts appear again in the cash flow statement. In the following listing of the income statement and balance sheet accounts, the notations to the right note where each item will appear again among the three sections of the cash flow statement: CFO = cash flow from operations; CFI = cash flow from investments; CFF = cash flow from financing. Each notated income statement item appears as it is in the cash flow statement, but it is the *change* in each balance sheet account (between each current and the prior period) that appears in the cash flow statement. Section 10.4 shows the cash flow statement that is the result.

Items in bold are sums. Italicized items are informational rows (such as margin percentages).

10.2 A FULL INCOME STATEMENT

Following is a listing of the chart of accounts for a typical industrial/manufacturing company's income statement.

Revenue	
Cost of goods sold	
Gross profit	
Gross margin	
SGA	
Other operating expenses	
EBITDA	
EBITDA margin	
Depreciation	CFO
Amortization of intangibles	CFO
EBIT	
EBIT margin	
Non-operating expenses	
Gain (loss) on asset sales	
Interest income	
Interest expense	
Earnings before taxes	
Provision for taxes	
Equity in earnings of affiliates	CFO

Minority interest in earnings	CFO
Net income	CFO
Net margin	
Extraordinary expense	CFO
Preferred dividends	CFF
Net available to common	
Common dividends	CFF
Net to retained earnings	

10.3 A FULL BALANCE SHEET

The following is a listing of the chart of accounts for a typical industrial/manufacturing company's balance sheet. Cash and excess cash are the end results of the total flows from the three sections. The change in retained earnings does not appear in the cash flow statement because this is equal to the net income before dividends from the income statement, which already appears as the first line in the cash flow statement.

10.3.1 Assets

Excess cash	[Result of total flows]
Operating cash	CFO
Short-term investments	CFI
Accounts receivable	CFO
Inventory	CFO
Other current assets	CFO
Current assets	
Net PPE	CFI
Investments in affiliates	CFI
Intangibles	CFI
Long-term assets	CFO
Total assets	

10.3.2 Liabilities

Revolver	[Result of total flows]
Notes payable	CFF
Accounts payable	CFO
Other current liabilities	CFO
Current liabilities	
Long-term debt 1	CFF
Long-term debt 2	CFF
Long-term debt 3	CFF
Long-term liabilities	CFO
Total liabilities	

10.3.3 Minority Interest

Minority interest is a sort of liability and sort of equity. It usually is listed in its own section in the right hand side of the balance sheet, between the total liabilities and the total shareholders' equity, as we are doing here. I have also seen it listed as part of total liabilities.

Minority Interest	CFF

10.3.4 Shareholders' Equity

Preferred stock	CFF
Common stock	CFF
Retained earnings	[does not appear]
Other equity account	CFF
Total shareholders' equity	

10.4 THE CASH FLOW STATEMENT

The cash flow statement tracks the use of cash. In this way, it can be used as a way to balance the balance sheet. Alternately, if the balancing is done through the balance sheet only, then the cash flow statement can be considered as a reconciliation table between the inflow or outflow of cash from income statement and sources and uses of cash on the balance sheet.

All accounts on the balance sheet, except the retained earnings, appear in the cash flow statement. Only several accounts from the income statement appear. These are: depreciation, amortization of intangibles and other non-cash expenses, net income, and other lines that appear below the net income in the income statement, including dividends.

The capital expenditures (or "capex") line appears in the cash flow statement only. In the model we are building, the input of this will appear as part of the inputs for the balance sheet Net PPE, as capex is most closely associated with this account.

The cash flow typically uses the convention that uses a positive value to indicate a source of cash, and a negative value to show a use of cash. An account that shows the label "(Incr) decr" means that an increase in that account is equivalent to a use of cash, and a decrease is a source (e.g., the accounts receivable account). Likewise, "Incr (decr)" means that an increase is a source of cash, and a decrease is a use (e.g., the debt account).

10.4.1 Cash from Operating Activities

Net income
Depreciation
Amortization of intangibles
(Equity in earnings of affiliates)
Minority interest in earnings
(Incr) decr in Deferred tax assets
Incr (decr) in Deferred tax liabilities
Extraordinary income (expense)

(Incr) decr in Accounts receivable
(Incr) decr in Inventory
(Incr) decr in Other current assets
Incr (decr) in Accounts payable

Incr (decr) in Other payables
Incr (decr) in Other current liabilities

(Incr) decr in Net working capital
(Incr) decr in Other long-term assets
Incr (decr) in Other long-term liabilities
Cash flow from operating activities

10.4.2 Cash from Investing Activities

(Incr) decr in Short-term investments
(Capital expenditures)
Dividends received from Investments in affiliates
(Incr) decr in Investments
Other (Incr) decr in Goodwill
Other (Incr) decr in Intangibles
Cash flow from investing activities

10.4.3 Cash from Financing Activities

Incr (decr) in Notes payable
Incr (decr) in Long-term debt 1
Incr (decr) in Long-term debt 2
Incr (decr) in Long-term debt 3
Incr (decr) in Long-term debt 4
Incr (decr) in Long-term debt 5
Incr (decr) in Subordinated debt
Incr (decr) in Subordinated debt 2
Other Incr (decr) in Minority interest
Incr (decr) in Preferred stock
Incr (decr) in Common stock
Incr (decr) in Other equity account
(Preferred dividends)
(Common dividends)
Cash Flow from Financing Activities

Total Cash Flow

10.5 RATIOS AND OTHER OUTPUT PAGES

Once the three financial statements are fully modeled, the other outputs of the model can be easily developed. Since all the results are now available from the financial statements, ratios of every type can be developed.

We can also add other modules, such as discounted cash flow ("DCF') valuation calculations into the model, that reference into the income statement, balance sheet, and the capital expenditures assumptions.

10.6 SAME SHEET OR DIFFERENT SHEETS

As we build out the model's various parts, we can put the various parts of the model on separate sheets, or all on one sheet, or any combination in between. There is no hard and fast rule about this; the final layout should be what works best for you and the colleagues with whom you are sharing the model. It would be natural, however, to plan on having multiple sheets as the model grows bigger, in keeping with the idea of building the model in modules (or sheets).

10.7 LAYOUT

In addition to including more accounts, but we also have to consider the layout for the different types of inputs. Because Excel's sheets are infinitely changeable, there is literally an unlimited number of possible layouts. Nevertheless, as a starting point, the layout should have these attributes:

- There should be room for historical data and forecast assumptions.
- Historical and forecast inputs should be in close proximity, to minimize navigation steps and provide easy visual reference.
- Forecast entries should allow for both hard-coded entries and assumptions based on other measures, such as growth or margin percentages.

- Performance trends should be visible so that users can have a basis for making forecasts.
- Scenarios can be accommodated.
- The layout helps guide the user in the data input process.

The layout that I will use in building our model is one approach, one that I have liked. This does not mean that it is *the* only way to do it. You may find that the inclusion of rows that calculate results right next to the input is distracting; or that the output being on a separate sheet from the input is not to your liking. By all means, develop your own model according to what best suits your needs.

10.7.1 Testing Layout No. 1

Figure 10-1 shows one layout that is often seen. This layout, shown here with just the revenue line as an example, uses two different input areas for the historical and projected numbers. The input entries are shown in bold.

1. We begin with the historical data on the top left. Inputs are entered here.

FIGURE 10-1

Layout No. 1

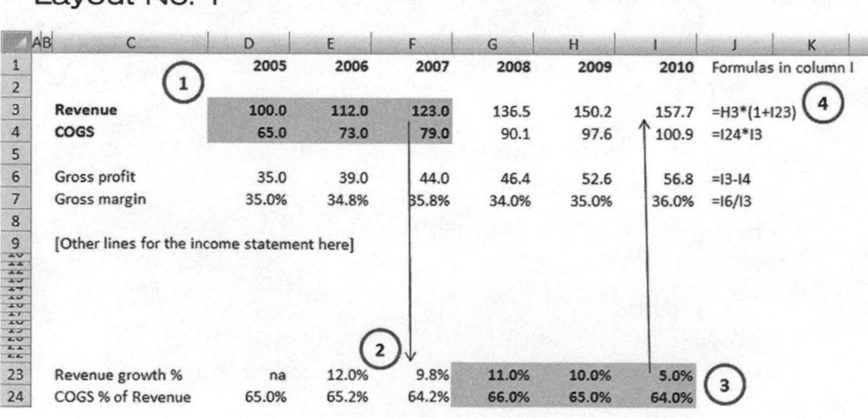

	C	D	E	F	G	H	I	J
1		2005	2006	2007	2008	2009	2010	Formulas in column I
2								
3	**Revenue**	**100.0**	**112.0**	**123.0**	136.5	150.2	157.7	=H3*(1+I23)
4	**COGS**	**65.0**	**73.0**	**79.0**	90.1	97.6	100.9	=I24*I3
5								
6	Gross profit	35.0	39.0	44.0	46.4	52.6	56.8	=I3-I4
7	Gross margin	35.0%	34.8%	35.8%	34.0%	35.0%	36.0%	=I6/I3
8								
9	[Other lines for the income statement here]							
23	Revenue growth %	na	12.0%	9.8%	**11.0%**	**10.0%**	**5.0%**	
24	COGS % of Revenue	65.0%	65.2%	64.2%	**66.0%**	**65.0%**	**64.0%**	

TABLE 10–1

Criteria	Layout No. 1
Historical and forecast	Yes
In close proximity	No
Hard-coded and percentage inputs	No
Performance trends visible	Yes
Layout helps the user	No

2. The model then calculates the implied growth from the historical data (bottom left). The user can review this output.
3. The user enters his or her own input (bottom right, for the first projected year).
4. The model calculates the result (top right).

As we build up the accounts for the income statement, not to mention the balance sheet, this layout gets bigger. At some point, the forecast input section could be one or two screens down, and far away from the result it produces. How well does this layout stack up against our criteria (Table 10-1)?

TABLE 10–2

Criteria	Layout No. 1	Layout No. 2
Historical and forecast	Yes	Yes
In close proximity	No	Yes
Hard-coded and percentage inputs	No	No
Performance trends visible	Yes	Yes
Layout helps the user	No	Yes

FIGURE 10-2

Layout No. 2

	AB C	D	E	F	G	H	I	J K
1		2005	2006	2007	2008	2009	2010	Formulas in column I
2								
3	Revenue	100.0	112.0	123.0	136.5	150.2	157.7	=H3*(1+I4)
4	Growth %	na	12.0%	9.8%	11.0%	10.0%	5.0%	
5								
6	COGS	65.0	73.0	79.0	90.1	97.6	100.9	=I7*I3
7	% of Revenue	65.0%	65.2%	64.2%	66.0%	65.0%	64.0%	
8								
9	Gross profit	35.0	39.0	44.0	46.4	52.6	56.8	=I3-I6
10	Gross margin	35.0%	34.8%	35.8%	34.0%	35.0%	36.0%	=I9/I3

10.7.2 Testing Layout No. 2

Layout No. 2 (Fig. 10-2) looks at each account as a complete modular unit, and in this way the physical and visual proximity of the inputs is much improved. This approach also makes adding additional accounts much more manageable.

In comparison with Layout No. 1, this satisfies more of the criteria we set out earlier (Table 10-2). However, it does not satisfy the criterion of being able to use either hard-coded numbers or a relational input (i.e., a growth rate, or a margin rate, etc.). We want the option of being able to enter hard-coded numbers for the forecast years because the model may be used to replicate the forecast already created in another model. The easiest way to do that would be to enter those forecast numbers directly into the model.

10.7.3 Testing Layout No. 3

This layout (Fig. 10-3) expands on the input lines for each account, and fulfills all criteria in our table.

10.7.3.1 The revenue input layout

Let's look at the pros and cons of the layout in detail (Fig. 10-4).

> Row 3: This is a row for hard-coded entries (Fig. 10-5), and spans both the historical and forecast years. Why the forecast years? Because the model may be used to replicate the

FIGURE 10-3

Layout No. 3

	C	D	E	F	G	H	I	J
1		2005	2006	2007	2008	2009	2010	Formulas in column I
2								
3	Revenue	100.0	112.0	123.0				
4	Growth %				10.0%	11.0%	12.0%	
5	Revenue	100.0	112.0	123.0	135.3	150.2	168.2	=IF(I3,I3,H5*(1+I4))
6	Growth %	na	12.0%	9.8%	10.0%	11.0%	12.0%	=IF(H5,I5/H5-1,0)
7								
8	COGS	65.0	74.0	83.0				
9	% of Revenue				68.0%	67.0%	65.0%	
10	COGS	65.0	74.0	83.0	92.0	100.6	109.3	=IF(I8,I8,I9*I$5)
11	% of Revenue	65.0%	66.1%	67.5%	68.0%	67.0%	65.0%	=IF(I$5,I10/I$5,0)
12	Gross profit	35.0	38.0	40.0	43.3	49.6	58.9	=I5-I10
13	Gross margin	35.0%	33.9%	32.5%	32.0%	33.0%	35.0%	=IF(I$5,I12/I$5,0)

FIGURE 10-4

The Revenue Section with Inputs

	C	D	E	F	G	H	I	J
1		2005	2006	2007	2008	2009	2010	
2								
3	**Revenue**	100.0	112.0	123.0				
4	Growth %				10.0%	11.0%	12.0%	
5	Revenue	100.0	112.0	123.0	135.3	150.2	168.2	**=IF(I3,I3,H5*(1+I4))**
6	Growth %	na	12.0%	9.8%	10.0%	11.0%	12.0%	**=IF(H5,I5/H5-1,0)**

FIGURE 10-5

Hard-Coded Forecast Inputs

	C	D	E	F	G	H	I	J
1		2005	2006	2007	2008	2009	2010	
2								
3	**Revenue**	100.0	112.0	123.0	135.3	150.2	168.2	
4	Growth %							
5	Revenue	100.0	112.0	123.0	135.3	150.2	168.2	**=IF(I3,I3,H5*(1+I4))**
6	Growth %	na	12.0%	9.8%	10.0%	11.0%	12.0%	**=IF(H5,I5/H5-1,0)**

forecast already created in another model. The easiest way to do that would be to enter those forecast numbers directly into the model. Another use of this is that the number of historical years can be expanded easily simply by changing the starting year to an earlier number; a "forecast" column will then serve as a "historical" column.

TABLE 10-3

Criteria	Layout No. 1	Layout No. 2	Layout No. 3
Historical and forecast	Yes	Yes	Yes
In close proximity	No	Yes	Yes
Hard-coded and percentage inputs	No	No	Yes
Performance trends visible	Yes	Yes	Yes
Layout helps the user	No	Yes	Yes

Row 4: This is a row for growth percentage assumptions. The inputs start on column 4, as there is no need for such entries in the three historical years.

Row 5: This is the row that shows the final revenue numbers. For the historical years, this row references the hard-coded inputs only. For the forecast years, this row has a formula that has an IF statement. The formula first reads the top row (hard-coded entries). If the row is a 0 or a blank, then the formula will calculate the revenue based on the prior year's revenue number multiplied by 1 + growth rate.

The test IF(I3, . . . in Cell I6 is the equivalent of =IF(I3<>0. The "<>0" can be dropped when writing formulas like this.

Row 6: This is a calculation that shows the growth rates across all the years (except the first year as there is no "prior" year). Once the historical data are entered, this row shows the historical trend and can inform the user on the appropriate growth rates to use for the forecast assumptions.

Additional advantages (Table 10-3):

- As seen in Figure 10-6, the layout also gives an immediate feedback of what the final result will be. When a 10% growth assumption for the Year 2008 is entered, the model shows that the revenue forecast is 135.3 (Cell G5).
- We can add a visual indication into the hierarchical order of the inputs by indenting the growth % input,

FIGURE 10-6

Mix-and-Match in Input Assumptions

	AB	C	D	E	F	G	H	I	J	K
1			2005	2006	2007	2008	2009	2010		
2										
3		**Revenue**	100.0	112.0	123.0		180.0			
4		Growth %				10.0%		12.0%		
5		Revenue	100.0	112.0	123.0	135.3	180.0	201.6	=IF(I3,I3,H5*(1+I4))	
6		Growth %	na	12.0%	9.8%	10.0%	33.0%	12.0%	=IF(H5,I5/H5-1,0)	

so indicate to the user that this row is subordinate to the first row. (Where we may have three input lines, the third line is indented even more.)

- The IF statement for the two layers of inputs provides a natural hierarchical system of using the inputs. This layout is simple and does not involve additional switches or toggles.
- This layout allows different assumptions for different years, e.g., 10% growth in one year and 12% in another.
- This layout allows a mix-and-match approach to the inputs: percentage growth assumptions in one year, a hard-coded number for another, and any combination thereof. Note in the illustration (Fig. 10-6) that the 12% growth in the final year (column I) now acts on a base of 180 to produce 201.6.

10.7.4 The COGS and SGA Inputs Layout

Figure 10-7 shows how we can continue to expand this output layout as we add the cost of goods sold (COGS) and Sales, General, and Administrative (SGA) entries. Rather than growth assumptions, COGS and SGA assumptions typically use a percent of revenue approach. Accordingly, the forecast output formulas (Rows 10 and 17) reflect this.

The gross profit line and gross margin (Rows 12 and 13) can be added to show the results as we proceed down the income statement.

FIGURE 10-7

The Revenue and COGS Inputs

	A B	C	D	E	F	G	H	I	J	K
1			**2005**	**2006**	**2007**	**2008**	**2009**	**2010**		
2										
3		**Revenue**	**100.0**	**112.0**	**123.0**					
4		Growth %				**10.0%**	**11.0%**	**12.0%**		
5		Revenue	100.0	112.0	123.0	135.3	150.2	168.2	**=IF(I3,I3,H5*(1+I4))**	
6		Growth %	na	12.0%	9.8%	10.0%	11.0%	12.0%	**=IF(H5,I5/H5-1,0)**	
7										
8		**COGS**	**65.0**	**74.0**	**83.0**					
9		% of Revenue				**68.0%**	**67.0%**	**65.0%**		
10		COGS	65.0	74.0	83.0	92.0	100.6	109.3	**=IF(I8,I8,I9*I$5)**	
11		% of Revenue	65.0%	66.1%	67.5%	68.0%	67.0%	65.0%	**=IF(I$5,I10/I$5,0)**	
12		**Gross profit**	35.0	38.0	40.0	43.3	49.6	58.9	**=I5-I10**	
13		Gross margin	35.0%	33.9%	32.5%	32.0%	33.0%	35.0%	**=IF(I$5,I12/I$5,0)**	
14										
15		**SGA**	**10.0**	**11.0**	**14.0**					
16		% of Revenue				**11.0%**	**11.0%**	**12.0%**		
17		SGA	10.0	11.0	14.0	14.9	16.5	20.2	**=IF(I15,I15,I16*I$5)**	
18		% of Revenue	10.0%	9.8%	11.4%	11.0%	11.0%	12.0%	**=IF(I$5,I17/I$5,0)**	

10.7.5 Some Excel Notes

The COGS section (Rows 8–11) can be used as a template for the SGA section and other input sections that look to a percentage of revenue inputs. Note the formula for Row 11 (% of Revenue) has an absolute reference to Row 5 (Revenue). When this formula is copied to other rows, this reference remains fixed. Indeed, to add the SGA section, we can copy the COGS section as a whole. At the new location (Rows 15–18), we change the labels to read SGA, and the formulas work without any other modifications.

10.7.6 The Rest of the Income Statement, and the Balance Sheet

This approach can be replicated to all the other inputs in the income statement, with some variation for particular accounts (such as the income tax calculation), as well as the balance sheet inputs.

10.7.7 The Number of Forecast Years

The number of forecast years can be extended to the right on the worksheet. Excel's limit for columns is well beyond the needs of reasonable forecasting: Excel 2003 has 256 columns across each worksheet; Excel 2007 has 16,384.

10.8 FORMATTING THE OUTPUT

As we expand each account's input section into multiple rows, it becomes clear that the input section itself can no longer be used as the final output section—there are simply too many lines. What we can do is to create separate output pages for the each of the three financial statements and other sheets for ratios and other types of

FIGURE 10–8

A Separate Output Sheet References the Input Sheet

	AB C	D	E	F	G	H	I	J K
1		2005	2006	2007	2008	2009	2010	
2								
3	**Revenue**	**100.0**	**112.0**	**123.0**				
4	Growth %				**10.0%**	**11.0%**	**12.0%**	
5	Revenue	100.0	112.0	123.0	135.3	150.2	168.2	**=IF(I3,I3,H5*(1+I4))**
6	Growth %	na	12.0%	9.8%	10.0%	11.0%	12.0%	**=IF(H5,I5/H5-1,0)**
7								
8	**COGS**	**65.0**	**74.0**	**83.0**				
9	% of Revenue				**68.0%**	**67.0%**	**65.0%**	
10	COGS	65.0	74.0	83.0	92.0	100.6	109.3	**=IF(I8,I8,I9*I$5)**
11	% of Revenue	65.0%	66.1%	67.5%	68.0%	67.0%	65.0%	**=IF(I$5,I10/I$5,0)**
12	**Gross profit**	35.0	38.0	40.0	43.3	49.6	58.9	**=I5-I10**
13	Gross margin	35.0%	33.9%	32.5%	32.0%	33.0%	35.0%	**=IF(I$5,I12/I$5,0)**
14								
15	**SGA**	**10.0**	**11.0**	**14.0**				
16	% of Revenue				**11.0%**	**11.0%**	**12.0%**	
17	SGA	10.0	11.0	14.0	14.9	16.5	20.2	**=IF(I15,I15,I16*I$5)**
18	% of Revenue	10.0%	9.8%	11.4%	11.0%	11.0%	12.0%	**=IF(I$5,I17/I$5,0)**

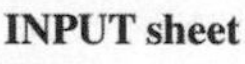

INPUT sheet

	AB C	D	E	F	G	H	I	J K
1		2005	2006	2007	2008	2009	2010	
2								
3	Revenue	100.0	112.0	123.0	135.3	150.2	168.2	**=Input!I5**
4	COGS	65.0	74.0	83.0	92.0	100.6	109.3	**=Input!I10**
5	**Gross profit**	35.0	38.0	40.0	43.3	49.6	58.9	**=I3-I4**
6	Gross margin	35.0%	33.9%	32.5%	32.0%	33.0%	35.0%	**=IF(I$3,I5/I$3,0)**
7								
8	SGA	10.0	11.0	14.0	14.9	16.5	20.2	**=Input!I17**

INCOME STATEMENT OUTPUT sheet

output (Fig. 10-8). Each output sheet references only the calculated results for a neater output look.

10.9 THE INPUT SHEET AS A COMPLETE MODELING ENGINE

In this layout, we can construct the historical and forecast numbers for all the accounts. Chapter 7's first pilot model shows that we can balance the balance sheet using only the income statement and the balance sheet. With that in mind, the input sheet has all the necessary parts to make it a full working modeling "engine." This engine sheet in turn drives the rest of the model's sheets. The next chapter, Chapter 11, shows the layout of the income statement and balance sheet for such an engine sheet.

CHAPTER 11

Building an Integrated Financial Model: Part 1

Let's build an integrated financial model. By the end of this chapter, you will have the framework of a working financial model using the income statement and the balance sheet, with the balancing being done on the balance sheet. The next chapter covers the development of the cash flow statement, and how to link the results of that statement for the balancing of the balance sheet.

11.1 SOME NOTES ON MODELING DISCIPLINE

At the risk of sounding overly fastidious, let me present some points to follow as you being a full-scale model.

11.1.1 The Normal Style

Excel has a default format in all its sheets. This format is a style, and is a global format that applies to all parts of the workbook. The default style is called Normal, and the default format for numbers is "General." The General format is an "intelligent" format in that it will apply a format to a cell based on what has been entered into it. Thus, if you enter 5.0%, that cell now carries the percent format, with one decimal place. Once the General format has done this, the cell now carries that format.

Although the General style is convenient for small models, it is less ideal for larger models, in which we want better control over what appears on the screen and output. For this reason, set the number format Normal style as described in Section 11.2.

11.1.2 The Percent Style

Likewise for the Percent Style, set it with the formatting code described in Section 11.2.

11.1.3 Start Formulas with =, Not +

Lotus 1-2-3, a predecessor spreadsheet software that was popular in the 1980s, began its formula with the plus (+) sign. Excel of course starts its formulas with the equal (=) sign. Nevertheless, I have seen formulas in models that were written using + as the starting point, with the result that the cell carries the formula that looks, say, like this:

=+C5

There is really no reason for this, and it adds to visual clutter. It also means an additional key stroke, since the + sign is a Shift key and the = sign. It is better to just hit the = sign.

11.1.4 Avoid Summing Blank Rows

When summing a range where there are blank rows, it is tempting to put a SUM formula that covers the whole range, including the blank rows (Column G in Fig. 11-1). As a matter of discipline, you should sum only those rows that have numbers to sum (Column C in Fig. 11-1).

11.1.5 The Line for Totals Is the Border at the Top of the Cell

In Figure 11-1, there is a line between Row 8 and the total in Row 9. You should make a habit that such a line should be the border at the *top* of the total cell, and not the border at the bottom of the last row in the range to be summed. In this way, if you add an additional row before the total, the line would still be correctly positioned.

FIGURE 11-1

SUM Only Rows with Numbers

	A	B	C	D	E	F	G	H	I	J
1										
2			DO				DON'T			
3										
4		Net Income	764.0				764.0			
5										
6		Depreciation	156.0				156.0			
7		Amortization of Intangibles	49.0				49.0			
8		(Incr) Decr in Working Capital	(128.0)				(128.0)			
9		Cash Flow from Operations	841.0	=C4+SUM(C6:C8)			841.0	=SUM(G4:G8)		
10								This sums the blank Row 5		
11										

11.2 LAYOUT

The model we are building has room 3 historical years, followed by 3 forecast years. The formulas for the historical columns will be simpler, since they will only be hard-coded inputs representing historical data. The forecast years will be more complicated, as they will have to work with multiple inputs (hard-coded numbers and percentage assumptions).

If you want to follow suit, start with a new Excel workbook, and create 6 sheets. Set each sheet to have the following format:

- Columns A and B: width of 2. These extra columns will be used for some interesting bells and whistles features for printing.
- Column C: width of 25
- Columns D and E: width of 4. These additional columns will be helpful in holding additional information that you may need.
- Set default column width to 10
- Set the Normal style to #,##0.0_);(#,##0.0);@_)
- The font in the Normal style is Calibri 10 point.
- Set the Percent style to 0.0%_);(0.0%);@_)

The cells that are the input cells are marked as pale yellow. I have used the lightest yellow on the color palette, modified so that it is a shade lighter than the default color. Feel free to choose the color that suits you best.

In the illustrations, the gridlines have been removed to minimize visual clutter. All numbers used in the illustrations are "dummy" numbers for illustrative purposes only, and do not reflect any real company's numbers.

11.3 HOW TO READ THE TABLES

Each section of the model will be illustrated first with a screen capture, followed by a table that has row-by-row descriptions of the illustration. For example, Table 11-1 shows a typical listing:

TABLE 11-1

Illustrative Sample

Row	Label in Column C	Formula in Column F (copy to G and H)	Formula in Column I (copy to J and K)
6	INCOME STATEMENT	*=DATE(YEAR(F6), MONTH(F6)+13,0)* *This formula is for Column G, as Cell F6 is the input cell for the staring column's fiscal year end*	=DATE(YEAR(H6), MONTH(H6)+13,0)
7			
8	Revenues	Input	Input
9	Percent growth %	*=IF(F10,G8/F10–1,0)* *This is a growth formula in Column G. Column contains only the notation "na" (not applicable) as there is no growth to measure for the first column.*	
10	Revenues	=F8	=IF(ISNUMBER(I8),I8, H10*(1+I9))
11			

The table has the following columns, reading from left to right:

1. The row number.
2. The label for Column C for that row.
3. The formula for Column F for that row, which should be copied to Columns G and H. Columns F to H are the historical years' columns.

   However, for some rows, the *italicized* and boxed formula means the formula is for Column G (i.e., **not** Column F). This should then be copied to column H. This occurs on those rows where the formula is not applicable for Column F.
4. The formula for Column I for that row, which should be copied to columns J and K. Columns I to K are the forecast years' columns.

   Once you have completed the model, you can copy Column K out further to create as many additional forecast years' columns as you need.

If the table is blank and is shaded gray, this means the row is an empty spacing row.

If the table has a blank row and is not shaded gray, this means that the row is an input row.

This format applies to all tables in this chapter.

11.4 THE INCOME STATEMENT INPUTS

We start with the income statement, shown section by section. After each screen capture, the formulas are listed for the two parts of the model: the historical years and the forecast years.

Use the screen captures to check your own formatting.

The Input sheet has additional lines for listing assumptions, so its format is not meant to be the final presentation-ready format. For this, we will add a separate output sheet with just the final numbers and without the additional lines for the assumption inputs.

11.4.1 Income Statement Revenue to EBIT (Rows 1–37)

FIGURE 11-2

Revenue to EBIT Input Layout

	C	F	G	H	I	J	K
1	**First Corporation**						
2							
3							
4							
5					**Proj**	**Proj**	**Proj**
6	**INCOME STATEMENT**	**Dec-05**	**Dec-06**	**Dec-07**	**Dec-08**	**Dec-09**	**Dec-10**
7							
8	Revenues	825.0	900.0	1,000.0			
9	Percent growth %	na	9.1%	11.1%	10.0%	10.0%	10.0%
10	Revenues	825.0	900.0	1,000.0	1,100.0	1,210.0	1,331.0
11							
12	COGS	450.0	490.0	550.0			
13	As % revenues	54.5%	54.4%	55.0%	55.0%	55.0%	55.0%
14	COGS	450.0	490.0	550.0	605.0	665.5	732.1
15	**Gross profit**	**375.0**	**410.0**	**450.0**	**495.0**	**544.5**	**599.0**
16	Gross margin	45.5%	45.6%	45.0%	45.0%	45.0%	45.0%
17							
18	SGA	125.0	135.0	150.0			
19	As % revenues	15.2%	15.0%	15.0%	15.0%	15.0%	15.0%
20	SGA	125.0	135.0	150.0	165.0	181.5	199.7
21							
22	Operating expenses	25.0	28.0	30.0			
23	As % revenues	3.0%	3.1%	3.0%	3.0%	3.0%	3.0%
24	Operating expenses	25.0	28.0	30.0	33.0	36.3	39.9
25	**EBITDA**	**225.0**	**247.0**	**270.0**	**297.0**	**326.7**	**359.4**
26	EBITDA margin	27.3%	27.4%	27.0%	27.0%	27.0%	27.0%
27							
28	Depreciation	60.0	75.0	80.0			
29	As % revenues	7.3%	8.3%	8.0%			
30	As % prior net fixed assets	na	8.6%	8.4%	8.5%	8.5%	8.5%
31	Depreciation	60.0	75.0	80.0	85.0	91.8	102.5
32							
33	Amortization of intangibles	4.0	4.0	4.0	4.0	4.0	4.0
34	Amortization of intangibles	4.0	4.0	4.0	4.0	4.0	4.0
35	**EBIT**	**161.0**	**168.0**	**186.0**	**208.0**	**230.9**	**252.9**
36	EBIT margin	19.5%	18.7%	18.6%	18.9%	19.1%	19.0%
37							

TABLE 11-2

Revenue to EBIT Input Formulas

	Label in Column C	Formula in Column F (copy to G and H)	Formula in Column I (copy to J and K)
6	INCOME STATEMENT	Input date in Column F Then enter this formula in Column G: *=DATE(YEAR(F6), MONTH(F6)+13,0)*	=DATE(YEAR(H6), MONTH(H6)+13,0)
7			
8	Revenues		
9	Percent growth %	Enter "na" in Column F Then enter this formula in Column G: *=IF(F10,G8/F10–1,0)*	
10	Revenues	=F8	=IF(ISNUMBER(I8),I8, H10*(1+I9))
11			
12	COGS		
13	As % revenues	=IF(F$10,F12/F$10,0)	
14	COGS	=IF(F12,F12,F13*F$10)	=IF(I12,I12,I13*I$10)
15	Gross profit	=F10–F14	=I10–I14
16	Gross margin	=IF(F10,F15/F10,0)	=IF(I10,I15/I10,0)
17			
18	SGA		
19	As % revenues	=IF(F$10,F18/F$10,0)	
20	SGA	=F18	=IF(I18,I18,I19*I$10)
21			
22	Operating expenses		
23	As % revenues	=IF(F$10,F22/F$10,0)	
24	Operating expenses	=F22	=IF(I22,I22,I23*I$10)
25	EBITDA	=F15–F20–F24	=I15–I20–I24
26	EBITDA margin	=IF(F$10,F25/F$10,0)	=IF(I$10,I25/I$10,0)
27			
28	Depreciation		
29	As % revenues	=IF(F$10,F28/F$10,0)	
30	As % prior net fixed assets	*=IF(F132,G31/F132,0)*	

(*continued on next page*)

TABLE 11-2 (CONTINUED)

	Label in Column C	Formula in Column F (copy to G and H)	Formula in Column I (copy to J and K)
		Formula for Column G	
31	Depreciation	=F28	=IF(I28,I28, IF(I29,I29*I10,I30*H I32))
32			
33	Amortization of intangibles		
34	Amortization of intangibles	=F33	=I33
35	EBIT	=F25–F31–F34	=I25–I31–I34
36	EBIT margin	=IF(F$10,F35/F$10,0)	=IF(I$10,I35/I$10,0)
37			

11.4.2 Non-Operating Expense to Earnings Before Taxes (Rows 38–62)

FIGURE 11-3

Non-Operating Expenses to EBT Input Layout

	C	F	G	H	I	J	K
38	Non-oper expenses	10.0	10.0	8.0	10.0	11.0	11.0
39	As % revenues	1.2%	1.1%	0.8%			
40	Non-oper expenses	10.0	10.0	8.0	10.0	11.0	11.0
41							
42	Gain (loss) on asset sales						
43	Gross proceeds from asset sales						
44	Book value of assets sold						
45	Gain (loss) on asset sales	0.0	0.0	0.0	0.0	0.0	0.0
46							
47	Interest income	3.0	4.9	5.5			
48	Excess cash				0.0	5.0	3.2
49	Cash				4.0	4.0	4.0
50	Marketable securities				1.7	1.7	1.8
51	Interest income	3.0	4.9	5.5	5.7	10.7	9.0
52							
53	Interest expense	50.0	50.0	49.4			
54	Revolver				0.0	0.0	0.0
55	ST notes				1.4	1.4	1.4
56	Debt 1				15.0	15.0	15.0
57	Debt 2				14.5	14.5	14.5
58	Debt 3				8.8	8.8	8.8
59	Interest expense	50.0	50.0	49.4	39.7	39.7	39.7
60	**Earnings before taxes**	**104.0**	**112.9**	**134.1**	**164.0**	**190.9**	**211.1**
61	EBT margin	12.6%	12.5%	13.4%	14.9%	15.8%	15.9%
62							

TABLE 11-3

Non-Operating Expenses to EBT Formulas

Row	Label in Column C	Formula in Column F (copy to G and H)	Formula in Column I (copy to J and K)
38	Non-oper expenses		
39	As % revenues	=IF(F$10,F38/F$10,0)	
40	Non-oper expenses	=F38	=IF(I38,I38,I39*I$10)
41			
42	Gain (loss) on asset sales		
43	Gross proceeds from asset sales		
44	Book value of assets sold		
45	Gain (loss) on asset sales	=F42	=IF(I42,I42,I43–I44)
46			
47	Interest income		
48	Excess cash		=I97
49	Cash		=I103
50	Marketable securities		=I109
51	Interest income	=F47	=IF(I47,I47,SUM(I48:I50))
52			
53	Interest expense		
54	Revolver		=I152
55	ST notes		=I157
56	Debt A		=I173
57	Debt B		=I179
58	Debt C		=I185
59	Interest expense	=IF(F53,F53,SUM(F54:F58))	=IF(I53,I53,SUM(I54:I58))
60	EBT	=F35–F40+F45+F51–F59	=I35–I40+I45+I51–I59
61	EBT margin	=IF(F$10,F60/F$10,0)	=IF(I$10,I60/I$10,0)
62			

11.4.3 Provision for Taxes to Net to Retained Earnings (Rows 63–91)

FIGURE 11-4

Provision for Taxes to Net to Retained Earnings Input Layout

	C	F	G	H	I	J	K
63	Provision for taxes	36.0	40.0	47.0			
64	Tax rate %	34.6%	35.4%	35.0%	35.0%	35.0%	35.0%
65	Provision for taxes	36.0	40.0	47.0	57.4	66.8	73.9
66							
67	Equity earnings in affiliates	5.0	5.0	6.0			
68	Percent growth %	na	0.0%	20.0%	4.0%	4.0%	5.0%
69	Equity earnings in affiliates	5.0	5.0	6.0	6.2	6.5	6.8
70							
71	Minority interest in earnings	11.0	12.0	13.0			
72	Percent growth %	na	9.1%	8.3%	10.0%	5.0%	5.0%
73	Minority interest in earnings	11.0	12.0	13.0	14.3	15.0	15.8
74	**Net income**	**62.0**	**65.9**	**80.1**	**98.5**	**115.6**	**128.3**
75	Net margin	7.5%	7.3%	8.0%	9.0%	9.5%	9.6%
76							
77	Extraordinary expense	5.0	5.0	6.0	3.0		
78	Extraordinary expense	5.0	5.0	6.0	3.0	0.0	0.0
79							
80	Preferred dividends	5.0	5.0	6.0			
81	Yield (see B/S for input)				6.0	6.0	6.0
82	Preferred dividends	5.0	5.0	6.0	6.0	6.0	6.0
83	**Net income available to common**	**52.0**	**55.9**	**68.1**	**89.5**	**109.6**	**122.3**
84							
85	Common dividends	10.0	12.0	11.0			
86	Payout ratio %	16.1%	18.2%	13.7%	10.0%	10.0%	10.0%
87	Common dividends	10.0	12.0	11.0	9.9	11.6	12.8
88	**Net to retained earnings**	**42.0**	**43.9**	**57.1**	**79.7**	**98.0**	**109.4**
89							
90							
91							

TABLE 11-4

Provision for Taxes to Net to Retained Earnings Formulas

Row	Label in Column C	Formula in Column F (copy to G and H)	Formula in Column I (copy to J and K)
63	Provision for taxes		
64	Tax rate %	=IF(F60,F63/F60,0)	
65	Provision for taxes	=IF(F63,F63,F60*F64)	=IF(I63,I63,I60*I64)
66			

TABLE 11-4 (CONTINUED)

Row	Label in Column C	Formula in Column F (copy to G and H)	Formula in Column I (copy to J and K)
67	Equity earnings in affiliates		
68	Percent growth %	*Formula for Column G* *=IF(F69,G67/F69–1,0)*	
69	Equity earnings in affiliates	=F67	=IF(ISNUMBER(I67), I67,H69*(1+I68))
70			
71	Minority interest in earnings		
72	Percent growth %	*Formula for Column G* *=IF(F73,G71/F73–1,0)*	
73	Minority interest in earnings	=F71	=IF(ISNUMBER(I71), I71,H73*(1+I72))
74	Net income	=F60–F65+F69–F73	=I60–I65+I69–I73
75	Net margin	=IF(F$10,F74/F$10,0)	=IF(I$10,I74/I$10,0)
76			
77	Extraordinary expense		
78	Extraordinary expense	=F77	=I77
79			
80	Preferred dividends		
81	Yield (see B/S for input)		
82	Preferred dividends	=F80	=IF(I80,I80,I81)
83	Net income available to common	=F74–F78–F82	=I74–I78–I82
84			
85	Common dividends		
86	Payout ratio %	=IF(F74,F85/F74,0)	
87	Common dividends	=F85	=IF(I85,I85,I74*I86)
88	Net to retained earnings	=F83–F87	=I83–I87
89			
90			
91			

11.5 THE BALANCE SHEET INPUTS

11.5.1 Current Assets (Rows 92–125)

FIGURE 11-5

Current Assets Input Layout

	A	B	C	D	E	F	G	H	I	J	K
92									Proj	Proj	Proj
93			**BALANCE SHEET**			**Dec-05**	**Dec-06**	**Dec-07**	**Dec-08**	**Dec-09**	**Dec-10**
94			**ASSETS**								
95			Excess cash						99.3	63.5	21.1
96			Interest rate %						5.0%	5.0%	5.0%
97			Interest income						0.0	5.0	3.2
98											
99			Operating cash			60.0	75.0	80.0	80.0	80.0	80.0
100			% of revenues			7.3%	8.3%	8.0%			
101			Operating cash			60.0	75.0	80.0	80.0	80.0	80.0
102			Interest rate %						5.0%	5.0%	5.0%
103			Interest income						4.0	4.0	4.0
104											
105			ST investments			30.0	32.0	33.0			
106			% growth			na	6.7%	3.1%	3.0%	3.0%	3.0%
107			ST investments			30.0	32.0	33.0	34.0	35.0	36.1
108			Interest rate %						5.0%	5.0%	5.0%
109			Interest income						1.7	1.7	1.8
110											
111			Account receivable			60.0	75.0	90.0			
112			% of revenues			7.3%	8.3%	9.0%			
113			Days of revenues			26.5	30.4	32.9	30.0	30.0	30.0
114			Account receivable			60.0	75.0	90.0	90.4	99.5	109.4
115											
116			Inventory			120.0	135.0	150.0			
117			% of revenues			14.5%	15.0%	15.0%			
118			Days of COGS			97.3	100.6	99.5	98.0	95.0	95.0
119			Inventory			120.0	135.0	150.0	162.4	173.2	190.5
120											
121			Other current assets			10.0	10.0	12.0			
122			% of revenues			1.2%	1.1%	1.2%	1.0%	1.0%	1.0%
123			Other current assets			10.0	10.0	12.0	11.0	12.1	13.3
124			**Current assets**			**280.0**	**327.0**	**365.0**	**477.1**	**463.3**	**450.4**
125											

TABLE 11-5

Current Assets Formulas

Row	Label in Column C	Formula in Column F (copy to G and H)	Formula in Column I (copy to J and K)
92			
93	BALANCE SHEET	=F$6	=I$6
94	ASSETS		
95	Excess cash		=MAX(I223,0)
96	Interest rate %		
97	Interest income		=I96*H95
98			
99	Operating cash		
100	% of revenues	=IF(F$10,F99/F$10,0)	
101	Operating cash	=F99	=IF(I99,I99, I100*I$10)
102	Interest rate %		
103	Interest income		=I102*AVERAGE (H101:I101)
104			
105	ST investments		
106	% growth	*Formula for Column G* *=IF(F107,G105/F107–1,0)*	
107	ST investments	=F105	=IF(I105,I105, H107*(1+I106))
108	Interest rate %		
109	Interest income		=I108*AVERAGE (H107:I107)
110			
111	Account receivable		
112	% of revenues	=IF(F$10,F111/F$10,0)	
113	Days of revenues	=IF(F$10,F111/F$10*365,0)	
114	Account receivable	=F111	=IF(I111,I111, IF(I112,I112*I$10, I113/365*I$10))
115			
116	Inventory		
117	% of revenues	=IF(F$10,F116/F$10,0)	
118	Days of COGS	=IF(F$14,F116/F$14*365,0)	

(continued on next page)

TABLE 11-5 (CONTINUED)

Row	Label in Column C	Formula in Column F (copy to G and H)	Formula in Column I (copy to J and K)
119	Inventory	=F116	=IF(I116,I116, IF(I117,I117*I$10, I118/365*I$14))
120			
121	Other current assets		
122	% of revenues	=IF(F$10,F121/F$10,0)	
123	Other current assets	=F121	=IF(I121,I121, I122*I$10)
124	Current assets	=F95+F101+F107+F114+F1 19+F123	=I95+I101+I107 +I114+I119+I123
125			

11.5.2 Net PPE to Total Assets (Rows 126–148)

FIGURE 11-6

Net PPE to Total Assets Input Layout

	C	F	G	H	I	J	K
126	Net PPE	870.0	950.0	1,000.0			
127	Capex	130.0	155.0	130.0			
128	% of revenues	15.8%	17.2%	13.0%	15.0%	18.0%	18.0%
129	Capex	130.0	155.0	130.0	165.0	217.8	239.6
130	Depreciation				(85.0)	(91.8)	(102.5)
131	Book value of assets sold				0.0	0.0	0.0
132	Net PPE	870.0	950.0	1,000.0	1,080.0	1,206.0	1,343.1
133							
134	Investment in affiliates	58.0	54.0	50.0			
135	Equity earnings in affiliates				6.2	6.5	6.8
136	Dividends received (enter as positive)				4.0		
137	Investment in affiliates	58.0	54.0	50.0	52.2	58.7	65.5
138							
139	Intangibles	50.0	54.0	58.0			
140	Amortization	(4.0)	(4.0)	(4.0)	(4.0)	(4.0)	(4.0)
141	Intangibles	50.0	54.0	58.0	54.0	50.0	46.0
142							
143	Long-term assets	100.0	116.0	142.0			
144	% of revenues	12.1%	12.9%	14.2%	14.0%	14.0%	14.0%
145	% growth	na	16.0%	22.4%			
146	Long-term assets	100.0	116.0	142.0	154.0	169.4	186.3
147	**Total assets**	**1,358.0**	**1,501.0**	**1,615.0**	**1,817.3**	**1,947.4**	**2,091.3**
148							

TABLE 11-6

Net PPE to Total Assets Formulas

Row	Label in Column C	Formula in Column F (copy to G and H)	Formula in Column I (copy to J and K)
126	Net PPE		
127	Capex		
128	% of revenues	=IF(F$10,F127/F$10,0)	
129	Capex	=F127	=IF(I127,I127, I128*I$10)
130	Depreciation		=–I31
131	Book value of assets sold		=–I44
132	Net PPE	=F126	=IF(I126,I126,H132+ SUM(I129:I131))
133			
134	Investment in affiliates		
135	Equity earnings in affiliates		=I69
136	Dividends received		
137	Investment in affiliates	=F134	=IF(ISNUMBER(I134), I134,H137+I135–I136)
138			
139	Intangibles		
140	Amortization	=–F34	=–I34
141	Intangibles	=F139	=IF(ISNUMBER(I139), I139,H141+I140)
142			
143	Long-term assets		
144	% of revenues	=IF(F$10,F143/F$10,0)	
145	% growth	*Formula for Column G* *=IF(F146,G143/ F146–1,0)*	
146	Long-term assets	=F143	=IF(I143,I143, IF(I144,I144*I$10, H146*(1+I145)))
147	Total assets	=F124+F132+F137+ F141+F146	=I124+I132+I137 +I141+I146
148			

11.5.3 Current Liabilities (Rows 149–168)

FIGURE 11-7

Current Liabilities Input Layout

	C	F	G	H	I	J	K
149	**LIABILITIES**						
150	Revolver				0.0	0.0	0.0
151	Interest rate %				10.0%	10.0%	10.0%
152	Interest expense				0.0	0.0	0.0
153							
154	Short-term notes	10.0	12.0	14.0	14.0	14.0	14.0
155	Short-term notes	10.0	12.0	14.0	14.0	14.0	14.0
156	Interest rate %				10.0%	10.0%	10.0%
157	Interest expense				1.4	1.4	1.4
158							
159	Accounts payable	60.0	70.0	80.0			
160	% of revenues	7.3%	7.8%	8.0%			
161	Days of COGS	48.7	52.1	53.1	55.0	55.0	55.0
162	Accounts payable	60.0	70.0	80.0	91.2	100.3	110.3
163							
164	Other current liabilites	10.0	20.0	20.0			
165	% of revenues	1.2%	2.2%	2.0%	2.0%	2.0%	2.0%
166	Other current liabilites	10.0	20.0	20.0	22.0	24.2	26.6
167	**Current liabilites**	**80.0**	**102.0**	**114.0**	**127.2**	**138.5**	**150.9**
168							

TABLE 11-7

Current Liabilities Formulas

Row	Label in Column C	Formula in Column F (copy to G and H)	Formula in Column I (copy to J and K)
149	LIABILITIES		
150	Revolver		=–MIN(I223,0)
151	Interest rate %		
152	Interest expense		=I151*H150
153			
154	Short-term notes		
155	Short-term notes	=F154	=I154
156	Interest rate %		
157	Interest expense		=I156*AVERAGE (H155:I155)
158			
159	Accounts payable		
160	% of revenues	=IF(F$10,F159/F$10,0)	
161	Days of COGS	=IF(F$14,F159/F$14*365,0)	

TABLE 11-7 (CONTINUED)

Row	Label in Column C	Formula in Column F (copy to G and H)	Formula in Column I (copy to J and K)
162	Accounts payable	=F159	=IF(I159,I159,IF(I160, I160*I$10,I161/365*I$14))
163			
164	Other current liabilities		
165	% of revenues	=IF(F$10,F164/F$10,0)	
166	Other current liabilities	=F164	=IF(I164,I164,I165*I$10)
167	Current liabilities	=F155+F162+F166	=I150+I155+ I162+I166
168			

11.5.4 Debt to Minority Interest (Row 169–197)

FIGURE 11-8

Debt to Minority Interest Input Layout

	A	B	C	D	E	F	G	H	I	J	K
169			Debt A			200.0	225.0	150.0			
170			New (amortization)								
171			Debt A			200.0	225.0	150.0	150.0	150.0	150.0
172			Interest rate %						10.0%	10.0%	10.0%
173			Interest expense						15.0	15.0	15.0
174											
175			Debt B			120.0	120.0	145.0			
176			New (amortization)								
177			Debt B			120.0	120.0	145.0	145.0	145.0	145.0
178			Interest rate %						10.0%	10.0%	10.0%
179			Interest expense						14.5	14.5	14.5
180											
181			Debt C			110.0	110.0	110.0			
182			New (amortization)								
183			Debt C			110.0	110.0	110.0	110.0	110.0	110.0
184			Interest rate %						8.0%	8.0%	8.0%
185			Interest expense						8.8	8.8	8.8
186											
187			Long-term liabilities			40.0	48.0	50.0			
188			% of revenues			4.8%	5.3%	5.0%	4.0%	4.0%	4.0%
189			% growth			na	20.0%	4.2%			
190			Long-term liabilities			40.0	48.0	50.0	44.0	48.4	53.2
191			**Total liabilities**			**550.0**	**605.0**	**569.0**	**576.2**	**591.9**	**609.2**
192											
193			**MINORITY INTEREST**								
194			Minority interest			58.0	70.0	83.0			
195			Minority interest in earnings			11.0	12.0	13.0	14.3	15.0	15.8
196			**Minority interest**			**58.0**	**70.0**	**83.0**	**97.3**	**112.3**	**128.1**
197											

TABLE 11-8

Debt to Minority Interest Formulas

Row	Label in Column C	Formula in Column F (copy to G and H)	Formula in Column I (copy to J and K)
169	Debt A		
170	New (amortization)		
171	Debt A	=F169	=IF(I169,I169, H171+I170)
172	Interest rate %		
173	Interest expense		=I172*AVERAGE (H171:I171)
174			
175	Debt B		
176	New (amortization)		
177	Debt B	=F175	=IF(I175,I175, H177+I176)
178	Interest rate %		
179	Interest expense		=I178*AVERAGE (H177:I177)
180			
181	Debt C		
182	New (amortization)		
183	Debt C	=F181	=IF(I181,I181, H183+I182)
184	Interest rate %		
185	Interest expense		=I184*AVERAGE (H183:I183)
186			
187	Long-term liabilities		
188	% of revenues	=IF(F$10,F190/F$10,0)	
		Formula for Column G	
189	% growth	*=IF(F190,G187/F190–1,0)*	
190	Long-term liabilities	=F187	=IF(I187,I187, IF(I188,I188*I$10, H190*(1+I189)))
191	Total liabilities	=F167+F171+F177+ F183+F190	=I167+I171+I177 +I183+I190

TABLE 11-8 (CONTINUED)

Row	Label in Column C	Formula in Column F (copy to G and H)	Formula in Column I (copy to J and K)
192			
193	MINORITY INTEREST		
194	Minority interest		
195	Minority interest in earnings	=F73	=I73
196	Minority interest	=F194	=IF(I194,I194, H196+I195)
197			

11.5.5 Shareholders' Equity and Balancing Formulas (Rows 198–223)

FIGURE 11-9

Shareholders' Equity Input Layout and Balancing Formulas

	C	F	G	H	I	J	K
198	**SHAREHOLDERS' EQUITY**						
199	Preferred stock	80.0	90.0	100.0	100.0	100.0	100.0
200	Preferred stock	80.0	90.0	100.0	100.0	100.0	100.0
201	Yield %				6.0%	6.0%	6.0%
202	Preferred dividends				6.0	6.0	6.0
203							
204	Common stock	460.0	480.0	550.0	650.0	650.0	650.0
205	Common stock	460.0	480.0	550.0	650.0	650.0	650.0
206							
207	Retained earnings	200.0	243.9	301.0			
208	Net to retained earnings		43.9	57.1	79.7	98.0	109.4
209	Retained earnings	200.0	243.9	301.0	380.7	478.7	588.1
210							
211	Other equity account	10.0	12.1	12.0			
212	% of revenues	1.2%	1.3%	1.2%	1.2%	1.2%	1.2%
213	Other equity account	10.0	12.1	12.0	13.2	14.5	16.0
214	**Shareholders' equity**	**750.0**	**826.0**	**963.0**	**1,143.9**	**1,243.2**	**1,354.1**
215	**Total liabs, min interest, equity**	**1,358.0**	**1,501.0**	**1,615.0**	**1,817.3**	**1,947.4**	**2,091.3**
216							
217	Balance check	0.0	0.0	0.0	0.0	0.0	0.0
218	**OK**	**OK**	**OK**	**OK**	**OK**	**OK**	**OK**
219							
220	Assets without excess cash	1,358.0	1,501.0	1,615.0	1,718.1	1,883.9	2,070.3
221	Liabs, SH Eq without revolver	1,358.0	1,501.0	1,615.0	1,817.3	1,947.4	2,091.3
222							
223	Excess cash (revolver)	na	0.0	0.0	99.3	63.5	21.1

TABLE 11-9

Shareholders' Equity and Balancing Formulas

Row	Label in Column C	Formula in Column F (copy to G and H)	Formula in Column I (copy to J and K)
198	SHAREHOLDERS' EQUITY		
199	Preferred stock		
200	Preferred stock	=F199	=I199
201	Yield %		
202	Preferred dividends		=I201*AVERAGE (H200:I200)
203			
204	Common stock		
205	Common stock	=F204	=IF(I204,I204,H205)
206			
207	Retained earnings		
208	Net to retained earnings		=I88
209	Retained earnings	=F207	=IF(I207,I207, H209+I208)
210			
211	Other equity account		
212	% of revenues	=IF(F$10,F211/F$10,0)	
213	Other equity account	=F211	=IF(I211,I211,I212*I $10)
214	Shareholders' equity	=F200+F205+F209+F213	=I200+I205+I209+I213
215	Total liabs, min interest, equity	=F191+F196+F214	=I191+I196+I214
216			
217	Balance check	=F215-F147	=I215-I147
218	OK	=IF(ROUND(F217,0)=0, "OK","Check")	=IF(ROUND(I217,0)=0, "OK","Check")
219			
220	Assets without SF	=F101+F107+F114+ F119+F123+F132+ F137+F141+F146	=I101+I107+I114+ I119+I123+I132+ I137+I141+I146
221	Liabs, SH Eq without NTF	=F155+F162+F166+ F171+F177+F183+ F190+F196+F214	=I155+I162+I166+ I171+I177+I183+ I190+I196+I214
222			
223	Excess cash (revolver)		=IF(ISERROR(I221–I220),0,I221–I220)

11.6 ADDING MORE LINES TO THE MODEL

Once you have created this model, you can add additional lines in the model. For example, if you wanted a fourth debt account (Debt D), do the following:

1. Copy the Debt C set of inputs, relabel them so that they carry the Debt D designation.
2. Make sure that the results of this module are included in the total liabilities total and the balancing formulas.

A good way to make sure that all new lines are connected is to use Excel's Formula Auditing tool. In the preceding example, use the Trace Dependents to trace all the Debt C module's dependent cells in the model; that is, all the locations in the model, especially those in the cash flow statement that have a connection to Debt C. In all those locations, make sure you add the same connections to the new Debt D lines.

11.7 REMOVING LINES

By the same token, you can use the same Formula Auditing tool approach to eliminate any lines not needed in the model. The model as described in this chapter has several accounts that make it more than a "simple" model:

- Gain (loss) on asset sales, with inputs on book value of asset sold and proceeds from the sale of assets
- Equity in earnings of affiliates (in the income statement) and investment in affiliates (in the balance sheet)
- Minority interest (in the income statement and the balance sheet)
- Three long-term debt accounts
- Preferred stock and preferred dividends

11.8 THE INCOME STATEMENT OUTPUT REPORT

FIGURE 11–10

The Income Statement Output

First Corporation

INCOME STATEMENT	Dec-05	Dec-06	Dec-07	Proj Dec-08	Proj Dec-09	Proj Dec-10
Revenues	825.0	900.0	1,000.0	1,100.0	1,210.0	1,331.0
COGS	450.0	490.0	550.0	605.0	665.5	732.1
Gross profit	**375.0**	**410.0**	**450.0**	**495.0**	**544.5**	**599.0**
Gross margin	45.5%	45.6%	45.0%	45.0%	45.0%	45.0%
SGA	125.0	135.0	150.0	165.0	181.5	199.7
Operating expenses	25.0	28.0	30.0	33.0	36.3	39.9
EBITDA	**225.0**	**247.0**	**270.0**	**297.0**	**326.7**	**359.4**
EBITDA margin	27.3%	27.4%	27.0%	27.0%	27.0%	27.0%
Depreciation	60.0	75.0	80.0	85.0	91.8	102.5
Amortization of intangibles	4.0	4.0	4.0	4.0	4.0	4.0
EBIT	**161.0**	**168.0**	**186.0**	**208.0**	**230.9**	**252.9**
EBIT margin	19.5%	18.7%	18.6%	18.9%	19.1%	19.0%
Non-oper expenses	10.0	10.0	8.0	10.0	11.0	11.0
Gain (loss) on asset sales	0.0	0.0	0.0	0.0	0.0	0.0
Interest income	3.0	4.9	5.5	5.7	10.7	9.0
Interest expense	50.0	50.0	49.4	39.7	39.7	39.7
EBT	**104.0**	**112.9**	**134.1**	**164.0**	**190.9**	**211.1**
EBT margin	12.6%	12.5%	13.4%	14.9%	15.8%	15.9%
Provision for taxes	36.0	40.0	47.0	57.4	66.8	73.9
Equity earnings in affiliates	5.0	5.0	6.0	6.2	6.5	6.8
Minority interest in earnings	11.0	12.0	13.0	14.3	15.0	15.8
Net income	**62.0**	**65.9**	**80.1**	**98.5**	**115.6**	**128.3**
Net margin	7.5%	7.3%	8.0%	9.0%	9.5%	9.6%
Extraordinary expense	5.0	5.0	6.0	3.0	0.0	0.0
Preferred dividends	5.0	5.0	6.0	6.0	6.0	6.0
Net income available to common	**52.0**	**55.9**	**68.1**	**89.5**	**109.6**	**122.3**
Common dividends	10.0	12.0	11.0	9.9	11.6	12.8
Net to retained earnings	**42.0**	**43.9**	**57.1**	**79.7**	**98.0**	**109.4**
OK	**OK**	**OK**	**OK**	**OK**	**OK**	**OK**

TABLE 11–10

The Income Statement Output

Row	Contents in Column C	Formula in Column F (copy to G to K)
6	INCOME STATEMENT	=Input!F6
7		
8	=Input!C10	=Input!F10
9	=Input!C14	=Input!F14
10	Gross profit	=F8-F9
11	Gross margin	=IF(F8,F10/F8,0)
12		
13	=Input!C20	=Input!F20
14	=Input!C24	=Input!F24
15	EBITDA	=F10–F13–F14
16	EBITDA margin	=IF(F$8,F15/F$8,0)
17		
18	=Input!C31	=Input!F31
19	=Input!C34	=Input!F34
20	EBIT	=F15–F18–F19
21	EBIT margin	=IF(F$8,F20/F$8,0)
22		
23	=Input!C40	=Input!F40
24	=Input!C45	=Input!F45
25	=Input!C51	=Input!F51
26	=Input!C59	=Input!F59
27	EBT	=F20–F23+F24+F25–F26
28	EBT margin	=IF(F$8,F27/F$8,0)
29		
30	=Input!C65	=Input!F65
31	=Input!C69	=Input!F69
32	=Input!C73	=Input!F73
33	Net income	=F27–F30+F31–F32
34	Net margin	=IF(F$8,F33/F$8,0)
35		
36	=Input!C78	=Input!F78
37	=Input!C82	=Input!F82
38	=Input!C83	=F33–F36–F37
39		
40	=Input!C87	=Input!F87
41	Net to retained earnings	=F38–F40
42		
43	=IF(COUNTIF(F43:K43,"Check"), "Check","OK")	=IF(ROUND(Input!F88–F41,0)=0, "OK","Check")

11.9 THE BALANCE SHEET OUTPUT REPORT

FIGURE 11–11

The Balance Sheet Output

First Corporation

BALANCE SHEET	**Dec-05**	**Dec-06**	**Dec-07**	**Proj Dec-08**	**Proj Dec-09**	**Proj Dec-10**
ASSETS						
Excess cash	0.0	0.0	0.0	99.3	63.5	21.1
Operating cash	60.0	75.0	80.0	80.0	80.0	80.0
ST investments	30.0	32.0	33.0	34.0	35.0	36.1
Account receivable	60.0	75.0	90.0	90.4	99.5	109.4
Inventory	120.0	135.0	150.0	162.4	173.2	190.5
Other current assets	10.0	10.0	12.0	11.0	12.1	13.3
Current assets	**280.0**	**327.0**	**365.0**	**477.1**	**463.3**	**450.4**
Net PPE	870.0	950.0	1,000.0	1,080.0	1,206.0	1,343.1
Investment in affiliates	58.0	54.0	50.0	52.2	58.7	65.5
Intangibles	50.0	54.0	58.0	54.0	50.0	46.0
Long-term assets	100.0	116.0	142.0	154.0	169.4	186.3
Total assets	**1,358.0**	**1,501.0**	**1,615.0**	**1,817.3**	**1,947.4**	**2,091.3**
LIABILITIES						
Revolver	0.0	0.0	0.0	0.0	0.0	0.0
Short-term notes	10.0	12.0	14.0	14.0	14.0	14.0
Accounts payable	60.0	70.0	80.0	91.2	100.3	110.3
Other current liabilities	10.0	20.0	20.0	22.0	24.2	26.6
Current liabilities	**80.0**	**102.0**	**114.0**	**127.2**	**138.5**	**150.9**
Debt 1	200.0	225.0	150.0	150.0	150.0	150.0
Debt 2	120.0	120.0	145.0	145.0	145.0	145.0
Debt 3	110.0	110.0	110.0	110.0	110.0	110.0
Long-term liabilities	40.0	48.0	50.0	44.0	48.4	53.2
Total liabilities	**550.0**	**605.0**	**569.0**	**576.2**	**591.9**	**609.2**
MINORITY INTEREST						
Minority interest	**58.0**	**70.0**	**83.0**	**97.3**	**112.3**	**128.1**
SHAREHOLDERS' EQUITY						
Preferred stock	80.0	90.0	100.0	100.0	100.0	100.0
Common stock	460.0	480.0	550.0	650.0	650.0	650.0
Retained earnings	200.0	243.9	301.0	380.7	478.7	588.1
Other equity account	10.0	12.1	12.0	13.2	14.5	16.0
Shareholders' equity	**750.0**	**826.0**	**963.0**	**1,143.9**	**1,243.2**	**1,354.1**
Total liabs, min int and SH equity	**1,358.0**	**1,501.0**	**1,615.0**	**1,817.3**	**1,947.4**	**2,091.3**
Balance check	0.0	0.0	0.0	0.0	0.0	0.0
OK	**OK**	**OK**	**OK**	**OK**	**OK**	**OK**

TABLE 11-11

The Balance Sheet Output

Row	Contents in Column C	Formula in Column F (copy to G to K)
6	BALANCE SHEET	=Input!F6
7	ASSETS	
8	Excess cash	=Input!F95
9	=Input!C101	=Input!F101
10	=Input!C107	=Input!F107
11	=Input!C114	=Input!F114
12	=Input!C119	=Input!F119
13	=Input!C123	=Input!F123
14	Current assets	=SUM(F8:F13)
15		
16	=Input!C132	=Input!F132
17	=Input!C137	=Input!F137
18	=Input!C141	=Input!F141
19	=Input!C146	=Input!F146
20	Total assets	=F14+SUM(F16:F19)
21		
22	LIABILITIES	
23	Revolver	=Input!F150
24	=Input!C155	=Input!F155
25	=Input!C162	=Input!F162
26	=Input!C166	=Input!F166
27	Current liabilities	=SUM(F23:F26)
28		
29	=Input!C171	=Input!F171
30	=Input!C177	=Input!F177
31	=Input!C183	=Input!F183
32	=Input!C190	=Input!F190
33	Total liabilities	=F27+SUM(F29:F32)
34		
35	MINORITY INTEREST	
36	=Input!C196	=Input!F196
37		
38	SHAREHOLDERS' EQUITY	
39	=Input!C200	=Input!F200
40	=Input!C205	=Input!F205
41	=Input!C209	=Input!F209
42	=Input!C213	=Input!F213
43	Shareholders' equity	=SUM(F39:F42)
44	Total liabs, min int and SH equity	=F33+F36+F43
45		
46	Balance check	=F44–F20
47	=IF(COUNTIF(F47:K47,"Check"), "Check","OK")	=IF(ROUND(F46,0)=0, "OK","Check")

11.10 THE COMMON-SIZE INCOME STATEMENT OUTPUT

In this output (Fig. 11-12), all values are shown as a percent of revenue. Essentially, this is an output of margins. The formulas are shown in Table 11-12.

FIGURE 11-12

The Common-Size Income Statement

First Corporation

INCOME STATEMENT	Dec-05	Dec-06	Dec-07	Proj Dec-08	Proj Dec-09	Proj Dec-10
Revenues	100.0%	100.0%	100.0%	100.0%	100.0%	100.0%
COGS	54.5%	54.4%	55.0%	55.0%	55.0%	55.0%
Gross profit	**45.5%**	**45.6%**	**45.0%**	**45.0%**	**45.0%**	**45.0%**
SGA	15.2%	15.0%	15.0%	15.0%	15.0%	15.0%
Operating expenses	3.0%	3.1%	3.0%	3.0%	3.0%	3.0%
EBITDA	**27.3%**	**27.4%**	**27.0%**	**27.0%**	**27.0%**	**27.0%**
Depreciation	7.3%	8.3%	8.0%	7.7%	7.6%	7.7%
Amortization of intangibles	0.5%	0.4%	0.4%	0.4%	0.3%	0.3%
EBIT	**19.5%**	**18.7%**	**18.6%**	**18.9%**	**19.1%**	**19.0%**
Non-oper expenses	1.2%	1.1%	0.8%	0.9%	0.9%	0.8%
Gain (loss) on asset sales	0.0%	0.0%	0.0%	0.0%	0.0%	0.0%
Interest income	0.4%	0.5%	0.6%	0.5%	0.9%	0.7%
Interest expense	6.1%	5.6%	4.9%	3.6%	3.3%	3.0%
EBT	**12.6%**	**12.5%**	**13.4%**	**14.9%**	**15.8%**	**15.9%**
Provision for taxes	4.4%	4.4%	4.7%	5.2%	5.5%	5.6%
Equity earnings in affiliates	0.6%	0.6%	0.6%	0.6%	0.5%	0.5%
Minority interest in earnings	1.3%	1.3%	1.3%	1.3%	1.2%	1.2%
Net income	**8.2%**	**8.1%**	**8.7%**	**9.7%**	**10.3%**	**10.3%**
Extraordinary expense	0.6%	0.6%	0.6%	0.3%	0.0%	0.0%
Preferred dividends	0.6%	0.6%	0.6%	0.5%	0.5%	0.5%
Net income available to common	**7.0%**	**7.0%**	**7.5%**	**8.9%**	**9.8%**	**9.9%**
Common dividends	1.2%	1.3%	1.1%	0.9%	1.0%	1.0%
Net to retained earnings	**5.8%**	**5.7%**	**6.4%**	**8.0%**	**8.8%**	**8.9%**

TABLE 11–12

The Common-Size Income Statement

Row	Contents in Column C	Formula in Column F (copy to G to K)
6	INCOME STATEMENT	=Input!F6
7		
8	=IS!C8	=IS!F8/IS!F$8
9	=IS!C9	=IS!F9/IS!F$8
10	Gross profit	=F8–F9
11		
12	=IS!C13	=IS!F13/IS!F$8
13	=IS!C14	=IS!F14/IS!F$8
14	EBITDA	=F10–F12–F13
15		
16	=IS!C18	=IS!F18/IS!F$8
17	=IS!C19	=IS!F19/IS!F$8
18	EBIT	=F14–F16–F17
19		
20	=IS!C23	=IS!F23/IS!F$8
21	=IS!C24	=IS!F24/IS!F$8
22	=IS!C25	=IS!F25/IS!F$8
23	=IS!C26	=IS!F26/IS!F$8
24	EBT	=F18–F20+F22–F23
25		
26	=IS!C30	=IS!F30/IS!F$8
27	=IS!C31	=IS!F31/IS!F$8
28	=IS!C32	=IS!F32/IS!F$8
29	Net income	=F24–F26
30		
31	=IS!C36	=IS!F36/IS!F$8
32	=IS!C37	=IS!F37/IS!F$8
33	=IS!C38	=F29–F31–F32
34		
35	=IS!C40	=IS!F40/IS!F$8
36	Net to retained earnings	=F33–F35

11.11 THE COMMON-SIZE BALANCE SHEET OUTPUT

In this output (Fig. 11-13), all values are shown as a percent of total assets. The formulas are shown in Table 11-13.

FIGURE 11-13

The Common-Size Balance Sheet

	A B C D E	F	G	H	I	J	K
1	**First Corporation**						
2							
3							
4							
5					**Proj**	**Proj**	**Proj**
6	**BALANCE SHEET**	**Dec-05**	**Dec-06**	**Dec-07**	**Dec-08**	**Dec-09**	**Dec-10**
7	**ASSETS**						
8	Excess cash	0.0%	0.0%	0.0%	5.5%	3.3%	1.0%
9	Operating cash	4.4%	5.0%	5.0%	4.4%	4.1%	3.8%
10	ST investments	2.2%	2.1%	2.0%	1.9%	1.8%	1.7%
11	Account receivable	4.4%	5.0%	5.6%	5.0%	5.1%	5.2%
12	Inventory	8.8%	9.0%	9.3%	8.9%	8.9%	9.1%
13	Other current assets	0.7%	0.7%	0.7%	0.6%	0.6%	0.6%
14	**Current assets**	**20.6%**	**21.8%**	**22.6%**	**26.3%**	**23.8%**	**21.5%**
15							
16	Net PPE	64.1%	63.3%	61.9%	59.4%	61.9%	64.2%
17	Investment in affiliates	4.3%	3.6%	3.1%	2.9%	3.0%	3.1%
18	Intangibles	3.7%	3.6%	3.6%	3.0%	2.6%	2.2%
19	Long-term assets	7.4%	7.7%	8.8%	8.5%	8.7%	8.9%
20	**Total assets**	**100.0%**	**100.0%**	**100.0%**	**100.0%**	**100.0%**	**100.0%**
21							
22	**LIABILITIES**						
23	Revolver	0.0%	0.0%	0.0%	0.0%	0.0%	0.0%
24	Short-term notes	0.7%	0.8%	0.9%	0.8%	0.7%	0.7%
25	Accounts payable	4.4%	4.7%	5.0%	5.0%	5.1%	5.3%
26	Other current liabilities	0.7%	1.3%	1.2%	1.2%	1.2%	1.3%
27	**Current liabilities**	**5.9%**	**6.8%**	**7.1%**	**7.0%**	**7.1%**	**7.2%**
28							
29	Debt 1	14.7%	15.0%	9.3%	8.3%	7.7%	7.2%
30	Debt 2	8.8%	8.0%	9.0%	8.0%	7.4%	6.9%
31	Debt 3	8.1%	7.3%	6.8%	6.1%	5.6%	5.3%
32	Long-term liabilities	2.9%	3.2%	3.1%	2.4%	2.5%	2.5%
33	**Total liabilities**	**40.5%**	**40.3%**	**35.2%**	**31.7%**	**30.4%**	**29.1%**
34							
35	**MINORITY INTEREST**						
36	Minority interest	**4.3%**	**4.7%**	**5.1%**	**5.4%**	**5.8%**	**6.1%**
37							
38	**SHAREHOLDERS' EQUITY**						
39	Preferred stock	5.9%	6.0%	6.2%	5.5%	5.1%	4.8%
40	Common stock	33.9%	32.0%	34.1%	35.8%	33.4%	31.1%
41	Retained earnings	14.7%	16.2%	18.6%	20.9%	24.6%	28.1%
42	Other equity account	0.7%	0.8%	0.7%	0.7%	0.7%	0.8%
43	**Shareholders' equity**	**55.2%**	**55.0%**	**59.6%**	**62.9%**	**63.8%**	**64.7%**
44	**Total liabilities and SH equity**	**100.0%**	**100.0%**	**100.0%**	**100.0%**	**100.0%**	**100.0%**
45							

TABLE 11–13

The Common-Size Balance Sheet

Row	Contents in Column C	Formula in Column F (copy to G to K)
6	BALANCE SHEET	=Input!F6
7	ASSETS	
8	=BS!C8	=BS!F8/BS!F$20
9	=BS!C9	=BS!F9/BS!F$20
10	=BS!C10	=BS!F10/BS!F$20
11	=BS!C11	=BS!F11/BS!F$20
12	=BS!C12	=BS!F12/BS!F$20
13	=BS!C13	=BS!F13/BS!F$20
14	Current assets	=SUM(F8:F13)
15		
16	=BS!C16	=BS!F16/BS!F$20
17	=BS!C17	=BS!F17/BS!F$20
18	=BS!C18	=BS!F18/BS!F$20
19	=BS!C19	=BS!F19/BS!F$20
20	Total assets	=F14+SUM(F16:F19)
21		
22	LIABILITIES	
23	=BS!C23	=BS!F23/BS!F$20
24	=BS!C24	=BS!F24/BS!F$20
25	=BS!C25	=BS!F25/BS!F$20
26	=BS!C26	=BS!F26/BS!F$20
27	Current liabilities	=SUM(F23:F26)
28		
29	=BS!C29	=BS!F29/BS!F$20
30	=BS!C30	=BS!F30/BS!F$20
31	=BS!C31	=BS!F31/BS!F$20
32	=BS!C32	=BS!F32/BS!F$20
33	Total liabilities	=F27+SUM(F29:F32)
34		
35	MINORITY INTEREST	
36	=BS!C36	=BS!F36/BS!F$20
37		
38	SHAREHOLDERS' EQUITY	
39	=BS!C39	=BS!F39/BS!F$20
40	=BS!C40	=BS!F40/BS!F$20
41	=BS!C41	=BS!F41/BS!F$20
42	=BS!C42	=BS!F42/BS!F$20
43	Shareholders' equity	=SUM(F39:F42)
44	Total liabilities and SH equity	=F33+F36+F43

CHAPTER 12

The Cash Flow Statement

This chapter adds the cash flow statement to the income statement and balance sheet created in the last chapter. There are two ways to think about the role of the cash flow statement in the model:

- The income statement and balance sheet already work together well, in that the balance sheet is now balanced; therefore, the cash flow statement can be viewed as a reconciliation table to track the cash flow from the income statement and other sources and uses of cash from the changes in the balance sheet. The cash flow statement calculates the total cash produced for each year, adds the prior year's excess cash or revolver, and arrives at the current year's excess cash. If the result is negative, then it is the current year's revolver. The ending excess cash or revolver for each year in the cash flow should equal the same results in the balance sheet.
- In an alternate modeling approach, however, the cash flow statement is viewed as the method by which the balance sheet is balanced. In this case, the excess cash or revolver plug that is calculated for each forecast year is calculated by the cash flow statement, and then used by the balance sheet.

In either approach, the final result in excess cash or revolver should be identical.

12.1 LAYOUT

The cash flow sheet uses the same layout format described in the last chapter.

12.2 TABLE OF FORMULAS HAS TWO DIFFERENT COLUMNS

Similar to the last chapter, each screen capture is followed by a table describing the formulas.

The table (see the example Table 12-1) has three columns. The first column gives the row number of the sheet. The next two columns are for the following:

1. The second column shows the formulas that you can use in Column C. You can refer to the headings already used by the sheets IS and BS, so that any changes made there will be automatically reflected in the cash flow statement. However, if you just want to create the cash flow statement quickly, you can skip this step and simply type in the labels as text.
2. The third column shows the formulas in the cash flow statement. There is no distinction in the cash flow statement between the historical and the forecast years, so on each row the formula shown is for Column G and it should be copied to Columns H to K.

As before, rows in the tables shaded gray indicate that they are blank spacing rows in the model.

12.3 THE CASH FLOW STATEMENT

The cash flow statement is shown in several sections. Let's start with Figure 12-1.

TABLE 12-1

Cash Flow Statement to Cash from Operations Formulas

Row	Contents in Column C	Formula in Column G (copy to H to K)
6	CASH FLOW	=Input!G6
7		
8	=IS!C33	=IS!G33
9		
10	Add back:	
11	=IS!C18	=IS!G18
12	=IS!C19	=IS!G19
13	(Gain) loss on asset sales	=–IS!G24
14	=IS!C31	=–IS!G31
15	=IS!C32	=IS!G32
16	Operating cash flow	=G8+SUM(G11:G15)
17		
18	="(Incr) decr in "&BS!C9	=BS!F9–BS!G9
19	="(Incr) decr in "&BS!C11	=BS!F11–BS!G11
20	="(Incr) decr in "&BS!C12	=BS!F12–BS!G12
21	="(Incr) decr in "&BS!C13	=BS!F13–BS!G13
22	="Incr (decr) in "&BS!C25	=BS!G25–BS!F25
23	="Incr (decr) in "&BS!C26	=BS!G26–BS!F26
24	(Inc) in Operating working capital	=SUM(G18:G23)
25		
26	=IS!C36	=–IS!G36
27	="(Incr) decr in "&BS!C19	=BS!F19–BS!G19
28	="Incr (decr) in "&BS!C32	=BS!G32–BS!F32
29	Cash from operations	=G16+G24+SUM(G26:G28)
30		

12.3.1 Cash Flow Statement to Cash from Operations (Rows 1–30)

12.3.1.1 Operating cash

Note that in the cash from operations section, changes in operating cash are included in the net working capital section. Recall that the

FIGURE 12-1

Cash Flow Statement to Cash from Operations Layout

	A B C D E	F	G	H	I	J	K
1	**First Corporation**						
2							
3							
4							
5					**Proj**	**Proj**	**Proj**
6	**CASH FLOW**	**Dec-05**	**Dec-06**	**Dec-07**	**Dec-08**	**Dec-09**	**Dec-10**
7							
8	Net income		65.9	80.1	98.5	115.6	128.3
9							
10	Add back:						
11	Depreciation		75.0	80.0	85.0	91.8	102.5
12	Amortization of intangibles		4.0	4.0	4.0	4.0	4.0
13	(Gain) loss on asset sales		0.0	0.0	0.0	0.0	0.0
14	Equity earnings in affiliates		(5.0)	(6.0)	(6.2)	(6.5)	(6.8)
15	Minority interest in earnings		12.0	13.0	14.3	15.0	15.8
16	Operating cash flow		151.9	171.1	195.6	219.9	243.7
17							
18	(Incr) decr in Operating cash		(15.0)	(5.0)	0.0	0.0	0.0
19	(Incr) decr in Account receivable		(15.0)	(15.0)	(0.4)	(9.0)	(9.9)
20	(Incr) decr in Inventory		(15.0)	(15.0)	(12.4)	(10.8)	(17.3)
21	(Incr) decr in Other current assets		0.0	(2.0)	1.0	(1.1)	(1.2)
22	Incr (decr) in Accounts payable		10.0	10.0	11.2	9.1	10.0
23	Incr (decr) in Other current liabilities		10.0	0.0	2.0	2.2	2.4
24	(Inc) in Operating working capital		(25.0)	(27.0)	1.3	(9.6)	(16.0)
25							
26	Extraordinary expense		(5.0)	(6.0)	(3.0)	0.0	0.0
27	(Incr) decr in Long-term assets		(16.0)	(26.0)	(12.0)	(15.4)	(16.9)
28	Incr (decr) in Long-term liabilities		8.0	2.0	(6.0)	4.4	4.8
29	**Cash from operations**		**113.9**	**114.1**	**175.9**	**199.3**	**215.6**
30							

balance sheet has two cash accounts: excess cash and operating cash. Excess cash is the balancing number and is derived from the total cash flow in the cash flow statement (i.e., total cash flow is the combined flow from cash from operations, cash from investments, and cash from financing). Operating cash is the cash that a business needs to have on hand for day-to-day operations. Think of it as "petty cash." Indeed, in forecasting this number for the balance sheet, an approach is to state it as a percentage of revenue. Operating cash is treated as being the result of an operating decision, rather than a financing decision, and is therefore included as a working capital item in this section.

12.3.2 Cash Flow Statement to the End (Rows 31–59)

For the next section (Fig. 12-2, and Table 12-2), the Cash from investments and Cash from financing sections have additional rows that refer to rows below the cash flow statement. These rows are from the reconciliation tables. For the moment, leave them blank and then fill in the formulas once the reconciliation tables are complete. See Section 12.5 for an explanation of the reconciliation tables.

12.4 GETTING FROM CASH FLOW TO THE EXCESS CASH OR REVOLVER NUMBER

Let's go over the last rows in the cash flow statement (Fig. 12-2 and Table 12-2, again), from Row 52 down.

FIGURE 12-2

Cash Flow Statement to Excess Cash (Revolver) Calculation Formulas

	A B C D E F	G	H	I	J	K
31	Capex	(155.0)	(130.0)	(165.0)	(217.8)	(239.6)
32	Proceeds from sale of assets	0.0	0.0	0.0	0.0	0.0
33	Other (Incr) decr in Net PPE	0.0	0.0	0.0	0.0	0.0
34	(Incr) decr in ST investments	(2.0)	(1.0)	(1.0)	(1.0)	(1.1)
35	Other (incr) decr in Investment in affiliates	9.0	10.0	4.0	0.0	0.0
36	Other (incr) decr in Intangibles	(8.0)	(8.0)	0.0	0.0	0.0
37	**Cash from investments**	(156.0)	(129.0)	(162.0)	(218.8)	(240.6)
38						
39	Incr (decr) in Short-term notes	2.0	2.0	0.0	0.0	0.0
40	Incr (decr) in Debt 1	25.0	(75.0)	0.0	0.0	0.0
41	Incr (decr) in Debt 2	0.0	25.0	0.0	0.0	0.0
42	Incr (decr) in Debt 3	0.0	0.0	0.0	0.0	0.0
43	Other incr (decr) in Minority interest	0.0	0.0	0.0	0.0	0.0
44	Preferred dividends	(5.0)	(6.0)	(6.0)	(6.0)	(6.0)
45	Common dividends	(12.0)	(11.0)	(9.9)	(11.6)	(12.8)
46	Incr (decr) in Preferred stock	10.0	10.0	0.0	0.0	0.0
47	Incr (decr) in Common stock	20.0	70.0	100.0	0.0	0.0
48	Other incr (decr) in Retained earnings	0.0	0.0	0.0	0.0	0.0
49	(Incr) decr in Other equity account	2.1	(0.1)	1.2	1.3	1.5
50	**Cash from financing**	42.1	14.9	85.3	(16.2)	(17.4)
51						
52	**Total cash flow**	0.0	0.0	99.3	(35.8)	(42.4)
53						
54	**Excess cash (revolver)**	0.0	0.0	99.3	63.5	21.1
55						
56	**B/S excess cash (revolver)**	0.0	0.0	99.3	63.5	21.1
57	Balance check	0.0	0.0	0.0	0.0	(0.0)
58	**OK**	**OK**	**OK**	**OK**	**OK**	**OK**
59						

TABLE 12-2

Cash Flow Statement to Excess Cash (Revolver) Calculation Formulas

Row	Contents in Column C	Formula in Column G (copy to H to K)
31	Capex	=–Input!G129
32	Proceeds from sale of assets	=Input!G43
33	=C70	=G70
34	="(Incr) decr in "&BS!C10	=BS!F10–BS!G10
35	=C78	=G78
36	=C85	=G85
37	Cash from investments	=SUM(G31:G36)
38		
39	="Incr (decr) in "&BS!C24	=BS!G24–BS!F24
40	="Incr (decr) in "&BS!C29	=BS!G29–BS!F29
41	="Incr (decr) in "&BS!C30	=BS!G30–BS!F30
42	="Incr (decr) in "&BS!C31	=BS!G31–BS!F31
43	=C92	=G92
44	=IS!C37	=–IS!G37
45	=IS!C40	=–IS!G40
46	="Incr (decr) in "&BS!C39	=BS!G39–BS!F39
47	="Incr (decr) in "&BS!C40	=BS!G40–BS!F40
48	=C99	=G99
49	="(Incr) decr in "&BS!C42	=BS!G42-BS!F42
50	Cash from financing	=SUM(G39:G49)
51		
52	Total cash flow	=G29+G37+G50
53		
54	Excess cash (revolver)	=F54+G52
55		
56	B/S excess cash (revolver)	=BS!G8–BS!G23
57	Balance check	=G54–G56
58	=IF(COUNTIF(G58:K58,"Check"), "Check","OK")	=IF(ROUND(G57,0)=0, "OK","Check")
59		

12.4.1 Row 52: Total Cash Flow

Row 52 adds the cash flows from the three categories that have been laid out in the cash flow statement (cash from operations, cash from investments, and cash from financing). This is how much cash the business has generated in the year. (Each column in the model is a year.) This is the cash *over* all the business needs as determined by all the changes in the balance sheet accounts between the prior year and the current year. In other words, all operating expenses, investments, and/or financing obligations have been covered by the company's cash flow and this is the resulting *excess cash flow* generated by the company.

Note that if the total cash flow is a negative number, it indicates the cash shortfall (or a negative cash flow) the business has.

12.4.2 Row 54: Excess Cash (Revolver)

Row 54 adds the current year's total cash flow (Row 52) to the prior year's excess cash (revolver) number. Note that the formula in Column G, which is the first column with formulas in the cash flow statement, looks to Column F, *which is empty*. Column F is a historical year and should have 0 as a balancing number in the excess cash (revolver) row, as all historical data are by definition balanced. So the fact that it is blank (which of course is equivalent to a 0 value) does not matter. What would matter is if the numbers in Column F balance sheet have not been correctly entered and there is an imbalance. In this case, the imbalance will be carried forward and there will appear to be an imbalance in subsequent years, too. So this is just a reminder that all historical numbers should balance, because if they do not, you will have a balancing error in the forecast years, even if your balancing formulas for the forecast years are working flawlessly.

Columns G and H are also historical years, and even though Row 54 has formulas for these columns, they should be zeros.

To illustrate with some sample numbers (Table 12-3): The starting point is the beginning or prior year's number. If there is excess cash, this prior year number is a positive number (cases 1, 3, and 4); if there is a revolver amount, this prior number is negative number (cases 2, 5, and 6).

TABLE 12-3

Calculation of Excess Cash or Revolver with the Current Year's Total Cash Flow

Case	Beginning–i.e., Prior Year–Value of Excess Cash (Revolver)	Current Year's Total Cash Flow	Ending–Current Year–Value of Excess Cash (Revolver)
1	50	(75)	(25)
2	(50)	75	25
3	100	(25)	75
4	100	25	125
5	(100)	(25)	(125)
6	(100)	25	(75)

The ending or current year's value depends on the amount of the total cash flow. It is possible that the current year's total cash flow is such that it reverses what was originally an excess cash position into a revolver position (case 1) and vice versa (case 2). In other situations, the current year's total cash flow may add or subtract to the original excess cash or revolver position, but there is no reversal of positions (cases 3–6): what was an excess cash position last year remains more or less so, and what was a revolver position likewise remains more or less so.

When the current year's total cash flow, which is a *flow* number, is added to the beginning excess cash (revolver) number, which is a *stock* number, we have the ending excess cash (revolver) number, another stock number. A stock number is a static value and is the accumulated total of all flows. All balance sheet accounts are stock accounts.

The ending value of excess cash is what appears on the balance sheet. If positive, it will appear as excess cash in the asset side of the balance sheet. If negative, it will appear (but shown as a positive) as the revolver in the liabilities account in the balance sheet.

12.4.3 Rows 55–57: Final Checks

These rows check that the balance sheet excess cash (revolver) numbers match the ones produced by the cash flow statement.

Cell C58 contains a check formula that counts the number of error messages that appear on the row to the right. In this way, Cell C58 becomes the master check cell for the cash flow statement.

12.5 RECONCILIATION TABLES

Reconciliation tables (sometimes referred to as control accounts) are ways to ensure that all flows are accounted for. A reconciliation table is useful in tracking those balance sheet accounts that are affected by an income statement account. An example is the investment account on the balance sheet, which is affected by the equity earning in affiliates in the income statement.

The role of a reconciliation table is to calculate any discrepancy between the change in the balance sheet account between the prior year and the current year, and the income statement flow in the current year. Should there be a discrepancy (e.g., investments account increases by 30, but the equity earnings in affiliates in the income statement expense is 35), then the reconciliation table should indicate that there is an additional—and unexplained—source of cash of 5. It is a source because the balance sheet account should have increased by 35 according to the income statement flow, but it is showing only a 30 increases. So there is an apparent decrease of 5 in the balance sheet. A decrease in an asset is a source of cash.

If such discrepancies are not accounted for, the cash flow statement will not foot correctly. The discrepancy can occur especially when the model is used to replicate the output from another model, which may have incorrect calculations. In this case, when the mismatched numbers are entered as hard-coded numbers in both the income statement and the balance sheet, the reconciliation tables can note the discrepancy and make the adjustment to the cash flow statement.

We will be building five reconciliation tables (Fig. 12-3 and Fig. 12-4). The five are for:

- Net PPE
- Investments in affiliates
- Intangibles
- Minority interest
- Retained earnings

FIGURE 12-3

Reconciliation Table Layouts for Net PPE, Investment in Affiliates, and Intangibles

	C	F	G	H	I	J	K
60					Proj	Proj	Proj
61	**RECONCILIATION**	**Dec-05**	**Dec-06**	**Dec-07**	**Dec-08**	**Dec-09**	**Dec-10**
62							
63	**Net PPE**						
64	Beginning amount		870.0	950.0	1,000.0	1,080.0	1,206.0
65	Capex		155.0	130.0	165.0	217.8	239.6
66	Depreciation		(75.0)	(80.0)	(85.0)	(91.8)	(102.5)
67	Book value of assets sold		0.0	0.0	0.0	0.0	0.0
68	Expected ending amount		950.0	1,000.0	1,080.0	1,206.0	1,343.1
69	B/S amount		950.0	1,000.0	1,080.0	1,206.0	1,343.1
70	Other (incr) decr in Net PPE		0.0	0.0	0.0	0.0	0.0
71							
72	**Investment in affiliates**						
73	Beginning amount		58.0	54.0	50.0	52.2	58.7
74	Equity earnings in affiliates		5.0	6.0	6.2	6.5	6.8
75	Note: how the table identifies the 4.0 dividends received in Dec-08						
76	Expected ending amount		63.0	60.0	56.2	58.7	65.5
77	B/S amount		54.0	50.0	52.2	58.7	65.5
78	Other (incr) decr in Investment in affiliates		9.0	10.0	4.0	0.0	0.0
79							
80	**Intangibles**						
81	Beginning amount		50.0	54.0	58.0	54.0	50.0
82	Amortization		(4.0)	(4.0)	(4.0)	(4.0)	(4.0)
83	Expected ending amount		46.0	50.0	54.0	50.0	46.0
84	B/S amount		54.0	58.0	54.0	50.0	46.0
85	Other (incr) decr in Intangibles		(8.0)	(8.0)	0.0	0.0	0.0
86							

FIGURE 12-4

Reconciliation Table Layouts for Minority Interest and Retained Earnings

	C	F	G	H	I	J	K
87	**Minority interest**						
88	Beginning amount		58.0	70.0	83.0	97.3	112.3
89	Minority interest in earnings		12.0	13.0	14.3	15.0	15.8
90	Expected ending amount		70.0	83.0	97.3	112.3	128.1
91	B/S amount		70.0	83.0	97.3	112.3	128.1
92	Other incr (decr) in Minority interest		0.0	0.0	0.0	0.0	0.0
93							
94	**Retained earnings**						
95	Beginning amount		200.0	243.9	301.0	380.7	478.7
96	Net to retained earnings		43.9	57.1	79.7	98.0	109.4
97	Expected ending amount		243.9	301.0	380.7	478.7	588.1
98	B/S amount		243.9	301.0	380.7	478.7	588.1
99	Other incr (decr) in Retained earnings		0.0	0.0	0.0	0.0	0.0
100							

TABLE 12-4

Reconciliation Table Formulas for Net PPE, Investment in Affiliates, and Intangibles

Row	Label in Column C	Label Formula in Column C	Formula in Column G (copy to H to K)
60			
61	RECONCILIATION	RECONCILIATION	=G6
62			
63	Net PPE	=Input!C132	
64	Beginning amount	Beginning amount	=BS!F16
65	Capex	Capex	=–G31
66	Depreciation	Depreciation	=–G11
67	Book value of assets sold	=Input!C131	=Input!G131
68	Expected ending amount	Expected ending amount	=SUM(G64:G67)
69	B/S amount	B/S amount	=BS!G16
70	Other (incr) decr in Net PPE	="Other (incr) decr in "&C63	=G68-G69
71			
72	Investment in affiliates	=Input!C134	
73	Beginning amount	Beginning amount	=BS!F17
74	Equity earnings in affiliates	=IS!C31	=IS!G31
75			
76	Expected ending amount	Expected ending amount	=SUM(G73:G75)
77	B/S amount	B/S amount	=BS!G17
78	Other (incr) decr in Investment in affiliates	="Other (incr) decr in "&C72	=G76–G77
79			
80	Intangibles	=Input!C141	
81	Beginning amount	Beginning amount	=BS!F18
82	Amortization	Amortization	=–G12
83	Expected ending amount	Expected ending amount	=SUM(G81:G82)
84	B/S amount	B/S amount	=BS!G18
85	Other (incr) decr in Intangibles	="Other (incr) decr in "&C80	=G83–G84
86			

12.5.1 Reconciliation Tables for Net PPE, Investment in Affiliates, and Intangibles

Table 12-4 describes the formulas in Figure 12-3.

12.5.2 Reconciliation Tables for Minority Interest and Retained Earnings

Figure 12-4 completes the reconciliation tables. See Table 12-5 for the description of the formulas.

TABLE 12-5

Reconciliation Table Formulas for Minority Interest and Retained Earnings

Row	Label in Column C	Label Formula in Column C	Formula in Column G (copy to H to K)
87	Minority interest	=BS!C36	
88	Beginning amount	Beginning amount	=BS!F36
89	Minority interest in earnings	=IS!C32	=IS!G32
90	Expected ending amount	Expected ending amount	=SUM(G88:G89)
91	B/S amount	B/S amount	=BS!G36
92	Other incr (decr) in Minority interest	="Other incr (decr) in "&C87	=G91-G90
93			
94	Retained earnings	=Input!C209	
95	Beginning amount	Beginning amount	=BS!F41
96	Net to retained earnings	Net to retained earnings	=IS!G41
97	Expected ending amount	Expected ending amount	=SUM(G95:G96)
98	B/S amount	B/S amount	=BS!G41
99	Other incr (decr) in Retained earnings	="Other incr (decr) in "&C94	=G98–G97

12.6 CONNECTING THE CASH FLOW STATEMENT TO THE BALANCE SHEET

The cash flow statement as developed so far is not used to balance the balance sheet. However, if we have done everything correctly, when we check the excess cash (revolver) results from the cash flow statement (Row 54) against the balance sheet values (Row 95 and Row 150 in the Balance Sheet model in Chapter 11), they should be identical. In fact, we can now go to the balance sheet and change the formulas for the excess cash row and the revolver row to read these cash flow statement results. In this case, we will then not be using the balancing formulas that we created at the bottom of the balance sheet.

Using the cash flow to balance the balance sheet is a common practice in creating integrated financial models. Even so, it is often useful to first build a balance sheet balancing system:

- The balance sheet method is quicker, since you do not have to build the cash flow statement.
- When it comes time to build a cash flow statement, you know the excess cash (revolver) numbers at which you should arrive. The cash flow statement is the most difficult to build because it is a compilation of many calculations, all of which have to work correctly to arrive at the correct result.
- The balance sheet balancing will work (and show where the imbalances are) for historical data, even for the first column in the model where there is no "prior" year. The cash flow balancing requires a "prior" year.

12.7 EXCESS CASH (REVOLVER) WORKS IN EITHER APPROACH

In either approach to building a balanced balance sheet, the excess cash (revolver) numbers—whether they are produced at the bottom of the balance sheet, or through the cash flow statement—will be correctly calculated. Keep this in mind as we go to the next chapter on cash sweeps.

CHAPTER 13

The Cash Sweep

The cash sweep is a modeling technique to automatically pay down debt in addition to any scheduled amortization payments. The sweep uses the excess cash line in the model. It does not use the cash line in the model.

The cash sweep can occur:

- In forecast years only
- When there is excess cash
- When there are tranches of long-term debt that are suitable for automatic repayment. Usually, this means only bank debt, and not issued bond debt.

Short-term debt by definition will be repaid in a year and so should not have the cash sweep applied to it. Certain long-term debt obligations such as bonds have either predetermined repayment schedules and/or penalties for being repaid early (prepayment penalties), so their holders cannot or do not want to repay them early. These obligations should not be part of the cash sweep.

13.1 CONCEPT

In a cash sweep, what we want to do is to make the model take the excess cash and reduce the long-term bank debt.

FIGURE 13-1

The Cash Sweep when the Excess Cash Is Less Than the Total Debt (Figure Not to Scale)

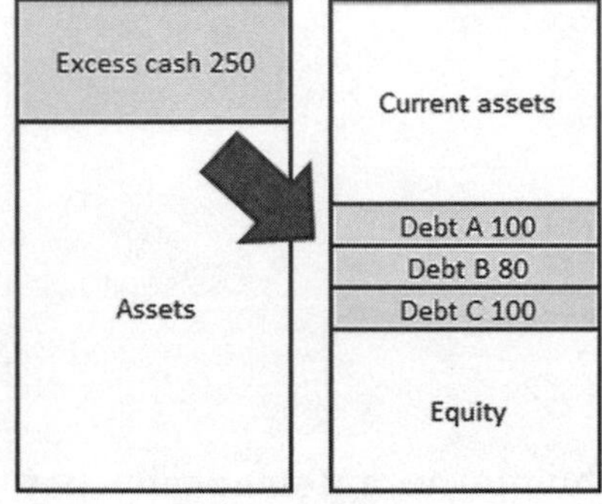

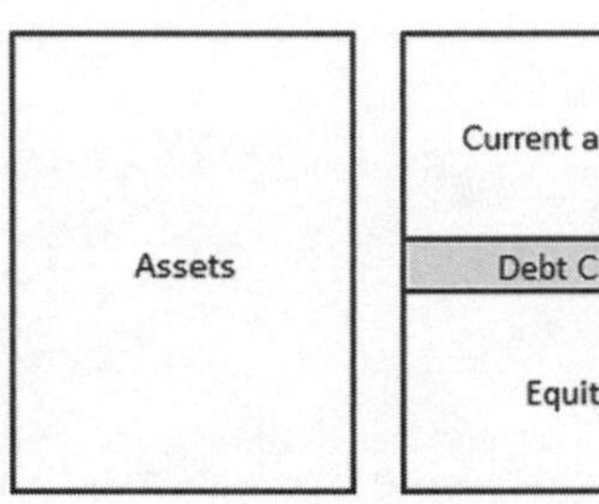

Figure 13-1 shows the case in which the excess cash (250) is less than the total debt that can be repaid (280). After the cash sweep, all excess cash has been used; 30 still remains of the Debt C tranche.

In Figure 13-2, the excess cash (300) is more than the total debt (280). In this case, after the cash sweep, 20 of the excess cash still remains on the asset side. All the debt has been repaid.

The cash sweep automatically adjusts for available excess cash. For example, as the tranche A of debt is repaid, the interest expenses associated with it is removed so the excess cash amount available for the remaining sweep increases. The same effect is seen as additional debt tranches are repaid.

13.1.1 Circular References

The cash sweep can work with or without the circular references caused by the calculation of interest income and expense on the excess cash and the revolver, respectively. If you want to use the average interest calculation on the plug numbers, make sure you turn Excel's iteration setting on.

FIGURE 13-2

The Cash Sweep When Excess Cash Is More Than Total Debt (Figure Not to Scale)

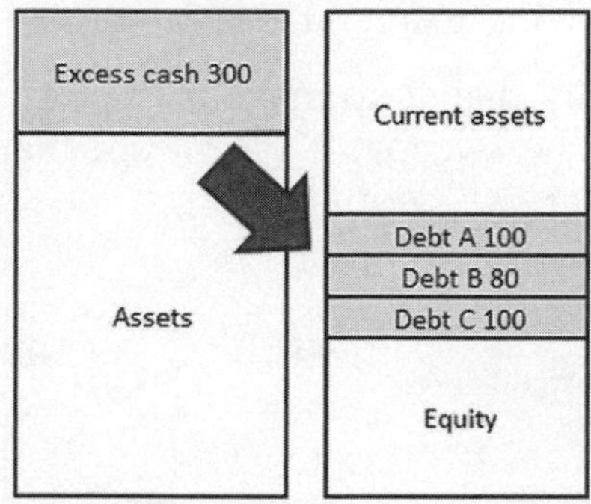

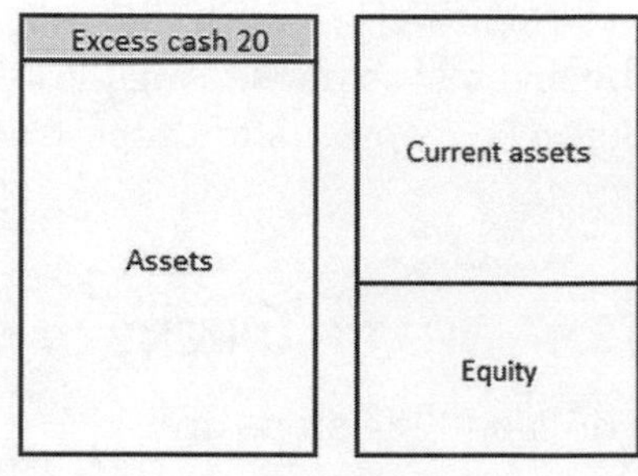

13.2 MODELING STRUCTURE FOR A CASH SWEEP

The illustration for the cash sweep can be generalized as follows (Fig. 13-3). The blocks shaded in gray are the items in the balance sheet that are affected as a result of the cash sweep. They are:

- Excess cash
- Repayable or sweepable debt

FIGURE 13-3

General Scheme for a Cash Sweep

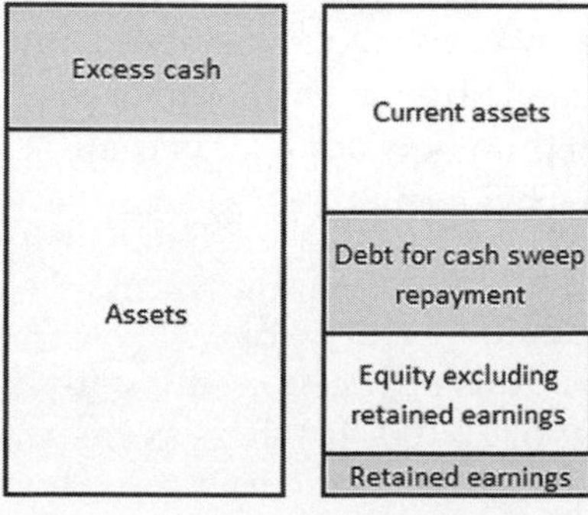

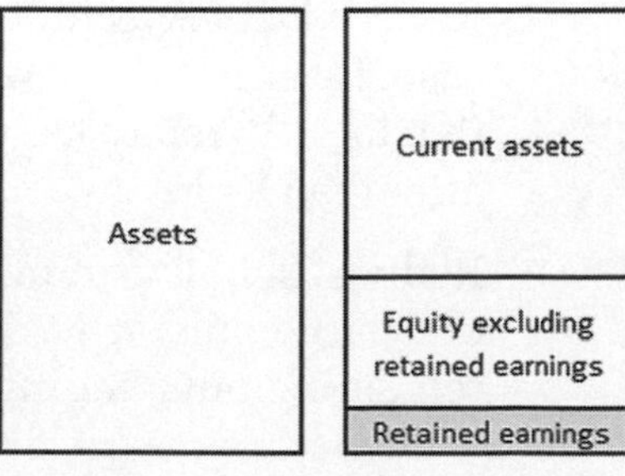

- Retained earnings. This is affected because the interest expense related to the debt being repaid decreases. At the same time, any interest income from the excess cash decreases. Because the interest rate on debt is typically higher than on excess cash, in a cash sweep there is usually a net decrease in interest expense and a corollary increase in the net income flowing to retained earnings.

On the income statement, the only change to make is to point the interest expense calculations on the sweepable debt from the before-sweep outstandings to the after-sweep outstandings.

13.3 WHAT HAPPENS IN A SWEEP

The modeling steps are:

1. Find the excess cash amount, if any. If there is no excess cash, there is no cash sweep. In this first calculation of excess cash in the "before" balance sheet, use the *before*-cash sweep debt amounts.

   Table 13-1 shows the flows in a cash sweep. Let's assume for this illustration that the numbers are as follows:

   a. Excess cash 80
   b. Debt A 40
   c. Debt B 60
   d. Debt C 20

   Let's also assume that we want to apply the available excess cash to pay down or sweep 100% of each debt's outstanding amount.
2. Reduce Debt A as much as possible by the available excess cash. In this case, there is more than enough excess cash (80) to fully repay Debt A (40). The ending excess cash after the Debt A sweep is 40.
3. Reduce Debt B as much as possible by the available excess cash, now only at 40. Thus, Debt B is reduced by 40, with a remaining outstanding amount of 20 (60–40). Excess cash is now a 0.

TABLE 13–1

Sweeps with Available Cash Applied for Repayment of 100% of Each Outstanding Debt Tranche

	Starting Amount		Excess cash	100% Sweep	Ending Amount
		Available at start	80		
Debt A	40			(40)	0
		Remaining after Debt A sweep	40		
Debt B	60			(40)	20
		Remaining after Debt A and Debt B sweeps	0		
Debt C	20			0	20
		Excess cash at the end	0		

TABLE 13–2

Sweeps with Available Cash Applied for Repayment of 60% of Each Outstanding Debt Tranche

	Starting Amount		Excess Cash	60% Sweep	Ending Amount
		Available at start	80		
Debt A	40			(24)	16
		Remaining after Debt A sweep	56		
Debt B	60			(36)	24
		Remaining after Debt A and Debt B sweeps	20		
Debt C	20			(12)	8
		Excess cash at the end	8		

4. Reduce Debt C as much as possible by the available excess cash. But by this stage, excess cash is 0. So Debt C remains at 20.
5. Create the "after" balance sheet by using the *after* cash sweep excess cash (revolver) plugs and *after* cash sweep debt outstandings.

In some cases, companies may want to use the available excess cash not for a full 100% repayment of the debt, but a lower percentage. Table 13-2 shows the flows when, for example, a 60% rate is used.

13.4 THE EXCESS CASH FOR SWEEP

The derive the excess cash amount, we can use either the balance sheet balancing approach or the cash flow balancing approach. Either one results in the same excess cash amount for the same modeling case.

In this chapter, we will build a cash sweep model for the balance sheet balancing method (see Section 13.5) and the cash flow balancing (see Section 13.6).

13.4.1 Excess Cash Before the Sweep and After the Sweep

It may seem contradictory that we can use the excess cash sweep to determine the cash sweep, when the cash sweep essentially reduces the ending cash amount. You may wonder if there is not some sort of a circular reference here.

The secret is that in the cash sweep we use two balance sheets for our calculations:

- The first balance sheet has the values of the debt before the cash sweep. This results in the pre-cash sweep excess cash. This excess cash is used to reduce the sweepable debt.
- The second balance sheet has the same assets, non-debt liabilities and equity as the first, but has the post-sweep debt outstandings, and the post-sweep excess cash.

This does not mean that we have to develop two balance sheets in the model, however. As pointed out in Section 13.3, only three parts of the balance sheet change in a cash sweep: the excess cash, the sweepable debt, and the retained earnings; all other parts do not change during the sweep calculations. With this in mind, to calculate the pre-sweep cash, we use the debt amounts *before* the cash sweeps with the other balance sheet accounts. When the sweep calculations are done, we present the final results using the debt amounts *after* the cash sweep and with the other (unchanged) balance sheet accounts.

There is a balance sheet already laid out in the model: this is the one that will appear as the second one that shows the *post*-cash sweep debt amounts. The first balance sheet is a virtual one and exists as nothing more than a row for the calculation of starting excess cash. This calculation uses the *pre*-cash sweep debt along with the assets, non-debt liabilities and equity already laid out.

13.4.2 Interest Calculations and Retained Earnings

Although the assets and non-debt liabilities show no differences between the before and after cash sweep states, retained earnings are affected because the cash sweep reduces the interest expense related to the debt being repaid. The cash sweep also reduces the interest income because interest income is reduced as the available excess cash is used for the sweep.

For the modeling, the interest income and interest expense calculations in the income statement should always be based on post-cash sweep debt amount. This calculation structure by itself does not create a circular reference. The circular reference occurs only if you choose to calculate the interest income and expense based on the average amounts of the current year and the prior year's values for excess cash and debt, respectively. The use of average amounts will cause by itself a circular reference, regardless of whether we are constructing a cash sweep calculation module or not.

13.4.3 Illustrative Calculations in a Cash Sweep

The following is a set of tables that show the calculations in a cash sweep. At the left of each table are reference letters for each line, with an explanation where needed in the second column. For example, Line K is Lines J less Line C.

Table 13-3 shows the elements that go into the calculation of the excess cash available for the cash sweep. Table 13-4 show the cash sweep calculations. The non-debt elements (assets A and B, liabilities D and H, and equity I) appear again in Table 13-5.

TABLE 13-3

The Starting Pre-Cash Sweep Balance Sheet

Line	Explanation	Item	Year 1	Year 2	Year 3
A to J are the before cash sweep balance sheet information used to calculate excess cash (revolver)					
A	Input in model	Current assets excluding excess cash	200	220	250
B	Input in model	Long-term assets	330	350	400
C		Total assets excluding excess cash	530	570	650
D	Input in model	Current liabilities excluding revolver	200	220	280
E	Prior yr's Line T	Starting Debt A (before each yr's sweep)[1]	40	40	0
F	Prior yr's Line U	Starting Debt B (before each yr's sweep)	60	60	20
G	Prior yr's Line V	Starting Debt C (before each yr's sweep)	20	20	20
H	Input in model	Other long-term liabilities	10	30	30
I	Input in model	Shareholders' equity	100	280	330
J		Total liabilities and equity excluding revolver	430	650	680
K	J-C	Excess cash (revolver) before sweep	(100)	80	30

[1] For the first year, Debts A-C are inputs into the model. In subsequent years, each uses each prior year's after-sweep amounts.

TABLE 13–4

The Cash Sweep Calculations

Line	Explanation	Item	Year 1	Year 2	Year 3
Cash sweep calculations begin					
L	MAX(K,0)	Excess cash available for cash sweep[2]	0	80	30
E		Starting Debt A (before sweep)	40	40	0
F		Starting Debt B (before sweep)	60	60	20
G		Starting Debt C (before sweep)	20	20	20
M	–MIN(L,E)	Sweep for Debt A: The sweep takes the smaller of the values of the excess cash available and Debt A	0	(40)	0
N	–MIN(L+M,F)	Sweep for Debt B: The sweep takes the smaller of the values of the excess cash available after the repayment in Line M, and Debt B	0	(40)	(20)
O	–MIN(L+M+ N,G)	Sweep for Debt C: The sweep takes the smaller of the values of the excess cash available after the repayment in Lines M + N, and Debt C	0	0	(10)
P	M+N+O	Total sweep	0	(80)	(30)
Q	E+M	Ending Debt A (after sweep)	40	0	0
R	F+N	Ending Debt B (after sweep)	60	20	0
S	G+O	Ending Debt B (after sweep)	20	20	10
T	K+P	Excess cash (revolver) after sweep	(100)	0	0

[2] This line shows only the available excess cash. In the first year, as the excess cash is negative (100), the value shows as 0 and there is no cash sweep.

TABLE 13-5

The Final Layout of the Balance Sweep with Post-Cash Sweep Numbers

The After Cash Sweep Balance Sheet. Note the Use of Accounts from the Before Sweep B/S					
U	MAX(T,0)	Excess cash	0	0	0
A		Current assets excluding excess cash	200	220	250
B		Long-term assets	330	350	400
V		Total assets	530	570	650
W	–MIN(T,0)	Revolver	100	0	0
D		Current liabilities excluding revolver	200	220	280
Q		Ending Debt A (after sweep)	40	0	0
R		Ending Debt B (after sweep)	60	20	0
S		Ending Debt B (after sweep)	20	20	10
H		Other long-term liabilities	10	30	30
I		Shareholders' equity	100	280	330
X		Total liabilities and shareholders' equity	530	570	650

The first illustration of the cash sweep modeling is based on the balance sheet balancing approach as opposed to the cash flow balancing approach. For the latter, please refer to Section 13.6 below.

Section 13.6.

In Table 13-4, the cash sweep calculations are shown.

With the cash sweep done, the pre- and post-sweep balance sheet numbers are brought together to present a final post-sweep picture (Table 13-5).

13.5 THE CASH SWEEP IN BALANCE SHEET BALANCING

Please use the model developed earlier in Chapter 11. The model is available in the book's Web site, www.buildingfinancialmodels.com.

13.5.1 Inserting New Rows in the Debt Section

Using the model that we have been working with, the first task is to insert additional rows in the model to distinguish debt before the cash sweep, the amount of the cash sweep itself, and the debt after the cash sweep. Figure 13-4 shows the changes in rounded boxes. Table 13-6 shows the formulas for the rows. Changes from the non-cash sweep version are shown in bold.

The historical formulas (Table 13-6) are not much different and simply connect to the original inputs.

Two important points:

1. For each of the IF formulas on the debt before the sweep (Row 171 for Debt A, Row 179 for Debt B, and Row 187 for Debt C), the reference to the prior year's number is to the *after*-cash sweep row (Rows 173, 181, and 189, respectively). This makes sure that for each debt the cash sweep reduction is carried into each subsequent year.

FIGURE 13-4

Insert the Rows Shown for Debts 1–3

	A	B	C	D	E	F	G	H	I	J	K
166			Other current liabilites			10.0	20.0	20.0	22.0	24.2	26.6
167			**Current liabilites**			**80.0**	**102.0**	**114.0**	**127.2**	**138.5**	**150.9**
168											
169			Debt A			200.0	225.0	150.0			
170			New (amortization)								
171			Debt A before sweep			200.0	225.0	150.0	150.0	150.0	150.0
172			Cash sweep						0.0	0.0	0.0
173			Debt A			200.0	225.0	150.0	150.0	150.0	150.0
174			Interest rate %						10.0%	10.0%	10.0%
175			Interest expense						15.0	15.0	15.0
176											
177			Debt B			120.0	120.0	145.0			
178			New (amortization)								
179			Debt B before sweep			120.0	120.0	145.0	145.0	145.0	145.0
180			Cash sweep						0.0	0.0	0.0
181			Debt B			120.0	120.0	145.0	145.0	145.0	145.0
182			Interest rate %						10.0%	10.0%	10.0%
183			Interest expense						14.5	14.5	14.5
184											
185			Debt C			110.0	110.0	110.0			
186			New (amortization)								
187			Debt C before sweep			110.0	110.0	110.0	110.0	110.0	110.0
188			Cash sweep						0.0	0.0	0.0
189			Debt C			110.0	110.0	110.0	110.0	110.0	110.0
190			Interest rate %						8.0%	8.0%	8.0%
191			Interest expense						8.8	8.8	8.8
192											

TABLE 13–6

Formulas for the New Debt Rows (Changes from Non-Cash Sweep Version in Bold)

Row	Label in Column C	Formula in Column F (copy to G and H)	Formula in Column I (copy to J and K)
169	Debt A		
170	New (amortization)		
171	Debt A before sweep	=F169	=IF(I169,I169,H173+I170)
172	Cash sweep		0 As we have not done the cash sweep formulas at this point, put a 0 or just leave this blank for the moment
173	Debt A	=F171	=I171+I172
174	Interest rate %		
175	Interest expense		=I174*AVERAGE (H173:I173)
176			
177	Debt B		
178	New (amortization)		
179	Debt B before sweep	=F177	=IF(I177,I177,H181+I178)
180	Cash sweep		0 As we have not done the cash sweep formulas at this point, put a 0 or just leave this blank for the moment
181	Debt B	=F179	=I179+I180
182	Interest rate %		
183	Interest expense		=I182*AVERAGE (H181:I181)
184			
185	Debt C		
186	New (amortization)		
187	Debt C before sweep	=F185	=IF(I185,I185,H189+I186)
188	Cash sweep		0 As we have not done the cash sweep formulas at this point, put a zero or just leave this blank for the moment

TABLE 13-6 (CONTINUED)

Row	Label in Column C	Formula in Column F (copy to G and H)	Formula in Column I (copy to J and K)
189	Debt C	=F187	=I187+I188
190	Interest rate %		
191	Interest expense		=I190*AVERAGE (H189:I189)
192			

2. Interest expense for each debt looks to the *after*-cash sweep outstandings.

The cash sweep rows will carry a negative sign to denote that a cash sweep is a reduction in debt. Thus, the formula on each ending debt (Rows 173, 181, and 189) is a sum of the before cash sweep amount and the calculated negative cash sweep amount.

13.5.2 Adding the Cash Sweep Rows

Figure 13-5 shows the balancing formulas expanded to show the cash sweep calculations. Because we have inserted additional rows in the debt section for the cash sweep rows (shown in Figure 13-4), the row numbers in this section have shifted downward when compared to Figure 11-9 in Chapter 11.

The new formulas are described below (Tables 13-7 to 13-11).

Note that in Table 13-7, as in previous chapters, the calculation for the excess cash or revolver is [total liabilities and equity without the revolver] minus [total assets without the excess cash]. This is shown in Rows 226 to 227.

Row 229 takes the difference between Rows 226 and 227. The ISERROR function is included because in the event there is an error message in the model, such as #DIV/0!, the ISERROR prevents such errors from propagating throughout the model and allows the model to automatically recover once the source of the error is removed.

FIGURE 13-5

The Formula Rows at the Bottom of the Balance Sheet

	A	B	C	D	E	F	G	H	I	J	K
217			Other equity account			10.0	12.1	12.0			
218			% of revenues			1.2%	1.3%	1.2%	1.2%	1.2%	1.2%
219			Other equity account			10.0	12.1	12.0	13.2	14.5	16.0
220			**Shareholders' equity**			**750.0**	**826.0**	**963.0**	**1,143.9**	**1,243.2**	**1,354.1**
221			**Total liabs, min interest, equity**			**1,358.0**	**1,501.0**	**1,615.0**	**1,817.3**	**1,947.4**	**2,091.3**
222											
223			Balance check			0.0	0.0	0.0	0.0	0.0	0.0
224						OK	OK	OK	OK	OK	OK
225			**Note: liabilities use pre-cash sweep amounts**								
226			Assets without excess cash			1,358.0	1,501.0	1,615.0	1,718.1	1,883.9	2,070.3
227			Liabs, SH Eq without revolver			1,358.0	1,501.0	1,615.0	1,817.3	1,947.4	2,091.3
228											
229			Excess cash (revolver)						99.3	63.5	21.1
230											
231			Excess cash enabled for cash sweep?					N	0.0	0.0	0.0
232											
233			Starting Debt A (before sweep)						150.0	150.0	150.0
234			Starting Debt B (before sweep)						145.0	145.0	145.0
235			Starting Debt C (before sweep)						110.0	110.0	110.0
236											
237			Sweep for Debt A						0.0	0.0	0.0
238			Sweep for Debt B						0.0	0.0	0.0
239			Sweep for Debt C						0.0	0.0	0.0
240			Total sweep						0.0	0.0	0.0
241											
242			**Excess cash (revolver) after sweep**						99.3	63.5	21.1
243											

In listing the Liabilities in Row 227 in Table 13-7, we use the before cash sweep debt amounts (Rows 171, 179, and 187). These rows include any scheduled amortizations or new funding.

In the cash sweep calculations, the assets side of the balance sheet, outside the excess cash row, does not change.

Row 231 (Table 13-8) is a toggle that turns on and off the cash sweep function. It turns off the sweep by setting the excess cash amounts to 0. This is a good feature to have. There may be cases, for example, in which you may want to see the numbers without the cash sweep; in this case, just set this to "N" to turn the cash sweep function off. The use of the MAX with the 0 means that this row shows only positive values or zeroes.

Rows 233, 234, and 235 bring the before-sweep debt amounts into this section of the model in preparation for the sweep formulas.

TABLE 13-7

Arriving at the Pre-Sweep Cash or Revolver Amounts

Row	Label in Column C	Formula in Column F (Copy to G and H)	Formula in Column I (Copy to J and K)
223	Balance check	=F221-F147	=I221-I147
224		=IF(ROUND(F223,0)= 0,"OK", "Check")	=IF(ROUND(I223,0)=0,"OK", "Check")
225	Note: liabilities use pre-cash sweep amounts		
226	Assets without excess cash	=F101+F107+F114+ F119+F123+F132+F137+ F141+F146	=I101+I107+I114+I119+I123 +I132+I137+I141+I146
227	Liabs, SH Eq without revolver	=F155+F162+F166+ F171+F179+F187+F196+ F202+F206+F211+ F215+F219	=I155+I162+I166+I171+I179 +I187+I196+I202+I206+I211 +I215+I219
228			
229	Excess cash (revolver)		=IF(ISERROR(I227–226),0, I227–I226)
230			

13.5.3 The Cash Sweep Formulas

This is where the cash sweep action takes place (Table 13-9). Let's look at the rows separately. Note: as configured here in building the cash sweep, the toggle for the cash sweep in Cell H231 is set to "N," so there are no cash sweep calculations at this point.

13.5.3.1 Debt A in row 237

The formula is:

=–MIN(I$231,I233)

This returns the lesser of the available excess cash (I$231) and the starting debt amount (I233). The available excess cash has an absolute reference for the row number to make it easier

TABLE 13-8

The Cash Sweep Formulas

Row	Label in Column C	No Formulas in Columns F to G	Formula in Column I (Copy to J and K)
231	Excess cash enabled for cash sweep?		=IF($H$231="Y",MAX (I229,0),0)
232			
233	Starting Debt A (before sweep)		=I171
234	Starting Debt B (before sweep)		=I179
235	Starting Debt C (before sweep)		=I187
236			

TABLE 13-9

The Sweep Formulas

Row	Label in Column C	No Formulas in Columns F to G	Formula in Column I (copy to J and K)
237	Sweep for Debt A		=–MIN(I$231,I233)
238	Sweep for Debt B		=–MIN(I$231+SUM (I$237:I237),I234)
239	Sweep for Debt C		=–MIN(I$231+SUM (I$237:I238),I235)
240	Total sweep		=SUM(I237:I239)
241			
242	Excess cash (revolver) after sweep		=I229+I240

as we copy this formula down to Rows 238 to 239. Of course, we will have to make some edits as we do this.

The MIN function used in this section has a minus sign in front of it as we want the sweep amount to be shown as a negative number.

13.5.3.2 Debt B in row 238

The formula is:

```
=–MIN(I$231+SUM(I$237:I237), I234)
```

This is an expansion of the formula in Row 237. The addition is a SUM function that adds the Debt A cash sweep to the starting available excess cash formula. It is a SUM because the Debt A cash sweep is a negative number, so this essentially reduces the available cash sweep for Debt B by the amount of the sweep for Debt A. I am using a SUM with an absolute reference for the front part of the range (on only on the row number) and not the back (I$237: I237). This makes it easy to copy the formula down to the next row for Debt C without having to make any changes.

13.5.3.3 Debt C in row 239

The formula is:

```
=–MIN(I$231+SUM(I$237:I238), I235)
```

This is similar to the formula for Debt B, but the reduction in the available excess cash now includes the cash sweeps for Debt A and Debt B as shown in the formula:

```
SUM(I$237:I238)
```

13.5.3.4 Excess cash (revolver) after sweep in row 242

This sums the starting excess cash or revolver (Row 229) and the total cash sweep (Row 240). This row is read by the excess cash and the revolver rows in the balance sheet.

Note that the excess cash or revolver row is Row 229, not Row 231. The latter is the row for excess cash only and it does

FIGURE 13-6

Change the Excess Cash Formula to Read the New Balancing Row

	A	B	C	D	E	F	G	H	I	J	K
94			ASSETS								
95			Excess cash						99.3	63.5	21.1
96			Interest rate %						5.0%	5.0%	5.0%
97			Interest income						0.0	5.0	3.2

show the negative values for the revolver. The reason we look to Row 229 is that we want to include negative numbers for the revolver values in this calculation, since we would need that for the balance sheet.

13.5.4 Adjusting the Balance Sheet Excess Cash and Revolver Rows

Change the excess cash formula in the balance sheet so that it reads Row 242, with the MAX ,0 (Fig. 13-6 and Table 13-10).

Change the revolver formula so that it reads Row 242, using the –MIN ,0. Don't forget the minus sign in front of the MIN function (Fig. 13-7 and Table 13-11).

13.5.5 Connect the Debt Input Section to the Cash Sweep

As the finishing touch, look at the rows listed in Table 13-12 and complete the formulas that we left blank as we began the cash sweep modifications.

TABLE 13-10

Formula for the Excess Cash Row

Row	Label in Column C	Formula in Column I (copy to J and K)
94	ASSETS	
95	Excess cash	=MAX(I242,0)
96	Interest rate %	
97	Interest income	=I96*H95

FIGURE 13-7

Change the Revolver Formula to Read the New Balancing Row

	A	B	C	D	E	F	G	H	I	J	K
149			LIABILITIES								
150			Revolver						0.0	0.0	0.0
151			Interest rate %						10.0%	10.0%	10.0%
152			Interest expense						0.0	0.0	0.0

13.5.6 Interest Expense Are on After Cash Sweep Values

We have already changed the interest expense calculations for the swept debt in the balance sheet (Section 13.5.1), and we made those look to the after-cash sweep amounts. The income statement in turn reads those formulas, so there is no need to make any changes in the income statement for the cash sweep. Of course, if the interest calculations had been put on the income statement, then we would have to make those changes in the income statement.

Now go to Cell H231 and set the toggle to "Y" to enable the cash sweep to run. You will see the model's numbers as shown in Figure 13-8. The numbers in the balance sheet for the debt and excess cash, and the related interest calculations in the income statement, will also reflect these changes. As you change your assumptions on the income statement and the balance sheet so that there is more or less available cash to pay down debt, the model will continue to calculate the cash sweep.

And we're done.

TABLE 13-11

Formula for the Revolver Formula

Row	Label in Column C	Formula in Column I (copy to J and K)
149	LIABILITIES	
150	Revolver	=–MIN(I242,0)
151	Interest rate %	
152	Interest expense	=I151*H150

TABLE 13–12

Fill in the Formulas to Bring the Cash Sweep Amounts to the Debt Section

Row	Label in Column C	Formula in Column F (copy to G and H)	Formula in Column I (copy to J and K)
...			
172	Cash sweep		=I237
...			
180	Cash sweep		=I238
...			
188	Cash sweep		=I239

FIGURE 13–8

The Cash Sweep Turned On

	A	B	C	D	E	F	G	H	I	J	K
223			Balance check			0.0	0.0	0.0	0.0	(0.0)	(0.0)
224						OK	OK	OK	OK	OK	OK
225			**Note: liabilities use pre-cash sweep amounts**								
226			Assets without excess cash			1,358.0	1,501.0	1,615.0	1,718.1	1,883.9	2,070.3
227			Liabs, SH Eq without revolver			1,358.0	1,501.0	1,615.0	1,820.3	1,851.2	1,997.4
228											
229			Excess cash (revolver)						102.2	(32.7)	(72.9)
230											
231			Excess cash enabled for cash sweep?					Y	102.2	0.0	0.0
232											
233			Starting Debt A (before sweep)						150.0	47.8	47.8
234			Starting Debt B (before sweep)						145.0	145.0	145.0
235			Starting Debt C (before sweep)						110.0	110.0	110.0
236											
237			Sweep for Debt A						(102.2)	0.0	0.0
238			Sweep for Debt B						0.0	0.0	0.0
239			Sweep for Debt C						0.0	0.0	0.0
240			Total sweep						(102.2)	0.0	0.0
241											
242			**Excess cash (revolver) after sweep**						0.0	(32.7)	(72.9)
243											

13.6 THE CASH SWEEP IN CASH FLOW BALANCING

When we use the cash flow balancing method, the cash sweep approach is essentially the same. The difference is in deriving the excess cash available for the cash sweep using the before cash sweep debt amounts. Let's go through the steps.

13.6.1 Inserting New Rows in the Debt Section

In terms of inserting rows, this is the same step seen in Section 13.5.1. However, when we complete this section, the cash sweep references will look to the cash flow sheet. Because the cash flow rows are not yet defined, leave the formulas for Rows 172, 180, and 188 blank for the moment. We will connect them later.

13.6.2 Modify the Cash Flow Statement Created in Chapter 12

The cash flow statement we created in the model in Chapter 12 will remain the same except for the following changes.

For the forecast formulas in Rows 40-42, change the formulas Column I, J and K so that they refer directly to the hard-code entries in the input (Fig. 13-9. See the formulas in top lines in Table 13-13). *This is an important step.* The original formulas looked

FIGURE 13-9

Inserting New Rows in the Cash Flow Sheet. This Is the Same Step as Figure 13-4 in Section 13.5.1

	A	B	C	D	E	F	G	H	I	J	K
39			Incr (decr) in Short-term notes				2.0	2.0	0.0	0.0	0.0
40			Incr (decr) in Debt A				25.0	(75.0)	0.0	0.0	0.0
41			Incr (decr) in Debt B				0.0	25.0	0.0	0.0	0.0
42			Incr (decr) in Debt C				0.0	0.0	0.0	0.0	0.0
43			Other incr (decr) in Minority interest				0.0	0.0	0.0	0.0	0.0
44			Preferred dividends				(5.0)	(6.0)	(6.0)	(6.0)	(6.0)
45			Common dividends				(12.0)	(11.0)	(10.2)	(11.9)	(13.3)
46			Incr (decr) in Preferred stock				10.0	10.0	0.0	0.0	0.0
47			Incr (decr) in Common stock				20.0	70.0	100.0	0.0	0.0
48			Other incr (decr) in Retained Earnings				0.0	0.0	0.0	0.0	0.0
49			(Incr) decr in Other equity account				2.1	(0.1)	1.2	1.3	1.5
50			**Cash from financing**				**42.1**	**14.9**	**85.0**	**(16.6)**	**(17.8)**

FIGURE 13-10

The Cash Sweep Section in the Cash Flow Statement

	A B C D E F	G	H	I	J	K
39	Incr (decr) in Short-term notes	2.0	2.0	0.0	0.0	0.0
40	Scheduled incr (decr) in Debt A	25.0	(75.0)	0.0	0.0	0.0
41	Scheduled incr (decr) in Debt B	0.0	25.0	0.0	0.0	0.0
42	Scheduled incr (decr) in Debt C	0.0	0.0	0.0	0.0	0.0
43	Other incr (decr) in Minority interest	0.0	0.0	0.0	0.0	0.0
44	Preferred dividends	(5.0)	(6.0)	(6.0)	(6.0)	(6.0)
45	Common dividends	(12.0)	(11.0)	(9.9)	(11.6)	(12.8)
46	Incr (decr) in Preferred stock	10.0	10.0	0.0	0.0	0.0
47	Incr (decr) in Common stock	20.0	70.0	100.0	0.0	0.0
48	Other incr (decr) in Retained earnings	0.0	0.0	0.0	0.0	0.0
49	(Incr) decr in Other equity account	2.1	(0.1)	1.2	1.3	1.5
50	**Cash from financing**	42.1	14.9	85.3	(16.2)	(17.4)
51						
52	**Cash flow before cash sweep**	0.0	0.0	99.3	(35.8)	(42.4)
53						
54	**Excess cash (revolver) before sweep**	0.0	0.0	99.3	63.5	21.1
55						
56	Excess cash enabled for cash sweep?		N	0.0	0.0	0.0
57						
58	Starting Debt A (before sweep)			150.0	150.0	150.0
59	Starting Debt B (before sweep)			145.0	145.0	145.0
60	Starting Debt C (before sweep)			110.0	110.0	110.0
61						
62	Sweep for Debt A			0.0	0.0	0.0
63	Sweep for Debt B			0.0	0.0	0.0
64	Sweep for Debt C			0.0	0.0	0.0
65	Total sweep			0.0	0.0	0.0
66						
67	**Excess cash (revolver) after sweep**		0.0	99.3	63.5	21.1

at the changes in the output balance sheet for each debt account. To calculate the cash flow available for the sweep, all changes in the debt accounts above this calculation must use the before-cash sweep values. The before-sweep changes here are only the scheduled amortizations, hence also the change in the title of the rows. (There is no need to change the historical periods' formulas.)

In Figure 13-10, Row 52 is the starting point for the cash sweep calculations. This row sums the cash flow from cash from operations, cash from investments, and cash from financing.

Recall that the basis of the sweep in each year is the available cash, *not* the available cash flow. Moreover, the sweep must have positive available cash. Rows 54 and 56 do this.

TABLE 13-13

Formulas for the Cash Sweep Section in the Cash Flow

Row	Label in Column C	Formula in Column I (Copy to Columns J and K)
40	Scheduled incr (decr) in Debt A	=Input!I170
41	Scheduled incr (decr) in Debt B	=Input!I178
42	Scheduled incr (decr) in Debt C	=Input!I186
51		
52	Cash flow before cash sweep	=I29+I37+I50
53		
54	Excess cash (revolver) before sweep	=IF(ISERROR(H67+I52),0,H67+I52)
55		
56	Excess cash enabled for cash sweep?	=IF($H$56="Y",MAX(I54,0),0)
57		
58	Starting Debt A (before sweep)	=Input!I171
59	Starting Debt B (before sweep)	=Input!I179
60	Starting Debt C (before sweep)	=Input!I187
61		
62	Sweep for Debt A	=–MIN(I$56,I58)
63	Sweep for Debt B	=–MIN(I$56+SUM(I$62:I62),I59)
64	Sweep for Debt C	=–MIN(I$56+SUM(I$62:I63),I60)
65	Total sweep	=SUM(I62:I64)
66		
67	Excess cash (revolver) after sweep	=I52+I65+H67
68		

Row 54 takes the current cash flow and adds it to the prior year's excess cash (revolver) amount *after* the cash sweep. This is Row 67.

Row 56 determines the amount of positive excess cash that is available. In this row, I have also added a toggle that can turn the cash flow sweep on and off, with an ISERROR statement to trap any errors.

Rows 58 to 60 bring in the before-debt amounts from the input.

Rows 62 to 65 are the cash sweep calculations similar to sweep formulas for the balance sheet balancing approach (Fig. 13-5).

Row 67 is the excess cash (revolver) after the cash sweep. Note that this looks to Row 54, the row for excess cash (and revolver) and not Row 56, which only has the positive numbers for the cash flow. This is the row that is referenced back to the balance sheet for the excess cash row and the revolver row.

13.6.3 Connect the Balance Sheet to the Cash Flow Statement Numbers

The cash sweep is happening in the cash flow statement. We now have to bring the after-sweep debt outstanding back into the balance sheet's input section.

13.6.3.1 Debt accounts

Write the formulas for the cash sweep amounts: Row 172 for Debt A brings the cash flow post-sweep debt into the balance sheet input area for Debt A. Do the same for Row 180 for Debt B and Row 188 for Debt C (Table 13-14) so that they read the correct rows in the cash flow statement.

13.6.3.2 Connect the excess cash and revolver

Change the excess cash formula in Row 95 and the revolver formula in Row 150 in the balance sheet so that it reads the correct rows in the cash flow statement (Table 13-15).

13.6.3.3 Turn on the cash sweep

Put a "Y" in Cell H56 in the CashFlow sheet, and check that everything is running properly. And we're done.

13.6.4 Output Format for the Cash Flow Statement

With the cash sweep formulas that we have added, the cash flow statement may lack the visual polish that a final presentation may require. It may be useful to create another sheet (let's call it Cash-

TABLE 13-14

Link the Cash Flow Cash Sweep Numbers to the Debt Sections on the Balance Sheet

Row	Label in Column C	Formula in Column I (Copy to Columns J and K)
169	Debt A	
170	New (amortization)	
171	Debt A before sweep	=IF(I169,I169,H173+I170)
172	Cash sweep	=CashFlow!I62
173	Debt A	=I171+I172
174	Interest rate %	
175	Interest expense	=I174*AVERAGE(H173:I173)
176		
177	Debt B	
178	New (amortization)	
179	Debt B before sweep	=IF(I177,I177,H181+I178)
180	Cash sweep	=CashFlow!I63
181	Debt B	=I179+I180
182	Interest rate %	
183	Interest expense	=I182*AVERAGE(H181:I181)
184		
185	Debt C	
186	New (amortization)	
187	Debt C before sweep	=IF(I185,I185,H189+I186)
188	Cash sweep	=CashFlow!I64
189	Debt C	=I187+I188
190	Interest rate %	
191	Interest expense	=I190*AVERAGE(H189:I189)
192		

FlowOutput) that presents the numbers in a more streamlined way (Figure 13-11). The top section of this new sheet will have the same rows as the CashFlow sheet. Shown below is just the section starting from the cash flow from financing section.

This presentation is favored by many analysts because it more clearly shows the cash flow from financing before the sweep, the sweep amounts themselves, and then the cash flow

TABLE 13–15

Link the Cash Flow Excess Cash and Revolver to the Balance Sheet

Row	Label in Column C	Formula in Column I (Copy to Columns J and K)
93	BALANCE SHEET	=I$6
94	ASSETS	
95	Excess cash	=MAX(CashFlow!I71,0)
96	Interest rate %	
97	Interest income	=I96*H95
. . .		
. . .		
149	LIABILITIES	
150	Revolver	=–MIN(CashFlow!I71,0)
151	Interest rate %	
152	Interest expense	=I151*H150
153		

FIGURE 13–11

Reformatting the Cash Flow Statement Output

	C	G	H	I	J	K
39	Incr (decr) in Short-term notes	2.0	2.0	0.0	0.0	0.0
40	Scheduled incr (decr) in Debt A	25.0	(75.0)	0.0	0.0	0.0
41	Scheduled incr (decr) in Debt B	0.0	25.0	0.0	0.0	0.0
42	Scheduled incr (decr) in Debt C	0.0	0.0	0.0	0.0	0.0
43	Other incr (decr) in Minority interest	0.0	0.0	0.0	0.0	0.0
44	Preferred dividends	(5.0)	(6.0)	(6.0)	(6.0)	(6.0)
45	Common dividends	(12.0)	(11.0)	(9.9)	(11.6)	(12.8)
46	Incr (decr) in Preferred stock	10.0	10.0	0.0	0.0	0.0
47	Incr (decr) in Common stock	20.0	70.0	100.0	0.0	0.0
48	Other incr (decr) in Retained earnings	0.0	0.0	0.0	0.0	0.0
49	(Incr) decr in Other equity account	2.1	(0.1)	1.2	1.3	1.5
50	**Cash from financing before cash sweep**	42.1	14.9	85.3	(16.2)	(17.4)
51						
52	Sweep for Debt A			0.0	0.0	0.0
53	Sweep for Debt B			0.0	0.0	0.0
54	Sweep for Debt C			0.0	0.0	0.0
55	**Cash from financing after cash sweep**	42.1	14.9	85.3	(16.2)	(17.4)
56						
57	**Cash flow after cash sweep**	0.0	0.0	99.3	(35.8)	(42.4)
58						
59	**Excess cash (revolver) after sweep**	0.0	0.0	99.3	63.5	21.1
60						

from financing after the sweep amounts. Row 57 is the total of the three sections of:

- Cash flow from operations
- Cash flow from investments
- Cash flow from financing after the cash sweep

The ending Row 59 shows the excess cash or revolver after the sweep. This is derived from Row 57 and the prior period's Row 59, which is the prior period's excess cash or revolver. Adding the cash flow to the existing excess cash or revolver gives us the current period's excess cash or revolver.

13.7 BELLS AND WHISTLES

A "bell and whistle" is a nice-to-have feature that is not a critical part of the model. As we put in our cash sweep modifications, we also added a bell and whistle in the form of a switch or toggle that

FIGURE 13–12

Additional Sweep Features in the Balance Sheet Balancing Method. Shown: The Input Sheet

	A B	C	D E F G	H	I	J	K
229		**Excess cash (revolver) before sweep**			102.2	(32.7)	(72.9)
230							
231		Excess cash enabled for cash sweep?		100.0%	102.2	0.0	0.0
232							
233		Starting Debt A (before sweep)			150.0	47.8	47.8
234		Percent to be paid			100.0%	100.0%	100.0%
235							
236		Starting Debt B (before sweep)			145.0	145.0	145.0
237		Percent to be paid			100.0%	100.0%	100.0%
238							
239		Starting Debt C (before sweep)			110.0	110.0	110.0
240		Percent to be paid			100.0%	100.0%	100.0%
241							
242		Sweep for Debt A			(102.2)	0.0	0.0
243		Sweep for Debt B			0.0	0.0	0.0
244		Sweep for Debt C			0.0	0.0	0.0
245		Total sweep			(102.2)	0.0	0.0
246							
247		**Excess cash (revolver) after sweep**			0.0	(32.7)	(72.9)
248							

can be used to enable or disable the cash sweep. This is seen in Cell H231 in the Input sheet for balance sheet balancing (Fig. 13-5) and in Cell H56 for the cash flow balancing (in Fig. 13-10).

13.8 PERCENTAGES OF AVAILABLE CASH FOR CASH SWEEP, OR DEBT TO BE SWEPT

Some of the features that can be added to a cash sweep mechanism are:

- Toggles associated with each debt tranche to determine whether it will be repaid or not as part of the cash sweep.

TABLE 13-16

Formulas for the Additional Features, for the Balance Sheet Balancing Approach

Row	Label in Column C	Formula in Column I (Copy to Columns J and K)
229	Excess cash (revolver) before sweep	=IF(ISERROR(I227-I226),0,I227-I226)
230		
231	Excess cash enabled for cash sweep?	=MAX(I229,0)*$H$231
232		
233	Starting Debt A (before sweep)	=I171*I234
234	Percent to be paid	
235		
236	Starting Debt B (before sweep)	=I179*I237
237	Percent to be paid	
238		
239	Starting Debt C (before sweep)	=I187*I240
240	Percent to be paid	
241		
242	Sweep for Debt A	=–MIN(I$231,I233)
243	Sweep for Debt B	=–MIN(I$231+SUM(I$242:I242),I236)
244	Sweep for Debt C	=–MIN(I$231+SUM(I$242:I243),I239)
245	Total sweep	=SUM(I242:I244)
246		
247	Excess cash (revolver) after sweep	=I229+I245

- A percentage input to determine if some percentage (not all) of the excess cash is to be used for the cash sweep.
- Inputs to determine if the cash sweep applies only to selected years for each debt tranche. This is useful when a debt facility may have a repayment grace period so that there is no repayment required (or perhaps allowed) in the beginning years.

13.8.1 For the Balance Sheet Balancing

Figure 13-12 shows how these three might be implemented in the model. The illustration in terms of the row numbers is based on the balance sheet balancing approach. The sheet shown is the Input sheet.

The formulas for the new additional features are shown in Table 13-16.

Note how the "Y" setting in the original setting on Row 231 has been changed to a percentage input. This in effect still

FIGURE 13-13

Additional Sweep Features in the Cash Flow Balancing Method. Shown: The CashFlow Sheet

	C	G	H	I	J	K
54	**Excess cash (revolver) before sweep**	0.0	0.0	99.3	(35.8)	(78.2)
55						
56	Excess cash enabled for cash sweep?		100.0%	99.3	0.0	0.0
57						
58	Starting Debt A (before sweep)			150.0	150.0	150.0
59	Percent to be paid			100.0%	100.0%	100.0%
60						
61	Starting Debt B (before sweep)			145.0	145.0	145.0
62	Percent to be paid			100.0%	100.0%	100.0%
63						
64	Starting Debt C (before sweep)			110.0	110.0	110.0
65	Percent to be paid			100.0%	100.0%	100.0%
66						
67	Sweep for Debt A			(99.3)	0.0	0.0
68	Sweep for Debt B			0.0	0.0	0.0
69	Sweep for Debt C			0.0	0.0	0.0
70	Total sweep			(99.3)	0.0	0.0
71						
72	**Excess cash (revolver) after sweep**		0.0	0.0	(35.8)	(78.2)
73						

retains the Y/N toggle (enter 100% or 0%, respectively) but has the added bonus that you can specify any level in between. This is the setting for the amount of excess cash that you want to use for the repayment.

The other percentage inputs also works as either a Y/N toggle for each debt tranche (enter 100% or 0% for all years for each tranche) or to set for sweeps on individual years (enter 0% for any year that you do not want to sweep, 100% for others). Additionally, you can set the level of payment to any value between 0% and 100%.

TABLE 13–17

Formulas for the Additional Features, for the Cash Flow Balancing Approach

Row	Label in Column C	Formula in Column I (Copy to Columns J and K)
54	Excess cash (revolver) before sweep	=IF(ISERROR(H72+I52),0,H72+I52)
55		
56	Excess cash enabled for cash sweep?	=MAX(I54,0)*$H$56
57		
58	Starting Debt A (before sweep)	=Input!I171*I59
59	Percent to be paid	
60		
61	Starting Debt B (before sweep)	=Input!I179*I62
62	Percent to be paid	
63		
64	Starting Debt C (before sweep)	=Input!I187*I65
65	Percent to be paid	
66		
67	Sweep for Debt A	=-MIN(I$56,I58)
68	Sweep for Debt B	=–MIN(I$56+SUM(I$67:I67),I61)
69	Sweep for Debt C	=–MIN(I$56+SUM(I$67:I68),I64)
70	Total sweep	=SUM(I67:I69)
71		
72	Excess cash (revolver) after sweep	=I52+I70+H72

13.8.2 For the Cash Flow Balancing

Figure 13-3 shows the same changes for the cash flow balancing approach. The sheet shown is the based on the CashFlow sheet.

13.9 ORDER OF CASH SWEEP

In this bell and whistle, we add the feature of being able to determine which debt tranche gets paid first. Essentially, we are putting into the model a capability to pay by a specified order.

To keep the illustration simpler, the formulas shown in the following do not include the changes made in Section 13.8.

13.9.1 Order of Cash Sweep by Balance Sheet Balancing

In this layout, we continue to use the same cash sweep engine (boxed area), but the numbers being worked on in this section

FIGURE 13-14

Cash Sweep by a Specified Order, Balance Sheet Balancing. Shown: The Input Sheet

	B C D E	F	G	H	I	J	K
229	Excess cash (revolver) before sweep	na	0.0	0.0	102.2	(32.7)	(72.9)
230							
231	Excess cash available for cash sweep			Y	102.2	0.0	0.0
232		Order of sweep					
233	Starting Debt A (before sweep)	3			150.0	150.0	150.0
234	Starting Debt B (before sweep)	1			145.0	42.8	42.8
235	Starting Debt C (before sweep)	2			110.0	110.0	110.0
236							
237	Starting First debt (before sweep)		1		145.0	42.8	42.8
238	Starting Second debt (before sweep)		2		110.0	110.0	110.0
239	Starting Third debt (before sweep)		3		150.0	150.0	150.0
240							
241	Sweep for First debt		1		(102.2)	0.0	0.0
242	Sweep for Second debt		2		0.0	0.0	0.0
243	Sweep for Third debt		3		0.0	0.0	0.0
244							
245	Sweep for Debt A	3			0.0	0.0	0.0
246	Sweep for Debt B	1			(102.2)	0.0	0.0
247	Sweep for Debt C	2			0.0	0.0	0.0
248	Total sweep				(102.2)	0.0	0.0
249							
250	**Excess cash (revolver) after sweep**				0.0	(32.7)	(72.9)
251							

have been reordered. The order of the sweep is defined in the yellow input cells in Cells F233 to F235. In the example, Debt B is the first debt which needs to be repaid first, followed by Debt C. Debt A is the last in the sweep order.

Once the numbers are calculated in the boxed area (note the debt tranches are now called First, Second, and Third in this area), the cash sweep amounts are resorted back to the order for the Debts A, B, and C. In this way, we can see the familiar parts of the previous cash sweep calculations being replaced.

The resorting of the order is done by the use of SUMIF formulas. The numbers 1, 2, and 3 in Columns F and G are used for the resorting or the order and the reversal back of the order (see Table 13-18 to Table 13-20).

Table 13-19 uses the same formulas as before.

Table 13-19 is the first part of the boxed area. Here, the use of the SUMIF function re-sorts the debt tranches so that within this area, the cash sweep can proceed in the usual 1, 2, 3 order. It is just that the First debt is not necessarily Debt A, the Second debt is not necessarily Debt B and likewise the Third debt is not necessarily Debt C (in our example, First is Debt B, Second is Debt C, and Third is Debt A).

TABLE 13–18

Getting the Numbers Together

Row	Label in Column C	Formula in Column I (Copy to Columns J and K)
229	Excess cash (revolver) before sweep	=IF(ISERROR(I227-I226),0,I227-I226)
230		
231	Excess cash available for cash sweep	=IF($H$231="Y",MAX(I229,0),0)
232		
233	Starting Debt A (before sweep)	=I171
234	Starting Debt B (before sweep)	=I179
235	Starting Debt C (before sweep)	=I187
236		

TABLE 13-19

Reordering the Rows Through a SUMIF Formula, for Column I Only

Row	Label in Column C	Formula in Column I (Copy to Columns J and K)
237	Starting First debt (before sweep)	=SUMIF($F$233:$F$235,$G237,I$233:I$235)
238	Starting Second debt (before sweep)	=SUMIF($F$233:$F$235,$G238,I$233:I$235)
239	Starting Third debt (before sweep)	=SUMIF($F$233:$F$235,$G239,I$233:I$235)
240		

In Table 13-20 we emerge from the boxed area. In Rows 245 to 247, we re-sort back the sweep calculations, again using the SUMIF function, so that they match the order for Debts A, B, and C.

TABLE 13-20

Bringing Everything Back to Debts A, B, and C

Row	Label in Column C	Formula in Column I (Copy to Columns J and K)
241	Sweep for First debt	=–MIN(I$231,I237)
242	Sweep for Second debt	=–MIN(I$231+SUM(I$241:I241),I238)
243	Sweep for Third debt	=–MIN(I$231+SUM(I$241:I242),I239)
244		
245	Sweep for Debt A	=SUMIF($G$241:$G$243,$F245,I$241:I$243)
246	Sweep for Debt B	=SUMIF($G$241:$G$243,$F246,I$241:I$243)
247	Sweep for Debt C	=SUMIF($G$241:$G$243,$F247,I$241:I$243)
248	Total sweep	=SUM(I245:I247)
249		
250	Excess cash (revolver) after sweep	=I229+I248

TABLE 13–21

References for the Repayment Order

Row	Label in Column C	Formula in Column F
245	Sweep for Debt A	=F233
246	Sweep for Debt B	=F234
247	Sweep for Debt C	=F235

An important point: make sure that Cells F245 to F247 have the references shown (Table 13-21).

The rest of the rows should look familiar. They follow the same format as seen in earlier illustrations.

One last thing: connect the cash sweep rows here to the rows in the debt inputs (Table 13-22).

13.9.2 Order of Cash Sweep by Cash Flow Balancing

Figure 13-15 repeats the same approach for determining the order of debt repayment, but for the cash flow balancing approach. Table 13-23 shows the formulas.

TABLE 13–22

Connect the Cash Sweep Rows to the Debt Input

Row	Label in Column C	Formula in Column I (Copy to Columns J and K)
169	Debt A	
172	Cash sweep	=I245
...		
177	Debt B	
180	Cash sweep	=I246
...		
185	Debt C	
188	Cash sweep	=I247

Shown: The Input sheet.

FIGURE 13–15

The Order of Repayment. Shown: The CashFlow Sheet

	B–E	F	G	H	I	J	K
54	Excess cash (revolver) before sweep		0.0	0.0	102.2	(32.7)	(72.9)
55							
56	Excess cash enabled for cash sweep?			Y	102.2	0.0	0.0
57		Order of sweep					
58	Starting Debt A (before sweep)	3			150.0	150.0	150.0
59	Starting Debt B (before sweep)	1			145.0	42.8	42.8
60	Starting Debt C (before sweep)	2			110.0	110.0	110.0
61							
62	Starting First debt (before sweep)		1		145.0	42.8	42.8
63	Starting Second debt (before sweep)		2		110.0	110.0	110.0
64	Starting Third debt (before sweep)		3		150.0	150.0	150.0
65							
66	Sweep for First debt		1		(102.2)	0.0	0.0
67	Sweep for Second debt		2		0.0	0.0	0.0
68	Sweep for Third debt		3		0.0	0.0	0.0
69							
70	Sweep for Debt A	3			0.0	0.0	0.0
71	Sweep for Debt B	1			(102.2)	0.0	0.0
72	Sweep for Debt C	2			0.0	0.0	0.0
73	Total sweep				(102.2)	0.0	0.0
74							
75	**Excess cash (revolver) after sweep**				0.0	(32.7)	(72.9)
76							

Note that the formulas in column F for Cells F70 to F72 (Table 13-24).

13.10 PARI PASSU CASH SWEEP

A variation of the repayment order is to allow all or selected tranches to be repaid in equal proportion to their total outstandings. This is a *pari passu* arrangement for debt facilities with equal levels of seniority.

13.10.1 Pari Passu Repayment with the Balance Sheet Approach

Expanding on the example for reordering the cash sweep (Fig. 13-16), we can make the model use the pari passu approach, whereby the available excess cash is used to repay all outstanding debt based on the pro-rata percentages of their outstandings. For the formulas, see Tables 13-25, 13-26, 13-27, 13-28, and 13-29.

TABLE 13-23

Formulas for the Order of Repayment for the CashFlow Sheet

Row	Label in Column C	Formula in Column I (Copy to Columns J and K)
54	Excess cash (revolver) before sweep	=IF(ISERROR(I52+H75),0,I52+H75)
55		
56	Excess cash enabled for cash sweep?	=IF($H$56="Y",MAX(I54,0),0)
57		
58	Starting Debt A (before sweep)	=Input!I171
59	Starting Debt B (before sweep)	=Input!I179
60	Starting Debt C (before sweep)	=Input!I187
61		
62	Starting First debt (before sweep)	=SUMIF($F$58:$F$60,$G62,I$58:I$60)
63	Starting Second debt (before sweep)	=SUMIF($F$58:$F$60,$G63,I$58:I$60)
64	Starting Third debt (before sweep)	=SUMIF($F$58:$F$60,$G64,I$58:I$60)
65		
66	Sweep for First debt	=–MIN(I$56,I62)
67	Sweep for Second debt	=–MIN(I$56+SUM(I$66:I66),I63)
68	Sweep for Third debt	=–MIN(I$56+SUM(I$66:I67),I64)
69		
70	Sweep for Debt A	=SUMIF($G$66:$G$68,$F70,I$66:I$68)
71	Sweep for Debt B	=SUMIF($G$66:$G$68,$F71,I$66:I$68)
72	Sweep for Debt C	=SUMIF($G$66:$G$68,$F72,I$66:I$68)
73	Total sweep	=SUM(I70:I72)
74		
75	Excess cash (revolver) after sweep	=I54+I73

TABLE 13-24

Formulas for Cells F70 to F72

Row	Label in Column C	Formula in Column F
70	Sweep for Debt A	=F58
71	Sweep for Debt B	=F59
72	Sweep for Debt C	=F60

Shown: The CashFlow Sheet.

The only changes made to the pari passu approach from the sweep reorder occur in Rows 241 to 244 (Table 13-27). With the toggle that can set the calculations to either the regular sweep or the pari passu sweep, we calculate the ratios in percentages

FIGURE 13-16

Changes for Pari Passu Repayment (Rows 241–247 Only). Shown: The Input Sheet

	A	B	C	D	E	F	G	H	I	J	K
229			Excess cash (revolver) before sweep			na	0.0	0.0	102.2	(32.7)	(72.9)
230											
231			Excess cash available for cash sweep					Y	102.2	0.0	0.0
232						Order of sweep					
233			Starting Debt A (before sweep)			3			150.0	150.0	150.0
234			Starting Debt B (before sweep)			1			145.0	42.8	42.8
235			Starting Debt C (before sweep)			2			110.0	110.0	110.0
236											
237			Starting First debt (before sweep)				1		145.0	42.8	42.8
238			Starting Second debt (before sweep)				2		110.0	110.0	110.0
239			Starting Third debt (before sweep)				3		150.0	150.0	150.0
240											
241							Pari passu?	N	35.8%	14.1%	14.1%
242									27.2%	36.3%	36.3%
243									37.0%	49.5%	49.5%
244											
245			Sweep for First debt				1		(102.2)	0.0	0.0
246			Sweep for Second debt				2		0.0	0.0	0.0
247			Sweep for Third debt				3		0.0	0.0	0.0
248											
249			Sweep for Debt A			3			0.0	0.0	0.0
250			Sweep for Debt B			1			(102.2)	0.0	0.0
251			Sweep for Debt C			2			0.0	0.0	0.0
252			Total sweep						(102.2)	0.0	0.0
253											
254			Excess cash (revolver) after sweep						0.0	(32.7)	(72.9)
255											

TABLE 13–25

Bringing the Debt Numbers In

Row	Label in Column C	Formula in Column I (Copy to Columns J and K)
229	Excess cash (revolver) before sweep	=IF(ISERROR(I227–I226),0,I227–I226)
230		
231	Excess cash available for cash sweep	=IF($H$231="Y",MAX(I229,0),0)
232		
233	Starting Debt A (before sweep)	=I171
234	Starting Debt B (before sweep)	=I179
235	Starting Debt C (before sweep)	=I187
236		

of each debt relative to the total. Shown here, the percentages are 35.8%, 27.2%, and 37.0%. Mathematically, on a proportionate repayment basis, these percentages should remain the same through the years, and in fact they do. There is no need to calculate them each year. However, for ease of column-by-column referencing, they are calculated each year.

TABLE 13–26

Reordering the Sweep Order

Row	Label in Column C	Formula in Column I
237	Starting First debt (before sweep)	=SUMIF($F$233:$F$235,$G237,I$233:I$235)
238	Starting Second debt (before sweep)	=SUMIF($F$233:$F$235,$G238,I$233:I$235)
239	Starting Third debt (before sweep)	=SUMIF($F$233:$F$235,$G239,I$233:I$235)
240		

TABLE 13–27

The Pari Passu Repayment Calculations

Row	Label in Column C	Formula in Column I (Copy to Columns J and K)
241		=IF(ISERROR(I237/SUM(I$237:I$239)),0,I237/SUM(I$237:I$239))
242		=IF(ISERROR(I238/SUM(I$237:I$239)),0,I238/SUM(I$237:I$239))
243		=IF(ISERROR(I239/SUM(I$237:I$239)),0,I239/SUM(I$237:I$239))
244		

The next changes (Table 13-28) are in the sweep formulas themselves, in Rows 245 to 247. The changes include the IF function so that there is a choice in the calculation between the regular cash sweep and the pari passu sweep. The pari passu calculation simply takes each debt's percentage portion and multiplies it by the available excess cash. Because the percentages total 100%, in each year, all available excess cash is used up. We also add a MIN function test so that the pari passu repayment does not exceed the total debt outstanding. For example, consider the case where the available excess cash is 600 and the total debt outstandings

TABLE 13–28

Heavy Duty Formulas: Option for a Normal or Pari Passu Sweep

245	Sweep for First debt	=IF($H$241="Y", –MIN(I$231,SUM(I$237:I$239))*I241, –MIN(I$231,I237))
246	Sweep for Second debt	=IF($H$241="Y", –MIN(I$231,SUM(I$237:I$239))*I242, –MIN(I$231+SUM(I$245:I245),I238))
247	Sweep for Third debt	=IF($H$241="Y", –MIN(I$231,SUM(I$237:I$239))*I243, –MIN(I$231+SUM(I$245:I246),I239))
248		

TABLE 13-29

Finishing Up

Row	Label in Column C	Formula in Column I (Copy to Columns J and K)
249	Sweep for Debt A	=SUMIF($G$245:$G$247,$F249,I$245:I$247)
250	Sweep for Debt B	=SUMIF($G$245:$G$247,$F250,I$245:I$247)
251	Sweep for Debt C	=SUMIF($G$245:$G$247,$F251,I$245:I$247)
252	Total sweep	=SUM(I249:I251)
253		
254	Excess cash (revolver) after sweep	=I229+I252

are 100, 100, and 100. We have a 33.3% proportional repayment for each debt or potentially 200 (33.3% of 600) to pay down each of the debt tranches. In this case, we want to make sure that we do not overpay, and the MIN function ensures that this does not happen.

Now with Table 13-27, we begin the pari passu calculations. The ISERROR function in Rows 241 to 243 ensures that the cells do not return a #DIV/0! error when all the debt is repaid.

The formulas in Rows 245 to 247 expand the original cash sweep formulas with an IF function. The pari passu option is enabled when the input cell in H241 is set to "Y." Note that the formulas for the pari passu repayment:

Row 245 –MIN(I$231,SUM(I$237:I$239))*$I241,

Row 246 –MIN(I$231,SUM(I$237:I$239))*$I242

Row 247 –MIN(I$231,SUM(I$237:I$239))*$I243

FIGURE 13-17

The Pari Passu Formula. Shown: The CashFlow Sheet

	A B C	D E F	G	H	I	J	K
54	**Excess cash (revolver) before sweep**		0.0	0.0	102.1	(33.0)	(73.6)
55							
56	Excess cash enabled for cash sweep?			Y	102.1	0.0	0.0
57		Order of sweep					
58	Starting Debt A (before sweep)	3			150.0	112.2	112.2
59	Starting Debt B (before sweep)	1			145.0	108.5	108.5
60	Starting Debt C (before sweep)	2			110.0	82.3	82.3
61							
62	Starting First debt (before sweep)		1		145.0	108.5	108.5
63	Starting Second debt (before sweep)		2		110.0	82.3	82.3
64	Starting Third debt (before sweep)		3		150.0	112.2	112.2
65							
66			Pari passu?	Y	35.8%	35.8%	35.8%
67					27.2%	27.2%	27.2%
68					37.0%	37.0%	37.0%
69							
70	Sweep for First debt		1		(36.5)	0.0	0.0
71	Sweep for Second debt		2		(27.7)	0.0	0.0
72	Sweep for Third debt		3		(37.8)	0.0	0.0
73							
74	Sweep for Debt A	3			(37.8)	0.0	0.0
75	Sweep for Debt B	1			(36.5)	0.0	0.0
76	Sweep for Debt C	2			(27.7)	0.0	0.0
77	Total sweep				(102.1)	0.0	0.0
78							
79	**Excess cash (revolver) after sweep**				0.0	(33.0)	(73.6)
80							

These have MIN functions to limit the amount of total repayment to the lesser of the available excess cash or the total debt outstanding. Also, note that they begin with the minus sign.

Table 13-29 shows the formulas to complete the pari passu calculations. We now have the option for the model to run either a normal cash sweep with a specified order of repayment, or on a pari passu basis.

13.10.2 Pari Passu Repayment with the Cash Flow Approach

Figure 13-17 shows the calculations for the CashFlow sheet. Table 13-30 shows the formulas.

TABLE 13–30

The Formulas for the Pari Passu Sweep on the CashFlow Sheet

Row	Label in Column C	Formula in Column I (Copy to Columns J and K)
56	Excess cash enabled for cash sweep?	=IF($H$56="Y",MAX(I54,0),0)
57		
58	Starting Debt A (before sweep)	=Input!I171
59	Starting Debt B (before sweep)	=Input!I179
60	Starting Debt C (before sweep)	=Input!I187
61		
62	Starting First debt (before sweep)	=SUMIF($F$58:$F$60,$G62,I$58:I$60)
63	Starting Second debt (before sweep)	=SUMIF($F$58:$F$60,$G63,I$58:I$60)
64	Starting Third debt (before sweep)	=SUMIF($F$58:$F$60,$G64,I$58:I$60)
65		
66		=IF(ISERROR(I62/SUM(I$62:I$64)),0,I62/SUM(I$62:I$64))
67		=IF(ISERROR(I63/SUM(I$62:I$64)),0,I63/SUM(I$62:I$64))
68		=IF(ISERROR(I64/SUM(I$62:I$64)),0,I64/SUM(I$62:I$64))
69		
70	Sweep for First debt	=IF($H$66="Y", –MIN(I$56,SUM(I$62:I$64))*I66, –MIN(I$56,I62))
71	Sweep for Second debt	=IF($H$66="Y", –MIN(I$56,SUM(I$62:I$64))*I67, –MIN(I$56+SUM(I$70:I70),I63))

(continued on next page)

TABLE 13–30 (CONTINUED)

Row	Label in Column C	Formula in Column I (Copy to Columns J and K)
72	Sweep for Third debt	=IF($H$66="Y", –MIN(I$56,SUM(I$62:I$64))*I68, –MIN(I$56+SUM(I$70:I71),I64))
73		
74	Sweep for Debt A	=SUMIF($G$70:$G$72,$F74,I$70:I$72)
75	Sweep for Debt B	=SUMIF($G$70:$G$72,$F75,I$70:I$72)
76	Sweep for Debt C	=SUMIF($G$70:$G$72,$F76,I$70:I$72)
77	Total sweep	=SUM(I74:I76)
78		
79	Excess cash (revolver) after sweep	=I54+I77

CHAPTER 14

Ratios

At this stage, we have a model with a complete set of the three financial statements. In this chapter, we will go through the types of ratios for showing how well a company is performing and a type of presentation called "common-size" that will show the income statement and balance sheet as nothing but ratios.

14.1 COMPARING NUMBERS AGAINST ONE ANOTHER

Once we have a complete model for a company, we can now use the numbers being produced to gain an understanding of the company. The historical numbers give us an insight into how well the company has been performing. From these, we can make forecast assumptions based on the historical trends and what we know of developments in the company's industry and see how well the company will perform based on these assumptions.

Numbers are most useful when we can compare them against other numbers to show ratios. For example, let's say there are two companies, each with a net income of $10 million. With just this information, the two may seem to be equals. But as the table shows, when we compare this against other numbers—in this case each company's revenues—we see a different picture:

	Company A	**Company B**
Net income	$10 million	$10 million
Revenues	$100 million	$200 million
Net margin	10%	5%

Now the fact emerges that the second company is only half as profitable on a net margin basis as the first.

By the same token, we can have two companies, one with profits twice as high as the other. Twice as profitable? Not necessarily:

	Company C	**Company D**
Net income	$10 million	$20 million
Revenues	$100 million	$200 million
Net margin	10%	10%

With one company's revenues twice as high as the other, the two have the same net margin profitability, even though they are of different sizes.

Ratios perform an indexing function—they bring different sets of numbers to a common yardstick; for example, revenues and net income are shown as one profitability index. Ratios allow us to look at performance of:

- A company across time
- Companies in an industry, even though they may vary in size
- Companies in different industries
- Companies in different countries
- Any combination of the above

Of course, one has to keep in mind factors such as economies of scale and different accounting treatments when comparing companies across disparate criteria. Nevertheless, ratios provide a good starting point for analysis.

In common-size statements, which we cover a little later in this chapter, we can also look at the performance of one company across time, even if that company has gone through considerable growth.

Different industries also have different ratio benchmarks, so it is important to limit ratio analysis to companies within an industry, but not across industries. And as you work with ratios, you should also keep in mind that companies often have some accounting approaches to manage their earnings numbers, to make their ratios look better. As an example, many department stores choose a fiscal year-end of January or February, when their inventory is at the lowest point after the end-of-the-year holiday sales. Companies can pay off their short-term working capital loans just before their reporting date, so that their debt ratios may be more favorable. They then draw down on their credit lines again after the reporting date passes.

14.2 NEGATIVE NUMBERS

From a modeling viewpoint, negative numbers present some problems. Here is a return on equity (net income/equity) calculation:

	Company E	**Company F**
Net income	\$10 million	(\$10 million)
Equity	\$100 million	(\$100 million)
Return on equity	10%	10%

It seems that both companies earn the same return on their equity, but obviously one is healthy, while the other one is dire straits. In such a case, you may want to use an IF statement that will calculate the ratio only if the denominator is positive and if not return a text message of "n/a" (for "not applicable").

Here is another example, with a negative dividend payout ratio (dividend/net income):

	Company G	**Company H**
Dividend	\$10,000	\$10,000
Net income	\$50,000	(\$50,000)
Payout ratio	20%	(20%)

A negative payout ratio does not mean that Company H has a lower payout ratio than Company G. If anything, Company H has an exorbitantly high payout ratio, given that it is paying dividends when in fact it has a net loss in earnings.

14.3 CATEGORIES OF RATIOS

When we look at companies and their ratios, there are six broad categories of metrics. These six apply to all types of companies, but within each category, there will be measures that are more important for some industries and less so for others:

- Size
- Liquidity
- Efficiency
- Profitability
- Leverage
- Coverage

14.3.1 Some Important Terms

EBIT, or earnings before interest and taxes, is an important number in the income statement, because it represents the company's ability to generate operating earnings before interest expense (a cost related to financing decisions, not operating decisions) and taxes (a cost related to running a business in a regulated economy). This is also called operating profit or operating income.

EBITDA is earnings before interest, taxes, depreciation, and amortization of intangibles. EBITDA is useful for comparing companies within and across industries, because it does not include the effects of many of the factors that differentiate companies in different sectors, such as interest (from different capital structures), depreciation (from different fixed asset bases), amortization (from different holdings of intangibles), and taxes (from different tax treatments). Because depreciation and amortization of intangibles are noncash expenses, EBITDA shows the amount of cash a company can generate from its operations. This is the source of cash for any interest payments, so this is a measure that a company's creditors would examine very closely.

Net debt is total debt minus cash and cash equivalents. Cash equivalents are accounts such as short-term investments or marketable securities, which can be easily turned into cash. Net debt represents the net debt load that a company has to bear after using its cash and cash equivalents. Companies with a large cash position relative to their total debt will have a negative net debt.

14.4 FOR SIZE

All things being equal, the larger the company as shown by the measures that follow, the sounder it is.

1. Revenues
2. Total assets
3. Total shareholders' equity

14.5 FOR LIQUIDITY

These measures give an indication of how much of a company's cash is invested in its current assets. However, they also show how well current assets can cover current liabilities if the company had to liquidate them into cash.

14.5.1 Working Capital

Working capital (sometimes also called net working capital) is current assets minus current liabilities. Working capital is a measure of the cushion that a company has for meeting obligations within the ordinary operating cycle of the business.

14.5.2 Operating Working Capital

Operating working capital (OWC) is a nonstandard term that means current assets without cash minus current liabilities without short-term debt (which includes any current portion of long-term debt). This measure looks at how much of its cash a company uses in maintaining its day-to-day operations. The higher the operating working capital, the less liquid a company is, because its cash is tied up in accounts such as accounts receivables and inventory.

14.5.3 The Current Ratio, or Current Assets/Current Liabilities

The current ratio is current assets divided by current liabilities. The ratio measures the multiple by which a company can use its current assets (if it could convert them all to cash) to cover all its current liabilities.

14.5.4 The Quick Ratio, or (Current Assets – Inventory)/ Current Liabilities

The quick ratio is similar to the current ratio but is a more severe ratio (the ratio will be a lower number than the current ratio) in that it takes inventory out of the numerator. Inventory is very illiquid and usually cannot be turned into cash at a moment's notice, at least without resorting to deep discounts and "fire sale" prices.

In regard to the last two ratios, both ratios are only indications since they do not include information about when the current liabilities are due. A company that can stretch its accounts payable over a longer period will have a better ability to pay its other bills than a second company with the same ratios but with a shorter payables payment period. These ratios are more popular in credit analysis than in mergers and acquisitions (M&A) work.

14.6 FOR EFFICIENCY

The ratios that follow indicate how well or efficiently a company makes use of its assets to generate sales. The first five look at the amount of balance sheet accounts that are tied up in the creation of earnings. The last two look at how well the company's assets are utilized for sales.

1. Accounts receivable/sales * 365
2. Inventory/cost of goods sold * 365
3. Accounts payable/cost of goods sold * 365
4. [(Current assets – cash) – (current liabilities – short-term debt)]/sales or Operating working capital/sales
5. Change in OWC and Change in OWC/sales

6. Sales/net fixed assets
7. Sales/total assets

14.6.1 Accounts Receivable/Sale * 365

Accounts receivable/sales * 365 shows how many days it takes a company to collect on its receivables: the higher the number of days, the worse its receivables management. If the company has made a sale but has not collected the money from it, it is literally extending an interest-free "loan" to that customer, tying up the cash that could be put to productive use elsewhere.

Without the * 365, the ratio shows the fraction of the year's sales that is still tied up in receivables. By multiplying the number of days in a year into the fraction, we get not a fraction, but the number of days that represents how long the average receivable remains uncollected. Thus, the result is usually called "receivable days." (You can use 360 as the number of days, but if you do, you should use the same number whenever you are calculating portions of years elsewhere in the model.)

Receivable days that have been increasing reflect declining sales and/or a poorly managed collection system.

A similar ratio to this is sales/accounts receivable, reversing the numerator and the denominator. This is a turnover ratio, and it describes how many times receivables turn over in the year (i.e., how many cycles of receivables are fully collected in the year). The higher the ratio, the better, since it would reflect a faster receivables collection system.

14.6.2 Inventory/Cost of Goods Sold * 365

Inventory/cost of goods sold * 365 shows how many days it takes a company to make use of a piece of inventory. The higher the number of days, the worse it is. Like the receivable days ratio, an "inventory days" ratio shows how long a company's cash is tied up in its inventory before that inventory is put into a product and sold. A high inventory days number suggests slowing sales and/or an inefficient production system.

Sales is sometimes used as the denominator and can show the same trend. However, if there are changes in the gross margin (i.e., in the relationship between sales and cost of goods sold), then the trend shown by the ratio using sales will be different from that using cost of goods sold.

Cost of goods sold/inventory is a ratio using the same numbers but in reversed positions, and without the 365 multiplier. This is a turnover ratio; it shows the number of times that inventory is turned over during the year. Think of this as the number of times that the inventory in the warehouse is completely moved out during the year.

14.6.3 Accounts Payable/Cost of Goods Sold * 365

Accounts payable/cost of goods sold * 365 shows how many days its takes a company to pay its suppliers. The higher the number of "payable days," the more favorable it is for the company. Not paying a supplier means that the company is able to get an interest-free "loan" from its supplier. (This is a receivables collection issue from the supplier's point of view.)

The denominator is cost of goods sold, and not sales, because the unpaid bills usually relate to purchases of inventory. In production, inventory is used up and that use is recognized as cost of goods sold.

A low payable days number means that the company has an efficient payment system, which is well and good in itself. A higher number can mean that the company has a strong enough buying power to delay its payments and still not have its suppliers abandon it. Beyond a certain limit, and this is a judgment call, a high number can mean the deterioration of its cash position, and therefore its ability to pay its bills.

Cost of goods sold/accounts payable is the payable turnover ratio. It shows how many times in the year that the company has completely repaid its suppliers.

14.6.4 [(Current Assets – Cash) – (Current Liabilities – Short-Term Debt)]/Sales

[(Current assets – cash) – (current liabilities – short-term debt)]/sales, or Operating working capital/sales, is an interesting ratio and bears some attention. The numerator is almost like working capital, but not quite. This is why I am using the term operating working capital, or OWC.

For highlighting the operating decisions of a company, working capital (or current assets minus current liabilities) has a flaw. Because it includes cash and cash equivalents and also short-term debt—both of which are related to financing decisions—working capital gives an unclear measure of the purely operating current investments a company has to make in its balance sheet. This is understandable as the original intent of working capital is to show the cushion that it has for meeting its current obligations.

For this reason, it is useful to look at current assets without cash and cash equivalents minus current liabilities without any sort of short-term debt. This will show only the company's operational investments, separate from financing effects. So, operating working capital is:

Current assets – cash
– (Current liabilities – short-term debt)
= Operating working capital

Thus the ratio OWC/sales is a measure of how much each dollar of sales is tied up in the current accounts of a company's balance sheet. OWC management is critical to a company's success, especially during periods of high growth.

Companies often fail during this growth spurt because their OWC goes out of control. They run out of cash as new buildups of receivables and inventory from the increased sales—combined with additional capital expenditures for expansion—lead to a depletion of their cash holdings, even if they manage to delay their payments to suppliers.

Important corollary measures of operating working capital are the change in OWC from one accounting period to the next as a dollar number, and change in OWC/sales in percentage terms. The dollar number is the ongoing amount that the company has to invest in its current accounts to sustain its operations. The higher the number, the more cash a company has to find and use. The ratio of the change over sales gives an indication of how well a company continues to manage these required investments as a percentage of its revenue stream. A trend of increasing percentages is a cautionary one as they reflect build-ups of OWC that proportionately take up more cash than what sales are bringing in.

14.6.5 Sales/Net Fixed Assets

Sales/net fixed assets measures sales as a percentage of the net fixed assets (i.e., gross fixed assets less accumulated depreciation). The higher the ratio, the more productively a company is making use of its fixed assets. This ratio is called the fixed asset turnover ratio. Another name for it is the asset intensity ratio. In general, industrial companies have lower ratios than service companies.

14.6.6 Sales/Total Assets

Sales/total assets measures sales as a percentage of the total assets of the company. This is the asset turnover ratio: the higher the ratio, the more productive the company. Comparing this ratio across companies in different industries is not particularly useful, as different industries can have significantly different average levels.

14.7 FOR PROFITABILITY

1. Gross margin, or gross profit/revenues
2. EBIT margin, or EBIT/revenue
3. EBITDA margin, or EBITDA/revenue
4. Net margin, or net income/revenue
5. Sales/(accounts receivable + inventory + net fixed assets)
6. EBIT/total invested capital
7. Return on average common equity
8. Return on average assets

The first four items listed in the preceding are metrics within the income statement. They look at how well the company manages its expenses relative to the revenues from sales, or alternatively, how well its pricing strategies are working. They define profitability in terms of earnings after expenses.

The final four items look at earnings relative to the balance sheet for a more complete picture and show how the earnings are relative to the investments that have been made to support those earnings. They define profitability in terms of returns on investment and compare earnings to different groups of balance sheet accounts. If revenues are small compared to the amount of assets on the balance sheet, this indicates the company is making an unproductive use of its assets.

14.7.1 Gross Margin

The gross margin shows how much as a percentage of sales the company can make after paying for the raw materials that go into sales. The raw materials expense is seen as a cost of goods sold.

14.7.2 EBIT Margin

The EBIT margin is the percentage of sales that the company can make after paying other operating expenses such as SG&A (sales, general, and administrative expenses). This is also called operating margin.

14.7.3 EBITDA Margin

The EBITDA margin is the percentage of sales that the company can make on the EBITDA basis, with the noncash depreciation and amortization expenses added to the EBIT measure.

14.7.4 Net Margin

The net margin is the percentage of sales that the company clears after payment of taxes.

14.7.5 Sales/(Accounts Receivables + Inventory + Net Fixed Assets)

This ratio shows the relationship between sales and the operating and investment assets. (Receivables, inventory, and net fixed assets are often called the core assets.) Accounts receivable is an operating investment, essentially the amount of cash "invested" in customers who have not paid for their purchases. Likewise, inventory represents the "investment" in the amount of goods already purchased and kept in storage ready for production. Net fixed assets are the capital equipment required to produce the company's products, net of depreciation.

14.7.6 Return on Average Common Equity

The return on average common equity, sometimes just called return on equity (ROE), is based on the average of the starting and ending common equity for the year. (The starting common equity in each year is equivalent to the ending number for the prior year.) This is because the earnings accrue over the year, so the return should be calculated over the common equity level that holds over the same period. The average of the beginning and ending numbers is the best proxy for this.

14.7.7 Return on Average Assets

Likewise, the return on average assets, sometimes just called return on assets (ROA), uses the same approach of using an average for the denominator.

14.8 FOR LEVERAGE

The following ratios measure leverage, or the amount of debt that the company has relative to investments or to its earnings flow. In either case, the higher the ratio, the higher the leverage and the higher the chances for default.

Cash is the measure of things for repaying debt, which is why EBITDA is the preferred number for leverage ratios.

1. Total debt/shareholders' equity
2. Net debt/shareholders' equity
3. Total debt/total invested capital
4. Bank debt/EBITDA
5. Senior debt/EBITDA

6. Total debt/EBITDA
7. Net debt/EBITDA

14.8.1 Total Debt/Shareholders' Equity

Total debt/shareholders' equity shows the ratio of debt to equity. A high ratio, within limits, is not necessarily bad. This should be looked at in the context of the company's ability to generate cash flow to cover its debt service (interest payments and principal repayments).

14.8.2 Net Debt/Shareholders' Equity

Net debt/shareholders' equity is a ratio similar to total debt/shareholders' equity. Net debt is total debt minus cash and cash equivalents. Cash equivalents are accounts such as short-term investments or marketable securities that can be turned into cash easily. Net debt shows the debt load of a company as if it had used its available cash to repay some of its debt. Companies with a large cash position relative to their total debt will have a negative net debt.

14.8.3 Total Debt/Total Invested Capital

The denominator is total invested capital—the combination of shareholders' equity, total debt, and minority interests.

14.8.4 Bank Debt/EBITDA; Senior Debt/EBITDA; Total Debt/EBITDA; Net Debt/EBITDA

These ratios with debt measures in the numerator and EBITDA in the denominator show the size of each debt measure relative to the cash operating earnings of the company. In an annual model, the EBITDA will be the annual earnings, so each ratio is a way of expressing that the debt is equivalent to so many years' earnings. If you start building models that have nonannual periods—for example, if each column contains quarterly data—these ratios will not be useful unless the quarterly EBITDA numbers are annualized. For quarterly EBITDA numbers, the easy "quick and dirty" way is simply to multiply them by 4. You should be careful with this approach if the company has highly seasonal flows.

14.9 FOR COVERAGE

Coverage refers to the ability of the company's cash flows to cover its interest expense or debt obligations.

1. Times interest earned: EBIT/interest expense
2. EBITDA/cash interest expense
3. (EBITDA – capital expenditures)/cash interest expense
4. Fixed charge coverage
5. Cash fixed charge coverage
6. Operating cash flow/total debt
7. Operating cash flow/net debt
8. Operating cash flow/average total liabilities

14.9.1 Times Interest Earned

Times interest earned (TIE) is a ratio that compares the company's EBIT to its interest expense. This ratio is important to the lending decisions made by banks. If a company has a TIE of 3.0×, this means that its EBIT is enough to pay its interest expense three times over. Put another way, EBIT has to shrink more than two-thirds before it defaults, or cannot pay its interest payments. Lending banks want to see a high ratio because it means there is less likelihood that a loan to the company will become a nonperforming loan.

14.9.2 EBITDA/Cash Interest Expense

EBITDA/cash interest expense is TIE on a cash basis. EBITDA is the cash earnings that a company has. The denominator uses the interest expense that is cash, as there are forms of debt in which the interest is not paid out in cash but instead added to the outstanding debt. This kind of debt is called accreting debt. It is also called payment-in-kind (or PIK, pronounced "Pick") debt. Thus, the denominator is total interest (which may have both cash and noncash interest) less noncash interest. This ratio gives an extra measure of insight for coverage analysis, because EBITDA as a measure of the cash earnings a company is being compared to the payment to cash interest expenses.

14.9.3 (EBITDA – Capital Expenditures)/Cash Interest Expense

(EBITDA – capital expenditures)/cash interest expense is a coverage measure of the ability to repay cash interest based on cash earnings after what usually is a required expense: capital expenditures. By accounting convention, capital expenditures do not appear in the income statement; they appear in the cash flow statement. By subtracting these expenditures from EBITDA, the ratio shows the company's ability to pay its cash interest expense. It may be that a company can reduce or defer its capital expenditures in order to pay its interest. But if it does so, it is likely to suffer diminished productivity in the long run (as its fixed assets age and fall into increasing disrepair) and jeopardize its interest-paying ability.

14.9.4 Fixed Charge Coverage

(EBIT + rent expense)/(interest expense + preferred dividends + rent expense). This ratio is more important in analyzing retail companies.

14.9.5 Cash Fixed Charge Coverage

This is similar to the ratio in the preceding, but we use (EBITDA + rent expense)/(cash interest expense + preferred dividends + rent expense). The cash interest expense makes a distinction between interest payments that are cash and those that are noncash.

14.9.6 Operating Cash Flow Ratios

Operating cash flow is an item from the cash flow statement and is the sum of net income (the first item on the statement) plus all the addbacks of noncash expenses. Put another way, this is net income on a cash basis and represents the cash earnings after interest and taxes from operations.

14.10 COMMON-SIZE STATEMENTS

Common-size statements, which typically are prepared for the income statement, and the balance sheet, express a firm's performance over time as a percentage of a base number. Common-size cash flow statements are less often seen.

For the income statement, the typical base is each year's revenue number. All the other income and expense numbers shown for each year are a percentage of that year's revenue. Revenue is shown as 100%. In effect, the whole income statement becomes a "margin statement." By expressing all the accounts in this manner, we can see how well the company maintains its margins, even if the underlying dollar numbers have undergone sizable changes over time.

For the balance sheet, the usual base is total assets, which are shown as 100%. Every other account on the balance sheet—whether assets, liabilities, or equity—are then shown as percentages of this total.

In addition to providing a yardstick for comparisons across time within a company, common-size statements also provide useful information for looking at the economic characteristics of different companies in the same industry, as well as in different industries.

You can add this to the model we have developed by adding an extra sheet for each financial statement you want to show in common-size terms. An easy way to do this is to make a copy of the sheet through the Excel commands:

1. Double-click on the sheet tab you want to copy, right-click and select "Move or copy…," select a position among the sheets shown in the list box, check the "Create Copy" check box, then click on OK.
2. You can then rename the duplicate sheet by clicking on the sheet tab, and typing in a new name for the sheet.
3. Then write the formulas this way. Let's say you have just made a duplicate of the "IS" sheet, and you have renamed the duplicate sheet "ISCS" (for Income Statement Common Size.) On "ISCS," create a formula that looks to its counterpart in "IS," but with a divisor of the Revenues

line for that column. For example, in ISCS cell B6 for the first year's revenues, write the formula that at its core is the calculation IS!B6/IS!B$6. Note the use of the absolute reference for the row in B$6. Because some of the rows in "IS" may be holding zeros, write the full formula as =IF(ISERROR(IS!B6/IS!B$6),0,IS!B6/IS!B$6) so that you do not get a DIV/0! Error when the formula encounters a zero.

4. In "ISCS," copy this formula down the column and across all the columns. As long as you have not made any changes to the "IS" and "ISCS" after you made the duplicate—i.e., each sheet has the same layout in rows and columns—this copying sequence can be done quickly, as you can be assured that the formula references from one sheet to the other are correct.
5. As you copy the formulas down, there may be some formatting that you want to keep, such as the underline before the subtotals. Make use of Excel's ability to copy only the contents of a cell (which means that the formatting of the cell you are pasting into is not affected). After the *Edit>Copy* command, use the *Edit>Paste Special>Formulas*. Then, format all the cells with the new formula in the Percent format.
6. As a final step, the original lines in "IS" had margin percentages. In "ISCS," you can delete these rows. The final "ISCS" sheet will be a few rows shorter than "IS."

Go through the same steps for creating a common-size balance sheet, but with the divisor for the formulas being the total assets for each column.

The "ISCS" sheet will look like Figure 14-1.

14.10.1 Common-Size Income Statement

As shown in Table 14-1, the labels are also formulas that read back to the IS sheet. This is not absolutely necessary; it is a nice touch in case labels get changed in the IS sheet, in which case the changes are automatically reflected on this sheet.

FIGURE 14-1

The Common-Size Income Statement

First Corporation

INCOME STATEMENT	Dec-05	Dec-06	Dec-07	Proj Dec-08	Proj Dec-09	Proj Dec-10
Revenues	100.0%	100.0%	100.0%	100.0%	100.0%	100.0%
COGS	54.5%	54.4%	55.0%	55.0%	55.0%	55.0%
Gross profit	**45.5%**	**45.6%**	**45.0%**	**45.0%**	**45.0%**	**45.0%**
SGA	15.2%	15.0%	15.0%	15.0%	15.0%	15.0%
Operating expenses	3.0%	3.1%	3.0%	3.0%	3.0%	3.0%
EBITDA	**27.3%**	**27.4%**	**27.0%**	**27.0%**	**27.0%**	**27.0%**
Depreciation	7.3%	8.3%	8.0%	7.7%	7.6%	7.7%
Amortization of intangibles	0.5%	0.4%	0.4%	0.4%	0.3%	0.3%
EBIT	**19.5%**	**18.7%**	**18.6%**	**18.9%**	**19.1%**	**19.0%**
Non-oper expenses	1.2%	1.1%	0.8%	0.9%	0.9%	0.8%
Gain (loss) on asset sales	0.0%	0.0%	0.0%	0.0%	0.0%	0.0%
Interest income	0.4%	0.5%	0.6%	0.5%	0.9%	0.7%
Interest expense	6.1%	5.6%	4.9%	3.6%	3.3%	3.0%
EBT	**12.6%**	**12.5%**	**13.4%**	**14.9%**	**15.8%**	**15.9%**
Provision for taxes	4.4%	4.4%	4.7%	5.2%	5.5%	5.6%
Equity earnings in affiliates	0.6%	0.6%	0.6%	0.6%	0.5%	0.5%
Minority interest in earnings	1.3%	1.3%	1.3%	1.3%	1.2%	1.2%
Net income	**7.5%**	**7.3%**	**8.0%**	**9.0%**	**9.5%**	**9.6%**
Extraordinary expense	0.6%	0.6%	0.6%	0.3%	0.0%	0.0%
Preferred dividends	0.6%	0.6%	0.6%	0.5%	0.5%	0.5%
Net income available to common	**6.3%**	**6.2%**	**6.8%**	**8.1%**	**9.1%**	**9.2%**
Common dividends	1.2%	1.3%	1.1%	0.9%	1.0%	1.0%
Net to retained earnings	**5.1%**	**4.9%**	**5.7%**	**7.2%**	**8.1%**	**8.2%**

14.10.2 Common-Size Balance Sheet

Figure 14-2 shows the balance sheet common-size statements, based on total assets.

TABLE 14–1

Formulas for the Common-Size Income Statement

Label in Column C	Formula in Column F (Copy to G and K)
INCOME STATEMENT	=Input!F6
=IS!C8	=IS!F8/IS!F$8
=IS!C9	=IS!F9/IS!F$8
Gross profit	=F8–F9
=IS!C13	=IS!F13/IS!F$8
=IS!C14	=IS!F14/IS!F$8
EBITDA	=F10–F12–F13
=IS!C18	=IS!F18/IS!F$8
=IS!H19/IS!H$8	=IS!F19/IS!F$8
EBIT	=F14–F16–F17
=IS!C23	=IS!F23/IS!F$8
=IS!C24	=IS!F24/IS!F$8
=IS!C25	=IS!F25/IS!F$8
=IS!C26	=IS!F26/IS!F$8
EBT	=F18–F20+F21+F22–F23
=IS!C30	=IS!F30/IS!F$8
=IS!C31	=IS!F31/IS!F$8
=IS!C32	=IS!F32/IS!F$8
Net income	=F24–F26+F27–F28
=IS!C36	=IS!F36/IS!F$8
=IS!C37	=IS!F37/IS!F$8
=Input!C78	=F29–F31–F32
=IS!C40	=IS!F40/IS!F$8
Net to retained earnings	=F33–F35

FIGURE 14–2

The Common-Size Balance Sheet

First Corporation

BALANCE SHEET	Dec-05	Dec-06	Dec-07	Proj Dec-08	Proj Dec-09	Proj Dec-10
ASSETS						
Excess cash	0.0%	0.0%	0.0%	5.5%	3.3%	1.0%
Operating cash	4.4%	5.0%	5.0%	4.4%	4.1%	3.8%
ST investments	2.2%	2.1%	2.0%	1.9%	1.8%	1.7%
Account receivable	4.4%	5.0%	5.6%	5.0%	5.1%	5.2%
Inventory	8.8%	9.0%	9.3%	8.9%	8.9%	9.1%
Other current assets	0.7%	0.7%	0.7%	0.6%	0.6%	0.6%
Current assets	**20.6%**	**21.8%**	**22.6%**	**26.3%**	**23.8%**	**21.5%**
Net PPE	64.1%	63.3%	61.9%	59.4%	61.9%	64.2%
Investment in affiliates	4.3%	3.6%	3.1%	2.9%	3.0%	3.1%
Intangibles	3.7%	3.6%	3.6%	3.0%	2.6%	2.2%
Long-term assets	7.4%	7.7%	8.8%	8.5%	8.7%	8.9%
Total assets	**100.0%**	**100.0%**	**100.0%**	**100.0%**	**100.0%**	**100.0%**
LIABILITIES						
Revolver	0.0%	0.0%	0.0%	0.0%	0.0%	0.0%
Short-term notes	0.7%	0.8%	0.9%	0.8%	0.7%	0.7%
Accounts payable	4.4%	4.7%	5.0%	5.0%	5.1%	5.3%
Other current liabilities	0.7%	1.3%	1.2%	1.2%	1.2%	1.3%
Current liabilities	**5.9%**	**6.8%**	**7.1%**	**7.0%**	**7.1%**	**7.2%**
Debt 1	14.7%	15.0%	9.3%	8.3%	7.7%	7.2%
Debt 2	8.8%	8.0%	9.0%	8.0%	7.4%	6.9%
Debt 3	8.1%	7.3%	6.8%	6.1%	5.6%	5.3%
Long-term liabilities	2.9%	3.2%	3.1%	2.4%	2.5%	2.5%
Total liabilities	**40.5%**	**40.3%**	**35.2%**	**31.7%**	**30.4%**	**29.1%**
MINORITY INTEREST						
Minority interest	**4.3%**	**4.7%**	**5.1%**	**5.4%**	**5.8%**	**6.1%**
SHAREHOLDERS' EQUITY						
Preferred stock	5.9%	6.0%	6.2%	5.5%	5.1%	4.8%
Common stock	33.9%	32.0%	34.1%	35.8%	33.4%	31.1%
Retained earnings	14.7%	16.2%	18.6%	20.9%	24.6%	28.1%
Other equity account	0.7%	0.8%	0.7%	0.7%	0.7%	0.8%
Shareholders' equity	**55.2%**	**55.0%**	**59.6%**	**62.9%**	**63.8%**	**64.7%**
Total liabilities and SH equity	**100.0%**	**100.0%**	**100.0%**	**100.0%**	**100.0%**	**100.0%**

TABLE 14-2

Formulas for the Common-Size Balance Sheet

Label in Column C	Formula in Column F (Copy to G and K)
BALANCE SHEET	=BS!F6
ASSETS	
=BS!C8	=BS!F8/BS!F$20
=BS!C9	=BS!F9/BS!F$20
=BS!C10	=BS!F10/BS!F$20
=BS!C11	=BS!F11/BS!F$20
=BS!C12	=BS!F12/BS!F$20
=BS!C13	=BS!F13/BS!F$20
Current assets	=SUM(F8:F13)
=BS!C16	=BS!F16/BS!F$20
=BS!C17	=BS!F17/BS!F$20
=BS!C18	=BS!F18/BS!F$20
=BS!C19	=BS!F19/BS!F$20
Total assets	=F14+SUM(F16:F19)
LIABILITIES	
=BS!C23	=BS!F23/BS!F$20
=BS!C24	=BS!F24/BS!F$20
=BS!C25	=BS!F25/BS!F$20
=BS!C26	=BS!F26/BS!F$20
Current liabilities	=SUM(F23:F26)
=BS!C29	=BS!F29/BS!F$20
=BS!C30	=BS!F30/BS!F$20
=BS!C31	=BS!F31/BS!F$20
=BS!C32	=BS!F32/BS!F$20
Total liabilities	=F27+SUM(F29:F32)
=BS!C35	
=BS!C36	=BS!F36/BS!F$20
SHAREHOLDERS' EQUITY	
=BS!C39	=BS!F39/BS!F$20
=BS!C40	=BS!F40/BS!F$20
=BS!C41	=BS!F41/BS!F$20
=BS!C42	=BS!F42/BS!F$20
Shareholders' equity	=SUM(F39:F42)
Total liabilities and SH equity	=F33+F36+F43

CHAPTER 15

Forecasting Guidelines

This chapter goes over the principles of good forecasting—the kind that will ensure that your analysis remains in the realm of realistic estimates, rather than going off into unreasonable assumptions.

By the way, now that you have built a working model from scratch, don't forget to pat yourself on the back.

15.1 KEY PRINCIPLES

- Good forecasts must be consistent with historical performance and the current industry outlook.
- Look at historical numbers in relationship to others and use these ratios, particularly the operating ratios, to make your projections.
- All forecasts are estimates and approximations. Spend the time thinking and developing your ideas about the big picture, not the trivial details.
- If the forecast looks too good to be true, it probably is. Re-examine your assumptions.
- Avoid the "hockey stick": historical trends show modest growth rates, but once the forecast begins, the rates

grow at a much steeper rate, looking like the profile of a hockey stick. Again, re-examine your assumptions.

15.2 INCOME STATEMENT ACCOUNTS

15.2.1 Revenues

For industrial/manufacturing types of companies, revenues drive the other numbers in the model. Here are things to think about as you make your forecast:

- Revenues are the result of three main components: price, industry growth, and market share. Isolating the price growth from inflation will give you the measure for volume growth. Understand that in the context of the economic cycle, and then concentrate on what the drivers for future industry growth and market share might be. Add back the inflation component (typically very low at 1–2% in the United States) to get the full estimate of future revenues growth.
- Think drivers, drivers, drivers. To forecast revenues, for example, it is useful to break down the components that drive the revenue, and in turn to analyze what are the drivers behind those drivers. In this way, the forecast can capture the dynamics of the market.
- Unless you are looking at new industries (new drugs, new telecommunications), most businesses are mature and should grow at around the growth of the economy. Gross domestic product (GDP) growth rates would be a good proxy. Your particular company's sales growth will also be affected at different points of the product cycle by new entrants and competing new technologies. Remember also that fast-growing businesses have very dramatic price and volume falls as the demand reaches a certain point. Consider the experience with cell phones now compared with when they first appeared. Cell phones are now low priced, if not free. Wireless companies are not selling phones; they are selling a monthly phone service, and they are happy to give away the phones if

it means that the customer can be locked into a 2-year contract. If your company does not have a position of advantage, it will lose market share, and your volume estimates must reflect that.

- If your company has product lines that have very different characteristics, it would be important to forecast the individual product lines. However, if they are similar enough, it is better to think in broad aggregate terms and forecast only one revenue line. There is no need to get super precise price and volume numbers for the forecast years.
- Take into account the characteristics of the industry your company is in. Some industries have price controls or regulatory restrictions, which would limit your own forecasts.

15.2.2 Margin Assumptions

- Analyze the trends in the historical accounts, such as cost of goods sold as percentage of sales, SGA (sales, general & administrative) as percentage of sales, etc. Your forecasts should be consistent with these trends, while taking into account what you know of any improvements or changes in the company's operating systems.
- If there have been striking changes in the margins, you should understand the reason.
- Look at the trends in the context of the economic and product cycles.

15.2.3 Depreciation

- Although it can be convenient to forecast depreciation as a percentage of revenue, the relationship to revenue is indirect. Depreciation is determined by net PPE (plant, property, and equipment), which in turn is affected by capital expenditures. Capex typically vary with revenue.

- If some precision is required, the best way to model depreciation is to lay out the depreciation that is associated with each year's new capital investments. This will mean creating a "depreciation triangle" as shown in Table 15-1. The longer the forecast period, the "deeper" the triangle has to be. However, it is generally acceptable to use the recent relationship between depreciation and the net PPE of the prior year.
- Depreciation for tax purposes and for book purposes can be different. This will lead to the creation of deferred taxes.

15.2.4 Interest Income

- Look to the effective rates of interest income that the company has been paying in the historical years. You can get this information simply by looking at interest income divided by the average of the beginning and

TABLE 15-1

A Depreciation Worksheet

Year	1	2	3	4	5	6
Capital Expenditures	80	60	100	80	120	120
Depreciation of Capex Year 1	4	8	8	8	8	8
Depreciation of Capex Year 2		3	6	6	6	6
Depreciation of Capex Year 3			5	10	10	10
Depreciation of Capex Year 4				4	8	8
Depreciation of Capex Year 5					6	12
Depreciation of Capex Year 6						6
Total Depreciation	4	11	19	28	38	50
Gross PPE	200	260	360	440	560	680
Accumulated Depreciation	4	15	34	62	100	150
Net PPE	196	245	326	378	460	530
Depreciation % Prior Net PPE		6%	8%	9%	10%	11%

Assumptions: 10-year life, straight life, 50% depreciation in the year of asset installation.

ending total interest-yielding assets. The average is used to capture the changes that have happened over the year. This may not be the actual interest earnings rate. Many companies keep cash as an operational cushion, and it is not necessarily in the bank earning interest. However, this effective interest rate is usually good enough for projections.

- Interest on cash should be less than the interest on debt.

15.2.5 Interest Expense

- Companies usually pay close to market rates, so get estimates of the benchmark being used (LIBOR, Prime, etc.) and then apply a spread over that. Check with the relationship banker or the debt pricing desk about what this spread should be. Generally speaking, the bigger and therefore the more creditworthy the company, the smaller the spread. Spreads can be quoted as basis points. One basis point is one one-hundredth of a percent; so 100 basis points is equivalent to 1%.
- Check also the historical effective interest rates that the company has been paying. (Remember to do so by dividing the interest expense by the average of the beginning and ending total debt.) If these rates seem very high, they may be due to seasonal borrowings. The company draws down on its line of credit during the year and therefore pays interest on that, but pays off the debt before the reporting date. The result is that there is a record of the interest expense in the income statement, but no record on the balance sheet of the debt that produced it. This is normal operating procedure, by the way, and there is nothing sneaky about it.

15.2.6 Taxes

- Taxes should be taxed at statutory rates, and they should also reflect local rules in effect for the company.

If there are any deviations from these rates, you should try to find out the reasons why, and if they are sustainable.

- Deferred taxes occur when the provision for taxes in the book basis is different from the actual taxes paid on the tax basis. These occur usually because of different book-basis and tax-basis depreciation schedules that the company has adopted, or from net operating losses. Their complexity puts them beyond the scope of this chapter.

15.2.7 Extraordinary Items

- This is a tricky line, since by its very nature items here are not easily forecast. If you have specific information about these items from the company, by all means include it. Otherwise, it may be best not to try to do any forecasts.

15.2.8 Dividends

The best way to forecast dividends is by multiplying the number of shares by a historic dividends per share number grown at a reasonable rate. However, you should watch out for the following:

- Use the correct number of shares, which is the weighted average shares outstanding. The plain shares outstanding refers to the number at the reporting date, but this does not take into account that there may have been changes in the shares outstanding over the year. It is also important to reflect the timing of the changes, which is why the weighted average number is used. Typically, this information is available in the annual reports. If you do not have this number, a proxy is to take the average of the shares outstanding at the beginning and the end of the reporting period.
- Compute the historic dividends per share numbers yourself. If they reconcile with the historic figures, then you have a good basis for using them as the basis for calculations of future dividends, plus a growth rate that

roughly equals the growth of the economy and/or the industry. If they do not reconcile, it may be because of stock splits or rights issues. Companies' dividends usually grow at a steady rate, but the growth can stop if earnings go into a dip.

15.3 BALANCE SHEET

15.3.1 Cash

There are two kinds of cash account in the model. One is the cash that the company needs to have on hand to handle day-to-day expenses. We can think of this as "minimum cash." You can attach an interest rate to this, but usually this cash is not kept in the bank and so it is not earning interest. Because this cash also reflects operational needs, it makes sense to forecast this as a percentage of sales, and to consider this as part of working capital.

The other is the cash that is automatically produced by the model when liabilities and equity exceed assets—the excess cash row. You do not forecast this account directly. Rather, it is a result of the forecast assumptions you make for other parts of the balance sheet and indeed the income statement, too. (It may be that your assumptions will create a need for additional debt, in which case you would see the revolver line, not the excess cash line.) To the extent that you will have excess cash, make sure that you enter an interest rate.

15.3.2 Short-Term Investments

If your company has this account, you may want to forecast the same level going forward, without any growth. By holding it steady, you will be able to see more clearly the rate of buildup in excess cash or revolver.

15.3.3 Operating Assets and Liabilities

A large part of the balance sheet is there to support sales. As sales grow, these operating assets and operating liabilities must also grow by a more-or-less proportionate rate. As a result, you can forecast them based on a relationship to revenues in the income statement.

15.3.3.1 The operating assets are:

- Accounts receivable
- Inventory
- Other current assets
- Net PPE
- Other assets. You should check if these are related to operations or investments; if the latter, they should be forecast at some growth rate, not as a percentage of sales.

15.3.3.2 The operating liabilities are:

- Accounts payable
- Other current liabilities

You can project these items on the basis of the last historical year, but you should take into account any variations from trends that are booming or reversing. Any unusual or extreme change is a call for delving further into the information to find out what the reasons may be.

The net PPE number is a tricky one to forecast, and the forecast numbers are determined by two main flows: capital expenditures (which add to the gross PPE number) and depreciation (which flows into accumulated depreciation and reduces the gross PPE number). The production base to support sales is a function of many things, including the product being produced, the technology in place, and the scale of production. These—and other factors—represent a "habit" of the production systems in the company. The net result is a net PPE number that should have some discernible and steady relationship to sales. Thus, a good way to forecast net PPE is first to determine the net PPE to sales ratio and then to use that as the basis of forecasting net PPE. If we have a depreciation schedule, then, in fact, the capital expenditures number becomes the "plug" number that we can back into in the calculation of net PPE.

Some pointers:

- If the latest net PPE to sales ratio is high, this probably reflects recent investments to modernize the plant. We can let this ratio trend down to the historical rates; as a result, future capex will also show a downward trend until the ratio meets the historical levels.
- If the ratio is low, this probably means that there will be a need for heavy investments soon.
- This measure of net assets to sales should be relatively steady over the forecast period. The logical test is to extend the projection period into perpetuity. If this ratio is trending upward, then we will have a company that will be extremely asset intensive. Likewise, if it is trending downward, we will have a company that will generate huge revenues on a sliver of a PPE base.

15.3.4 Other Assets

You should find out if these other assets are operating or investment assets, and then forecast them accordingly. If they are operating, you should forecast them in some relationship to sales; if they are investments, then they should grow at some rate.

15.3.5 Other Liabilities

These can be either operating or financing assets. You should project them accordingly. Sometimes, when you have no information, the best recourse would be to hold them steady at the last reported date levels.

15.3.6 Taxes Payable

You should forecast these as a percentage of current taxes. Taxes payable reflect the part of taxes not paid until the next year.

15.3.7 Dividends Payable

This should be forecast as a percentage of current dividends. Like taxes, a part of dividends is not paid out until the following year.

15.3.8 Debt

You should forecast the debt based on known amortization schedules. Where debt is being amortized, you may find that the assets side of the balance sheet is now "higher" than the liabilities and equity side. In this case, a plug debt line appears that is the Necessary to finance line in our model.

15.3.9 Common Stock and Other Equity Accounts

Unless you have specific information about these accounts, hold them at the level of the last historical year.

15.3.10 Retained Earnings

Retained earnings in the equity account should not be directly projected in the balance sheet. Instead, this should grow in the model as a result of the flows from net income, which in turn have been produced by the assumptions in use in the income statement.

CHAPTER 16

Discounted Cash Flow Valuation

There are many different ways to value a company, but one that makes use of a projection financial model is the Discounted Cash Flow (DCF) valuation method. This is based on the concept that the value of an entity is based on the future cash flows it can generate. The value is arrived at when those cash flows are discounted (or present-valued) at a discount rate that represents the risk of those cash flows.

DCF is not limited to just valuing a company. It can be used to value a division of a company, a project, an asset—basically any enterprise that generates a cash flow. For this reason, we will use the term *entity* instead of *company* in describing the elements of a DCF valuation.

The elements of a DCF analysis are:

- The weighted average cost of capital
- The free cash flows
- The terminal value
- The enterprise value
- The equity value

16.1 WEIGHTED AVERAGE COST OF CAPITAL

Weighted average cost of capital (or WACC, pronounced "wack") is the blended cost of the equity and debt capital of the entity.

The cost of equity is the return required by equity holders for the risk of investing their capital into the company. The cost of debt is the return required by debt holders. However, because debt interest is tax deductible, the cost of debt required is really the after-tax cost of debt [interest rate % * (1-tax rate %)]. The blended value is based on the portion of equity and debt in the entity's capitalization.

In an acquisition scenario where there is an acquirer and a target, and the target is being valued by DCF, the WACC to use in valuing the target is the *target's* WACC, not the acquirer's. The reason is that discount rate should reflect the risk of the cash flows; the risk in this case is attached to the cash flows of the target.

16.2 FREE CASH FLOW

The cash flows in a DCF are called "free cash flows" (FCF). The free cash flow is comprised of:

- The operating earnings of the entity. For a company, this is typically the EBIT line. The rationale here is that the cash flows should derive from the operations of the company. The FCF should also be unlevered, i.e., they do not reflect the interest costs of debt (or "leverage"). The FCF should also be the amount before any dividends are subtracted out for the equity holders.
- Less: Taxes on the EBIT. This is obviously an artificial number (tax in the income statement is on the earnings after interest, not on the EBIT), but because taxes are a real cost, this is computed. The taxes are on EBIT, not EBITDA, because depreciation and amortization are tax-deductible.
- Add back depreciation and amortization. These are noncash expenses so they are added back.
- Add back any increases in deferred tax liability. An increase in this balance sheet account represents taxes that have been deferred (typically because of different

book and tax-basis basis calculations), and represents cash that the entity still has in hand.

- Less: any increases in operating working capital. Any increase in net working capital is a use of funds. Operating working capital is defined as [current assets excluding cash and short-term investments] less [current liabilities less short-term debt and current portion of long-term debt].
- Less: Capital expenditures

The increase in operating working capital and capital expenditures reduces the free cash flow. They are included in the calculation of FCF because they represent the cash that must be invested in order to sustain the operations.

In DCF terminology, the EBIT after taxes is called EBIAT, or earnings before interest after taxes. A parallel terminology is operating profit for EBIT, and NOPAT, or net operating profit after taxes for EBIAT. We will use the terms EBIT and EBIAT.

The free cash flow of each projected year is discounted back to the valuation date at the WACC. There are two ways of discount the free cash flows.

16.2.1 Discounting by the Year-End Convention

In year-end discounting, the free cash flows are recognized at the end of each year. For example, if the valuation date is the beginning of the year of 2010 and the discount rate is 10%, a free cash flow of $100 for the year 2010 as of the valuation date is discounted by a full year, since the $100 is recognized only at the end of 2010. The discounted value is $90.9 ($100/(1+10%)). By the same token, the free cash flow for 2011 will be discounted a full 2 years to the valuation date, etc.

16.2.2 Discounting by the Mid-Year Convention

In this approach, the free cash flow are recognized at the mid-point of the year, as the average point for the free cash flows that occur in each month during the year. In this method, if a valuation date is the beginning of the year 2010 and the discount rate is 10%, then

FIGURE 16-1

Year-End vs Mid-Year Discounting

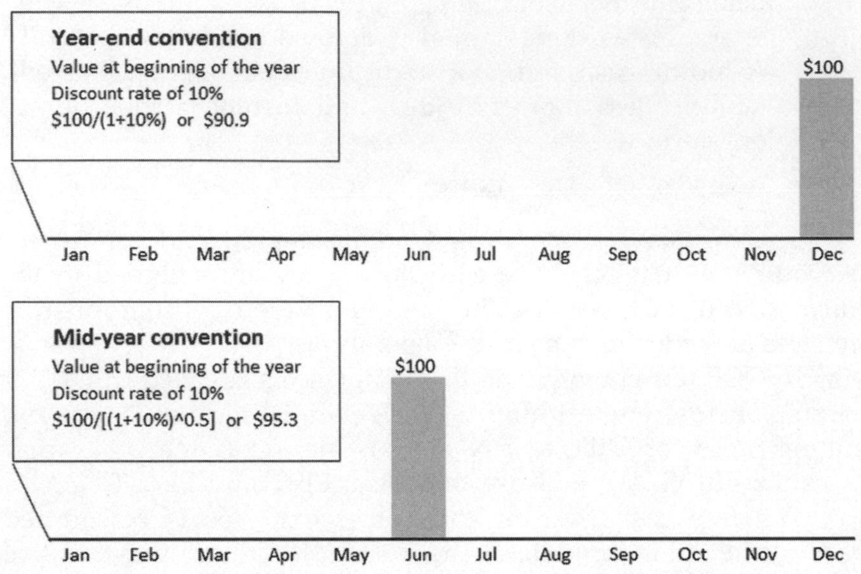

the free cash flow of $100 for the year 2010 is discounted by only half a year, since the free cash flow is recognized as of the mid-point of 2010. The discounted value is $95.3 ($100/[(1+10%)^0.5]). All things being equal, the mid-year results in a higher valuation of the free cash flows than the year-end convention (Fig. 16-1).

16.3 TERMINAL VALUE

Terminal value (TV) is the estimate of the value of the firm from the end of the projected period to perpetuity. It is based on the assumed growth into perpetuity of the FCF at the last projected year ($Year_n$). The TV can also be derived by using an "exit multiple" of Revenue, EBIT, or EBITDA. In our model, we will use the growth option and the EBITDA option. A net income multiple would not be appropriate, because that is a flow after interest expense and thus net income represents the flows available to the equity holders only. (The debt holders are out of the picture since they have already received their interest payments.) The basis of DCF is to use flows available to both equity and debt holders.

Since a DCF relies on a limited time horizon of 5 to 10 years, the terminal value represents the value of all the free cash flows extending from beyond the last projected year. Another way to think of this is to consider the TV as the price that a buyer would buy the entity at Year_n.

The terminal value is a large number and can be in the region of 50%–80% of the enterprise value. Thus, assumptions regarding the TV are critical.

The TV is recognized at the last projected year, Year_n (and *not* Year_{n+1}). It is discounted back to the valuation date at the rate of the WACC.

16.3.1 Year-End or Mid-Year Discounting for Terminal Value

If the TV value is derived from the perpetuity growth assumption, then it should be discounted using the same method for the FCF. Thus, for a year-end convention, the TV is recognized at the end of Year_n; for the mid-year convention, the TV is recognized at the middle of Year_n.

If the TV is derived using an exit multiple of Revenue, EBIT, or EBITDA, it should be discounted using the year-end convention, even if the FCF values are being discounted using the mid-year convention. This is because the multiples are looking to year-end values for Revenue, EBIT, or EBITDA, so the exit multiple value is a year-end value.

16.4 ENTERPRISE VALUE

The enterprise value is the total of the present value of the free cash flows and the terminal value. It represents the value of the entity to both the equity and debt holders.

16.5 EQUITY VALUE

The equity value is the enterprise value less the market value of debt plus the cash on the balance sheet. This represents the value to the equity holders. If you divide the equity value by the number of shares outstanding, you get to the equity value per share. You can compare this value, the market price of the entity's shares, if they are publicly traded, and from this you can get a sense of whether the market overvalues or undervalues the entity.

16.6 SCHEMATIC OF A DCF VALUATION

Figure 16-2 shows the schematic of the flows in a DCF valuation. Here, we assume that the projection period covers only 5 years. Beyond this, the company is assumed to continue to produce free cash flows into perpetuity (dark bars). The value of those cash flows is captured in a terminal value (TV).

The series of free cash flows (FCF1 to FCF5) are discounted to the valuation date (Year 0) at the WACC. The TV is value recognized at the end of the projection period (FCF5 in this case) and is discounted to the valuation date at the WACC. The two are added together to arrive at the enterprise value.

FIGURE 16-2

Flows in a DCF

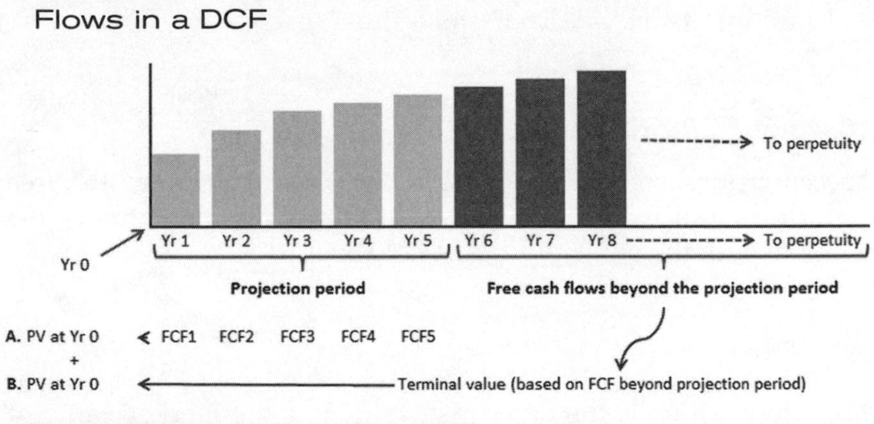

16.7 CHALLENGES

DCF analysis relies on projected numbers (there is no such thing as a DCF using historical numbers), so getting the projections right is important. There are several areas that require attention:

- Do the projections properly, with due care in defining the drivers in the income statement from the revenue down to EBIT, the assumptions for the working capital, and the estimates for capital expenditures. These are the components for the free cash flows. If the projections are overly optimistic, all things being equal, this will overstate the value of the entity; the reverse is also true. If you see the "hockey stick" trend (historical trends show consistently low growth and projected growth show a steep increase; the result is the outline of a hockey stick), it is time to revisit your projections.
- If possible, have a 10-year time horizon in the projections. This enables you to cover the operations of the entity within a business cycle, which typically runs 5 to 10 years. A longer time horizon than, say, only 5 years, also allows you to model the company so that as it reaches toward the last projected year, it has the profile of a company in a "steady state" with no major fluctuations in its operating flows or investment requirements in working capital and capital expenditures. The danger of a company that is not in a steady state is that the last projected year may present an upswing or downswing year. The TV will then be overestimated in the former and underestimated in the latter.
- Get the correct estimate for the WACC. All things being equal, a WACC that is too low will result in a higher valuation, and vice versa.

16.8 CONTINUING THE MODEL

The illustrations that follow are from the model from Chapter 11 and show a valuation model that includes the types of calculations for the DCF analysis. This layout is just one example that can be used for a DCF analysis module.

This DCF sheet uses as inputs the outputs from the model that we have been developing in earlier chapters; the inputs for the elements of the free cash flow look to the output rows in that model. Of course, this DCF model could be built as a standalone module on its own, with the free cash flow entries reading inputs from other locations. As before, each figure is a screen shot, followed by a table that lists the formula entries in the cells shown in the illustration. The cells marked with the fine dotted lines are the input cells.

In the layout of this DCF sheet, you may notice that there are four columns (Columns D, E, F, and G) that appear to have no particular use. Why not just one regular-width column instead of four narrow-width columns? These columns are spacer columns so that the first year's column on this DCF sheet is aligned with the first projected year's column on the other sheets. This makes it easier to check for errors in the referencing across the sheets.

Figure 16-3 shows the inputs for the valuation date, WACC, the discounting for the flows, and the terminal value setting.

FIGURE 16-3

Inputs for the DCF

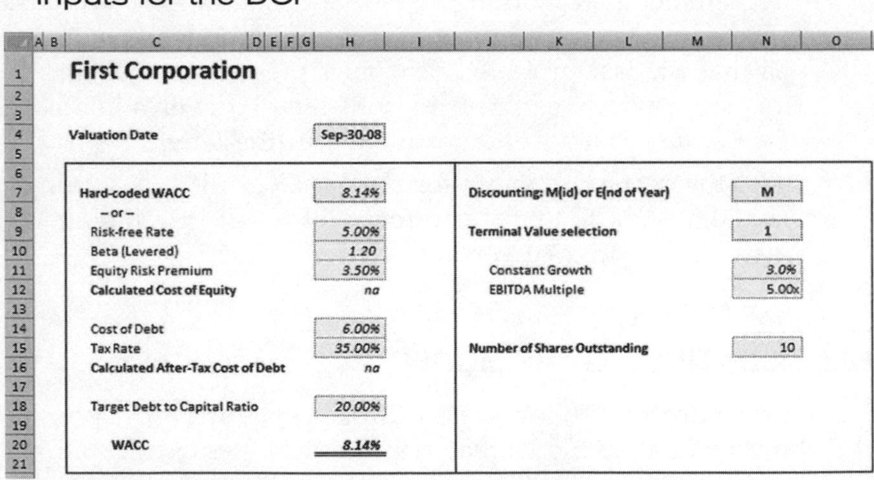

Row	C	H	J	N
1	**First Corporation**			
2				
3				
4	Valuation Date	Sep-30-08		
5				
6				
7	Hard-coded WACC	8.14%	Discounting: M(id) or E(nd of Year)	M
8	-- or --			
9	Risk-free Rate	5.00%	Terminal Value selection	1
10	Beta (Levered)	1.20		
11	Equity Risk Premium	3.50%	Constant Growth	3.0%
12	Calculated Cost of Equity	na	EBITDA Multiple	5.00x
13				
14	Cost of Debt	6.00%		
15	Tax Rate	35.00%	Number of Shares Outstanding	10
16	Calculated After-Tax Cost of Debt	na		
17				
18	Target Debt to Capital Ratio	20.00%		
19				
20	WACC	8.14%		
21				

16.8.1 The Valuation Date

The starting point is the Valuation Date (Cell H4), which defines the point in time to which the flows will be discounted.

16.8.2 Calculation of the WACC

The model has room for two approaches to the Weighted Average Cost of Capital: there is a cell for a hard-coded input (Cell H7), or several other input cells that allow you to enter the components of the WACC calculation. The final WACC result is shown in Cell H20. The hard-coded entry in Cell H7 has the first priority in defining the result in Cell H20. With this hard-coded entry, inputs in Cells H9 to H18 are ignored (Fig. 16-4). This design allows a quick WACC input but gives the option of deriving it from the components. In the illustrations that follow, we will use the 8.14% rate.

The WACC calculation is as follows:

Cost of equity	Risk-free rate + (Beta x Equity risk premium)
Cost of debt	Cost of debt * (1 – tax rate %)

F I G U R E 16–4

Hard-Code Entry in Cell H7 Disables Calculations of WACC Components

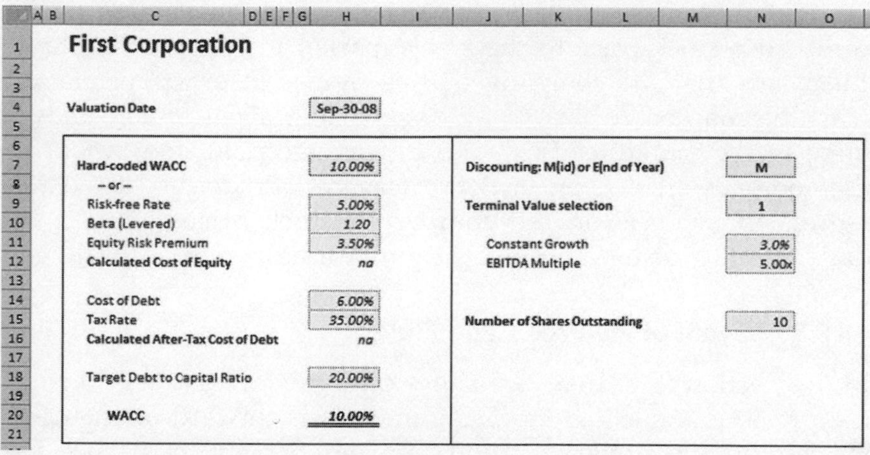

TABLE 16-1

Formula for the WACC Inputs

Row	Formula in Column H
12	=IF(H7,"na",H9+H10*H11)
16	=IF(H7,"na",H14*(1–H15))
20	=IF(H7,H7,H12*(1–H18)+H16*H18)

WACC	Cost of equity x percent of equity in capital structure + Cost of debt x percent of debt in capital structure

Table 16-1 shows the formulas for the rows shown. Other rows in this section, including those in Column N, are inputs and do not have formulas.

The 10-year U.S. Treasury bond rate is often used as representative of the risk-free rate. Be sure to check with your colleagues about which rate is the appropriate one to use as the risk-free rate and the equity risk premium. There are no hard and fast standards for these rates, and they can differ significantly from firm to firm.

Beta is a measure of the sensitivity of the movement of the company's stock price to the stock market in general. A beta of 1.0 means that the company's price moves in exact correlation with the market. A beta of 1.3 means that a percentage movement in the market causes a 1.3 percentage point movement in the company's stock price. Beta measures are derived by using regression analysis on the company's stock price sampled by daily, weekly, or monthly over a given time period.

16.8.3 Layout of the Free Cash Flows

In this section (Fig. 16-5), we show only the forecast period from the previous model, as the DCF analysis is forward-oriented. In fact, as we have set the valuation date to be September 30, 2008, we

FIGURE 16-5

Layout of the FCF

	C	I	J	K	L	M
23		*3 mos*				
24	**VALUATION**	**Dec-08**	**Dec-09**	**Dec-10**	**Dec-11**	**Dec-12**
25						
26	**Revenue**	1,100	1,210	1,331	1,464	1,611
27	*Growth %*	*na*	*(72.5%)*	*10.0%*	*10.0%*	*10.0%*
28	EBITDA	297	327	359	395	435
29	Depreciation and amortization	(89)	(96)	(107)	(118)	(131)
30	EBIT	208	231	253	277	304
31	Tax	(72)	(82)	(89)	(97)	(106)
32	*Tax rate %*	*34.6%*	*35.4%*	*35.0%*	*35.0%*	*35.0%*
33	**EBIAT**	**136**	**149**	**164**	**180**	**198**
34						
35	Depreciation and amortization	89	96	107	118	131
36	(Incr) decr in Operating Working Capital	1	(10)	(16)	(18)	(19)
37	Capital expenditures	(165)	(218)	(240)	(264)	(290)
38	Full year Free Cash Flow	61	17	15	17	19
39	Less: Pre-valuation date flows	(46)				
40	Discountable Free Cash Flow	15	17	15	17	19
41						
42	Terminal Value: 3.0% Constant Growth					384
43						

should not take into account the FCF that occur before this date. The first year of the FCF layout shows the full year's numbers. But note that in Cell I39, there is an adjustment to subtract 75% of the full-year's free cash flow (75% is the portion that is historical relative to the valuation date), to arrive at the estimate of the FCF for only the last (forecast) 3 months of 2008.

The Revenue row (Row 26) is not strictly needed because we are not using it as an option for a TV multiple. However, some people like to show it as part of the valuation calculations so that they can check the reasonableness of the revenue, EBITDA, and EBIT values.

Table 16-2 lists the formulas for the FCF section. Additionally, Table 16-3 shows the formula for the label in Cell C42, to show the label that can display information related to the terminal value option in use.

Row 23: This calculates the number of months based on the valuation date and date of the end of the first year. The DAYS360 function assumes a 360-day year with each month having 30 days. With the result divided by 30, this makes it easy to calculate the number of months. Once this calculation is done,

TABLE 16-2

Formulas for the FCF Section

Row	Formula in Column I (copy to Columns J to M, except as noted otherwise)	
23	=DAYS360(H4,I24)/30	*This is only for Column I*
24	=IS!I6	
25		
26	=IS!I8	
27	=IF(H26,I26/(H26*IF(H23,12/H23,1))−1,"na")	
28	=IS!I15	
29	=−SUM(IS!I18:I19)	
30	=SUM(I28:I29)	
31	=−I30*I32	
32	=IF(ISERROR(IS!F30/IS!F27),0,IS!F30/IS!F27)	
33	=I30+I31	
34		
35	=−I29	
36	=CashFlow!I24	
37	=CashFlow!I31	
38	=I33+SUM(I35:I37)	
39	=−I38*(1−I23/12)	
40	=I38+I39	
41		
42	=IF(ISBLANK(J40)=TRUE,CHOOSE($N$9,I40*(1+$N$11)/($H$20−$N$11),I28*$N$12),"")	

TABLE 16-3

Formula for the Label in C42

Row	Formula in Column C Only
42	="Terminal Value: "&CHOOSE($N$9,TEXT($N$11,"#0.0%")&" "&J11,TEXT($N$12,"#0.0x")&" EBITDA Exit Multiple")

the cell is formatted using the Custom format of 0 "mos" so that the number 3 in this example appears as "3 mos." Although it appears to hold a combined value and text, the cell in actually still holds only the number 3. This allows this cell to be used in calculations elsewhere.

16.8.4 The Terminal Value Formula

Row 42: This formula can be entered only in Column M. This is the formula that calculates the terminal value, and should make its appearance only in the last projected year. The formula is constructed, however, so that the formula could be entered anywhere along the projection period, but it will appear only in the last projected year because of the test that looks to the column to the right. Only if that cell is blank (which is the case if we were in the last projected year) does the formula show its results. You might want the formula to be present in the other columns in case you want to have a reduced number of years in your forecast.

Extending the forecast number of years is just a matter of copying Column M out to add the number of forecast years that you want. Other formulas in this DCF sheet assume that you will not go any further than a total of 10 forecast years.

Let's examine the terminal value formula a bit more. Let's look at the formula in column M:

```
=IF(ISBLANK(N40)=TRUE,CHOOSE($N$9,M40*(1+$N$11)/
          ($H$20-$N$11),M28*$N$12), " ")
```

Let's simplify it. The ISBLANK test is to hide the results if we are not at the last projected year. So let's eliminate that. We are then left with:

```
=CHOOSE($N$9,M40*(1+$N$11)/($H$20-$N$11),M28*$N$12)
```

The CHOOSE function gives the formula a way to show two different calculations, based on the toggle in Cell N9. To break it down further:

```
If Cell N9=1   then   M40*(1+$N$11)/($H$20-$N$11)
If Cell N9=2   then   M28*$N$12
```

The label in Cell C42 is constructed to that it can reflect the TV selection (Table 16-3).

16.8.5 The Constant Growth Formula for Terminal Value

The constant growth approach (also known as the perpetuity growth or the Gordon Growth) has this form:

Last projected FCF * (1+terminal growth rate) /
(WACC – terminal growth rate)

Remember to grow the last projected year by one year. Omitting this is a common mistake. Even so, with this extra growth step, the final result of the terminal value appears at the last projected year, and not 1 year later. The discounting of the TV, whether for the constant growth or the exit multiple, is from the last projected year.

This terminal growth rate could well be 0%. It appears both in the numerator and the denominator. In the denominator, you should take care that the WACC and the terminal growth rate are not close to each other. If they are, the denominator becomes small, with the effect that the final value (from the numerator being divided by a very small number) becomes hugely multiplied.

16.8.6 The Exit Multiple Formula for Terminal Value

This is a straightforward calculation using EBITDA in the last projected year and the input for the multiple.

16.9 DISCOUNTING FACTORS

Excel has functions for arriving at the present value, but sometimes it is better in terms of clarity and control to develop our own formulas for discounting. And in fact the formulas are not that complicated. The section in the model here (Fig. 16-6) lays out the discount factors—the exponents we want to use—if we wanted to use the mid-year or year-end conventions (Rows 44–45). It also shows the discounting in use for the FCF and the TV (Rows 47–

FIGURE 16-6

Discounting Factors and the Final Results

	C	H	I	J	K	L
44	Year-End to Valuation Date		*0.25*	*1.25*	*2.25*	*3.25*
45	Mid-Year to Valuation Date		*0.13*	*0.75*	*1.75*	*2.75*
46						
47	Discount Exponent for FCF		*0.13*	*0.75*	*1.75*	*2.75*
48	Discount Exponent for TV		-	-	-	-
49						
50	Discounted FCF		15	16	13	14
51	Discounted TV		0	0	0	0
52						
53	PV of FCF		73	*20.3%*		
54	PV of Terminal Value		286	*79.7%*		
55	**Enterprise Value**		**359**	*100.0%*		
56	+ Excess cash + ST investments		0	<== excludes Operating Cash		
57	- Debt		342			
58	**Equity Value**		**17**			
59						
60	Equity Value per Share	$	1.69			
61						

48). The discounted values for the FCF and the TV, based on the discounting approach used, are shown in Rows 50 and 51.

16.9.1 Year-End and Mid-Year Discounting Factors

Table 16-4 shows the formulas. Three columns are shown because Columns I, J, and K show different formulas in Rows 44 and 45.

16.9.1.1 Year-end discounting

Row 44 calculates the discount factor calculations for the year-end convention. For Column I (i.e., Cell I44), the formula calculates the stub year based on the three-month portion of the year from September 30 to December 31, 2008. Using the DAYS360 function, we get a factor of 0.25.

For all years after the stub period, the factor to use in year-end discounting is the stub period factor + 1. This is shown in Figure 16-7.

TABLE 16-4

Formulas for the Discounting Factors

Row	Formula in Column I	Formula in Column J	Formula in Column K (copy to Cols L–M)
44	=DAYS360(H4,I24)/360	=I44+1	=J44+1
45	=I44/2	=I44+0.5	=J45+1
46			

16.9.1.2 Mid-year discounting

Row 45 calculates the discount factor calculations for the mid-year convention. For the stub year, the "mid-year" is really the "mid-period" approach. The FCF is recognized at the midpoint of the 3 months of the stub—in effect at October 15, 2008—so the discounting exponent used is not 0.25 but 0.125.

The discounting for the first full year after the stub is the *full* stub factor, plus 0.5 for the full year, or 0.75. This is seen in Figure 16-8.

Table 16-5 shows the formulas for selecting the discounting conventions. Rows 47 selects the factors for the discounting the FCF, depending on the toggle for the year-end or mid-year setting in Cell N7. Row 48 selects the factors for the discounting of

FIGURE 16-7

FCF Recognition Point to the Valuation Date for Year-End Convention

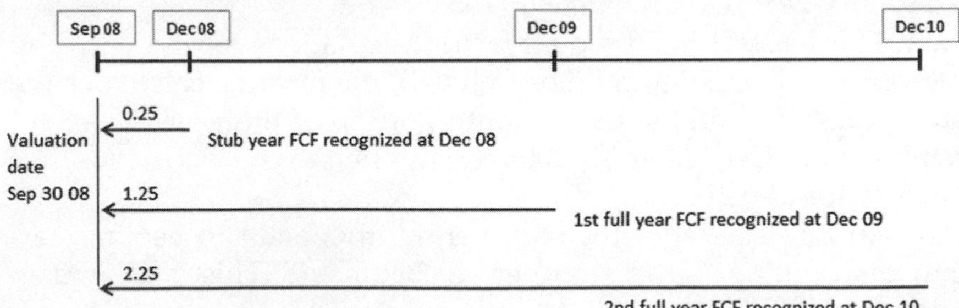

FIGURE 16-8

FCF Recognition Point to the Valuation Date for Mid-Year Convention

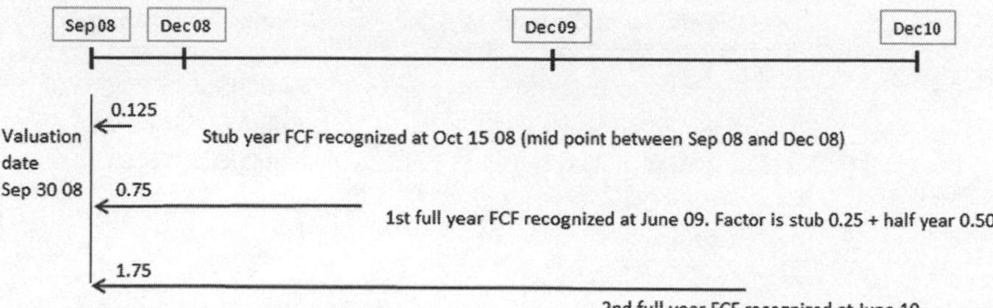

the TV, depending on the toggle for constant growth or EBITDA multiple toggle in Cell N9.

Row 50 is the factor applied to the FCF for each column. Row 51 is the factor applied to the TV. The calculation works only for the last column when the TV appears. In columns before this, the TV line has the "" entry and will return an error if it is used in a formula. This is the reason for the IF-ISERROR in the formula.

16.9.2 Final Results

Table 16-6 shows the formulas for arriving at the final equity value and the equity value per share. These formulas are not meant to be copied across.

TABLE 16-5

Formulas for Selecting Discounting Conventions

Row	Formulas in Column I (copy to Columns J–M)
47	=IF($N$7="E",I44,I45)
48	=IF(I42="","–",IF($N$9=1,I47,I44))
49	
50	=I$40/(1+$H$20)^I$47
51	=IF(ISERROR(I42/(1+$H$20)^I48),0,I42/(1+$H$20)^I48)

TABLE 16-6

Formulas for Final Results

Row	Formulas in Column I	Formulas in Column J
53	=SUM($I50:$R50)	=IF($I$55,I53/$I$55,0)
54	=SUM($I51:$R51)	=IF($I$55,I54/$I$55,0)
55	=SUM(I53:I54)	=IF($I$55,I55/$I$55,0)
56	=J64	
57	=J69	
58	=I55+I56-I57	
59		
60	=IF(N15,I58/N15,0)	

Row 53 shows how we can arrive at the present value (PV) of the FCF by simply summing Cells I50:R50. The values in each of these cells already have been discounted to the valuation date by virtue of the appropriate discount rate having been applied to them. All values in these cells are thus "as of" the valuation date. Summing them allows us to arrive at the total PV of al FCF.

The range defined is Column I to Column R. This represents the 10-year projections span that we expect to be the model to have. If you are building your model with a longer time horizon, this range should be adjusted accordingly.

Row 54 is the present value of the TV.

Row 55 adds the two rows above it. This gives us the enterprise value.

Row 56 and 57 are the excess cash, short-term investments less debt. Operating cash is not included as it is already included in the operating working capital.

Row 58 is the equity value.

Rows 60 is the calculation of the equity value per share, based on the number of shares specified in Cell N15.

16.9.2.1 Cash and debt at the valuation date

If you do not have specific inputs for the cash and debt at the valuation date, you can create a table that looks at the prior year end

FIGURE 16-9

Cash and Debt at Valuation Date

	A	B	C	D	E	F	G	H	I	J
62			For Base Model					0.25	0.75	Deal Date
63			Estimated value at Deal Date					Dec-07	Dec-08	Sep-08
64			Excess Cash					0	0	0
65			Cash					80	80	80
66			ST Investments					33	34	34
67			Total					113	114	114
68										
69			Debt					419	317	342
70										

and current year end values of these items, and do an estimate based on their prorated relative weights in each year and relative to the valuation date (Fig. 16-9).

The formulas are shown in Table 16-7. Columns H and I look to the model. Column J uses the stub year factor and its obverse. However, note that at the September 30, 2008 point, we

TABLE 16-7

Cash and Debt at Valuation Date

Row	Formulas in Column H	Formulas in Column I	Formulas in Column J
62	=DAYS360 (H4,I24)/360	=1−H62	
63	=BS!H6	=BS!I6	=H4
64	=BS!H8	=BS!I8	=$H$62*H64+$I$62*I64
65	=BS!H9	=BS!I9	=$H$62*H65+$I$62*I65
66	=BS!H10	=BS!I10	=$H$62*H66+$I$62*I66
67	=SUM(H64:H65)	=SUM(I64:I65)	=SUM(J64:J65)
68			
69	=SUM(BS!H23: BS!H24)+SUM (BS!H29:H31)	=SUM(BS!I23: BS!I24)+SUM (BS!I29:I31)	=$H$62*H69+$I$62*I69

want to use 0.75 of the value at December 31, 2008 and 0.25 of the value of the prior year end of December 31, 2007.

For the value of cash, we should look to both cash and short-term investments. Cash should include any excess cash produced by the model.

For debt, take care to include not only the long-term debt but also short-term debt, including any current portion of long-term debt that you may have included in your model.

CHAPTER 17

Introduction to Visual Basic for Applications

Visual Basic for Applications (VBA) is the language for writing macros in Excel. This chapter describes basic VBA macros to perform various tasks in Excel that you otherwise would have to do through the keyboard or with the mouse.

17.1 MACROS

Macros are programmed sequences that replicate actions done through the keyboard or mouse. More advanced macros can work with linking Excel to other applications and transferring data, but they are outside the scope of discussion for this chapter.

In VBA terminology, macros are called subroutines. In this chapter, the terms "macro" and "subroutine" are interchangeable.

17.2 THE VISUAL BASIC EDITOR

Access the Visual Basic Editor (VBE) by any one of these methods:

- Alt + F11
- *Developer>Visual Basic* (Excel 2007 only)
- *Tools>Macros>Visual Basic Editor* (Excel 2003 only)

The VBE is shown in Figure 17-1. It has three main areas:

- The top left corner area is Project Explorer. If this is not in view, press Ctrl+R. The Project Explorer can contain three types of programming objects:
    - The worksheet "objects"—the worksheets in the workbook not as the spreadsheets but as "objects" which can carry macros, typically those that might be directly linked to the worksheet. For example, if you have out an on-screen button on the worksheet named Sheet1, the macro linked to that button could be written in the Sheet1 worksheet object in VBE.
    - Modules for the macros. Think of them as notepads in the VBE. You can write all the macros in one module, just as you can put all your spreadsheet formulas on one worksheet. However, as the VBE allows multiple modules to be inserted, it makes

FIGURE 17-1

The Look of the Visual Basic Editor

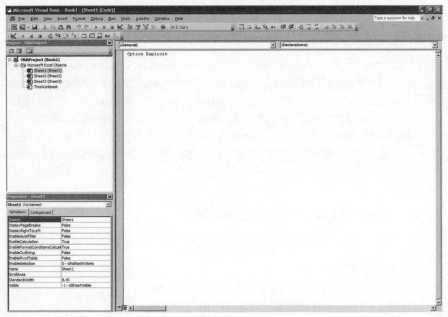

sense to group macros for different functions in different modules, just as it makes sense to put different sets of calculations on different worksheets.

- User-designed forms that are used as part of the macro sequences. An example of a form would be a custom print form to allow the user to select sheets to be printed, the printer settings, etc.

- The lower left corner area is called the Properties Window. If this is not in view, press F4. This lists the properties of whichever object has been selected in the Project Explorer. For example, you can click on the Sheet1 object in the Project Explorer, and the Properties Window will show the properties of Sheet1. In this window, for example, you can set the Visible property to Hidden. This is equivalent to setting the worksheet format to Hide in the workbook. (Or you can set to VeryHidden, which means that it is hidden in the workbook, and there is also no indication that there is a hidden sheet.)

- The large area on the right that takes up about two-thirds of the screen is the Code area. If this is not in view, press F7.
  The Code area shows the coding space related to the object selected in the Project Explorer. Click on Sheet1 in the Project Explorer, and anything written in the Code area is linked to Sheet1. Insert a module in the Project Explorer and click on that, and macros written in the Code area are part of that module.
  There is no limit to the number of lines in the Code area.

17.2.1 Returning to Excel

To return to Excel from the VBE, you can do any of the following:

- Press Alt+F11.
- Click through *View>Microsoft Excel* on the menu bar.
- Click on the Excel icon on the toolbar.

- Click on *File>Close* and Return to Microsoft Excel. This last one will close the VBE, however. The shortcut for this is Alt+Q.

17.3 THE STRUCTURE OF A MACRO

Macros begin with the keyword Sub and end with the keyword End Sub. Try this as a start. Type the following in the VBE in the Code section:

```
Sub FirstMacro
MsgBox "This is my first macro."
End Sub
```

You do not have to enter the () when you write Sub FirstMacro. You will find that when you press Enter after typing Sub First-Macro that the VBE will automatically add the () at the end, as well as inserting the End Sub keywords. All you have to do is write the code between the starting and ending points. This macro uses a VBA function that is already built-in: MsgBox. MsgBox (for Message Box) will display the argument that follows in a message box in the middle of the screen.

Once the macro is done, you can launch it from the VBE by putting your cursor anywhere in the macro, and then pressing F5. The message box (Fig. 17-2) appears. Click on OK to close the message box, and the macro to finish executing.

FIGURE 17-2

The Message Box

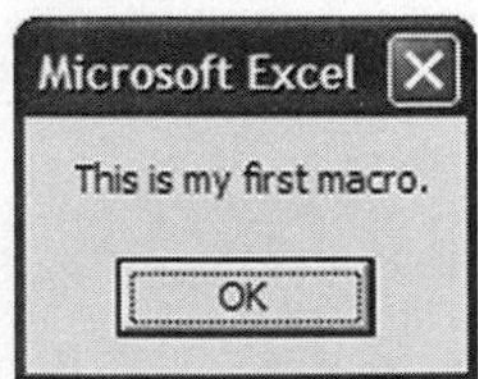

17.4 RUNNING THE MACRO

You can launch this macro from the VBE itself and also from Excel itself. From the VBE:

- With the cursor anywhere in the macro, press F5.
- With the cursor anywhere in the macro, click on the *Run>Run Sub/UserForm* command in the menu bar.
- With the cursor anywhere in the macro, click on the *Run Sub/Userform* button on the Standard toolbar.
- Click on *Tools>Macros* and then select the name of the macro from the list of available macros. Then click on the Run button.

From Excel:

- In Excel 2007, *Developer>Macros*. Select the macro to run and then click Run.
- In Excel 2003, *Tools>Macro>Macros*. Select the macro to run and then click Run.

17.5 RECORDING A MACRO

The easiest way to start writing your own macros is to record a macro as you go through the keyboard steps of what you want to do. By examining what and how Excel has recorded your actions, you can begin to learn how to write your own macros.

17.5.1 How to Record a Macro

- In Excel 2007, *Develop>Record Macro*
- In Excel 2003, *Tools>Macro>Record NewMacro*

17.5.2 How to Stop Recording

- In Excel 2007, *Develop>Stop Recording*. Note: this command is in the same place as the "Record Macro": the command label changes when you start recording.
- In Excel 2003, *Tools>Macro>Stop Recording*

17.5.3 Record Your First Macro

Let's say that you are now in Sheet1 of a new workbook, which also has Sheet2. From Excel, let's start the recording sequence (see 17.5.1). Now do the following:

1. Go to cell C1 and enter 10.
2. Go to cell C2 and enter 20.
3. Go to cell C3 and enter 30.
4. Go to cell C4 and enter = SUM(C1 : C3).
5. Copy the range C1:C4 to Sheet2, cell D1.
6. Go to Sheet2 and apply the Bold and Italic formats to cell D4.
7. Go to Cell A1 of Sheet1.

Stop the macro recording (see Section 17.5.2).

Did we record the macro properly? Let's check by deleting all the entries in Sheet1 and Sheet2. (Don't delete the sheets; just delete the entries.) Now go back to Sheet1 and launch the macro. (See the last part of Section 17.3.) The sets of numbers with the formulas and the bolding of the Cell D4 in Sheet2 appear again.

17.6 RUNNING A MACRO WITH A SHORTCUT KEY

Instead of going through the menu steps to launch a macro, you can provide a short cut to quickly launch a macro. For example, you could designate that pressing Ctrl+Shift+M could be the shortcut to launch the macro that we just wrote, or for that matter any other macro. The way to do this is as follows:

- Go through the same steps to bring up the macro form (see Section 17.8).
- Click on the Options button to have the Macro Options form appear:
- Enter the key that will work with Ctrl+[letter]. Since we want the shortcut combination to be Ctrl+Shift+M, then use the Shift key as we enter. Essentially, we are entering the upper case M. (When we do not use the Shift key, Excel shows the shortcut combination as Ctrl+M, as opposed to Ctrl+m.)

FIGURE 17-3

Enter the Shortcut Key Combination

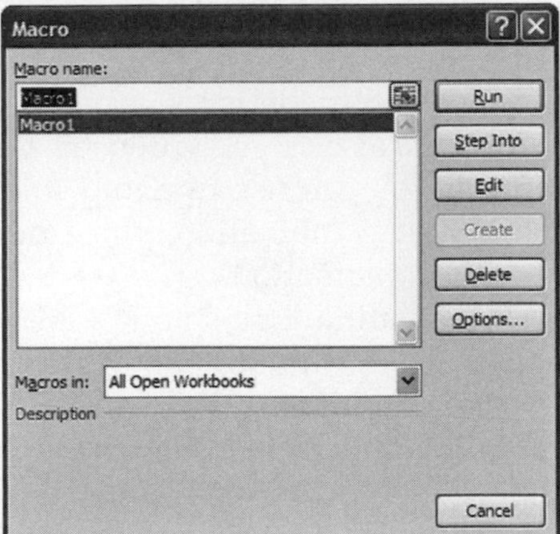

TABLE 17-1

Excel's Native Shortcut Keys

a	To select everything in the sheet; equivalent to clicking on the corner where the column letter A and the row number 1 meet
b	Apply bold type
c	Copy
d	Copy the row above
f	Find
h	Find and replace
i	Apply italic type
n	Insert new worksheet
o	Open file
p	Print
r	Copy to fill the highlighted row to the right
s	Save
u	Apply underline format
v	Paste
x	Cut
y	Redo
z	Undo

Whenever you specify shortcut keys, be careful that you do not specify a letter that is already used by Excel. For example, Table 17-1 shows the keys used by Excel in combination with the Ctrl key. (I have used the lowercase letter to indicate that you do not need to apply the Shift key.)

If you do use one of these letters for a shortcut key, the native command in Excel will be overridden by your shortcut setting. A good approach you can use to avoid this kind of mix-up is to use the Ctrl + Shift combination, since none of the shortcuts in Excel uses this combination.

Let's put the combination Ctrl + Shift + M in the dialog box shown as Figure 17-3. This will allow us to run this macro again just by pressing this combination. You can set (and reset) this shortcut key combination later on, by the way.

17.7 RUNNING THE MACRO FROM VBA

Place the cursor anywhere in the body of the macro and use the following keys:

F5	Run the macro
F8	Run the macro one line at a time
F9	Place a breakpoint so that the macro stops at that point

17.8 CHECKING THE MACRO

We can check the macro that was just recorded from Excel:

- *Developer>Macros* (in Excel 2007) or *Tools>Macro>Macros* (in Excel 2003) to see the Macro form (Fig. 17-4).
- Select the macro name, in this case Macro1 as the default name for the first macro in VBE, and click on Edit.

Or we can go directly to the VBE and look for it in Module1 under Modules in the Project Explore box.
The macro will be like this:

```
Sub Macro1()
Range("C1").Select
```

FIGURE 17-4

Locating the Macro

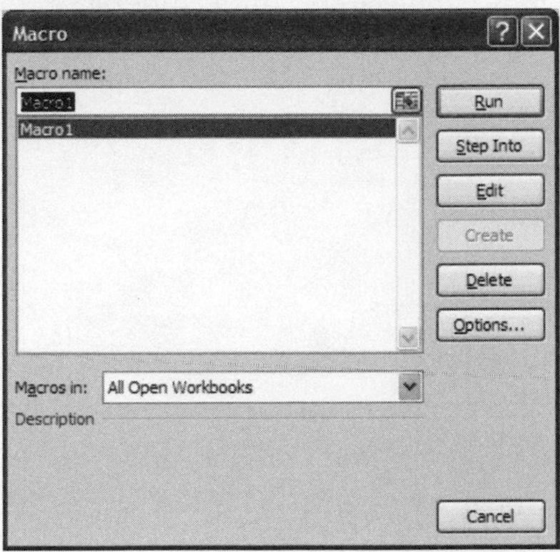


```
ActiveCell.FormulaR1C1 = "10"
Range("C2").Select
ActiveCell.FormulaR1C1 = "20"
Range("C3").Select
ActiveCell.FormulaR1C1 = "20"
Range("C4").Select
ActiveCell.FormulaR1C1 = "=SUM(R[-3]C:R[-1]C)"
Range("C1:C4").Select
Selection.Copy
Sheets("Sheet2").Select
Range("F1").Select
ActiveSheet.Paste
Range("F4").Select
Selection.Font.Bold = True
Sheets("Sheet1").Select
```

```
Range("A1").Select
End Sub
```

At first glance, this looks indecipherable, but just a little study will reveal how it works. VBA code is wonderful in one aspect: its code is reasonably close to normal English language. So let's try to decipher it line by line. Here is the translation in plain English of each line (Table 17-2):

TABLE 17-2

The Macro Deciphered

Range("C1").Select	Select cell C1.
ActiveCell.FormulaR1C1 = "10"	In the active cell (i.e., the one that we just selected, C1), enter the formula "10." Because there is no equal (=) sign within the double quotes, the formula is the number itself.
Range("C2").Select	Select cell C2.
ActiveCell.FormulaR1C1 = "20"	In the active cell (C2), enter the number 20.
Range("C3").Select	Select cell C3.
ActiveCell.FormulaR1C1 = "30"	In the active cell (C3), enter the number 30.
Range("C4").Select	Select cell C4.
ActiveCell.FormulaR1C1 = "=SUM(R[−3]C:R[−1]C)"	This code writes the formula that begins with =SUM and then defines the rows from 3 rows above C4 to 1 rows above C4 and adds the closing parenthesis. If you remember, we were writing a formula for SUM(C1:C3).
Range("C1:C4").Select	Select the range C1 to C4.
Selection.Copy	Copy the selection.
Sheets("Sheet2").Select	Go to Sheet2.
Range("D1").Select	Go to Cell D . . .
ActiveSheet.Paste	. . . and Paste.
Range("D5").Select	Go to Cell D5.
Selection.Font.Bold=True	In the selection (D5), apply Bold formatting . . .
Selection.Font.Italic=True	. . . And in the same election, apply Italic formatting.
Sheets("Sheet1").Select	Go to Sheet1.
Range("A1").Select	Go to cell A1.

17.9 EDITING A MACRO

Once we have recorded a macro, we can edit it.

For example, when we started the recording this, we were already on Sheet1. Consequently, there was no need to specify that we should first go to Sheet1. However, consider the fact that we may be launching this macro from another sheet, in which case the first block of formulas would be written on that active sheet, and not on Sheet1. So just add this as the very first line of code:

```
Sheets("Sheet1").Select
```

17.9.1 Adding Comments to Our Code

It is easy to add comments to your lines of code. After the code itself, type an apostrophe, and then add your comment. Comments are important for reminding yourself or telling others about what the code is supposed to do. For example, having added that line, we may want to add a comment to explain why. That line will now look like this:

```
Sheets("Sheet1").Select   'This ensures that we start on Sheet1
```

17.9.2 Commenting Out

The apostrophe is also useful in another way: you can put it as the first thing on a line of code, which has the effect of turning that code into a comment. In this way, that line is ignored by VBA.

17.10 EDITING THE MACRO

Once you have seen the recorded VBA code, you may notice that it gets to be repetitious. The fact is, when it is recording a macro, Excel records every step without any attempt of being streamlined. When you do write your own code, you can directly write the code in a way that is more streamlined than what the VBE is recording. Let's see if we can streamline the recorded code.

Following are some beginning hints on streamlining the code.

17.10.1 Entering Values into a Cell

```
Range("C1").Select
ActiveCell.FormulaR1C1 = "10"
```

The two steps described here involve bringing the cursor to the cell, and then entering a value into it. In VBA, you can enter a value directly into a cell without selecting it, so this could be simplified into:

```
Range("C1").FormulaR1C1 = "10"
```

An even simpler way to do this is to write:

```
Range("C1").Value = "10"
```

Any time you wish to specify a value, Value will work as well as FormulaR1C1. You can even simplify it further and write Range("C1") = "10" but it is better as a programming style to specify what it is you want with that Range. In this case, the instruction to the VBE is "let the value of the Range be" x, so you should always specify Value. By the way, you should also use Value even if you are entering text. That's a "value," too, according to VBA.

17.10.2 Writing Formulas

The recorder constructs the code based on relative addresses. This is why you see:

```
"=SUM(R[-3]C:R[-1]C)"
```

which describes the action of highlighting a range 3 rows to 1 row above (notice the negative sign) the current active cell. If you know the range that you want to specify, then:

```
Range("C4").Select
ActiveCell.FormulaR1C1 = "= SUM(R[-3]C:R[-1]C)"
```

could be rewritten as:

```
Range("C4").Value = "=SUM(C1:C3)"
```

Notice that we use Value even for writing formulas. To write a formula, start with an equals (=) sign and then write the formula within the double quotes. The code literally enters into the cell whatever it is told to, so in this case, with the beginning equal sign, it is writing the format that is required for entering formulas.

17.10.3 Copy and Paste

As already shown, we can shorten the Copy part from:

```
Range ("C1:C5").Select
Selection.Copy
```

Any time you see a Select followed by a Selection in the next line, you can combine the two lines while omitting those two words, like this:

```
Range ("C1:C5").Copy
```

The next step specifies a different sheet. It's best to leave it as is for the moment:

```
Sheets ("Sheet2").Select
Range ("D1").Select
ActiveSheet.Paste
```

17.10.4 Commenting

I mentioned that you can write descriptive comments in your code by entering an apostrophe and then writing the text after that. Comments are great for reminding you what the code is doing. You may think that you do not need comments as you will remember the purpose of the code, but it is easy to forget some of the thinking that has gone into writing the lines of code.

There is another use of the comment apostrophe, by the way: If you need to turn off code, simply put an apostrophe in front of it and it will be ignored by VBA.

17.11 GETTING OUT OF THE MACRO WHEN THERE IS AN ERROR

Sometimes, when you are developing a macro and are doing test runs, VBA will stop when it encounters an error. In this case, go to the VBE and the Code area should be showing you the row where the error has occurred. To get out of the macro run so that you can begin to edit and correct the macro, use the *Run>Reset* command. The Reset icon (a small square button) is also visible on the toolbar and you can click that.

CHAPTER 18

A VBA Primer

Now that we have gone over how to work between the Visual Basic Editor and Excel, and have had a first look of what a macro looks like, here is an overview of how VBA works. VBA is a rich programming language on its own and deserves full-length books, but hopefully this summary can give you a leg up on how to become adept at this language.

Note: This is a necessarily limited introduction to VBA, but it should allow you to work with VBA to do tasks in Excel that require repetitive keyboard actions. Knowing VBA adds to your ability to create even more powerful and functional models, and there are tremendous resources available in bookstores and online for more advanced information on this programming language. I invite you to turn to these other sources for continuing your learning.

To understand the basics of VBA, we need to understand:

- Objects
- Properties and methods
- Variables
- Dimensioning a variable
- Forced variable declaration
- Object variables

- Scope of variables
- Control structures
- If Then Else
- If Then ElseIf Then Else
- For Next
- While Wend
- Do Loop
- Select
- For Each Next
- The With statement

In this chapter, I will use the term "procedure" for what we have been calling macros or subroutines.

18.1 OBJECTS

An object in Excel is something that can be programmed and therefore controlled. The biggest object in Excel is Excel itself, and this is referred to in VBA code as Application.

```
Application.Calculate
```

This is the line of code that you would put in to have the procedure run the calculation, the equivalent of pressing the F9 key in Excel. In plain English, it means "take the Application (which is Excel) and calculate."

Objects in Excel have a hierarchy, starting from the Application object. In turn, the Application object has these objects: Workbooks object (a collection of all Workbook objects), Windows object (a collection of all Window objects), AddIns (a collection of all AddIn objects), etc.

All of these subjects hold other objects, The Workbooks collection holds a Workbook object, and a Workbook object contains objects such as Worksheets (a collection of Worksheet objects), Charts, Names, etc. For the moment, it is enough to know that for "things" in Excel that you need to work with and manipulate, the right word to use is "objects."

18.2 PROPERTY AND METHOD

Once you have defined the object you want to manipulate, then you have a choice of working with the property or the method. A good way to remember these terms is that a property describes what an object is, and a method describes what you do with it.

18.2.1 Property

Every object has a property, property in this case being the standard definition of an "essential or defining attribute." If the range that you are looking at contains the number 170853 in italics, then you can say that the range has the Value property of 170853 and the Format property of italics (or, more specifically, the Font Italic property is TRUE). A property always has a value, whether it is a string value, a numeric value, a Boolean value, or some other value.

18.2.2 Method

A method is an action that is performed with an object. Copying the range to another range is an example of the copy method. Of course, this action has the effect of changing the property of the destination cell.

If you are wondering how to tell a command for property and a command for method part, the command for property has an equal (=) sign by itself. Here is the code to enter 100 into the Cell A1, or in VBA lingo, to change the value property of Range("A1") from whatever it was to the numer 100:

```
Range("A1").Value=100
```

You may see an equal sign in a command for method, but you will see this with a colon (":=") when the method has to show arguments that are part of the method command. Here is an example of copying and pasting using the paste-value method:

```
Range("A1").Copy
Selection.PasteSpecial Paste:=xlPasteValues
```

18.2.3 Follow the Hierarchy

In a VBA procedure, whether you want to apply a property or a method to an object, the way to do it is to start identifying it from within the hierarchy, from the largest object to the smallest. Most of the time, you do not have to specify the object that is Excel itself (the Application object), and you can start with the workbook. In the fullest approach, you would define it in this order:

- The workbook
- The worksheet
- The range

Each of these is separated from the next by a period. The period is called the "dot operator." Here is an example of the hierarchy structure if you want to put the number "123" in cell C10 in the sheet named "MySheet." The workbook is named "MyFile.xls." Write this as one line.

```
Workbooks("MyFile.xls").Sheets("MySheet").Range("C10").Value = "123"
```

We can also write it in a shortened form, like this:

```
Range("C10").Value = "123"
```

But note that in the latter case, as there is no definition of the workbook or the sheet, Excel will perform this command on whatever worksheet is currently active. So long as you are certain about where you are as the subroutine is launched, you can make the code short. However, when you are making the subroutine work across many worksheets or even many workbooks, it helps to write the longer code, specifying the hierarchy tree, so you can specify exactly where the procedure should work.

The .Value you see at the end of the code (note the dot operator) is another example of being specific. IF we write:

```
Range("C10")="123"
```

this works, too, but Excel has to evaluate what you mean by this. It is always better to be very specific so that Excel can work in the most immediate way to accomplish the task.

18.3 VARIABLES

Variables are used to represent values or data during a procedure's run. Think of algebra and x = 3. In this case, x is the variable and has been assigned the value of 3. In the same manner, VBA uses variables to which values or data have been assigned.

The best practice approach in programming is that you have to declare or "dimension" what type of variable you wish to use. The dimension of data determines how much memory in Excel's VBA is being used, but as memory is relatively inexpensive these days, the dimensioning of data is more important as a way to keep track of what types of data are being used.

18.4 DIMENSIONING A VARIABLE

You can work with VBA without declaring or dimensioning the variable, but it is good practice to do so. To declare a variable, you use a statement that will look like this:

```
Dim MyVariable As Integer
```

Write this line at the beginning of the procedure, just after you write the name of the procedure in the line that begins with Sub. This makes the variable usable for that procedure. If you want to this variable to be used by other procedures in the same module, write it at the very top of the module sheet, i.e., above even with the first procedure. This makes it usable by all the procedures in the module. See also Section 18.5 for setting the variable to be usable across all modules.

The components are:

Dim	For "Dimension." This Is the VBA keyword to indicate a variable declaration.
MyVariable	The name of the variable. This is anything that you wish to make it.
As	VBA keyword to separate the variable name from the data type.
Integer	The data type. This is one of 12 standard data types.

18.4.1 Data Types for VBA Variables

The following lists the data types for VBA variables. Each type is followed by the type of information the variable can hold. For example, the Boolean variable can only hold a True or False value. If you try to assign a value such as 1 or the text "true" to it, you will have an error in your VBA code.

Data Type	Range of Values
Boolean	True or False
Byte	0 and 255
Currency	-922,337,203,685,477.5808 to 922,337,203,685,477.5807
Date	January 1, 0100 to December 31, 9999
Double	-1.79769313486231E308 to -4.94065645841247E-324 4.94065645841247E-324 to 1.79769313486231E308
Integer	-32,768 to 32,767
Long	-2,147,483,648 to 2,147,483,647
Object	Object variable that can be used to represent any Excel object
Single	-3.402823E38 to -1.401298E-45 1.401298E-45 to 3.402823E38
String	0 to approximately 2 billion
Variant	Can be used for any data type. Useful when the data type may vary depending on other user input or other calculations
User-defined	Varies

Of these twelve, the ones you are most likely to use—and you can get by just knowing—are Boolean, Integer, Long, String, and Variant.

The usual practice is to write each Dim statement as separate lines:

```
Dim MyVariable As Integer
Dim MyCellAddress As String
Dim MySetting As Boolean
```

However, you can also write them as one line starting with one Dim keyword, and separating one variable from the other with a comma:

```
Dim MyVariable As Integer, MyCellAddress As String, MySetting As Boolean
```

Even if the variables are of the same data type, you must still use the As specifier for each one. If you do not, the ones that do not use the As specifier are declared as Variant. In the following, MyVariable and MyVariable1 are Variant data types.

```
Dim MyVariable, MyVariable2, MyVariable3 As Integer
```

18.4.2 Advantages in Using Variables

Using a variable means that your procedure can run faster, especially when the variable has been set to a value or a piece of data from Excel. In this case, VBA can use the value without having to get the data from Excel every time it is required. Additionally, variables make the code easier to read.

18.4.3 Making the Variable Declaration Mandatory

You can set VBA so that you have to declare variables by including this in the first line at the very top of each VBA module:

```
Option Explicit
```

With this statement, VBA will stop if it runs into a variable that has not been declared. You can have VBA automatically put this statement in for any VBA module that you insert. In the VBE, click on *Tools>Options* and in the Options form (Fig. 18-1), check the box for Require Variable Declaration.

18.5 SCOPE OF VARIABLES

A variable's scope sets which modules or procedures the variables can be used in. There are three levels:

FIGURE 18-1

The Options Form in the VBE

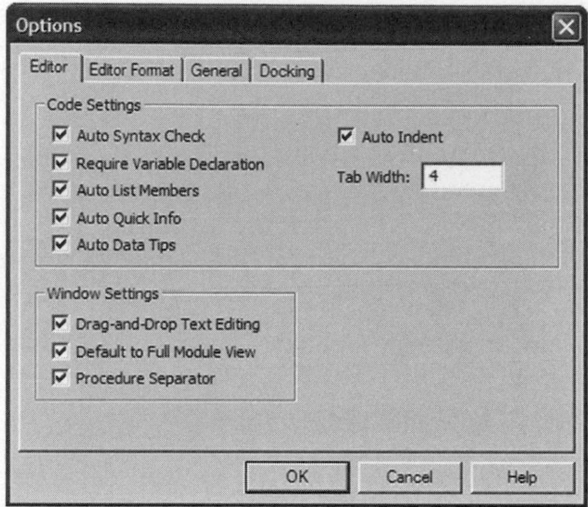

Scope	How declared
Single procedure	Write the Dim statement within the procedure.
Module wide	Write the Dim statement before the first procedure in the module.
All module	Write it before the first procedure in any module, but use Public instead of Dim when writing the declaration.

18.6 OBJECT VARIABLES

An object variable is a variable that refers to an object. You need to declare the object variable as any other, with a slight difference. Here is an example:

```
Sub TestRun()
   Dim MyRange As Object
   Set MyRange = Worksheets("Sheet1").Range("A1")
   MyRange.Value=1000
End Sub
```

After the Dim statement, we have to use a Set [object] = in order to assign the Cell A1 in the Sheet1 worksheet to that object. What we are saying to Excel is: (a) I am putting in the dimensions of a new variable called Range1, and the variable is an object. (b) This new object variable is going to represent the Range object for Cell A1 in the worksheet Sheet1.

You can Dim the object variable as a usable module-wide or across all modules, but the Set assignment keyword has to be part of the procedure that is being run.

In the preceding example, we used Dim and declared the MyRange as an Object. In this case, we are declaring it using the generic classification. We could also have specifically declared it as a range:

```
Dim MyRange As Range
```

This has the advantage of making the procedure run faster, but as the procedures we are writing here are very short and uncomplicated, the time savings would not be perceptible.

18.7 CONTROL STRUCTURES

The real programming work in VBA is done by control structures that can control the flow of execution in the procedures. The most commonly used ones are described in the following sections.

18.7.1 If Then Else

This is the equivalent of the IF function in Excel. The structure is similar to the IF function.

```
Sub IfThenElse()
    If ActiveSheet.Name = "Input" Then
        Range("C10").Select
    Else
        Range("H20").Select
    End If
End Sub
```

When run, this procedure brings the cursor to Cell C10 if the active sheet is "Input." Otherwise, it sets to cursor to Cell H20.

Of course, the command that you run can be much more complicated than the single line of cursor setting as shown here.

No matter how complicated though, the basic If-Then-Else structure will continue to work.

18.7.2 If Then ElseIf Then Else

This is a variation of the If Then Else structure, and allows additional conditions to be tested. You can add as many elseif conditions as required. Here is an example:

```
Sub IfThenElseIfElse()
        If ActiveSheet.Name = "Input" Then
            Range("C10").Select
        ElseIf ActiveSheet.Name = "Output" Then
            Range("H20").Select
        ElseIf ActiveSheet.Name = "Ratios" Then
            Range("B6").Select
        Else
            Range("A1").Select
        End If
End Sub
```

18.7.3 For Next

For Next lets you run the same action a specified number of times. It has a built-in counter in that you specify a starting number and an ending number (e.g., 1–100). The starting number can be any number (e.g., 0, -20, 187); and there is no limit to that ending number. You can even set it so that the sequence runs backwards (100–1). In either direction, you can also set whether you want to count to go by 1 step or a different multiple.

```
Sub ForLoop()
       Dim x As Integer
       Worksheets("Sheet1").Activate
      For x = 1 To 100
          If Range("A" & x).Value <> 0 Then
                 Range("A" & x).Copy Range("C" & x)
          Else
                 Exit For
          End If
      Next x
End Sub
```

In the example, the For-Next loop is set to run from 1 to the upper limit of 100. The variable x is defined as integer within this procedure. Be default, the count goes up from 1 to 100, in steps of 1. To make it run from 100 down to 1 in counts of 2, the `For x = 1 To 100` line is rewritten as starting with the higher number:

```
For x = 100 To 1 Step -2
```

18.7.4 Additional Notes

- The starting number, ending number, and the step count could be variables reading entries in Excel. In this way, you can control how the VBA procedure runs without having to go to the VBE.
- The test that the procedure is performing goes down the Excel worksheet Sheet1 by virtue of connecting the Range address to the x variable. Thus, at the beginning of the For-Next loop, the code `Range("A" & x).Value` is looking at the equivalent of `Range("A1").value`. At the next loop, it is looking at `Range("A2").value`, etc. If the first row had been, say, row 12, then it would have been just as easy to start the For-Next loop with `For x = 12 To 111`.

  Note the use of:

  ```
  Exit For
  ```

  as a way to break out of the For-Next loop when a particular condition is met. In this way, once that condition is met, the For-Next loop does not need to run through to the end.
- A recorded macro for copying Cell A1 to Cell C1 would be something like this:

  ```
  Range("A1").Copy
  Range("C1").Select
  ActiveSheet.Paste
  ```

- The example I used shortens this so that it looks like this:

```
Range("A1").Copy Range("C1")
```

- For most of the instances where a repeated action is required, I find that the For-Next loop offers the most straightforward approach, compared to the While-Wend and the Do-Loop.

18.7.5 While-Wend

This is similar to the For-Next loop. The difference is that instead of looping a specified number of times, While-Wend loops as long as a specified test condition returns a True. The test condition is specified at the beginning of the loop. The danger is that the condition does not reach a False, and the While-Wend loop continues without stopping. Compare this with the For-Next loop, which has an ending limit.

Also, because While-Wend does not have a built-in counter, the way the x variable acted as a counter in the For-Next loop, While-Wend does not lend itself immediately for use where the looping is used to drive an action that works through the rows or across the column. Of course, adding a variable called Counter that can work. This procedure does the same as the action as the For-Next example:

```
Sub WhileWendExample()
    Dim x As Integer
    x = 1
        While Range("A" & x).Value <> 0
        Range("A" & x).Copy Range("C" & x)
        x = x + 1
    Wend
End Sub
```

18.7.6 Do-Loop

Do-Loop is similar to While-Wend. However, in the Do-Loop, the test condition can be specified either at the beginning or the end of the loop. (While-Wend can only do this at the beginning.) The Do-

Loop also has the test of continuing the loop until a test is met, or while a test is met.

```
Sub DoLoopExample_While()
    Dim x As Integer
    x = 1
    Do While Range("A" & x).Value <> 0
        Range("A" & x).Copy Range("C" & x)
        x = x + 1
    Loop
End Sub

Sub DoLoopExample_Until()
    Dim x As Integer
    x = 1
    Do Until Range("A" & x).Value = 0
        Range("A" & x).Copy Range("C" & x)
        x = x + 1
    Loop
End Sub
```

The following shows the same Do-Loops, but with the test placed at the end of the loop. This ensures that the loop will execute at least once.

```
Sub DoLoopExample_WhileEnd()
    Dim x As Integer
    x = 1
    Do
        Range("A" & x).Copy Range("C" & x)
        x = x + 1
    Loop While Range("A" & x).Value <> 0
End Sub

Sub DoLoopExample_UntilEnd()
    Dim x As Integer
    x = 1
    Do
        Range("A" & x).Copy Range("C" & x)
        x = x + 1
    Loop Until Range("A" & x).Value = 0
End Sub
```

18.7.7 Select Case

Select Case is similar to using If-then-elseif-then-else structure, and is a good alternative. Here is an example for selecting which sheets in the model to hide or unhide, depending on the entry in a cell in Excel itself. The entry cell is a range named ModelRunMode, which will hold any one of three options: Review, Merger or LBO.

```
Sub SelectExample()
    Dim RunMode As String
    RunMode = Range("ModelRunMode").Value
    Select Case RunMode
        Case "Review"
            ActiveWorkbook.Worksheets("Company1").Visible = True
            ActiveWorkbook.Worksheets("Company2").Visible = False
        Case "Merger"
            ActiveWorkbook.Worksheets("Company1").Visible = True
            ActiveWorkbook.Worksheets("Company2").Visible = True
        Case "LBO"
            ActiveWorkbook.Worksheets("Company1").Visible = False
            ActiveWorkbook.Worksheets("Company2").Visible = True
    End Select
End Sub
```

Case Select can also be used for a range of values. Note that the Case starting value is followed by the To keyword. In this procedure, a score of 80 would be a C. A score of over 80 and up to 90 would be a B.

```
Sub SelectExample_2()
    Dim TestScore As Single
    TestScore = Range("ModelTestScore").Value
    Select Case TestScore
        Case 0 To 40
            MsgBox "Your grade is F."
        Case 40 To 60
            MsgBox "Your grade is D."
        Case 60 To 80
            MsgBox "Your grade is C."
        Case 80 To 90
            MsgBox "Your grade is B."
        Case 90 To 100
            MsgBox "Your grade is A."
    End Select
End Sub
```

18.7.8 For Each Next

For-Each-Next allows a looping through all of the objects in a collection. This is a good control structure to use for going through all the worksheets in workbook, for example. Here is an example for placing the cursor in the top left corner of each sheet, with the procedure then returning to the first sheet in the workbook.

```
Sub ForEachNext_Example()
    Dim ws As Worksheet
    For Each ws In Worksheets
        ws.Activate
        Application.Goto Range("A1"), True
    Next
    Worksheets(1).Select
End Sub
```

18.7.9 The With Statement

The With statement is a way to abbreviate object references. There are three main advantages in With statements: 1) they shorten the code 2) they make it easier to read and 3) they improve the performance of the procedure.

Here is a procedure for setting the attributes of a cell without the With statement:

```
Sub Without_With()
 ActiveWorkbook.Worksheets(1).Range("A1").Font.Name = "Calibri"
 ActiveWorkbook.Worksheets(1).Range("A1").Font.Size = 11
 ActiveWorkbook.Worksheets(1).Range("A1").Font.Italic = True
 ActiveWorkbook.Worksheets(1).Range("A1").Font.Color = -4165632
 ActiveWorkbook.Worksheets(1).Range("A1").Interior.Pattern = xlSolid
 ActiveWorkbook.Worksheets(1).Range("A1").Interior.Color = 10092543
 ActiveWorkbook.Worksheets(1).Range("A1").Borders(xlEdgeLeft).LineStyle =
xlContinuous
 ActiveWorkbook.Worksheets(1).Range("A1").Borders(xlEdgeTop).LineStyle =
xlContinuous
 ActiveWorkbook.Worksheets(1).Range("A1").Borders(xlEdgeBottom).LineStyle =
```

```
xlContinuous
  ActiveWorkbook.Worksheets(1).Range("A1").Borders(xlEdgeRight).LineStyle =
xlContinuous
End Sub
```

Here is the same procedure for setting the attributes of a cell with the With statement:

```
Sub With_With()
    With ActiveWorkbook.Worksheets(1).Range("A1")
        With .Font
            .Name = "Calibri"
            .Size = 11
            .Italic = True
            .Color = -4165632
        End With
        With .Interior
            .Pattern = xlSolid
            .Color = 10092543
        End With
        .Borders(xlEdgeLeft).LineStyle = xlContinuous
        .Borders(xlEdgeTop).LineStyle = xlContinuous
        .Borders(xlEdgeBottom).LineStyle = xlContinuous
        .Borders(xlEdgeRight).LineStyle = xlContinuous
    End With
End Sub
```

The With statement identifies the common portions of an object definition. Once that is part of the With statement, the following lines can simply start with the dot. You can use With statements within another With statement, as you can see with the Font property and the Interior property.

18.8 CONTROLLING WHAT YOU DO WITH YOUR CURSOR

Here are some helpful hints for controlling the movement of your cursor in Excel. As always, anytime you are looking for the VBA code to do something and are not sure where to start, use the Record Macro in Excel. In this way, Excel gives you an initial map of the coding that is required.

18.8.1 Where You Are

To specify in VBA where the cursor is, use:

```
ActiveCell
```

Followed by the dot operator and then the next method that you want to use, such as:

```
ActiveCell.Copy
```

Of course, if you want to specify a specific starting location that is not where the cursor is, and you want to use, say, Cell C10, then:

Range("C10").Select	To select that cell
Range("C10").Copy	To copy that cell

And so on.

If you are using a named range, then it would be:

```
Range("MyRange1").Select
Range("MyRange1").Copy
```

And so on.

In the following sections, I will assume that we will start always from the ActiveCell. If you want to use the examples that follow as a template for your own coding, and you are starting from locations other than the active cell, simply substitute the ActiveCell portion of the code with the specific cell address or named range that you wish to use.

18.8.2 Working with Many Workbooks

Often, you may find yourself working with many workbooks open at the same time. In order to minimize errors, you may want to use the following.

Use ThisWorkbook to indicate to the macro which workbook it should be working in. ThisWorkbook refers to the workbook where the procedure resides.

```
Sub WorkingWithWorkbooks()
    ThisWorkbook.Sheets("Sheet1").Select
    Range("A1").Select
End Sub
```

18.8.3 Selecting a Range

To select a one-cell range, add Select.

```
Sub RangeSelect()
    Range("A1").Select
End Sub
```

To select a range that is more than one cell, use Resize.

```
Sub ActiveCellResize()
    ActiveCell.Resize(3, 5).Select
End Sub
```

This example highlights a range that is 3 rows deep going down and five rows wide going to the right. Note the order of the arguments in Resize: like Excel itself, VBA uses the convention of row first, column second.

The row and column arguments cannot be less than 1,1 because that is the minimum size of a range. What this means is that ActiveCell.Resize(1,1).Select would be the same as ActiveCell.Select.

18.8.3.1 Selecting a whole column or row

If you want to select a whole column, use:

```
Sub ActiveCellWholeColumn()
    ActiveCell.EntireColumn.Select
End Sub
```

If you want to select a whole row, use:

```
Sub ActiveCellWholeRow()
    ActiveCell.EntireRow.Select
End Sub
```

18.8.4 Moving to Another Location

18.8.4.1 In the same worksheet

To shift from one location to another within the same worksheet, use Offset:

```
Sub ActiveCellOffset()
    ActiveCell.Offset(5, 10).Select
End Sub
```

In this example, we are selecting a cell that is five rows below and 10 rows to the right of the current cell. Again, the arguments in Offset is row first, column second. Like the Excel function OFFSET, you can specify 0,0 as the arguments, which means that you are selecting the same cell as the active cell. You can also include negative numbers. A negative row argument means a location above the current cell, and a negative column argument means a location the left of the current cell.

18.8.4.2 To another worksheet

To shift to another worksheet, you will have to specify the worksheet first:

```
Sub ActiveCellWorksheet()
    Worksheets("Sheet2").Select
    Range("A1").Select
End Sub
```

18.8.4.3 Selecting a range from another location

To select a range from another location, even from another worksheet, you can combine all the commands we have covered so far. Here are some examples:

Selecting the Range G11:J14 in Sheet2, from Cell A1 in Sheet2: Note that we could have been starting from another worksheet, or we could be in Sheet2 already. For the latter, the line of code to specify the Worksheet("Sheet2").Select would be redundant but would not have caused an error.

```
Sub ActiveCellAnotherRange()
    Worksheets("Sheet2").Select
    Range("A1").Offset(10, 6).Resize(4, 4).Select
End Sub
```

Selecting three whole columns D, E, F from the starting cell of Cell A1: To get to Column D, we need an Offset first. The row argument is not important and can be left at 0. In Resize, the column argument of 3 is what defines the number of columns that EntireColumn will act on. The row argument is not important and can be left at 1.

```
Sub ActiveCellOffsetThreeColumns()
    Range("A1").Offset(0, 3).Resize(1, 3).EntireColumn.Select
End Sub
```

18.8.5 Finding a Cell on a Worksheet

Sometimes, you may need to find the location of a cell from which to start to highlight a range (or mark the end of a highlight) for other purposes. You can use the Cells.Find command. The easiest way to get the right syntax is to record a macro from Excel. For example, here is a recorded macro for find the Cell that contains the word "BS Output":

```
Sub Macro1()
    Cells.Find(What:="BS Output", After:=ActiveCell, LookIn:=xlFormulas, _
        LookAt:=xlPart, SearchOrder:=xlByRows, SearchDirection:=xlNext, _
        MatchCase:=False, SearchFormat:=False).Activate
End Sub
```

If you are not specifying anything out of the default parameters in the Find command, you edit the macro so that it only reads as follows:

```
Sub Macro1_Edited()
    Cells.Find(What:="BS Output").Activate
End Sub
```

18.8.5.1 *Get the address of what you found*

To get the row number of the location of the test you were looking for, just change the Activate to Address. You will have to use declare a variable to hold this value, so the procedure would look like this:

```
Sub FindAddress()
    Dim MyAddress As String
    MyAddress = Cells.Find(What:="BS Output").Address
End Sub
```

18.8.5.2 *Get the row of what you found*

To get the row number of the location of the test you were looking for, just change the Activate to Row. You will have to use declare a variable to hold this value, so the procedure would look like this:

```
Sub FindRow()
    Dim MyRow As Integer
    MyRow = Cells.Find(What:="BS Output").Row
End Sub
```

18.8.5.3 *Find the last cell*

In Excel, every worksheet is allocated memory based on its contents. If you have used no more than a 10 row by 10 column area for your work, and have not touched any of the other cells, the "last cell" in that worksheet would be Cell J10. You can locate this and also determine the VBA macro for it be recording the macro as you press Ctrl+End. The recorded macro looks like this:

```
Sub Macro1()
    ActiveCell.SpecialCells(xlLastCell).Select
End Sub
```

You can have the same variations as before of finding the address or the row of the last cell:

```
Sub LastCellAddress()
    Dim MyAddress As String
    MyAddress=ActiveCell.SpecialCells(xlLastCell).Address
End Sub
```

```
Sub LastCellRow()
    Dim MyRow As Row
    MyAddress=ActiveCell.SpecialCells(xlLastCell).Row
End Sub
```

18.8.6 Going to a Specific Cell and Making It the Top Left Corner

To go to a specific cell and to make it the top left corner, use the GoTo command. The argument of True for the Scroll is what makes the selected cell be located at the top left corner.

```
Sub HomeCorner()
    Application.Goto reference:=Range("H10"), scroll:=True
End Sub
```

Or in simpler form:

```
Sub HomeCorner_Simple()
    Application.Goto Range("H10"),True
End Sub
```

18.8.7 Selecting Sheets

To duplicate the action of selecting in sheets in Excel, i.e., the equivalent of clicking on individual tabs while pressing on the Shift key, use a form of Select. The example here selects the sheets between Worksheet(1), the leftmost tab, and Worksheet(5), the fifth sheet from the left.

```
Sub SelectSheets()
    Dim x As Integer
    For x = 1 To 5
            ThisWorkbook.Worksheets(x).Select False
    Next x
End Sub
```

Without the False, this sequence will simply select each tab in turn. The False is the equivalent of having the Shift key down so that all tabs remain selected.

There is another way of selecting sheet which require arrays. In the spirit of keeping everything simple, I will not venture there.

18.9 CALLING ONE PROCEDURE FROM ANOTHER

As you write your procedures, it would make sense to break them apart into separate subroutines. You can run a procedure from a master level, and then have the procedure branch off to other subroutines and then come back to the main procedure again. This kind of branching off is called a call. To call one procedure from another, use Call and the procedure name. For example, a print procedure may look like this:

```
Sub PrintSequence()
    Call FormatPages
    Call SelectSheets
    ActiveWindow.SelectedSheets.PrintOut Copies:=1
End Sub
```

18.10 ON-SCREEN BUTTONS

In Chapter 8, one of the ways of correctly calculating interest income and expense on the excess cash and revolver, respectively, without using circular references is to use a cut-and-paste approach. A macro would be most helpful in this case, as it would automate the sequence. To launch such a macro, an on-screen button would be a welcome touch of user-friendliness.

In both Excel 2003 and 2007, you can add an on-screen control through the Forms toolbar or the Control Toolbox toolbar. You then assign a macro to such a control. Additionally, for relatively simple controls such as buttons, in both versions of Excel, you can also insert a drawing shape and assign a macro to that.

The Control Toolbox controls are fully-programmable ActiveX controls and have some additional features that make them more flexible for serious developers. However, for what we are covering in this chapter, the controls from the Forms toolbar and the Control Toolbox toolbar are interchangeable.

FIGURE 18–2

The Model for the Balancing

	A	B	C	D	E	F	G	H	I	J
1				Hist	Proj	Proj				
2		INCOME STATEMENT		Year 1	Year 2	Year 3	Formulas in column F			
3		Revenue		160.0	200.0	390.0	Input			
4		COGS		80.0	90.0	190.0	Input			
5		SGA		29.0	45.0	80.0	Input			
6		EBIT		51.0	65.0	120.0	=F3-SUM(F4:F5)			
7										
8		Interest: Excess cash	3.0%	0.0	0.5	0.5	=$C$8*AVERAGE(E18:F18)			
9		Interest: Revolver	6.0%	0.0	0.0	1.3	=$C$9*AVERAGE(E23:F23)			
10		Interest: Debt	6.0%	19.2	20.1	20.7	=$C$10*AVERAGE(E24:F24)			
11		EBT		31.8	45.4	98.5	=F6+F8-F9-F10			
12										
13		Tax	40.0%	12.7	18.2	39.4	=$C$13*F11			
14		Net income		19.1	27.2	59.1	=F11-F13			
15										
16				Hist	Proj	Proj				
17		BALANCE SHEET		Year 1	Year 2	Year 3				
18		Excess cash		0.0	32.2	0.0	=MAX(F34,0)			
19		Current assets		200.0	250.0	350.0	Input			
20		Long-term assets		350.0	375.0	400.0	Input			
21		Total assets		550.0	657.2	750.0	=SUM(F18:F20)			
22										
23		Revolver		0.0	0.0	43.7	=-MIN(F34,0)			
24		Debt		320.0	350.0	340.0	Input			
25		Common stock		50.0	100.0	100.0	Input			
26		Retained earnings		180.0	207.2	266.3	=E26+F14			
27		Total liabs and equity		550.0	657.2	750.0	=SUM(F23:F26)			
28										
29		Balance sheet check			0.0	0.0	=F27-F21			
30										
31		Assets without excess cash			625.0	750.0	=SUM(F19:F20)			
32		Liabs, equity without revolver			657.2	706.3	=SUM(F24:F26)			
33		Excess cash (revolver) as calculated			32.2	(43.7)	=IF(ISERROR(F32-F31),0,F32-F31)			
34		Excess cash (revolver) pasted as values			32.2	(43.7)	Hard-coded number			
35										
36										

Plugs refer to row 34, not 33

In the following steps, we will go through the steps of adding basic button as a way to launch a macro.

Figure 18-2 shows the layout of the model we were working with. This is the screen of Figure 8-7.

18.10.1 Creating Three Range Names

First, let's create three range names, with each named range covering the Columns E and F. Figure 18-3 shows the locations of the new ranges.

FIGURE 18–3

The Three New Ranges

	A	B	C	D	E	F	G
16				Hist	Proj	Proj	
17		BALANCE SHEET		Year 1	Year 2	Year 3	
18		Excess cash		0.0	0.0	0.0	=MAX(F34,0)
19		Current assets		200.0	250.0	350.0	Input
20		Long-term assets		350.0	375.0	400.0	Input
21		Total assets		550.0	625.0	750.0	=SUM(F18:F20)
22							
23		Revolver		0.0	0.0	0.0	=-MIN(F34,0)
24		Debt		320.0	350.0	340.0	Input
25		Common stock		50.0	100.0	100.0	Input
26		Retained earnings		180.0	206.9	266.5	=E26+F14
27		Total liabs and equity		550.0	656.9	706.5	=SUM(F23:F26)
28							
29		Balance sheet check			31.9	(43.5)	=F27-F21
30							
31		Assets w…			625.0	750.0	=SUM(F19:F20)
32		Liabs, equity without revolver			656.9	706.5	=SUM(F24:F26)
33		Excess c… ted			31.9	(43.5)	=IF(ISERROR(F32-F31),0,F32-F31)
34		Excess c… values					Hard-coded number
35							
36						FALSE	=OR(MAX(E29:F29)<0.001,MIN(E29:F29)>-0.001)
37							

Range: CopyCalc
Range: PasteVal
Range: BSCheck

- The first range is CopyCalc. This range is Cells E33 and F33. These two cells show the current imbalance as calculated in each of the two years in the model. The macro will be copying this calculation to the second range.
- The second range is PasteVal. This range is Cells E34 and F34. These two cells will be read by the model's excess cash (Row 18) and revolver (Row 23) row. The CopyCalc range will be copied onto the PasteVal range as hard-coded values, and not as live formulas.
- The third range is called BSCheck. This range is Cell F36, and contains the formula =OR(MAX(E29:F29)<0.001,MIN(E29:F29)>-0.001). Cells E29 and F29 are the balancing check cells. This range is the catch-all test of whether the balance sheet is balanced within the tolerance of absolute 0.001. If the balancing is off by this, the cell returns FALSE ("The balance sheet is not

balanced, keep calculating). If it is less than this, the cell returns TRUE ("The balance sheet is balanced. You can stop calculating.")

18.10.2 To the VBE

We go to the Visual Basic Editor. In a module, we write the following code:

```
Sub BalancingMacro()
Dim x As Integer
        Range("PasteVal").ClearContents
        For x = 1 To 100
                Range("CopyCalc").Copy
                Range("PasteVal").PasteSpecial Paste:=xlPasteValues
                If Range("BSCheck").Value = True Then Exit For
        Next x
        Application.CutCopyMode = False
End Sub
```

I am using the for-loop here, using x as the integer variable as the count. The maximum iterations I have set is 100, to follow the iterations setting default. The first command is to clear any values in the PasteVal range from any prior calculations. For each iteration, the step is to copy the range "CopyCalc" and paste as values to the range "PasteVal". After this sequence, check if the range BSCheck is FALSE (the balance sheet is not balanced) or TRUE (the balance sheet is balanced). If FALSE, do the copy-paste-value step again; if TRUE, then get out of the for-loop using the VBA step of Exit For.

The Application.CutCopyMode = False command is a housekeeping step to remove the "dancing ants" copy border around the CopyCalc range.

18.10.3 Creating the On-Screen Control Button

Now that we have the macro ready, we can link it to a button that we can add on the screen. Figure 18-4 shows the three types of controls for a button, arranged from left to right in terms of ease of creation.

FIGURE 18-4

Three Types of On-Screen Controls

	A	B	C	D	E	F	G	H
23		Revolver		0.0	0.0	0.0	=-MIN(F34,0)	
24		Debt		320.0	350.0	340.0	Input	
25		Common stock		50.0	100.0	100.0	Input	
26		Retained earnings		180.0	206.9	266.5	=E26+F14	
27		Total liabs and equity		550.0	656.9	706.5	=SUM(F23:F26)	
28								
29		Balance sheet check			31.9	(43.5)	=F27-F21	
30								
31		Assets w			625.0	750.0	=SUM(F19:F20)	
32		Liabs, equity without revolver			656.9	706.5	=SUM(F24:F26)	
33		Excess c	ted		31.9	(43.5)	=IF(ISERROR(F32-F31)	
34		Excess c	values				Hard-coded number	
35								
36						FALSE	=OR(MAX(E29:F29)<0	
37								
38								
39		Balance		Balance			Balance	
40								
41								

Range: CopyCalc

Range: PasteVal

Range: BSCheck

18.10.4 Inserting a Shape

The first one is inserting a shape onto the worksheet.

In Excel 2003, this done from the Drawing toolbar. Click on AutoShapes, point to a category, and then click the shape you want. Actually, the rectangle is one of the shapes immediately visible on the toolbar, so you can just click on that directly. In Excel 2007, *Insert>Shapes* and then click on the shape you want.

Once you have selected your shape, click on the location in the workbook where you want to insert the shape. Then right-click and choose Assign Macro. In the form that appears, select BalancingMacro for the name of our macro and click on OK.

To write or edit the label, right-click on the shape and select Edit Text. The font and font size can be set from the menu bar or the menu ribbon.

18.10.5 Inserting a Form Button

In Excel 2003, the steps are *View>Toolbars>Forms* and then select *Button.* In Excel 2007, it's *Developer>Insert>Button (Form Control).*

Note: if in Excel 2007 you cannot find the Developer tab, you must first set it to be visible by *Office Button>Excel Options>Popular,* check the checkbox "Show the developer tab in the ribbon."

Once you have selected your button, click on the location in the workbook where you want to insert the shape. The Assign Macro form automatically appears after insertion. At this point, select BalancingMacro for the name of our macro and click on OK.

To write or edit the label, right-click on the shape and edit in the object. The font and font size can be set from the menu bar or the menu ribbon.

18.10.6 Inserting a Control Toolbox Button

In Excel 2003, the steps are *View>Toolbars>Control ToolBox* and then select *Command Button.* In Excel 2007, it's *Developer>Insert>Command Button (ActiveX Control).* Note: if in Excel 2007 you cannot find the Developer tab, you must first set it to be visible by *Office Button>Excel Options>Popular,* check the checkbox "Show the developer tab in the ribbon."

Once you have selected your button, click on the location in the workbook where you want to insert the shape. To assign the macro, you right-click on the button and click on View Code. This will then take you to the VBE window in the code window attached to the worksheet that you are working on. You will see something like this:

```
Private Sub CommandButton1_Click()
End Sub
```

At this point, insert the call for the macro, so that the final code look like this

```
Private Sub CommandButton1_Click()
        Call BalancingMacro
End Sub
```

To edit the text, right-click on the button again and click on Properties to see this form (Figure 18-5):

Change the Caption to the text you want. The Font property allows changes in the font and font size. Other properties

FIGURE 18-5

The Properties Form

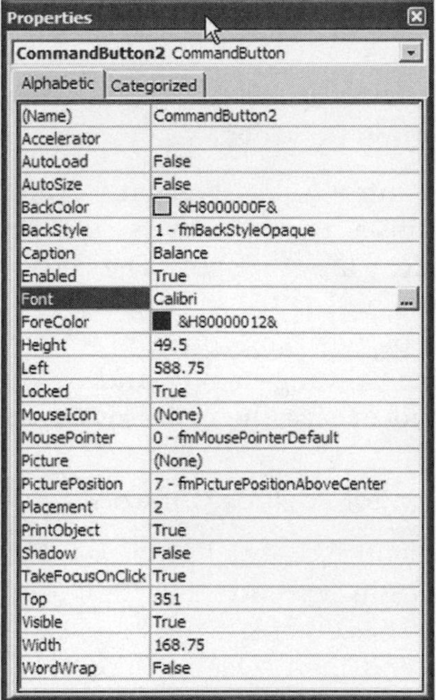

can also be customized, including foreground and background color and other programming settings.

Once you have completed your edits to the Control Toolbox button, you must click on the Exit Design Mode icon. In Excel 2003, this is at the top left corner of the Control Toolbox toolbar (*View>Toolbars>Control Toolbox*). In Excel 2007, this is at *Developer>Controls*. This "locks in" your edits. To edit the button again later, you must click on the Design Mode icon again. This is a nice feature intended to prevent inadvertent changes to the button, as can happen with the Forms toolbar button. In Excel 2003, the Design Mode icon is also part of the Visual Basic toolbar.

18.11 OTHER ON-SCREEN CONTROLS

Other types of on-screen controls, such as checkboxes, drop-down boxes, spinners, are also available through these steps. Unlike the button for launching a macro, these other controls interact with the model by selecting from a list of options and then storing the selection in a cell. Describing each of these controls would expand this chapter beyond its intended scope, so I leave you with these few points:

18.11.1 For the Forms Controls

Right-click on the control, select Format Control. For any control that uses a list of items as its selection list, this has to be defined on the Control tab under "Input range". The cell where the selection is stored is the "Cell link" on the same tab.

Under the Properties tab, you can select whether the control shows up in the printing or not, and determine its behavior when you move and or size the cell around the control.

18.11.2 For the Control Toolbox Controls

Right-click on the control, select Properties. For any control that uses a list of items as its selection list, the input range is the ListFillRange property. The cell link is the LinkedCell property.

Right-clicking and then selecting Format Control gives you some additional settings. Under the Properties tab (not to be confused with selecting Properties on the first-level menu when you right-click), you can select whether the control shows up in the printing or not, and determine its behavior when you move and or size the cell around the control.

CHAPTER 19

Tips and Tricks

Here are some additional notes and comments to make the model you are building functional.

19.1 SCENARIOS

Scenarios are for the forecast years only and allow the model to run different what-if conditions. In this way, you can see what the likely outcomes are given changing inputs in the forecast assumptions. Usually, there are three types of scenarios to look at: the base case, the high case, and the low case.

It is not critical that we change every account in the model for the three scenarios. We need only to look at the main accounts that most affect the model's outcomes. In our model, there are only seven such accounts, called *drivers*:

- Revenue
- COGS
- SGA
- Accounts receivable
- Inventory
- Accounts payable
- Capital expenditures

FIGURE 19-1

The Original Rows in the Input Sheet

	C	F	G	H	I	J	K	L	M
1	**First Corporation**								
2									
3									
4									
5					**Proj**	**Proj**	**Proj**	**Proj**	**Proj**
6	**INCOME STATEMENT**	**Dec-05**	**Dec-06**	**Dec-07**	**Dec-08**	**Dec-09**	**Dec-10**	**Dec-11**	**Dec-12**
7									
8	Revenues	825.0	900.0	1,000.0					
9	Percent growth %	na	9.1%	11.1%	10.0%	10.0%	10.0%	10.0%	10.0%
10	Revenues	825.0	900.0	1,000.0	1,100.0	1,210.0	1,331.0	1,464.1	1,610.5
11									

These seven drivers set a company's profitability and cash needs. The simplest arrangement is for all seven to move in tandem following one toggle, and that is what the following illustration shows. If you want to have more possibilities, you can set seven toggles, one for each of the drivers, so that you can get permutations of combinations (base case on revenue, but high case on COGS, low case on SGA, etc.). From an analysis point of view, however, this may be overdoing things and leads to too many permutations to be useful.

FIGURE 19-2

Layout of the Scenario Inputs

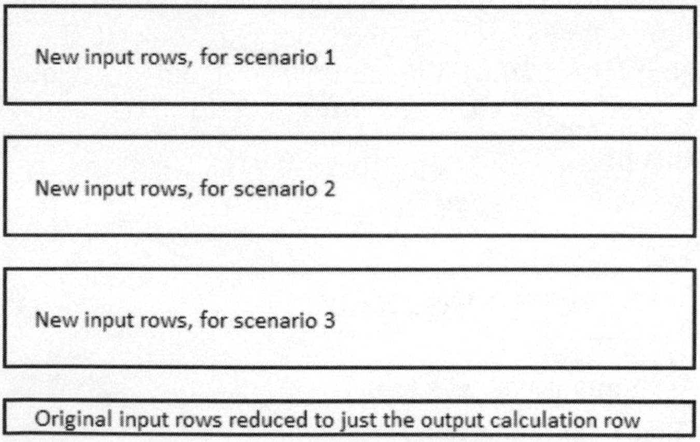

New input rows, for scenario 1

New input rows, for scenario 2

New input rows, for scenario 3

Original input rows reduced to just the output calculation row

To add scenarios in our model, we change only the input sheet in the model. Rather than one set of input rows for each of the drivers, we create additional input rows. A toggle (where we enter, say, 1, 2, or 3) determines which of the input rows are read by the outputs in the model.

19.1.1 Layout of the Scenario Rows

Let's illustrate how to add scenarios by just looking at the Revenue inputs. The basic idea is to retain the links from the calculation row (Row 10 in Fig. 19-1) into the rest of the model. In this way, we do not have to remap any of the formulas in the model that read the revenue section. We do this by inserting the additional scenario input rows above Row 10 (the original Row 10 is then pushed several rows down). The layout is shown in Figure 19-2.

19.1.2 Layout of the Model with the Full Scenario Inputs

Figure 19-3 shows one example of how the inputs can be arranged. We designate Cell I8 as the input cell for the toggle to determine which scenario is being run. The entries for this cell are 1, 2, and 3.

FIGURE 19-3

Layout with the Scenario Inputs

	C	F	G	H	I	J	K	L	M
1	**First Corporation**								
2									
3									
4									
5					Proj	Proj	Proj	Proj	Proj
6	INCOME STATEMENT	Dec-05	Dec-06	Dec-07	Dec-08	Dec-09	Dec-10	Dec-11	Dec-12
7									
8				Scenario	1				
9									
10	Revenues	825.0	900.0	1,000.0					
11	Percent growth %	na	9.1%	11.1%	10.0%	10.0%	10.0%	10.0%	10.0%
12	Revenues Case 1	825.0	900.0	1,000.0	1,100.0	1,210.0	1,331.0	1,464.1	1,610.5
13									
14	Revenues								
15	Percent growth %				12.0%	12.0%	12.0%	12.0%	12.0%
16	Revenues Case 2	825.0	900.0	1,000.0	1,120.0	1,254.4	1,404.9	1,573.5	1,762.3
17									
18	Revenues								
19	Percent growth %				5.0%	5.0%	5.0%	5.0%	5.0%
20	Revenues Case 3	825.0	900.0	1,000.0	1,050.0	1,102.5	1,157.6	1,215.5	1,276.3
21	Revenues Case 1	825.0	900.0	1,000.0	1,100.0	1,210.0	1,331.0	1,464.1	1,610.5
22									

The formulas for this layout are shown in Table 19-1.

Note the label in Column C for Row 21 contains a formula with a CHOOSE function. In this way, the labels for the individual scenarios can also be read.

The historical revenues for Scenarios 2 and 3 read the output for Scenario 1. The forecast revenues retain their individual calculations (Rows 12, 16, and 20). Row 21, which was the original calculation in the one-scenario input (Row 10 in Figure 19-1.), reads the appropriate scenario output based on the setting of the toggle in Cell I8.

19.1.3 Layout with Abbreviated Scenario Inputs

The layout illustrated in Section 19.1.2 (Fig. 19-3) is easy, in that you simply have to copy the original input rows without any

TABLE 19-1

Formulas for the Scenario Inputs

Row	Label	Column F (Copy to G and H)	Column I (Copy to J to M)
10	Revenues		
11	Percent growth %	na	
12	Revenues Case 1	=F10	=IF(ISNUMBER(I10), I10,H12*(1+I11))
13			
14	Revenues		
15	Percent growth %		
16	Revenues Case 2	=F12	=IF(ISNUMBER(I14), I14,H16*(1+I15))
17			
18	Revenues		
19	Percent growth %		
20	Revenues Case 3	=F12	=IF(ISNUMBER(I18), I18,H20*(1+I19))
21	=CHOOSE($I$8, C12,C16,C20)	=CHOOSE($I$8, F12,F16,F20)	=CHOOSE($I$8,I12,I16,I20)

modifications. This can be made easier if the thinking in scenarios may require only the percentage growths (or margin percentages for other drivers, such as COGS, etc). In this case, we can simplify the layout to be like this (Fig. 19-4):

FIGURE 19-4

Condensed Scenario Inputs

	C	F	G	H	I	J	K	L	M
1	**First Corporation**								
2									
3									
4									
5					Proj	Proj	Proj	Proj	Proj
6	INCOME STATEMENT	Dec-05	Dec-06	Dec-07	Dec-08	Dec-09	Dec-10	Dec-11	Dec-12
7									
8				Scenario	1				
9									
10	Revenues	825.0	900.0	1,000.0					
11	Percent growth %	na	9.1%	11.1%	10.0%	10.0%	10.0%	10.0%	10.0%
12	Percent growth %				12.0%	12.0%	12.0%	12.0%	12.0%
13	Percent growth %				5.0%	5.0%	5.0%	5.0%	5.0%
14	Revenues Case 1	825.0	900.0	1,000.0	1,100.0	1,210.0	1,331.0	1,464.1	1,610.5
15									

19.1.4 Other Layouts

There are other layouts that you can use for scenarios, such as having the inputs off to the right, starting from a few columns beyond M. That layout reduces the confusion that might come with having three sets of inputs one on top of the other.

19.2 DATA VALIDATION

With Data Validation, you can make your data entries more foolproof by limiting the types of data that can be entered. The simplest limit may be the type of data (e.g., allow only integers, or values within a range, etc.), but you can also have it function with more sophistication, such as providing you with easy-to-build lists of the items that the worksheet can accept.

Additionally, Data Validation also has pop-up boxes that alert you to the wrong type of data being input. You can use these pop-up boxes as a type of cell comment in their own right.

FIGURE 19-5

The Data Validation Form

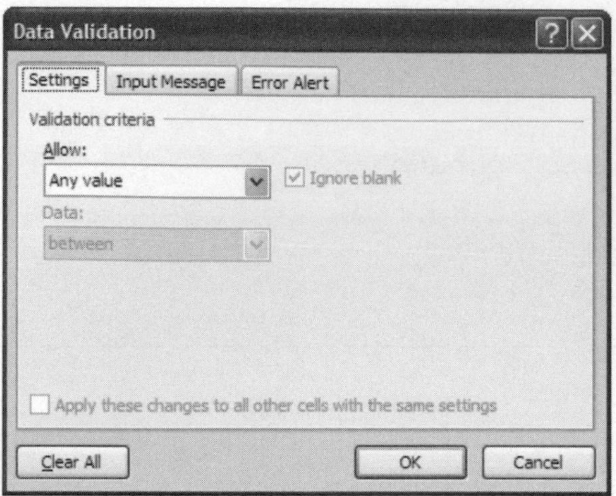

FIGURE 19-6

Options for the Allow Setting

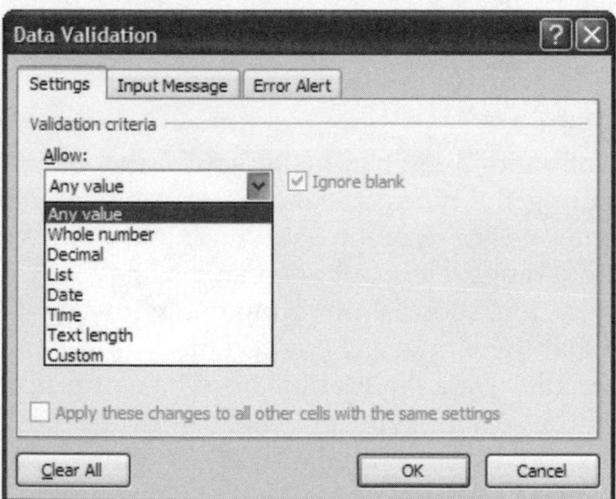

Start Data Validation by the following steps:

1. Put your cursor on the cell or cells for which you want to validate the data. In Excel 2007, go to *Data>Data Validation*. In Excel 2003, it's *Data>Validation*. A user form (Fig. 19-5) appears.
2. Click on the Settings tab. Specify the type of data that can be entered by clicking on the list box "Allow:" (Fig. 19-6). Selecting one of the options gives you another set of input options. For example, the Whole Number setting (Fig. 19-7) shows that you can select a range of integers in a range. You set the range of "between" a minimum and a maximum number. The "between" is not the only setting, though (Fig. 19-8). An explanation of the types of data you can enter:
   - i. **Any value**: This is the default and essentially does not provide any limitations on the entries.
   - ii. **Whole number:** Integers only.
   - iii. **Decimal:** Numbers with decimals.

FIGURE 19-7

Settings for Whole Number

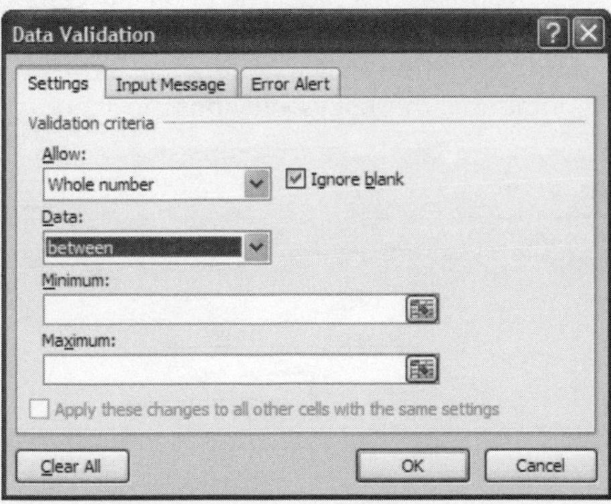

FIGURE 19-8

Settings for Data

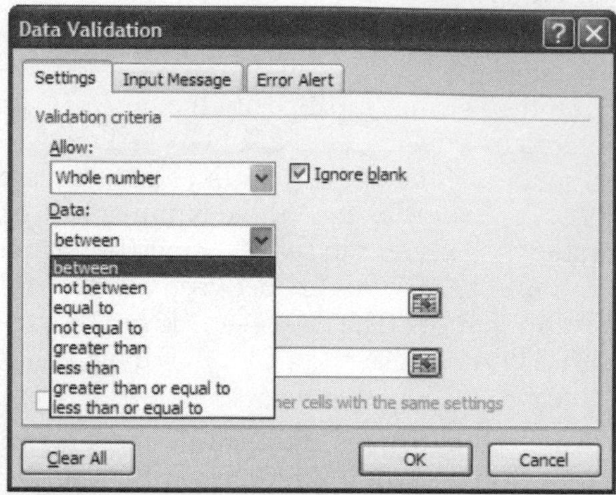

iv. **List**: You can enter for example "1,2,3" directly here or as a reference (write the "1,2,3" elsewhere and enter the range address here) and these are the only values that the data validation allows into the cell. Bonus feature: the 1,2,3 appears as a drop down box (Fig. 19-9).

You can also enter a range of cells that lists the contents of the list box. If you are doing a data validation cell in one sheet but the range containing the list is on another sheet, you must

FIGURE 19-9

A List Box

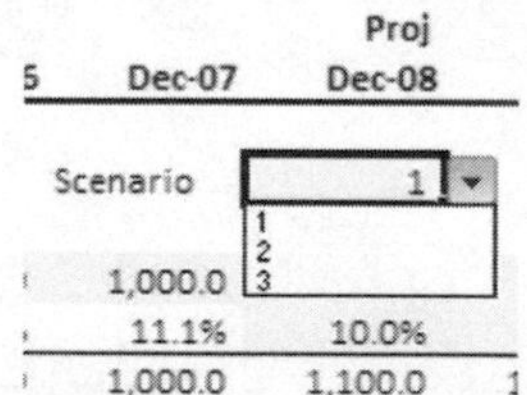

use a range name to read that list across the sheets.

v. **Date:** Dates only

vi. **Time:** Time only

vii. **Text length:** Any entry, with a defined limit on the number of characters.

viii. **Custom:** Here is an interesting trick. In the Formula box, enter FALSE. The cell will not allow itself to be changed!

These set the primary data validation settings. The next two steps are optional, but they add a nice level of control for what happens before and after you enter the data.

1. Select the "Input Message" tab. With the check box for "Show input message when cell is selected" checked, you can enter the message or information that appears when you put the cursor on this cell.

   You may want to have this function by itself, in lieu of cell comments, without the data filtering that we set on the "Settings" tab. In that case, simply leave the "Allow:" entry on that tab to read "Any value."

2. Select the "Error Alert" tab. If this is undefined, Excel will show a default error message after the invalid message is entered. To define your own message, enter it as shown in Figure 19-10:

   This tab also has the setting for what to do if invalid data are entered. Under the "Style:" list box, you can choose to have the sequence stopped as shown, or only have a warning or information icon show up. The Stop option is the default and does not allow data outside the defined parameters to be entered. The other two allows data that are outside the defined parameter to be entered, but will flash a message first.

19.3 FORMATS

Excel's features for formatting numbers are quite well developed. The menus under Format show the different ways that values

FIGURE 19-10

The Error Alert Tab

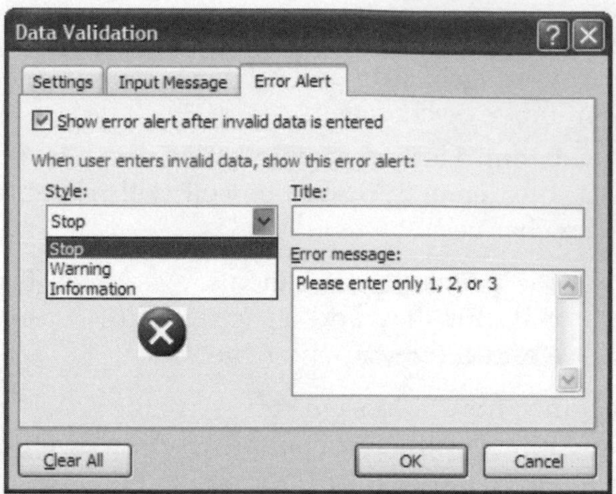

can be formatted. In addition to this, you should know that Excel can make a distinction among positive, negative, and zero values and give different formats to each type of value. You can format a number to appear as if it were a text or a combination of number and text. So 0 can appear as "n/a" and will not cause any formulas reading the value to go into error, which they would do if the cell actually did contain the text "n/a." Likewise, you can make a number, say 8, appear as "8 months" and still be read as a value.

19.3.1 Different Formats for Different Values

Excel's formats have four different sections. They are in the following order, separated by semicolons:

Format for positives; format for negatives; format for zero; format for text

Here is an example of all four sections:

#,##0.0_);(#,##0.0);"-"_);@_)

FIGURE 19-11

Custom Format Example

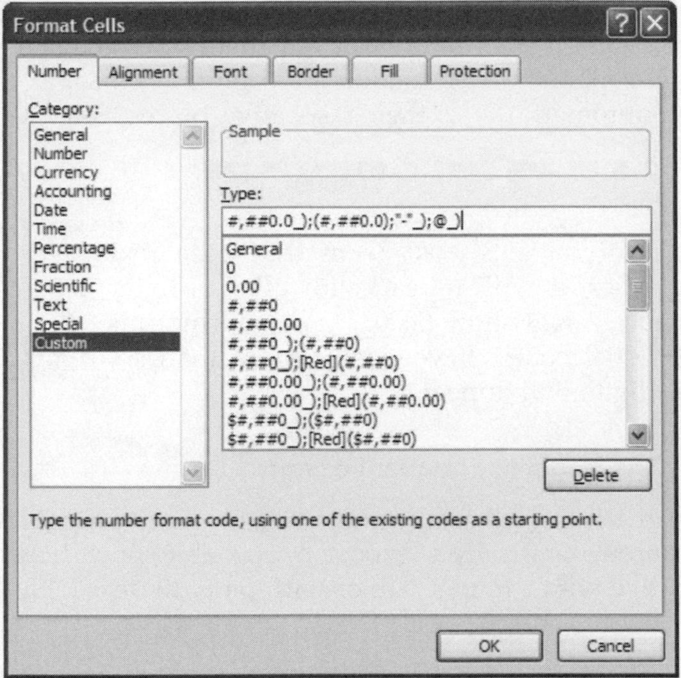

You would enter this within the Format Cells form under the Custom setting (Fig. 19-11).

The format for positive numbers is required, but the other three are optional. If the other three are not specified, Excel will use the format for the positive as the default for all types of numbers.

You can set a different format, including a different color, for each of the three number formats. For example, you could have the positive show two decimal places; the negative no decimal places; and the zero show what appears to be a text "n/a." To do this, you will have to define a custom format in Excel.

19.3.2 The Positive Number Format

Let's look at a format. This one is to show numbers with one decimal place, with a comma for the thousand separators:

#, ##0

The 0 means that at the very least a cell with this format will show one digit. The pound (#) mark means that if there additional digits, these will appear and there will be a comma as a thousand separator. (The million and billion, etc., separators also come in automatically at their respective places.)

000000

This format of six 0s means that even if you enter a one digit number, it will appear with all six digits (e.g., Entering the number 7 will show 000007). This format may be useful for some product codes. If you enter more than six digits, the additional digits will appear.

19.3.3 The Negative Number Format

The negative number format comes after the positive number format. The two are separated by a semicolon. The table shows how to show the negative with a minus sign or with parentheses (Table 19-2):

TABLE 19-2

Negative Formatting for Minus or Parentheses

Format	How 1234.56 Will Appear	How –1234.56 Will Appear
#,##0.0; #,##0.0	1,234.6	–1,234.6
#,##0.0; (#,##0.0)	1,234.6	(1,234.6)

19.3.3.1 Making positive and negative numbers have aligned decimals

When you have a column of positive and negative numbers, using the format #,##0.0; (#,##0.0) is problematical in that the decimals will not be aligned: both numbers will be flush right in the cells, but as the negative numbers have the ending parenthesis, the extra space taken up by the ending parenthesis pushes all the numbers to the left, misaligning the decimals.

You can solve this by using the format:

#,##0.0_); (#,##0.0)

The positive format now has the additional formatting _) at the end. The underscore in Excel formatting means "leave a space equivalent to the next character." The next character is shown here as the ending parenthesis. The result of this is that positive number will have an extra space equivalent to the width of an ending parenthesis at the end. This aligns the numbers over the decimal point. This is shown in Figure 19-12:

FIGURE 19-12

Aligning Decimals (Example at Right)

	A	B	C	D	E
1		Formatted with		Formatted with	
2		#,##0.0;(#,##0.0)		#,##0.0_);(#,##0.0)	
3					
4		1,234.6		1,234.6	
5		(1,234.6)		(1,234.6)	
6		678.5		678.5	
7		(345.0)		(345.0)	
8					

19.3.4 The Zero Format

The zero format follows the negative format.

#,##0.0_); (#,##0.0); "-"_)

With this setting, a cell with 0 will show a hyphen. We are also using the _) code, so there is a space equivalent to the ending parenthesis at the end of the hyphen to align with the other positive and negative numbers. Even though cell appears to have a text string (the hyphen), it is actually still carries the 0 value. This means that it can still be used in formula references without causing any errors.

19.3.5 The Text Format

The text format the last format. It begins with the @ sign. The text format can follow the positive format if the negative and zero formats are not defined. The text format cannot be put between other formats; it must always be the last of the number of formats defined.

You can make your text also align with the positive and negative numbers by adding the _) at the end.

```
#,##0.0_); (#,##0.0); "-"_);@_)
```

19.3.6 Not Defining a Format

You can leave a format undefined by leaving its space between the semicolons unoccupied.

```
#,##0.0_); (#,##0.0);;
```

This formatting means that if the cell contains a 0 or a text, those entries will not appear at all. The extreme would be if you define the format as:

```
;;;
```

With this format (three semicolons) any entry is invisible, as there are no formats assigned to it.

19.3.7 Other Formatting Tips

You can add a comma at the end of a regular format and it has the effect of dropping the "thousand" digits in the display of the cell (Table 19-1). The cell content does not change. Add two commas, and this drops the "million" digits. This is a good formatting approach to know in order to quickly display numbers in different scales, without changing the underlying numbers.

TABLE 19-3

Other Tips

Format	Entry	How It Appears
#,##0.0	1234567.89	1,234,567.9
#,##0.0,	1234567.89	1,234.6
#,##0.0,,_);(#,##0.0,,)	−1234567.89	(1.2)
0 "months"	8	8 months

The last example in Table 19-3 shows that you can specify a format so that text appears in the cell. Nevertheless, the cell's content remains a number so it can still work in formulas without producing any errors.

19.4 CONDITIONAL FORMATTING

Conditional formatting changes the attributes of a cell depending on criteria that you set. You can change:

- The color/bold/italic of the font
- The border settings for the cell
- The background (pattern) color of the cell

19.4.1 Conditional Formatting in Excel 2007

Conditional formatting in Excel is considerably expanded compared to the features in Excel 2003. Much of the improvement is centered on easily formatting groups of numbers so that their relative values can be visually.

19.4.2 Defining Conditional Formats

Start by putting your cursor on the cells you want to format. Then *Home>Conditional Formatting*, then select *New Rule* (Excel 2007) to see the formatting form in Figure 19-13. This section will describe Conditional Formatting as seen in Excel 2007. In Excel 2003, the

FIGURE 19-13

Conditional Formatting Rules

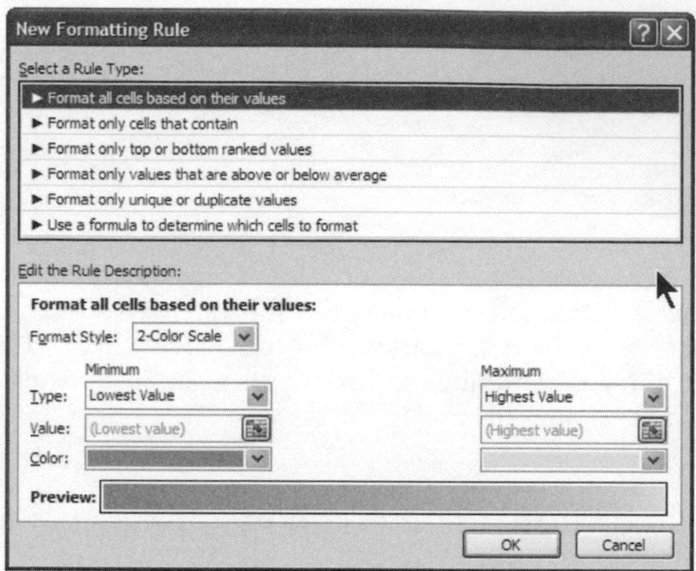

menu commands for conditional formatting is *Format>Conditional Formatting*.

The options on this form are:

1. Format all cells based on their values.
2. Format only cells that contain.
3. Format only top or bottom ranked values.
4. Format only values that are above or below average.
5. Format only unique or duplicate values.
6. Use a formula to determine which cells to format.

Options 2 and 6 are the only ones seen in Excel 2003.

19.4.2.1 Option 1: Format all cells based on their values

For each option, the bottom half of the form shows the properties that you can change. For example, in the option 1 highlighted in Figure 19-13, you can set the format to be a two-color scale, with colors that you can choose. You can also select how to define the minimum and also the maximum (Fig. 19-14).

Let's look at the other conditional formatting options.

19.4.2.2 Option 2: Format only cells that contain

In this option, you format only the cells that contain items specified in the first dropdown box (Fig. 19-15). This is an expanded list from what was available in Excel 2003, which only asked for the "cell value." Once this is set, then select the property of that value as seen in the second dropdown box. Then fill in the values in the input boxes shown (when set for other than "between" and "not between," there is only one input box).

Once you have defined the trigger for the conditional formats, click on the Format button to define the various attributes of the cell. If the starting cell has the plain, regular formatting, and you want to change many of its attributes (e.g., to a

F I G U R E 19–14

Options for Defining the Minimum. The Maximum Option Setting is Identical

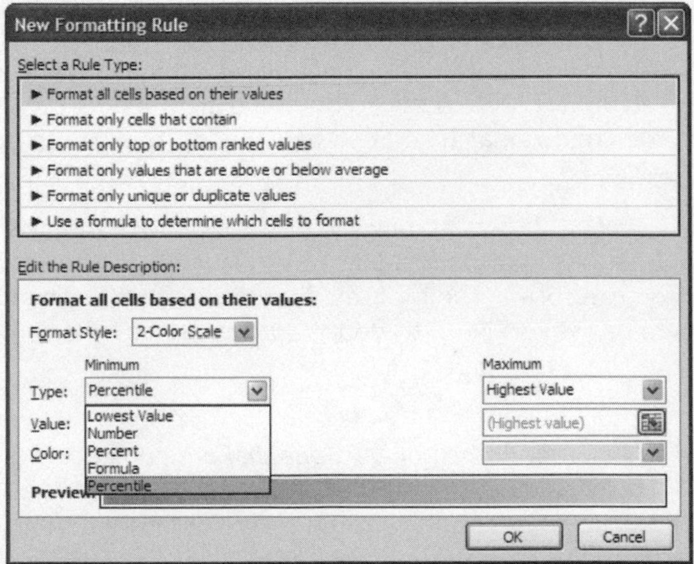

FIGURE 19-15

Option 2 Settings

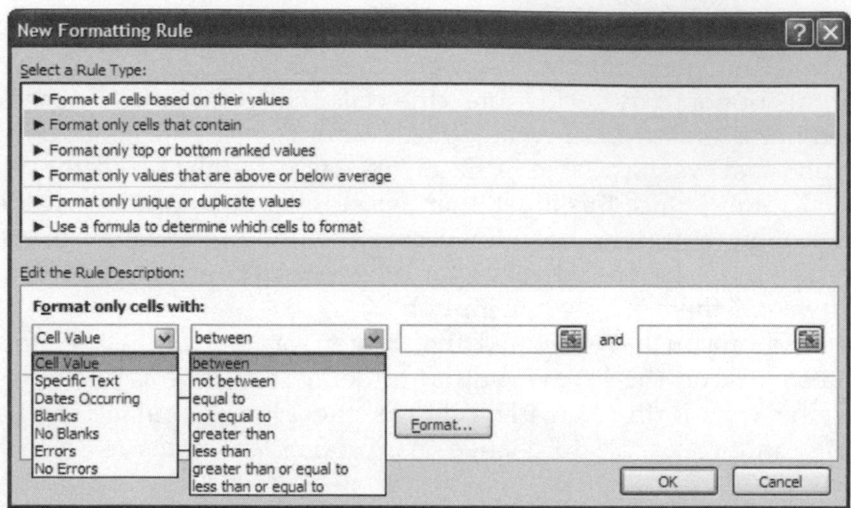

cell with a bold, italic font, with borders and a different pattern background), it may be easier to "flip" how the conditional format works. In other words, make the starting cell carry the fancy attributes and have the conditional format be the "plain, regular" attributes. Of course, you have to make sure that the logic of the conditional format is working in the correct way.

19.4.2.3 Option 3: Format only top or bottom ranked values

This option allows you to format the top or bottom values. For example, you can format the top, say, 5 or the bottom 7. The number of items to be ranked is up to you. You can also set the ranking as percents of the total range.

19.4.2.4 Option 4: Format only values that are above or below average

This option allows not only a simple above or below but also standard deviation measures.

FIGURE 19-16

Option 4 Settings

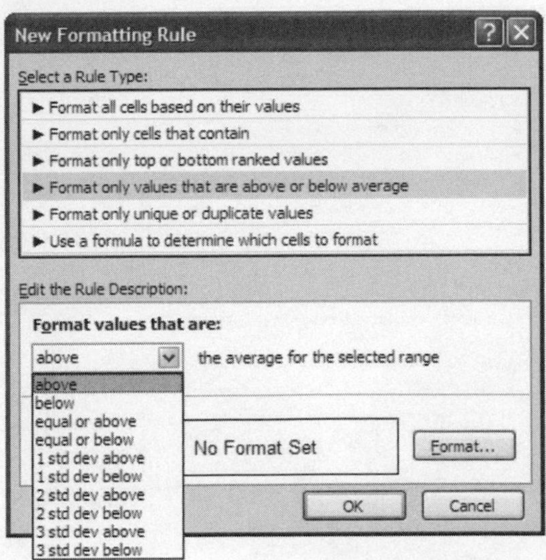

19.4.2.5 Option 5: Format only unique or duplicate values

You can format to highlight unique or duplicate values in the cells with this conditional formatting.

19.4.2.6 Option 6: Use a formula to determine which cells to format

This option (Fig. 19-17) is also available in Excel 2003 as the "Formula Is" option.

In the rule description input box, write the formula the way you write a formula in a cell. In other words, begin the formula with the equal (=) sign. Otherwise, the formula is regarded by Excel as a text string. If you have written a conditional formatting formula and it does not seem to be working, go back to this dialog box and make sure that it has not been recognized as a text string.

19.4.3 Finding Cells That Have Conditional Formats

A good way to check the location of cells that hold conditional formats (which can remain apparently undifferentiated on the screen)

FIGURE 19-17

Option 6 Settings

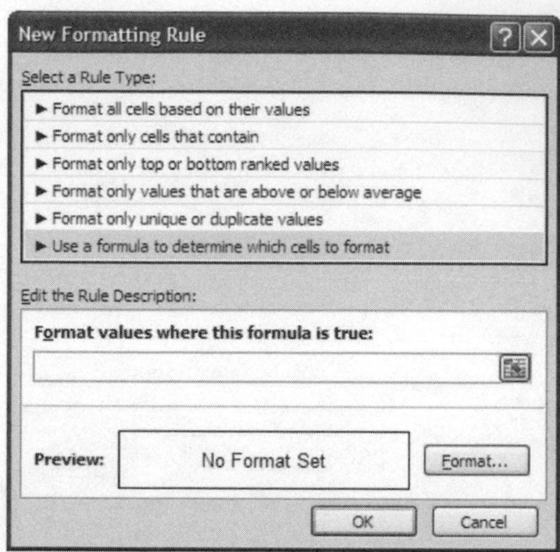

is to use the F5 (Go to) key and then to click on the Special button on that dialog box. On the Special form, click on the Conditional Formats. This causes any cells on the screen with conditional formats to be highlighted.

19.5 HIDING ROWS FOR PRINTING

In this model or any other model that you are building, there are often rows that have been developed such as Current Assets 1, Current Assets 2, etc. that have been included in the development but are not always used. Thus the print output may have these "zero rows"—rows that contain only zeroes and really do not need to be printed. These zero rows should be hidden, but not deleted. (They may not be zero rows in the next modeling run.)

19.5.1 Hiding Rows with the Group Command

Use the *Data>Group* and *Outline>Group* command to selectively hide these zero rows. This involves first highlighting the row or rows you want and then going through this sequence. A margin automatically appears on the left edge of the screen, which shows you the rows that you can hide. By clicking on the Minus button, you can hide the rows bracketed by the grouping line. The Minus button changes to a Plus button after you do this; clicking on this unhides the rows again. Alternately, you can click on the small numbers buttons at the top of the margin space. This hides and unhides according to the levels.

Although this method gives a way of quickly hiding and unhiding rows, the disadvantage is that you have to do this for each company being modeled. Different companies' data use different rows in the model, so this requires that you go through the grouping sequence for each company run before this can work properly.

19.5.2 Hiding Rows with Formulas

Another way of hiding the zero rows is to use formulas combined with the autofilter command. This works automatically for any set of numbers that you have in the model.

The autofilter feature allows only those rows that contain the desired marker to appear. Put another way, it hides rows that do not meet the criteria we set. In our case, we will use the letter "y" (for "yes") to indicate that the row should continue to be shown; the letter "n" (for "no") indicates that the row should be hidden. This method uses an IF statement to return a "y" when there are values other than 0 in the row. The autofilter is then set to show only rows with "y".

The following shows the steps for setting this up. If your model has labels in Column A, simply insert a new column so you have a new Column A that is empty.

1. In Column A, enter the formula. For this example, we are on Row 8.

   ```
   =IF(OR(MAX(F8:H8)>0.001,MIN(F8:H8)<–0.001),"y", "n")
   ```

   The range of columns is from F to H to reflect the illustration shown in Figure 19-18. Modify the range of columns depending on your model. The columns should cover the columns with numerical data.

FIGURE 19-18

Worksheet with Autofilter Formulas in Column A

	A	B	C	D	E	F	G	H
1	▾		**First Corporation**					
2	y							
3	y							
4	y							
5	y							
6	y		**INCOME STATEMENT**			**Dec-05**	**Dec-06**	**Dec-07**
7	y							
8	Y		Revenues			825.0	900.0	1,000.0
9	Y		COGS			450.0	490.0	550.0
10	Y		Gross profit			375.0	410.0	450.0
11	Y		Gross margin			45.5%	45.6%	45.0%
12	y							
13	Y		SGA			125.0	135.0	150.0
14	N		Operating expenses			0.0	0.0	0.0
15	Y		EBITDA			250.0	275.0	300.0
16	Y		EBITDA margin			27.3%	27.4%	27.0%
17	y							
18	Y		Depreciation			60.0	75.0	80.0
19	Y		Amortization of intangibles			4.0	4.0	4.0
20	Y		EBIT			186.0	196.0	216.0
21	Y		EBIT margin			19.5%	18.7%	18.6%
22	y							
23	N		Non-oper expenses			0.0	0.0	0.0
24	N		Gain (loss) on asset sales			0.0	0.0	0.0
25	Y		Interest income			3.0	4.9	5.5
26	Y		Interest expense			50.0	50.0	49.4
27	Y		EBT			139.0	150.9	172.1
28	Y		EBT margin			12.6%	12.5%	13.4%
29								

The formula uses the MAX and MIN functions to test for the presence of nonzero values. We test for values above 0.001 and below -0.001, and not 0. In this way, small values that show up in the row will not cause the row to be printed.

2. For other rows that you always want to be shown (i.e., not hidden by the auto filter), type a hard-coded "y" in Column A. An example of such a row would be a title row (e.g., Rows 1–7 in Fig. 19-18) or a blank row required for spacing (e.g., Row 12).

   Type "n" in Column A for those rows that you always want to be hidden by the autofilter. An example of such a row would be intermediate calculations that you would want to see on the screen only, and not in the printout.

It may be useful to type the hard-coded "y" and "n" in lowercase letters, and use capital letters for the same letters in the IF autofiltering formulas. In this way, you can view quickly which rows have hard codes and which rows have dynamic formulas.

3. Click on the column letter A to highlight Column A. Apply the autofilter by *Data>Sort & Filter>Filter* (Excel 2007) or *Data>Filter* (Excel 2003). With the autofilter turned on, select to show only "y" (Fig. 19-19).
4. The rows are automatically hidden (Fig. 19-20). The row numbers turn blue when the autofilter is on. When you print this range, the zero rows (Rows 14, 23, and 24 in the layout) remain hidden. After printing, click on the autofilter button again and select "Select All." All the hidden rows appear again.

   You can create a macro that does the hiding, printing and then unhiding automatically.

FIGURE 19–19

With Autofilter Turned On, then Selecting So Show "y" Rows Only

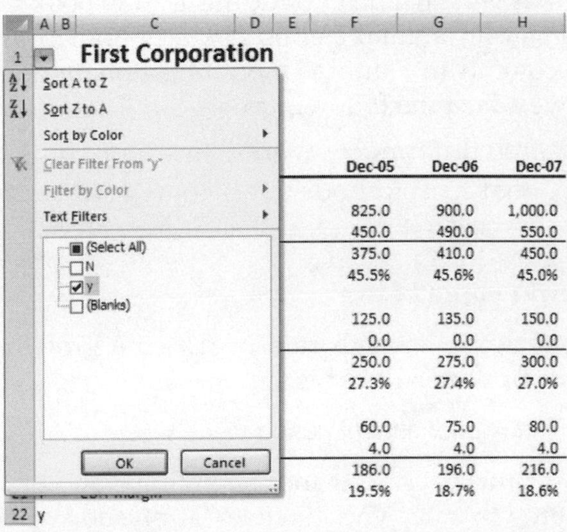

FIGURE 19–20

The Final Range with Zero Rows Hidden (Rows 14, 23, and 24)

	A	B	C	D	E	F	G	H
1			**First Corporation**					
2	Y							
3	Y							
4	Y							
5	Y							
6	Y		**INCOME STATEMENT**			**Dec-05**	**Dec-06**	**Dec-07**
7	Y							
8	Y		Revenues			825.0	900.0	1,000.0
9	Y		COGS			450.0	490.0	550.0
10	Y		Gross profit			375.0	410.0	450.0
11	Y		Gross margin			45.5%	45.6%	45.0%
12	Y							
13	Y		SGA			125.0	135.0	150.0
15	Y		EBITDA			250.0	275.0	300.0
16	Y		EBITDA margin			27.3%	27.4%	27.0%
17	Y							
18	Y		Depreciation			60.0	75.0	80.0
19	Y		Amortization of intangibles			4.0	4.0	4.0
20	Y		EBIT			186.0	196.0	216.0
21	Y		EBIT margin			19.5%	18.7%	18.6%
22	Y							
25	Y		Interest income			3.0	4.9	5.5
26	Y		Interest expense			50.0	50.0	49.4
27	Y		EBT			139.0	150.9	172.1
28	Y		EBT margin			12.6%	12.5%	13.4%

19.6 NONANNUAL PERIODS

The model that we have been building in this book assumes that each column in an annual period. In addition to adjusting the dates from column to column, modeling nonannual periods requires that we adjust the following:

- How growth formulas work
- Ratios that look to both the income statement and the balance sheet

19.6.1 Growth Formula

Assuming an annual growth rate of $n\%$, the growth formula to find the value of x after 1 year is:

$$x = \text{prior annual period value} * (1 + n\%)$$

For nonannual periods, and assuming you continue to use an annual growth rate, you have to apply an exponent. For a quarter-to-quarter growth rate, to find the value of x after one quarter, the formula is:

$$x = \text{prior quarter value} * (1 + n\%)^{0.25}$$

The 0.25 represents the quarter of the year. For semiannual growth, the exponent should be 0.50, etc. The n% is always the annual percentage growth rate.

19.6.2 Quarterly Growth

When you work with quarterly models, the usual calculation for calculating quarterly growth rates is not quarter-to-quarter growth. Instead, it is to look at the growth from the quarter of a year ago to the current quarter. This means that you would still be using an annual growth rate; it is just that the base value you are using is not the annual value, but the quarterly value.

19.6.3 Ratios

Ratios whose numerators and denominators look to the same financial statement (e.g., net income/revenue for net margin; debt/total capital for leverage) are not affected by the periodicity of your model. However, we have to be careful with those that look across the statements. Table 19-4 shows examples of adjustments that would be required, with a quarterly periodicity used as an illustration, in order to maintain the formulas on an annual basis. There may be cases, of course, where you would want to look at the formulas on a quarterly basis, in which case these adjustments would not be required.

Multiplying the income statement values by 4 is a "quick and dirty" way of annualizing them, but if the company is highly seasonal and most of its sales happen in specific quarters, this multiplication approach would not be very useful.

19.7 ADDITIONAL SOURCES

A quick visit to the bookstore or to websites such as amazon.com will give you a view of the many books on modeling that have

TABLE 19-4

Example of Adjustment for Ratios

Ratio	Annual Formula	Quarterly Formula
Receivable days on revenue	Receivables/revenue x 365	Receivables/revenue x 91*
Inventory days on COGS	Inventory/COGS x 365	Inventory/COGS x 91*
Payable days on COGS	Payables/COGS x 365	Payables/COGS x 91*
EBIT/Total capitalization	EBIT/Total capitalization	(EBIT* 4)/Total capitalization
Return on avg total assets	Net income / Avg total assets	(Net inc * 4) / Avg total assets
Return on avg total equity	Net income / Avg total equity	(Net inc * 4) / Avg total equity
Asset turnover	Revenue / Total assets	(Revenue * 4) / Total assets

* Actual number of days in quarter, to be consistent with the 365-day year. You can use 90 days for the quarter, but the annual formula should then use a 360-day year.

been published, and I would encourage you to explore what is available now. The website for this book is www.buildingfinancialmodels.com.

The following are other sources of accounting or finance expertise that you might want to look to as you progress in your financial modeling skills:

Castillo, Jerilyn J. and Peter J. McAniff, *The Practitioner's Guide to Investment Banking, Mergers & Acquistions, Corporate Finance*. Circinus Business Press, 2007. This is a superbly comprehensive reference manual for professionals new to or in M&A and corporate finance. Available through www.scoopbooks.com,

Morris, James E., *Accounting for M&A, Equity and Credit Analysts,* McGraw-Hill, 2004. This book covers topics not touched upon in run-of-the-mill accounting books, with a special emphasis on modeling the issues being discussed.

Tracy, John A., *How to Read a Financial Report: Wringing Vital Signs Out of the Numbers (How to Read a Financial Report)*, John Wiley & Sons, 2004. The book does an excellent job in explaining the accounting concepts behind the balance sheet, the income statement, and the cash flow statement, and how the three statements fit together.

Walkenbach, John. Any book by him, deservedly known as "Mr. Spreadsheet." His website is www.j-walk.com.

There are also many internet public forums on Excel where queries on various aspects of Excel (and other Office applications) usually get answered within the hour by the many visitors to and readers of the sites. The discussion groups under Google at http://groups.google.com/group/microsoft.public.excel/topics with other side forums for Excel functions, programming, miscellaneous, etc., are particularly rich sources of information for those times when you are absolutely stumped by an Excel problem.

A P P E N D I X

Abbreviations

A/P	Accounts Payable
A/R	Accounts Receivable
B/S	Balance Sheet
C/F	Cash Flow Statement
CFF	Cash Flow from Financing
CFI	Cash Flow from Investments
CFO	Cash Flow from Operations
COGS	Cost of Goods Sold
DCF	Discounted Cash Flow
EBIAT	Earnings Before Interest After Taxes
EBIT	Earnings Before Interest and Taxes
EBITDA	Earnings Before Interest, Taxes, Depreciation, and Amortization
EBT	Earnings Before Taxes
FCF	Free Cash Flow
IRR	Internal Revenue of Return
Inv	Inventory
I/S	Income Statement
Liabs	Liabilities
NI	Net Income
NPV	Net Present Value
OCF	Operating Cash Flow
OWC	Operating Working Capital

PPE	Plant, Property and Equipment
QAT	Quick Access Toolbar (Excel 2007 feature)
SGA	Sales, General and Administrative
SH	Shareholders
SHE	Shareholders' Equity
TA	Total Assets
TFCF	Terminal Free Cash Flow
TL	Total Liabilities
TV	Terminal Value
WACC	Weighted Average Cost of Capital
WC	Working Capital

INDEX

F

ABOUT THE AUTHOR

John S. Tjia (pronounced "*Chee*-ah") has 20 years of experience in developing financial models, including 7 years as head of the Models Group J.P. Morgan (now known as JPMorgan Chase) in New York. He was responsible for designing, developing, and providing the training for the firm's standard analysis and execution financial models for the Mergers & Acquisitions and Investment Banking divisions worldwide. Prior to that, he was an investment banker in the firm's Hong Kong office and had assignments in credit analysis and financial advisory in New York. Now a founding partner of the TMG & Associates, LLC modeling consulting company (*www.tmga.com*), he lives in Pleasantville, New York, with his wife and two children. He can be contacted at johntjia@buildingfinancialmodels.com.